Worn

Worn

A People's History of Clothing

Sofi Thanhauser

Pantheon Books, New York

All rights reserved. Published in the United States by Pantheon Books, a division of Penguin Random House LLC, New York, and distributed in Canada by Penguin Random House Canada Limited, Toronto.

Pantheon Books and colophon are registered trademarks of Penguin Random House LLC.

Library of Congress Cataloging-in-Publication Data
Name: Thanhauser, Sofi, author.
Title: Worn : a people's history of clothing / Sofi Thanhauser.
Description: First Edition. New York : Pantheon Books, 2022.
Includes bibliographical references and index.
Identifiers: LCCN 2021014453 (print). LCCN 2021014454 (ebook).
ISBN 9781524748395 (hardcover). ISBN 9781524748401 (ebook).
Subjects: LCSH: Clothing and dress—History. Clothing and dress—
Social aspects. Fashion—History. Fashion—Social aspects. Textile
fabrics—History.
Classification: LCC GT511 .T53 2022 (print) | LCC GT511 (ebook) |
DDC 391.009—dc23
LC record available at lccn.loc.gov/2021014453
LC ebook record available at lccn.loc.gov/2021014454

www.pantheonbooks.com

Jacket art by Hollie Chastain
Jacket design by Janet Hansen

Printed in Canada

First Edition

9 8 7 6 5 4 3 2 1

For my father, SRJ Thanhauser

Contents

WOOL

Introduction

I like clothes.

Not far from the house in which I grew up on the island of Martha's Vineyard is a place that we locals call the Dumptique. There are too many *New York Times* Travel Section pieces devoted to giving away islander secrets for me to describe its exact location here in good conscience, but imagine it in a low-lying field edged with gnarled, wind-stunted oaks: a small uninsulated shack set a few hundred yards out from the municipal landfill. The Dumptique is stuffed to its corrugated metal roof with pots, pans, books, old lamps, worn-out puzzles, and several bins of used clothing.

Everything at the Dumptique is free, and every year wealthy summer residents of Martha's Vineyard leave behind extraordinary garments that end up buried among unwanted craft kits, waiting to be discovered by a sharp eye. I went to the Dumptique every Saturday of my adolescence to scavenge, and in this way garments I would never otherwise have touched, let alone owned, came into my possession. To wit: A loden coat. A Barbour jacket. A pink silk cocktail dress from the 1950s with a cream-colored taffeta lining. A green Marimekko Design Research dress from the 1970s. Swiss-made camisoles with delicate scalloped edges. Camel hair shirts. Arche boots. Slowly, ineluctably, these treasures drained any possible enthusiasm I could have felt for the clothes in the Falmouth TJMaxx, which was the other place I shopped at that time. I became, irrevocably, a clothing snob.

In the Dumptique I began to notice that the older clothes were almost invariably better and more durably made than the newer ones. I noticed the same thing when I watched old films. Lauren Bacall's tailored suits, Anna Karina's perfect jersey tops, even in celluloid, retained markers of an integrity and formal thoughtfulness that was totally absent in, say, one of Jennifer Aniston's limp rayon blouses.

The record on film and in the Dumptique could not take me back much further than the early twentieth century. But about three miles west of the Dumptique stands a house built around 1740, beside a brook dammed by a Puritan patriarch who made his name as a general in King Philip's War. Like many colonial-era American homes, the house was designed with no closets. Rather, a single hook or a peg rail sufficed. This was testament to a time when each member of the family owned two sets of clothing: one for Sunday, and one for every other day of the week. These clothes must have been durable indeed.

It seemed to me that the quality and durability of American clothing had seen a steady decline and fall. My mother's reminiscences about her past were further testimony. My mother grew up in Sheffield, Massachusetts, in the 1950s and 1960s. When she was in high school, a common joke was "what does she, make her own clothes?" to refer to a nerdy or unpopular girl. This was really, my mother recalls, a coded way of saying that the girl was poor. What this points to (beyond the barbarity of American high schoolers) is that in the 1960s it was still cheaper to make your own clothes than to buy them in a store. And no wonder: garment manufacture was union work at which highly skilled workers labored and earned a living wage and health benefits. At the time, the International Ladies' Garment Workers' Union was one of the largest unions in the U.S.

Today, it is no longer cheaper to make your own clothes than to buy them. A task that once fell within the province of the ordinary household is now an esoteric hobby, requiring skills out of reach to most ordinary Americans. It can even be cost prohibitive, since to buy the cloth to make a shirt will often cost more than the price of a new shirt. A curious reversal.

Ralph Tharpe, the former design engineer at Cone Mills in North Carolina, and the man responsible for making denim for Levi's 501s during the 1970s, put the question to me this way: "Why is it that from 1960 to today the price of a Ford truck has increased ten times over and the price of a pair of dungarees has stayed the same?" This question becomes even more puzzling when one considers that many mass-manufacturing processes have been automated since the 1960s but sewing is not one of them. The process one follows to sew a garment has not changed materially since the advent of the sewing machine. Fabric is a fussy and unpredictable material, unlike sheet metal, that still requires the subtle manipulation of tension that can only be done by a real human hand.

How then, did this happen?

f it were possible to travel back in time five hundred years, we would be dazzled by the beauty and diversity of the clothing that people made and wore. We would see huipil woven of handspun cotton dyed with cochineal, silk kimono, shibori dyed using indigo, Hezhe dresses made of salmon skin, Kuba textiles woven from palm leaf fiber, embroidered with complex geometric patterns and stained red with dye from the heartwood of a tropical tree, and Russian peasant shifts made from linen, embroidered with threads dyed a deep mauve using local lichen. We would see the flora and fauna of thousands of microenvironments transformed into cloth: like the scratchy wool of the Herdwick sheep, which thrive on the rocky terrain of the Cumbrian fells of northern England, perfect for the local tweed. The colors of the clothes were drawn from lichen, shells, bark, indigo, saffron, roots, beetles. The fabric constructions and patterns themselves were astonishing, containing special regional weaves and knits, number magic, protective prayers, and clan symbols, collectively honed motifs, and individual flourishes. This localism coexisted with trade. And a type of small-scale textile manufacturing thrived among every group of agriculturalists across the world.

In our present world, whether we traveled to England or Russia, China or Mexico, Kenya or Uruguay, we would see T-shirts, jeans, jackets, and skirts made predominantly of two materials: cotton and petroleum. At the same time, the system of production responsible for making all these clothes has everywhere become more extractive, centralized, and concentrated among a few megacorporations. In 2019, global retail sales of apparel and footwear reached 1.9 trillion U.S. dollars. That's more than double that year's global sales of consumer electronics and four times global arms sales. Meanwhile, Nike's market capitalization is more than four times that of the Ford Motor Company. And what had once been the world's most common and widely distributed popular art—making textiles—has almost disappeared from the hands of the artisan.

In the preindustrial period, anthropologists estimate, humans devoted at least as many labor hours to making cloth as they devoted to producing food. It is almost impossible to overstate how enormous the change was in the daily rhythm when textile work disappeared from everyday life and moved into the factory. The worlds on either side of this schism differed from one another completely: or at least as much as the two different kinds of cloth.

The contemporary clothing trade may be valuable, but the clothes produced are not. Between 2000 and 2014, clothing production around the world doubled. This was possible because clothing had become almost completely disposable. Over the course of this almost fifteen-year period consumers came to buy, on average, 60 percent more clothes than they used to, but kept each garment for half as long. By 2017, one garbage truck of clothes (5,787 pounds) was burned or sent to landfills every second.

Alarm bells have been ringing about fast fashion's evils: its toxicity and exploitativeness. These aren't new problems. What *is* new is their scale. Textile and garment work have been dangerous to laborers since industrialization, but three of the four deadliest garment factory disasters in history occurred during the 2010s. Textile making has been damaging the environment for centuries, but today the industry produces a full fifth of global wastewater, and emits one tenth of global carbon emissions.

"Fast fashion" didn't spring from a void in the 1990s, the decade during which this term came into circulation. It isn't a thirty-year-old problem, but the newest symptom of a problem that is centuries old. I wanted to go digging for its roots, and discover how our modern clothing system came to be.

This book is not meant to be the all-encompassing history of fabric and its production and importance in the world. Rather, I want to tell the story of what I found, of how we went from making fabric for ourselves as part of our everyday work to dressing in clothes that come from a complex, inscrutable system that has divorced us from the creative act, from our land, from our rights as consumers and workers.

I t may not be intuitive to everyone who does not sew that clothes are made by people, not just machines. In fact, it was not until I started making clothes myself—I was nine years old and I wanted to replicate the cream-colored blouse that Jennifer Connelly's character wears in *The Labyrinth*—that I really understood clothes *are made*. This probably sounds absurd. I remember watching a young man who had grown up in Manhattan learn that if you planted an apple seed, an apple tree could grow. These things can happen in a culture as divorced from agriculture and industry as the one in which we live today. Once I started sewing, clothes revealed themselves as assemblages of tubes and planar surfaces: two-dimensional cloth arrayed on three-dimensional bodies, pierced with holes, spangled with buttons, folded and tucked to make pleats, rounded under at the edges to make hems. Making clothes demanded that I examine the way the tube of the arm connects to the tube of the torso, and the full range of motion of the shoulder joint. I realized that a neck opening had to be large enough to allow the hard cantaloupe of the head to pass through it, and then fastened up with buttons if the shirt was to be snug around the neck. I came to understand clothes as a very particular kind of sculpture, made to echo the body's shape but also to transform that shape: a puffy shoulder to make the arm billow out like a bird's, a flared leg to make the shape of the human calf into an ecstatic bell. Experiments with sewing taught me to appreciate clothes, and the art and labor that goes into them.

I learned to appreciate *cloth* when I tried to make clothing without it.

I was a polemical teenager. One day shortly before New Year's Eve 2002, I announced that the human race had been tragically closed-minded regarding the material for clothing, insisting, as they had since the beginning of time, that it be made of cloth, when there were clearly many other suitable materials readily available. I proposed that this year for New Year's Eve my friends and I wear dresses made only of paper.

We gathered at Lila's house, down a long dirt road by the Tisbury Great Pond, where her family's sheep grazed in pasture running up to the water. My family had kept sheep, too, before we moved to Massachusetts from rural Vermont in 1995. My friends and I started in the late morning, and spread out a massive pile of newspapers, magazines, and packing material. Hannah used only the covers of *Vogue* and clear plastic tape and let her boyfriend Colin adjust the hemline with a pair of scissors, which he did until you could almost see her ass. Luke made himself a handsome newspaper suit. Lila made herself a pleated skirt out of Stop & Shop glossy inserts, and for the top of the ensemble she used the cardboard rainbow spinner wheel removed from a Candy Land board game, placed right over her solar plexus, with bands of white printer paper radiating out over her shoulders and around her narrow chest. Kate made a series of concentric paper hoops held together by a strip down the front. I made a newspaper dress and earrings out of toilet paper rolls. We all crimped our hair.

At the party, our dresses revealed a design flaw. They ripped. It started as we exited the car, and continued as we danced, walked, sat, or even lifted our arms to take swigs of our forties. By the time we went home, we were all more or less naked. This experience gave me a respect for fabric.

Clothing is made from cloth. Cloth can come from plants (cotton, linen), animals (sheep, silkworm), and, since the nineteenth century, from synthetic materials and processes, namely plant-derived cellulose liquefied and then extruded into strands (rayon) and various chemical recombinations of petroleum (nylon, spandex, polyester).

This book begins with the story of linen. Northern Europeans dressed from the Paleolithic Age through the nineteenth century primarily in a fabric that is now rarely worn except by small numbers of the elite: linen. The oldest fabric in the archeological record is made from linen or related vegetal fibers, and this section looks to fabric's early beginnings. Clothmaking has in many cultures been women's work. Women represent more than two thirds of the modern garment workforce. The value of women's labor and women's wages has been shaped by cloth production, and vice versa, and this section looks at the importance of women's work at the dawn of industrial fabric production.

Next comes cotton. Cotton is an incredibly thirsty crop, and it is also chemically intensive, accounting for almost 20 percent of the global usage of pesticides. In this section, I journey to sites where cotton agriculture is causing ecological disaster, while examining the colonial armatures that set up these modern systems of production. The cotton industry has shown its workers no more mercy than its land. Cotton has been a central part of the stories of the colonization of India, slavery in the American South, and the modern-day eco-genocide of the Uyghur people of Xinjiang in western China.

Third comes silk. Silk is almost synonymous with luxury, and this section traces the course of luxury clothing and its use as a status marker. Humans carefully clothe their hierarchies, and political power is not just advertised by forms of clothing; it is sometimes achieved through skillful use and manipulation of both personal dress and the national textile trade. This section interrogates clothing's deep interpenetration with power and hierarchy, from ancient China to Louis XIV, to the modern mega brand.

Fourth is the story of synthetics. From the ancient silk route, we move to more contemporary trade routes and regimes, by tracing the rise of synthetic fabric in the twentieth and early twenty-first centuries. Between 2000 and 2008, petroleum-based fabrics supplanted cotton as the most commonly worn fabric on the planet. In the previous century, clothing manufacture briefly moved out of the sweatshop, and then back into it while governments aided and abetted this backslide in basic workers' rights. Today, synthetic fabrics and low-wage labor join to make cheap clothes that are, like fast food, bad for the land and the people who make them.

Finally, in the story of wool, we discover that what once was known as a commoner's fabric is now in the avant-garde of radical textile experiments. These experiments seek both to resuscitate handcraft and find ways to use textile machinery that serve human life, rather than threaten it. This section looks at regenerative projects that rely on small-scale production models. It celebrates some of the many people who are helping tell new stories about clothing and the connections between people, their work, their ancestors, and the land.

There is scarcely a part of the human experience, historic or current, that the story of clothes does not touch. The history of clothing has been also the history of a human quest for warmth, and both have been tied, in turn, to the story of human migrations. Researchers believe humans began wearing clothes well after they lost their body hair, and that clothing may have been the technology that enabled the first humans to migrate out of Africa and encounter the conditions of the Ice Age. If possessing clothing has driven migration, so has coveting it: in the seventeenth century, the earliest forays by Europeans into the interior of what is now the United States and Canada were made in order to trade with the native inhabitants for furs.

Clothing drives government policy, and demarcates environmental use. Economies have risen on the back of its manufacture. Meanwhile, our daily human interactions are mitigated by the presence of clothing and its innumerable signals, whether we are receiving a traffic ticket, attending a graduation, or determining a stranger's social class. Virginia Woolf observed that clothes "change our view of the world and the world's view of us." A clearinghouse of social codes, clothing also springs from concrete exchanges of resources, work, and wealth. Understanding these very particular objects with any precision means coming to terms with our own location within a plenitude of hierarchies. Decoding the global system that makes our clothes, and how it came to be, might also change the way we view the world.

This book blends reportage with historical research. Although I traveled widely to research this book: to China, Vietnam, Honduras, India, England, and throughout the U.S., the history and reportage it contains is weighted toward understanding the U.S.'s role in building a global garment trade that touches every corner of the world. And, with this, to interrogate the fact that despite its handiwork the U.S. remains aloof in international conversations to do with the ethics of this trade. The garment factory collapse in Dhaka in 2013, which killed over one thousand workers in a day, galvanized European consumers to band together to pressure brands, some of which have taken concrete and meaningful actions to prevent future disasters. No movement of parallel force has emerged in the United States, nor has any such meaningful response come from U.S. brands like The Gap and Walmart, who continue on as before.

I discovered much that was heartbreaking in the years that I spent researching and writing this book, but also much to celebrate. I met many people who are finding ways to create fabric on their own terms, claiming the right to make something both useful and beautiful. My first interview was with Jay Ardai of Fingerlakes Woolen Mill, who invented a way to use repurposed early-twentieth-century machinery to card and spin batches of wool from small-flock owners, to allow them to knit and weave their own fleeces. Later, I met Navajo women in Phoenix learning traditional weaving in an old high school, mending a line of transmission that had been severed by racist assimilation policies. I visited a country store on I-80 selling wool all dyed with local plants. I met sheep breeders in Cumbria who match their sheep to the geology and the ground cover to build sustainable systems. I met Rabbit Goody, who runs her weaving shop in upstate New York along nineteenth-century socialist cooperative lines.

Cloth is often used to symbolize the web of connections between people, as phrases like "the social fabric" or "the community was rent apart" or "an alliance was stitched together" or "moral fiber" attest. On a literal level cloth and clothing, with which we live in such intimate proximity from cradle to grave, link us together with the people who made our garments, people we will never meet. These relations between maker and wearer can be very difficult to decipher, but I hope this book will be a guide.

As a child I had a great fondness for the factory segment on *Mister Rogers*, which ushered curious children into a toothpaste factory one week and a crayon-making plant the next. I registered a note of the uncanny in being surrounded by everyday objects, like clothing, whose origins were mysterious. I found this odd and demoralizing. Part of this project is an answer to that impulse, or craving, to know where things come from. After all, our clothes don't just come ready-made from factories or from the countries named on their tags. They come from our histories.

Linen

The Last Linen Shirt in New Hampshire

For peril is bothe fyr and tow t' assemble . . .

—WIFE OF BATH'S PROLOGUE, GEOFFREY CHAUCER,
CANTERBURY TALES

n 2012, my mother and I drove up from Woods Hole, Massachusetts, through the gutted former textile hubs of Fall River and New Bedford, to visit a museum exhibit located inside the restored Sylvanus Brown House in Pawtucket, Rhode Island. The Sylvanus Brown House was a family dwelling from mid-eighteenth-century New England, arranged to give the visitor an idea of its inhabitants' daily lives. We were there for the displays of textile tools used to make linen in colonial New England, before the arrival of the factory production.

Linen is a fabric made from flax, a plant with a slender stalk that grows to two or three feet tall and bears a light blue flower. Inside the hard husks of *Linum usitatissimum,* otherwise known as linseed or flax, are soft, silky strands. When these are twisted together, the brittleness of each strand alone is surmounted by group strength, and the resulting cord or thread can then become longer than any of the individual strands. These threads are woven together to make linen.

The thicker flax is sown in the ground, the finer the stalk, and subsequently, the thread. New Englanders planted their flax at the end of March or early in April. "Flax should be sowed promiscuously (as Wheat or Oats, &.c.) but somewhat thicker . . . it will take a Bushel and a Half to sow one Acre of Land to make it fit for Linen or Thread," instructed John Wily, in *A Treatise on the Propagation of Sheep, the Manufacture of Wool, and the Cultivation and Manufacture of Flax*. The plants were pulled in July when the leaves turned yellow and left to dry. Then the dry plants were pulled through a rippling comb to strip the seeds, and retted—a process employing moisture to rot and soften the outer cellular tissue of the plant—in a stream or a dewy field. "It is out of the Power of any Man to tell the exact Number of Days it will take to water or dew rot Flax," wrote Wily, leaving much to the farmer's own discretion. After the flax had been retted it was crushed down the line of the stalk until all the coarse outer bark known as tow had been broken; then it was scutched—struck and scraped with a wood knife until the tow fell to the ground. The inner fibers of the flax were then drawn through a hackling comb to remove smaller pieces of tow, then carded, and spun, and woven into fabric.

Our tour guide at the Sylvanus Brown House was in period costume, with a long skirt, a shawl around her shoulders, and bonnet atop her head. She was a heavyset woman with a thick Rhode Island accent. She showed us the flax break, which looked like a large wooden paper cutter, and demonstrated with a sheaf of dried flax how to crush the bark, bringing down the wooden blade every inch or so. She showed us the iron spikes of the hackling comb and the carding brushes, which were lined with rows and rows of teasel, the spiky head of a flowering plant ideal for drawing multitudinous fibers into parallel rows.

Upstairs, our tour guide brought us to see the loom, which presided over an entire room. Finally she showed us the spinning wheel, and the groove in the wooden floor beside it that was made by the woman who was spinning as she walked back and forth, back and forth, a motion required by this particular kind of spinning wheel, dubbed the "walking wheel," in order to draw the fiber away from the spindle and lengthen it before giving it a twist. The wheel would have been moved every so often in order to avoid wearing a groove too deep into the floor, the guide said. My mother and I looked at each other, making our eyes wide. She then announced to us, without ceremony or regret, in that frank manner that New Englanders have, that her shift was over.

I reflected on the bittersweetness in that phrase, "my shift is over." On the one hand, textile making was the shift that was *never* over for the New England farm woman, as the grooves by the side of the walking wheel could so amply attest. On the other hand, the thread she had spun and woven—indeed all the materials to make her family's clothing—came from a few acres around her own house. The American essayist, activist, and farmer Wendell Berry has said that "eating is an agricultural act." So is getting dressed. Mrs. Brown would have known where her meal was grown and exactly where her clothing had been harvested. This was part of a long-standing tradition. The type of linen making that was being practiced on the New England farm before the Industrial Revolution was one that had persisted through thousands of years of human history. On this unlikely patch of New England soil, unbeknownst to anyone, it was living out its twilight years.

Humans developed an upright stance, and modern hands and feet, about four million years ago, oral speech between 150,000 and 100,000 years ago, and writing 3,500 years ago. The advent of string, according to Elizabeth Wayland Barber, professor emerita of linguistics and archeology at Occidental College, who specialized in using techniques from both archeology and linguistics to study ancient textiles, comes well after people had learned to speak, and before they learned to write.

The first clothes were most likely made of animal skins. Researchers using the DNA of lice have determined that humans most likely began clothing themselves in hides and pelts about 170,000 years ago. Then, at some critical moment in the long and leisurely waste of preliterate human time, people learned to weave plant fibers into textiles. Because cloth is rarely preserved at archeological sites, it is difficult to identify its earliest use with any level of certainty. In 2009, a Georgian, Israeli, and U.S. research team discovered more than one thousand fibers of the flax plant in the Dzudzuana Cave in the foothills of the Caucasus Mountains in what is now the Republic of Georgia. The microscopic fibers were found in layers radiocarbon dated to as early as 36,000 years ago. A small number of fibers were colored black, turquoise, gray, and pink, and the research team concluded they had been dyed. This pulverized fiber powder is the earliest evidence we have of humans making use of linen.

Cloth is made from hundreds of strings interlaced with one another at right angles, or knit together in multitudinous knots. Before they could make cloth, humans had to learn to make thread. String making began during the Upper Paleolithic, a period during which humans migrated from Africa to every econiche on the globe. According to Barber, these two developments are connected: the advent of string made the rapid expansion of the zone of human habitation possible. With string, people could make nets, snares, tethers, leashes, fishing lines, and ways to bind objects together to make complex tools—new ways to catch prey and gather food.

Some of the earliest representations of humans wearing clothing made from vegetal fiber (rather than hides or sinew) show them wearing not cloth, but string. These so-called Venus statuettes made from bone and carved stone were discovered in what is now Russia and Eastern Europe, in a zone that represented the eastern end of what archeologists have termed the Gravettian culture. Most of these statuettes show naked women but some—the earliest of which dates to 20,000 BC—depict women wearing skirts made of twisted cords, distinguishable from strands of sinew because the artist carefully carved the fraying ends of each of the strings. These skirts were more ceremonial than practical, used to signify and enhance fertility, and to protect women during childbearing. One such statuette, the Venus of Gagarino, wears a string skirt that hangs only in front, above the pubic bone and below the breasts, covering neither.

Representations of women in string skirts exist in this geographical area for the next twenty thousand years, and beginning around 1300 BC actual string skirts are preserved or partially preserved in the archeological record. The first physical evidence of cordage made of vegetal fiber dates much earlier, to 15,000 BC, and comes from the

Lascaux caves in southern France, where an abbot working on copying cave paintings "picked up a compact lump of clay" and broke it open to find, inside, "the carbonaceous imprint of a sort of fillet with twisted lines stretching the entire length of the lump." All the earliest string in the archeological record is from plant fiber such as flax, hemp, jute, ramie, yucca, elm, linden, willow.

The first intact cloth in the archeological record, like those microscopic remnants from the Georgian cave, is also of linen. In 1988 archeologists digging in Çayönü, Turkey, found a linen fragment wrapped around the handle of a tool made from antler that had miraculously been preserved because of contact with calcium in the bone. The cloth was radiocarbon dated to 7000 BC. Analysis of seed types at the archeological site demonstrated that, unlike the wild flax that was used to make the linen found in the Georgian cave, this flax was domesticated. The world's first farmers, planters of wheat and barley at the headwaters of the Tigris, had also domesticated flax, and farmed the materials for their clothing, as they had for their food.

Barber has argued that textile production up until the Bronze Age, which began in the Near East around 3000 BC, was in almost all human societies women's work, in large part because it is an activity that is compatible with childrearing and safe for children to be around, unlike hunting. Toward the end of the Bronze Age, roughly 1200 BC, men begin to weave, not for household use, but for profit (or in some cases, if they were enslaved, for a slave owner's profit) in a period of increasing trade and specialization. In Egypt, men began weaving decorative, patterned cloth at around 1500 BC. For this, they used upright, vertical looms, today called tapestry looms, which provide a suitable orientation for producing expensive fabrics with designs in them. By that time, women in the region had been weaving plain linens on horizontal looms for three thousand years.*

Perhaps because of this deep-rooted association with women, textiles have often been treated as less important archeological artifacts

---

* This did not mean that women were not also sometimes textile entrepreneurs, like the woman in Apollonia, Egypt, who, in AD 298, records show spending three hundred troy ounces of silver on a loom to set up a profit-making weaving shop.

than other kinds of ancient objects. Textiles also break down quickly. Where they have survived, physically, their second-class status has threatened them with a more avoidable kind of historical annihilation. This was almost the fate of the oldest shirt in the archeological record. The shirt was found in a First Dynasty Egyptian tomb at Tarkhan, and dates to 3000 BC. Excavating the tomb in 1912 and 1913, the British archeologist Sir William Matthew Flinders Petrie dug it up among numerous other linens and placed it among his findings. The shirt went on to languish at University College London in a storage container marked "funerary rags" until two female curators exhumed it in 1977 and discovered what it was: a meticulously crafted shirt with an elaborate system of pleats that allowed its wearer to move their limbs comfortably, while still enjoying a fitted silhouette.

Growing flax to make linen was one of the oldest human activities in Europe, particularly in the Rhineland. Archeologists have found linen textiles among the settlements of Neolithic cultivators along the shores of Lake Neuchâtel in the Jura Mountains west of Bern, Switzerland. These were elaborate pieces: Stone Age clothmakers of the Swiss lakeshores sewed pierced fruit pits in a careful line into a fabric with woven stripes. The culture spread down the Rhine and into the lowland regions.

The Roman author Pliny observed in the first century AD that German women wove and wore linen sheets. By the ninth century flax had spread through Germany. By the sixteenth century, flax was produced in many parts of Europe, but the corridor from western Switzerland to the mouth of the Rhine contained the oldest region of large-scale commercial flax and linen production. In the late Middle Ages the linen of Germany was sold nearly everywhere in Europe, and Germany produced more linen than any other region in the world.

At this juncture, linen weavers became victims of an odd prejudice. "Better skinner than linen weaver," ran one cryptic medieval German taunt. Another macabre popular saying had it that linen weavers were worse than those who "carried the ladders to the gallows." The reason why linen weavers were slandered in this way, historians suspect, was that although linen weavers had professionalized and organized themselves into guilds, they had been unable to prevent homemade linen from getting onto the market. Guilds appeared across Europe between the twelfth and fifteenth centuries but many of the items they produced for exchange, like textiles and soap, were also produced at home right up through the nineteenth century. The intricate regulations of the guilds—determining who could join, how they would be trained, what goods they would produce, and how these could be exchanged—were mainly designed to distinguish guild work from this homely labor. That linen making continued to be carried out inside of households—a liability for guilds in general—lent a taint to the linen guild in particular.

In the seventeenth century, guilds came under pressure from a new, protocapitalist mode of production. Looking for cheaper cloth to sell on foreign markets, entrepreneurs cased the Central European countryside offering to pay cash to home producers for goods. Rural households became export manufacturing centers and a major source of competition with the guilds. These producers could undercut the prices of urban craftsmen because they could use the unregulated labor of their family members, and because their own agricultural production allowed them to sell their goods for less than their subsistence costs.

The uneasiness between guild and household production in the countryside erupted into open hostility. In the 1620s, linen guildsmen marched on villages, attacking competitors, and burning their looms. In February 1627 Zittau guild masters smashed looms and seized the yarn of home weavers in the villages of Oderwitz, Olbersdorf, and Herwigsdorf.

Guilds had long worked to keep homemade products from getting on the market. In their death throes, they hit upon a new and potent weapon: gender. Although women in medieval Europe wove at home for domestic consumption, many had also been guild artisans. Women were freely admitted as masters into the earliest medieval guilds, and statutes from Silesia and the Oberlausitz show that women were master weavers. Thirteenth-century Paris had eighty mixed craft guilds of men and women and fifteen female-dominated guilds for such trades as gold thread, yarn, silk, and dress manufacturing. Up until the mid-seventeenth century, guilds had belittled home production because it was unregulated, nonprofessional, and competitive. In the mid-seventeenth century this work was identified as *women's* work, and guildsmen unable to compete against cheaper household production tried to eject women from the market entirely. Single women were barred from independent participation in the guilds. Women were restricted to working as domestic servants, farmhands, spinners, knitters, embroiderers, hawkers, wet nurses. They lost ground even where the jobs had been traditionally their own, such as ale brewing and midwifery, by the end of the seventeenth century.

The wholesale ejection of women from the market during this period was achieved not only through guild statute, but through legal, literary, and cultural means. Throughout the sixteenth and seventeenth centuries women lost the legal right to conduct economic activity as *femes soles*. In France they were declared legal "imbeciles," and lost the right to make contracts or represent themselves in court. In Italy, they began to appear in court less frequently to denounce abuses against them. In Germany, when middle-class women were widowed it became customary to appoint a tutor to manage their affairs. As the medieval historian Martha Howell writes, "Comedies and satires of this period . . . often portrayed market women and trades women as shrews, with characterizations that not only ridiculed or scolded them for taking on roles in market production but frequently even charged them with sexual aggression." This was a period rich in literature about the correction of errant women: Shakespeare's *The Taming of the Shrew* (1590–94), John Ford's *'Tis Pity She's a Whore* (1629–33), Joseph Swetnam's "The Araignment of Lewde, Idle, Froward, and Unconstant Women" (1615). Meanwhile, Protestant reformers and Counter-Reformation Catholics established doctrinally that women were inherently inferior to men.

This period, called the European Age of Reason, successfully banished women from the market and transformed them into the sweet and passive beings that emerged in Victorian literature. Women accused of being scolds were paraded in the streets wearing a new device called a "branks," an iron muzzle that depressed the tongue. Prostitutes were subjected to fake drowning, whipped, and caged. Women convicted of adultery were sentenced to capital punishment.

As a cultural project, this was not merely recreational sadism. Rather, it was an ideological achievement that would have lasting and massive economic consequences. Political philosopher Silvia Federici has argued this expulsion was an intervention so massive, it ought to be included as one of a triptych of violent seizures, along with the Enclosure Acts and imperialism, that allowed capitalism to launch itself.

Meanwhile, over the course of the sixteenth and seventeenth centuries, England's large landowners seized control of land that had traditionally been held in common, or leased by families to use for their own purposes. Some peasants no longer had common pasture, while others were forcibly evicted. Enclosure spelled the end of subsistence, and the end of the peasant family's ability to support itself on the land. Women were often the fiercest resisters and were accused of devil worship, and burned as witches.

Part of why women resisted enclosure so fiercely was because they had the most to lose. The end of subsistence meant that households needed to rely on money rather than the production of agricultural goods like cloth, and women had successfully been excluded from ways to earn. As labor historian Alice Kessler-Harris has argued, "In pre-industrial societies, nearly everybody worked, and almost nobody worked for wages." During the sixteenth and seventeenth centuries, monetary relations began to dominate economic life in Europe. Barred from most wage work just as the wage became essential, women were shunted into a position of chronic poverty and financial dependence. This was the dominant socioeconomic reality when the first modern factory, a cotton-spinning mill, opened in 1771 in Derbyshire, England, an event destined to upend still further the pattern of daily life.

Meanwhile, another story was unfolding across the ocean. While in England enclosure created a landless workforce that soon would be drawn into the new spinning mills, in North America it looked as though a new golden age for independent, small-scale agriculture was dawning. Late-seventeenth- and eighteenth-century America was a world, in the words of historian Laurel Thatcher Ulrich, "where any man might own land," and in which "cloth making was an extension of farming."

The region of New England that became most famous for its linen was Londonderry, New Hampshire. Londonderry linen was sold, bartered, and exchanged each year at country festivals. Although grown on individually held plots, diarists from the time record how villagers shared the labor of harvesting and processing flax. "Break flax for Jam Henry forenoon and for myself in afternoon," wrote one resident. On another day: "Break 18 Bundles Jamison swingle 14 for mee." Men helped with the work of harvesting and breaking the flax while women skutched, hackled, carded, combed, spun, and wove the fiber. Fishing, farming, and flax making commingled in rural self-sufficiency.

This pastoral setting in which early American industry was born was not as utopian as it appeared. While the linen makers enjoyed plentiful land and the freedom to use their labor as they willed, others were not so lucky.

The tow, the hard bark skutched from the long, soft, inner fiber of the flax plant, was spun and woven to make tow cloth, "which is exported to the Southern States, to Clothe the Negroes, who labor on the plantations," as Jeremy Belknap recorded in 1792. The land itself had been newly evacuated. Shortly before the Ulster Scotts arrived, in 1713 Massachusetts and New Hampshire officials had met in Casco Bay, Maine, with representatives of several groups of Abenaki—Algonquian-speaking peoples whose homeland had extended across most of what is now northern New England and into Quebec and the Maritimes—to sign "Articles of Pacification," rendering the Abenaki subjects of Queen Anne, and promising colonists freedom to hunt, fish, and develop in the "Eastern Parts." North of Londonderry's idyllic country fairs, in a raid on an Abenaki camp in St. Francis in 1759, one participant recalled that soldiers were ordered to kill all the women and children, but when a "papoose" looked up at him he faltered. "Nits become lice," his commander said, and killed her himself. As settlers moved to take possession of territories in the New World, they justified the massacre of Native American Indians (beginning during King Philip's War) by accusing them of being devil worshippers, an echo of how women had been accused of being possessed by the devil during the European witch hunts if they resisted the enclosure movements and clung stubbornly to communal land rights.

Londonderry had once been the favorite fishing spot for the Penacook people. At Amoskeag Falls, the largest drop in the Merrimack River, the Penacook had gathered in autumn to fish for the last ten thousand years when the alewife, shad, lamprey, and salmon ran out to sea, and in spring when the fish ran upriver to spawn. Salmon return to the tiny pools where they were born to lay their eggs. Just before they die, offering their decomposing bodies for their offspring's first food, they lay several thousand eggs. It is this incredible fecundity, says the archeologist Elizabeth Wayland Barber, that led both the Greeks and early Slavs to treat fish as totems of fertility, to use their images as decorative motifs to support the making of life, like those early string skirts worn by the Gravettian people for thousands of years. To the Atlantic salmon, the Merrimack River was life itself, so it must seem to them a bitter historical irony that their own bodies were used to entice the two consecutive waves of development on the Merrimack that proved to be their undoing: drawing in settlers who would overfish them, and then dam the river outright.

The settlers who arrived were Ulster Scots, transplanted to northern Ireland in the early seventeenth century when they were offered cheap rent on large, fertile estates as the British attempted to populate the area with Protestants. Ulster, which had a good, damp climate for flax, was a thriving center for linen.

When they arrived on the banks of the Merrimack—lured there by the promise of "more Salmon & all manner of fish than in any place in the World"—these settlers swiftly made the region famous not for salmon, but for linen. Such was the reputation of Londonderry linen

that the townsfolk demanded their name be protected from coun-
terfeiters advertising any old linen as *Londonderry*. A resolution in
the New Hampshire legislature in 1731 decried the "deceit practiced
by persons travelling in this Province by selling of Foreign Linnens
under pretence they were made at Londonderry." Citizens at a 1748
town meeting demanded the creation of a seal such that "the Credate
of our Manefactors may be keept up and the bayers and purchers of
our linens may Not be Imposed upon with foreign and outlandish
Linens in the name of ours."

Although Londonderry linen was highly prized in New England,
colonial linen in general was rustic and amateurish by European
standards. English policy forbade commercial linen production from
developing in the New World in order to protect sales of English cloth
in America, so colonial American linen making did not evolve to the
scale or level of specialization seen in England. While the southern
colonies quickly developed tobacco and hemp as resources to trade
with England for finished goods, and were able thus to keep wearing English fabric, the Massachusetts Bay colonists lacked these raw
materials and thus relied on homespun yarn and handwoven fabric.
Every foreign visitor who described the New England economy at
the end of the seventeenth century made some mention of small-scale
textile production, which to European eyes appeared retrograde.

Another thing that would have seemed odd from a European perspective was that colonial weavers were largely women. The colonists
who came from East Anglia to New England in the 1630s left a sophisticated manufacturing economy where men, not women, did the
weaving, and they brought this gender division of labor with them.
In the New World, however, weaving would soon become, again, a
female occupation as other commercial opportunities appeared for
men. In New Hampshire weaving passed into the female domain in
exactly the same time that the colony's woodworking economy was
maturing.

Although its commercial implications were largely submerged
within household economies, spinning and weaving were still work,
and sometimes the workers rebelled. At midnight on January 20,
1767, as the court's indictment would later record, Sarah Bartlet, "spin-

ster," of Hadley, Massachusetts, took a candle with her right hand and voluntarily, *with malice,* set fire to "a Certain Bundle of Linnen Yarn and also a certain Bundle of Flax and Tow."

Flax, like the straw it resembles, is highly flammable. So is tow, the outer bark of the flax plant, and so too is linen thread, spun from the flax plant's soft inner fibers. Still, we cannot be certain that Sarah *intended* to burn down her employer's house when she set her spinning materials on fire. According to the diary of a neighbor girl, Elizabeth Porter, "Sarah Bartlet that Lived with Captain Marsh was brought to own that she willfully set his house on fire . . . to burn some yarn that she had been discovered to make false ties in." Perhaps Sarah only meant to burn the yarn, false ties and all.

Sarah, like other New England girls from poor families, had been boarded out to live with another family, where her spinning labor paid for room and board, and sometimes allowed her to accrue extra yarn to put toward a trousseau. Spinners like Sarah were paid by the length of the thread they spun—marked off in ties. To make false ties was to defraud the employer. Records from this period show that some young women found themselves in debt to their employers even after months of work, a fate Sarah may have been trying to avoid.

The annals of early New England fabric making are littered with small acts of intransigence, not all of them so dramatic as Sarah Bartlet's fire. In Rutland, Vermont, the angry husband of a wife who failed to be prolific in clothmaking published the following poem in the local newspaper in the early nineteenth century to announce that he would no longer pay any debts incurred by her:

> *For she will neither spin nor weave,*
> *But there she'll sit, and take her ease;*
> *There she'll sit, and pout, and grin,*
> *As if the devil had entered in;*
>
> *She would neither knit nor sew,*
> *But all in rags I had to go:*
> *So, farewell Sukey: and farewell, wife!*
> *Till you can live a better life.*

The reference to the devil entering in ought not to be taken as merely one husband's attention to meter and metaphor: it was not a century since the close of the witch hunts.

Scandals, however, are by definition exceptional. To rifle more broadly through the late-eighteenth-century American woman's diary is to hear the uninterrupted hum of industry, and also to get a sense of the enormous amount of time that went into making cloth.

Betty Foot wrote from Colchester, Connecticut, in 1775, "I have been knitting all day stiddy as a priest and so has Nab too." A week later, "I am knitting yet." Mid-March she begins spinning linen, every day but Sunday.

Betty was training to be a schoolteacher, and because of that she had some variation to her days, as when one Sunday she "stay'd at home and Learnt to read and cypher." Even with her math training one must note that in Betty's, as in all of the women's diaries, there is a wrinkle in the ciphering: the math is odd. Because women were not compensated for their labor, one must consult a man's diary from the same period to balance the equation.

Matthew Patten, a Scots-Irish farmer who lived in Bedford, New Hampshire, just across the Merrimack River from Londonderry, wrote in his accounts on July 13, 1781, "I went to Robert Spears in Goffstown and lent him 237 Dollars of Continental old money for which he is to pay me New money when he sells the fine cloath his wife is now making." Mrs. Spears's cloth could yield currency when she stood next to her husband, as though she were a cipher and he the integer, and so that by proximity she increased his value by ten.

Only unmarried women, born to well-off families, were able to earn money in colonial New England by spinning and weaving. In the 1790s, Hannah Matthews, working under her father's well-provisioned roof, kept her own accounting books. She carefully recorded debts on the left and credits on the right, in her journal, balancing her own labor in spinning, weaving, and combing worsted with goods received: corn, flax, mutton, hogs, lard, and occasional cash. She included an alphabetical index and title to the book, "The Property of Hannah Matthews Yarmouth June the 11th 1790." However, Hannah's accounts abruptly end when she marries. And rather than waste the rest of the pages, her provident husband simply turned her journal over and began to use it to do his own accounting.

The long, unmarked hours that New England women spent by their spindles and looms burst suddenly out from the private diary and into the spotlight in the late eighteenth century, as fabric making moved center stage in the fight for national independence. In the 1760s Parliament's effort to tax the colonies provoked boycotts of British goods. Suddenly, homespun fabric became charged with political meaning. Newspapers devoted front-page spreads to spinning meetings organized by New England's "daughters of liberty."

In his 1791 *Report on Manufactures,* Alexander Hamilton argued that the United States would cement its political independence from England by become economically self-sufficient. How? By developing its textile manufacture. To do this, Hamilton argued, Americans would have to rely on their most pliable resources: water, women, and children. In a nation where "the defect of hands constitutes the greatest obstacle to success," Hamilton wrote, the new textile machinery being developed in England would make women "more useful, and the [children] more early useful."

Hamilton rejected the pastoral vision for America espoused by Thomas Jefferson, who wanted to retain an unindustrialized agrarian economy. Although Hamilton's model may indeed have been the best way for the U.S. to maintain its independence in the face of expansionist colonial powers in Europe, it is easy to see why others like Jefferson remained attached to an America where farmers dressed in flax grown and spun on the family plot. Londonderry seemed far preferable to the desolate sight of hollow-cheeked women and children bent over industrial machinery that emerged quickly from England's industrial North, as the first cotton mill in Derbyshire was joined by scores of imitators. If, as archeologists suggest, textile work was originally assigned to women because it was an activity that was safe to do with children nearby, the new logic of assigning mechanized fabric production to both women and children forwent this consideration entirely. Women and children were to enter together into factories where *neither* would be safe: where blowing cotton destroyed lungs, ears were deafened by the sound of machinery, and belts regularly tore off scalps.

The argument Hamilton made and his willingness to exploit two cheap resources—women and nature—became ubiquitous. Cheap women's labor and expendable land have been the foundation of the garment industry ever since.

Industrial spinning soon arrived in America, where it swiftly brought about the end of home-manufactured flax. In the early 1790s, an industrial saboteur named Samuel Slater broke the British law forbidding engineers with knowledge of the new textile machinery to emigrate, and arrived in the U.S. with working plans for a drawing frame stitched in the lining of a coat pocket. In 1793 Slater, along with investor Moses Brown, opened the first industrial cotton-spinning mill in America in Pawtucket, Rhode Island, known as the Slater Mill. The same year, Eli Whitney invented the cotton gin. The metal teeth of Whitney's gin could process as much short staple cotton in under an hour as a team of slaves had formerly been able to process in a day. Linen was out, cotton was in, and it was big money.

Slater Mill copycats popped up quickly across New England. Townspeople in Londonderry voted in 1810 to change the town's name to *Manchester,* after the British city by then famous for its textiles. A small mill with new spinning equipment was set up on the west side of the roaring Amoskeag Falls. In 1822, Samuel Slater received a "fine specimen of a salmon" that had been caught at the Falls to entice him to invest in the new mill. Slater was intrigued and brought in the Boston Associates, a group of investors who had made eighteenth-century shipping fortunes in the triangle of rum, slaves, and sugar, and built up factory cities at Cabot and Lowell. Together, they bought up houses, farms, and water rights, until they controlled the water down the entire length of the Merrimack. The company installed a massive, U-shaped dam on the river, and laid out an entire town around it, replete with factories, boardinghouses, family worker housing, schools, and churches—an entire city built for one reason: to make cloth.

For thousands of years, human beings had worked within the constraints of the natural environment to make cloth. Here in Manchester they had made cloth by bending the environment completely to their will. Achieving a total domination of nature, as the Boston Group had, was fantastically productive: in its heyday, Amoskeag Mill, the largest in the country, produced fifty miles of cloth an hour.

The days of homespun linen had come to an end. By 1831, the *New England Farmer* reported, "a domestic manufactured linen shirt [was] as rare as a white colt." The historian of Hadley, Massachusetts, Sylvester Judd, wrote in 1863 that "the flax dresser, with the shives, fibres and dirt of flax covering his garments, and his face begrimed with dust, has disappeared; the noise of his brake and swingling knife has ended, and the boys no longer make bonfires of his swingling tow. The sound of the spinning wheel, the song of the spinster and the snapping of the clock-reel have all ceased." He might have continued the dirge directly from Ecclesiastes, "And the doors are shut toward the street, when the sound of the grinding is subdued, and they rise up at the voice of the bird, and all the daughters of song are brought low."

The salmon that used to populate Amoskeag Falls are long gone, so are the linen fairs, and the cotton factories: Manchester's citizens no longer fish, nor make flax, nor spin cotton. Manchester is a dreary postindustrial town, where rehabs and treatment centers now flourish. I was in town to attend a local residency in the summer of 2017, and planned a visit to a museum converted from what was formerly Mill no. 3 in the historic Amoskeag Millyard. Stephanie, whom I had met in a local coffee shop, decided to come along with me. She had grown up in Manchester, but told me she had never learned about the mills in school.

At the opening of the museum's exhibition, an interpretive text beside a grinding tool carved with the head of a deer read: "The native peoples of the Merrimack were self-sufficient. They created all the objects they needed for everyday life within the tribal group. Although they had no metal tools, they made many kinds of stone implements—making them the first 'industrialists' of New Hampshire!"

A hall reconstructed Manchester in its "heyday," with a soda shop, shoe store, and candy store. What had become of the city since the mills were shuttered in this one-industry town? The museum's plaques acknowledged that the legendary industrial center that once belched fifty miles of cotton fabric an hour is now defunct. But they boasted that there are *dozens of small businesses* in the refurbished buildings that once housed the machinery and the workers. There are *dentists* and *hairdressers* and *restaurants*. *Coca-Cola* has built a machine to purify water in the *Third World*. The giant Lego model of the Amoskeag Mill at the children's museum is the *Largest in North America*. The exhibit concluded with a wall of tributes to Manchester celebrities: To "the far-sighted investors who had developed the textile centers downriver at Lowell and Lawrence [and] took on the challenge of harnessing the tremendous power of the Amoskeag Falls for manufacturing." To Revolutionary War general John Stark, "Honored Patriarch." To the founders of McDonald's, Richard and Maurice McDonald. To Adam Sandler.

In the gift shop I bought a T-shirt that said, "The Mill Girl, Forging a New Path for Women." I could only imagine the skepticism with which an actual "Mill Girl" would have greeted this T-shirt.

Unlike their British counterparts, shoved off the land and into factories, New England girls often came from families who still had their farms, but their main economic function had been usurped. When New England women went to work in industrial textile mills, or as some historians have said, "followed" their work out of the house and into the factory, they found it almost as difficult to make money at it that way as they had before. "I have tended four looms nearly a year & a half & have only ninety dollars in the bank," one young textile worker in Lowell, Massachusetts, named Deborah Hibbard would write to her sister Sarah on October 8, 1845.

Despite what Manchester's museum curators may proclaim, in the mid-nineteenth century, observers of New England's mills noted their oppressive conditions. Transcendentalist Orestes Brownson wrote in the 1840s of the factory girls in Lowell: "The great mass wear out their health, spirits, and morals without becoming one whit better off than when they commenced labour. The bills of mortality in these factory villages are not striking, we admit, for the poor girls, when they can toil no longer, go home to die."

The years a young woman spent at Lowell would traditionally have been the period in which she spun and wove, along with female relatives, a store of linens to supply herself for marriage. With the rise of industrial machinery, manufacturers tried to frame a very new situation in terms of old ideas, emphasizing the ways factory work would allow a young woman to support her family from afar, and prepare for her future marriage. But the new labor arrangements would come to threaten the very unit—the family—from which industrial employers derived their convoluted justifications for paying women so little. To maintain a source of cheap workers, employers did their best to conceal these contradictions. But as we have seen, under family economies lie stains and strains, and linens have a particular way of storing secrets. The very thing that likes to keep itself hidden: the underlinen, has a lot to reveal.

2

Underthings

. . . last night you were in my room
And now my bedsheets smell like you.

—ED SHEERAN, "SHAPE OF YOU"

Number 5 on *Bustle*'s "17 Ways to Take Care of Yourself After a Breakup so You Can Move On in the Healthiest Way Possible" is: "Wash everything. The clothes you've been avoiding, towels, bedsheets (especially). You know what? If the relationship was a long one and you can afford it, buy new sheets. High thread-count ones. But seriously, getting the smell and~presence~of your ex off all your fiber belongings is a good start."

This advice is reiterated on numerous online and print magazines. The lifestyle experts agree: extirpation is the better part of healing.

The first thing to note about this prescription is that in much of the contemporary world, sheets are closely bound up with sex and love. The word "sheet" makes its first appearance as bedding in 1250: "Schene vnder schete, and þeyh heo is schendful," which loosely translates to "she looks lovely in the sheet, but she's a whore." Earlier usages refer to the sheet as a bandage at about AD 725 and shroud sometime around AD 1000, establishing the sheet as companion to the wound and the corpse prior to its service as the casement of the lover. By 1347, in Chaucer, the sheet has become a commonplace, if not a right: "No down of fetheres ne no bleched shete Was kyd to hem."

Sheets, like undergarments, had been made of linen from their earliest appearance up until the advent of cheap, mass-manufactured cotton fabric in the late eighteenth century and *linen* became metonymically linked with both sheets and underthings in the Middle Ages, yielding "lining," "linen closet," and "lingerie." In France, the word "linen" migrated from adjective to noun in the thirteenth century, as its use to refer to household linen and undergarments became universal. Property inventories for wealthy medieval families started to list clothes worn next to the body, usually made from finer cloth than outer garments. In comparison to household linen like sheets, shrouds, tablecloths, napkins, and *toualles* (a combination of a napkin and a towel), body linen remained rare in this period but was not unknown even among the poor. The seventeenth-century linen draper dealt both household linen (*linger*) and underwear (*lingerie*), and in the seventeenth and eighteenth centuries the French spoke of these as "great" and "small" linen (*gros linge* and *menu linge*). A seventeenth-century dictionary demarcated linen's many types: there was table linen and fine linen, great linen, day and night linen.

By the eighteenth century, the use of underlinen became general throughout the population.* These undergarments bore little resemblance to ours, however. An inventory drawn up by the meticulous Mme de Schomberg in the 1760s listing all the items of her wardrobe showed she owned a great deal of underlinen: underskirts, shirts, mantles (nightgowns), mantelets (short, sleeveless capes), furbelows (flounces to adorn an underskirt), caps, cuffs, stockings formed her arsenal of lingerie.

The rise of modern-day underwear awaited indoor plumbing: the threat of thrush, which warmth invites, discouraged women from wearing a garment close in against her crotch until regular bathing and laundering were possible. Women in Europe and America wore, rather, long skirts with petticoats right up into the early twentieth century. Knickers, or drawers, had been worn occasionally since

---

* Linen's broader use was fed by its falling price, which in turn was owed to the advances of the merchants who contracted directly with peasants to avoid the expensive labor of guild manufacturing.

the fifteenth century by upper-class women in Europe, though the vogue largely died out by the seventeenth century. These were tied at the waist and above or below the knee with a ribbon or string drawn tight at the closures (yielding "drawers"). The design of contemporary underwear awaited two colonial products: cotton, and rubber, which was used to make elastic.

Despite looking quite different from our contemporary undergarments, body linen, like bed linen, was closely associated with the illicit in the medieval European imagination. In its first recorded use to signal "undergarment," linen appears in a fourteenth-century chronicle: "Alle þei fled on rowe, in lynen white as milke,"* and costumes the tryst in a 1607 Jacobean revenge tragedy when "He and the Duchesse, By night meete in their linen."

Shakespeare, the most prodigal of phrase-smiths, seems to have coined "between the sheets," in *Much Ado About Nothing* (1600): "O when she had writ it, and was reading it ouer, she found Benedicke and Beatrice betweene the sheete." However, the church had already acknowledged the link between sheets and sex in a bizarre sixteenth-century public shaming ritual that was brought to North America with English colonists. Adulterers or fornicators were made to stand in a public marketplace or church wearing nothing but a white sheet and holding either a candle or a rod. As a chronicle from 1587 records, "Harlots and their mates by . . . dooing of open penance in sheets, in churches and market steeds are . . . put to rebuke." This connection to respectability and its opposite was to cling quite stubbornly to linen.

From the sixteenth century onward, the social position of both men and women was hitched closely to the fineness and cleanness of their linen. At a time when the body was understood to be porous, susceptible to attack by waterborne miasmas, washing with water was done sparingly, and immaculate white linen became a kind of proxy for cleanliness. Linen *did* cleanse somewhat, insofar as when a shirt was changed, sweat was removed, but its primary function was to serve as a marker of status.

---

* "They all fled in rows, in linen white as milk."

One tenet of the early modern "civilization of manners" was that dirty clothing indicated a tarnished soul. A manual of manners published in 1740 emphasized the importance of clean linen: "for if your clothes are clean, and especially if your linen is white, there is no need to be richly dressed, you will feel your best, even in poverty." For the poor, adhering to the ideal of clean linen was difficult. In cities, water was scarce and expensive, fabrics were broken down by repeated washing, and to be clean it was necessary to own enough linen and clothes to allow time for them to *be* cleaned.

Advertising a family's superior morality by keeping its linens white was a burden that fell largely to women, under whose care linen was placed. In the sixteenth through eighteenth centuries, as we have seen, the juridical and social status of European women eroded, and a new feminine identity emphasized women's role within the household. They became housewives, dependent within the family economy, confined to keeping up both their own personal appearance and the appearance of the household at large: including attending to the cleanliness of clothes and linens.

Europeans grew more and more obsessed with the whiteness of their linen as they dirtied their hands in brutal colonial ventures. In the early 1780s it became fashionable in Paris to send one's linens to be bleached to a blue white in the sun of what was then called Saint-Domingue, and is now called Haiti. Although soap became commonly used for laundry, replacing ashes, by the eve of the French Revolution, Parisian linen still carried a yellowish tinge. Linen bleached in the equatorial sun with native indigo achieved a luminous, bluish tint: it had "a fineness and an azure whiteness entirely different from the linen of France," according to the comte de Vaublanc. In 1782, after a fleet of one hundred ships arrived from the colonies, Vaublanc recalled that "Paris was full of men and women who wore the handsome linen bleached in Saint-Domingue. This linen drew everyone's eyes. . . . One compared the whiteness of this linen to the slightly yellow color of that of Paris. From that day the laundering of linen changed entirely; it became very difficult."

. . .

n New England, fine white linen displayed caste, and the most prosperous colonists draped their cupboards in lace-trimmed linen, damask, and diaper. In first-generation New England, the Puritan gentry worried whether an attachment to fine linen could be spiritually compromising. John Winthrop, governor of Massachusetts whose 1630–49 journal has provided much of our knowledge of early colonial Massachusetts, tells the story of a Boston woman who brought with her from London "a parcel of very fine linen of great value, which she set her heart too much upon." Her maid dropped candle snuff on it one night and it all was burned, "but it pleased God that the loss of this linen did her much good . . . in taking off her heart from worldly comforts," Winthrop wrote, indicating a cultural milieu in which it was both necessary to display the fine linen and view it with the appropriate level of detachment.

Country and city girls lavished time and attention on their trousseaus, producing wardrobes full of household and personal linen beyond what would ever be needed, clothing historian Daniel Roche has argued. This was linen that would be exhibited on the wedding day, and never sold. Women prepared trousseau textiles together with their mothers, in preparation for marriage. Some of these textiles would be inherited in turn by the daughter's daughters, connecting generations of women. The matrilineal side was called the "distaff side," a distaff being a part of a spinning wheel, just as the word "wife" appears to be connected etymologically to the word "weave."

For most women, linen was the only property they could own. Daughters received their portions at marriage rather than at the death of their fathers. In early modern Europe and America, real estate was transmitted by inheritance from father to son, while daughters received their inheritance in goods that could easily be moved from one dwelling to another: cattle, and household goods known as "movables." The "movables" that formed the core of a New England inheritance usually consisted of furniture and textiles, and of these two textiles were by far the more valuable. In eighteenth-century New England, the parlor cupboard listed in the household inventory of a man named John Pynchon was valued at £3, while the table linens kept in it were worth more than £13. As the American historian Laurel Ulrich has noted, "The possession of real property secured male authority. In such a system, women themselves became movables, changing their names and presumably their identities as they moved from one male headed household to another."

Women's property rights in America were set by the English common-law concept of coverture. Upon marriage, a woman's legal existence as an individual was suspended under "marital unity," a legal fiction by which the husband and wife became a single entity: the husband.[*]

Under coverture, married women legally owned nothing, but by custom they possessed the linens. The word "coverture" appeared in English for the first time around 1200 and was originally a term used for a coverlet or quilt. Beneath this quilt, appropriately enough, lay the rightful territory of women: the linens. Under coverture, women had no rights to their children, so that if a wife divorced, where it was permitted, or left a husband, she would not see her children again. A husband could claim any wages generated by his wife's labor and had an absolute right to sexual access. Within marriage, a wife's consent was implied, so under the law, all sex-related activity was legitimate.

With rights neither to land, nor wealth, nor their own children or bodies, women made their mark on linen. Unlike land, which can be traced in deeds, movables flowed, by definition, outside the law. However, it is possible to trace, albeit sketchily, lines of female inheritance, because women took care to mark linens with their own initials if not their full names. One property survey noted: "two pair of sheets marked EC, new sheets marked MC, and a pair of sheets called Hannah's." Women adorned linens with their names, their insignia, and sometimes with the desire not to sink into obscurity, like the eighteenth-century woman who stitched:

---

* Coverture lasted in England until the Married Women's Property Act of 1882. Coverture was disassembled in the United States through legislation at the state level beginning in Mississippi in 1839 and continuing into the 1880s. Real estate, a relatively more abundant trade commodity, played a different role in the United States than it did in England. In Canada, coverture was repealed by statute in the 1970s.

When I am dead and in my grave,
And all my bones are rotten.
When this you see remember me,
That I won't be forgotten.

Before the Industrial Revolution transformed the nature of work, the family was a unit of production. In the nineteenth century, this productive function was stripped away. Homespun became factory cloth, the vegetable plot and canning became tinned foods. Some tasks, however, clung stubbornly within the walls of the private family home. Caring for children and other family members who might have been able to contribute to life on a farm, but not able to work for wages—the disabled and the elderly, for instance—became the responsibility of women, who were simultaneously cut off from equal participation with men in paid work.

The bourgeois ideal of the family pervasive from the mid-nineteenth century onward was one in which only the man earned money, and the wife performed unpaid labor in the home, which in turn was imagined as a haven away from business and competition. It was an extension of the "domestic code" that had evolved in the eighteenth century, labor historian Alice Kessler-Harris argues, in which a role inside the home was the measure of morality for women.

Francis Cabot Lowell attempted to make factory work for women compatible with the domestic code by hiring the young single daughters of farm families and enticing them with the notion that they could save money for a trousseau, to send a brother through college, or to help pay off a family mortgage. At the Lowell, Massachusetts, mill he opened in 1821, he offered strictly supervised boardinghouses for young women, and assured their parents that hard work and discipline would render the women better wives and mothers. In the dormitories, matrons enforced a 10 p.m. curfew and, as the *Boston Associate* announced, "the company will not employ anyone who is habitually absent from public worship on the Sabbath or known to be guilty of immorality." The working day lasted 12.5 or 13.5 hours, weekly wage set at about $2.50, with $1.25 deducted each week for board.

In the 1840s, although only one in ten American women worked in the paid labor force, they made up half of the country's factory population. The proportion of women was even higher in textiles, hats, and shoes, and some New England mills were staffed by 80–90 percent women. It was no wonder that factories wanted to hire women: they were cheap. Throughout the nineteenth century, women's wages hovered between one third and one half of men's: not enough to support a single woman, let alone a family. And yet, evidence pointed to the fact that women factory workers frequently became the family breadwinner. In England, Karl Marx's collaborator Friedrich Engels observed in 1845 that factory owners preferred cheap female and child labor to more expensive male labor. This arrangement "unsexes the man and takes from the woman all womanliness," Engels despaired. He perceptively added, however, that "if the reign of the wife over the husband, as inevitably brought about by the factory system, is inhuman, the pristine rule of the husband over the wife must have been inhuman too."

Even with ample evidence to the contrary, employers continued to justify women's inadequate wages by asserting that her family would supplement them.

The "domestic code" that insisted women's place was in the home was not a description of reality. It was an ideology, and in the United States it worked to punish women along racist and classist lines. After all, if a woman's respectability depended on her staying out of the labor force, those excluded from respectability were disproportionately immigrants and Black women. While less than 20 percent of all white women could be found in the paid labor force at any time before 1900, among African American women that proportion was at least double. The absence of good jobs for Black men and the prevalence of poverty among the newly emancipated population made their wages necessary to support a household.[*]

If it was a myth that women deserved to be paid less because they could count on a family to support them, it was also a myth that the

---

[*] Black women were broadly excluded from work in textile factories, which was more desirable than work as a domestic servant, until 1964.

home was a haven away from commerce. Indeed, women did much of their wage work *in* the home, in the form of piecework. In the eighteenth century, women embroidered their linens. In the nineteenth century, a whole new generation of women picked up their needles at home to earn a paltry wage.

Sewing ready-to-wear clothing emerged as a livelihood in American cities in the 1820s, right when the daughters of New England were going to work in textile mills. Indeed, one enabled the other. In an age of handwoven fabric, the time and expense to make fabric more than merited taking, also, the time and expense of hand tailoring. Manufactured cloth was so much cheaper that it made the prospect of mass-producing whole garments a logical next step. Ready-made clothes were cut out and distributed by wholesalers to women who took the pieces home or worked on them in the cutter's shop. Until the 1840s, most of the ready-to-wear being produced was undergarments for men: shirts and pantaloons, joined in the 1850s by corsets.

The nineteenth century saw the exaltation of the corset, or what costume historian Daniel Roche has termed the "cult of underwear." It arrived along with the triumph of a bourgeois dress that, for women, meant massive skirts and a painfully attenuated waist: a costume in which it was difficult to move, let alone work, "epitomizing," according to Roche, "the image of the unproductive woman, pure display, pure consumption, whilst silence temporarily reigned on the subject of sexuality." While bourgeois women's corsets flaunted a lack of fitness for work, the seamstresses producing these undergarments typically worked fourteen-hour days.

A mid-nineteenth-century American woman tasked with supporting herself had very few options outside of factory work. In Europe she might have become a governess, but American families seldom hired them. She could open a shop or start a school, but both required capital. Without capital, taking in sewing was the only alternative left, besides working on the street. Employers took advantage of this extreme lack of options to exploit women without fear of protest.

The misery of nineteenth-century seamstresses was notorious. "We know of no class of workwomen who are more poorly paid for their work or who suffer more privation and hardship," wrote the *New York Herald* in 1853. "A tailor gets five dollars for a coat taking two days, a shirt woman gets a maximum of one and a half dollars, working 12 or 14 hours a day." Working on this per-shirt basis, shirt sewers earned an average of $2.50 a week, although a quarter of them made only $1.50 a week. The average seamstress could barely afford, the English poet Thomas Hood wrote, to stitch herself a shroud. For these women, Thomas Hood wrote the popular ditty "Song of the Shirt."

> *With fingers weary and worn,*
> *With eyelids heavy and red,*
> *A woman sat, in unwomanly rags,*
> *Plying her needle and thread,*
> *Stitch! Stitch! Stitch!*
> *In poverty, hunger and dirt;*
> *And still with a voice of dolorous pitch—*
> *Would that its tone could reach the rich!—*
> *She sang this "Song of the Shirt!"*

While women had few options in nineteenth-century America, white men were allowed upward social mobility. Indeed, this was the age that defined the American myth of the self-made man. One of the greatest of the rags-to-riches stories of the mid-nineteenth century was that of Isaac Merritt Singer.

In 1829 Rochester, New York, was a bustling city, drawing young men from the neighboring countryside. Among them was the seventeen-year-old Isaac Singer. He had left his father's house in Oswego, New York, at the age of twelve and moved in with an older brother in Rochester. In 1830, at eighteen, Singer apprenticed himself at a shop that made and repaired machines for farmers and craftsmen. After four months he picked up a contract in Auburn, to make some lathe-making machinery, and left the apprenticeship. He had that restlessness Alexis de Tocqueville commented on among the Americans he had observed in 1831: Americans had, he said, "No inveterate habits, no spirit of routine. . . . Everybody here wants to grow rich and rise in the world."

Singer joined an itinerant theater troupe after winning over the troupe leader, Edwin Dean, with a monologue from *Richard III*. Later in life he liked to boast he had been "one of the best Richards of his day." Although, tellingly, he was not without his detractors: one contemporary critic described his performances as "crude and bombastical." In 1835 or '36 he moved to New York City, taking a job in a print shop. But Singer could not shake his theater bug. The next spring, he took off with a company of strolling players as an advance agent, leaving a wife and a child behind. He drifted, supporting himself with labor jobs when acting work was scarce.

The Erie Canal's success had encouraged a spate of canal construction. In 1839 Singer was working as a laborer in Chicago, where one of his brothers was a contractor for the new Illinois and Michigan Canal. It was here that Singer produced his first invention: a crank-operated machine for drilling rock. He was able to sell the patent for $2,000, a small fortune at the time. Having made some money, he convinced his mistress, Mary Ann Sponsler, to come out to meet him in Chicago. There they formed a family theater troupe they called the Merritt Players, performing temperance dramas and Shakespeare. Although Singer never capitulated to Mary Ann's demand that he divorce his first wife and marry her, she was to become the public Mrs. Singer, a compromise she apparently accepted. They lived this itinerant life until 1844 when the players (by now comprised of Isaac and Mary Ann, plus their children Gus, Voulettie, John, and Fannie) settled in Fredericksburg, Ohio, where Singer got a job carving wooden typeface.

Newspaper headlines in America were at that time set in wooden type that had to be carved laboriously by hand. Singer went to work on creating a machine that could automatically carve wood type. He had made money once before by inventing, and now he hoped to strike it rich again. He found an investor, George Zieber, who brought Singer to Boston, then the center of the book manufacturing trade, to look for a buyer. In one of the other rented rooms on the first floor at 19 Harvard Place where Singer was laboring over the wood type carving machine, a group of mechanics was working on fixing a glitch in another novel machine, manufactured by Lerow and Blodgett and based on a model that had been patented by Elias Howe in 1846. It was a machine designed to do something that had only ever been done by hand: to sew.

Howe's early model had a curved needle and a shuttle that made a circular motion, and could only sew in one direction, making it only useful for straight seams. In addition to that flaw, it was constantly breaking down. When George Zieber suggested Singer take a break from the wood type machine and try to tinker with the sewing machine, he is alleged to have responded, "What a devilish machine . . . you want to do away with the only thing that keeps women quiet, their sewing."

Despite his misgivings, Singer fixed and improved upon the machine so that it could sew in any direction. His efforts yielded the first sewing machine that worked in a practical way, powered by a convenient foot pedal. Elated, Zieber set about getting a patent. A company was formed with Singer, Zieber, and a third man, Orson Phelps, who owned the shop where they worked. Singer was a big man, six foot five. He didn't want his own name on such an effeminate machine, so he first called his sewing machine "The Jenny Lind," after the singer P. T. Barnum had just brought over from Europe. After some consideration, Singer and his investors decided that the name might one day go out of fashion, and renamed the machine "The Singer."

By the time Singer encountered it in 1850, the sewing machine had been invented at least four times already. In 1790 an English cabinetmaker, Thomas Saint, had taken out a patent for a device that contained many of the features later to be incorporated into the Singer. This machine, however, had never been produced, and the drawing was buried in a patent outlining new ways to use adhesive in making shoes.

Another sewing machine was invented by a journeyman tailor named Barthélemy Thimonnier in Amplepuis, near the textile center of Lyon, France. The machine Thimonnier patented in 1830 was slow and clumsy, and produced only a chain stitch (unlike a lock stitch, a chain stitch can be easily unraveled if the thread is cut). Nonetheless, he found a backer and set up a workshop in Paris. In 1831 he had eighty seamstresses working for him, tailoring army uniforms. Two hundred journeyman tailors, sensing their livelihoods were threatened by Thimonnier's machine, stormed the workshop and threw the machines out the window. Thimonnier returned to Amplepuis and developed a new, improved machine he called the *couso-brodeur*. But just as he was getting back on his feet the start of the French Revolution of 1848 threatened to destroy his workshop again, and he fled to England.

In 1834 the sewing machine was invented for the third time on Amos Street, in New York, by Walter Hunt. Hunt, inventor of, among other things, the safety pin and the rotary street-sweeping machine, offered the machine to his daughter Caroline to make corsets with. She objected that this might harm the many seamstresses then living so precariously and her father dropped the idea as well as the machine.

Soon after, another American invented a sewing machine. Elias Howe both produced and patented it, in 1846, and went out looking for a market. Here, Howe struggled. His first buyer was a corset manufacturer in Cheapside, London, who so badly took advantage of Howe that he returned to America penniless. He was so poor, in fact, that the day his wife and children left for America ahead of him, they couldn't afford to pick up their linens from the washerwoman.

The sewing machine had thus remained a novelty, one whose value was not immediately recognized. At the Great Exhibition, held at the Crystal Palace in London in 1851, several sewing machines were on display, and were not much noticed. A reporter from the Italian *Giornale di Roma* gave the following, highly colorful account of them:

A little further on, you stop before a small brass machine, about the size of a quart pot, you fancy it is a meat roaster; not at all. Ha! Ha! It is a tailor! Yes, a veritable stitcher. Present a piece of cloth to it; suddenly it becomes agitated, it twists about, screams audibly—a pair of scissors are projected forth—the cloth is cut; a needle sets to work; and lo and behold, the process of sewing goes on with feverish activity, and before you have taken three steps a pair of inexpressibles are thrown to your feet, and the impatient machine, all fretting and fuming, seems to expect a second piece of cloth at your hands.

The sewing machine had been invented by many people, and each of the major American sewing machine manufacturers that appeared in the 1840s and 1850s had soon applied for and obtained patents for various improvements to it, until eventually each was consumed in suing the others for infringement.

When Howe returned home penniless from England, he was dogged in suing anyone who manufactured a similar machine. By 1853 the four biggest sewing machine manufacturers, apart from Singer, had accepted Howe's terms and were manufacturing under his license. Singer flew into a rage when Howe offered to sell him rights, and threatened to kick Howe down the stairs of the machine shop.

In October 1856 things came to a head: representatives from three major competing manufacturers—Singer, Wheeler and Wilson, and Grover and Baker—met in Albany, where the cases in which each accused the other of infringement were to be tried. Orlando Potter, a lawyer for Grover and Baker, proposed an elegant alternative. The group formed the Sewing Machine Combination, pooling their patent rights. Howe was eventually convinced to join. Anyone who wanted to manufacture the machines could be granted a license by the Combination, for a price of $15 per machine sold, and an additional $5 to Howe. This legal innovation proved to be crucial in the making of automobiles, radios, and other goods. The Anti-Trust Division of the U.S. Department of Justice was created in large part to deal with the lasting effects of the patent pool.

Because sewing machines were the first complex machines to be mass-produced for the consumer market, the tools to produce them only existed in armories, which is where the first sewing machines were manufactured. By the 1860s sewing machine manufacture emerged in its own right. A journalist for the *New York Daily Tribune* toured a factory in 1863, and rhapsodized that the parts were all "so exactly alike that a thousand pieces are finished and thrown into a box together, and each one forming a part of a machine, and never requiring the stroke of a file to adjust it." In 1858 the English *Mechanic's Journal* explained to its readers, "in the United States, the manufacture of sewing machines is carried out by improved machinery, in large factories specially devoted to the purpose, and consequently the machines themselves are, as pieces of mechanism, of the most perfect construction."

The Singer Company bragged in its 1857 *Gazette* that the new factory it had constructed on Mott Street, in Manhattan, was worth $400,000. This marked the first time an investment of this scale had been made to manufacture any consumer good other than guns. Production exploded. In 1856 I. M. Singer & Co. manufactured 2,564 machines. In 1890 they manufactured 13,000.

Singer outperformed his competition because he was a born publicist. His background in theater was paying off, and he was about to play his greatest role: Singer went on national tours, gave demonstrations in hired halls, fairs, and carnivals, even offered his own heart-rending rendition of "The Song of the Shirt." He had to convince the spendthrift Yankee farmer that he needed a contrivance that he had never needed before: initial asking price, $125.

Among all the challenges the sewing machine manufacturers faced, the largest one was that of selling them in a United States still filled with largely self-sufficient farmers. Historically, everything a household needed could either be manufactured at home such as linens and furniture or bought cheaply like pots and pans. The exception to this was guns. But for a gun, there was no substitute. It provided food, and on the frontier, protection. There *was* a substitute for the sewing machine: a woman's time and effort. In 1859 *Frank Leslie's Illustrated Weekly* ran a cartoon in which "Mr. Plumley, tired of stitching up his own coats, concludes to get himself a sewing machine. He accordingly gets one that will not get out of order, and will cost nothing to keep in repair [the picture shows a young woman]. After a few months of marriage, Mr. Plumley finds to his great dismay, that said machine does cost something" [the picture shows she has become a nagging wife].

The concept of machinery that would perform domestic labor was a new one, and although mechanical innovation had been made welcome on the farm and in the factory in labor-hungry America, it achieved an uncertain welcome into the home. Because men were typically making the purchase of a sewing machine, while a woman would be the one to use it, the purchase raised the question of what benefit, if any, would come from a device that saved women time. What would she do with her free hours? In 1866 *Harper's Weekly* ran a cartoon showing a salesman demonstrating a sewing machine to a group of ladies with a caption: "A most Wonderful Invention, indeed, Mum, and it really Executes the Work so Efficiently and Quickly that, 'pon my Word, I think there's nothing left for the ladies to do now but to *Improve their Intellects!*"

From the beginning, Singer's ad copy targeted women. One Singer booklet announced, "The great importance of the sewing machine" was that it freed up countless hours that could be spent "In the increase of time and opportunity for that early training of children, for lack of which so many pitiful wrecks are strewn along the shores of life." It bragged also of "the numberless avenues it has opened for women's employment; and in the comforts it has brought within the reach of all, which formerly could be attained only by the wealthy few."

The observers, like Caroline Hunt, the inventor's daughter, who worried that the shirt women would lose an occupation because of the sewing machine, need not have. Women who had plied the needle became sewing machine operators. Unlike sewing machines themselves, whose cast iron parts could be forged by machines, clothing manufacturers could never manage to eliminate (and still have not) the immense amount of human labor necessary to handle fabric. And mass manufacturers, looking to squeeze profit, often assigned this task to women.

The sewing machine did not create the concept of ready-to-wear, which started in the 1820s, but it vastly accelerated and consolidated it. At the end of the nineteenth century, as the sewing machine came into general use, it sped up the centralization of the garment industry and increased competition for work. Conditions in garment shops became notorious. Just as the shirt woman with her needle and thread had walked the line with starvation, sewing machine operators were exploited to the full. Bosses manipulated clocks to cheat on hours, locked factory doors to prevent unauthorized bathroom breaks, and handed out tiny, easy-to-lose paper tokens that had to be saved up toward a paycheck. And the industry was rife with the practice of trading easy tasks for sexual favors.

n an age when "reputable" women were barred from industry jobs, but poor women were worked to death, another great hypocrisy was perpetrated in the arena of sexual mores. While bourgeois women were supposed to be chaste, among working-class women, prostitution was rampant. Indeed, for the whole of the nineteenth century, the brothel and the sewing needle were like poles for a penniless female underclass to vacillate between.

Dr. William W. Sanger, a resident physician at New York's Blackwell's Island, estimated in 1857 that the majority of the female inhabitants of Blackwell's Island were prostitutes: about 50 percent of the women in the almshouse, and close to 100 percent of those in the penitentiary. The fact that many women turned to prostitution to supplement income from other jobs illustrates how desperately low was the pay offered them. In 1888 a U.S. Commission of Labor report found that nearly a third of the 3,866 prostitutes who were interviewed by the study had been "in service" either in private homes or hotels and restaurants. Another third had no other wage work. And the final third had come from a variety of other unskilled, low-paid occupations. Where appearances mattered, employers took certain steps: in the 1880s, department store managers refused to hire salesclerks who did not live in families, worried that financial need would drive them to prostitution.

In the 1889 Chekhov story "An Attack of Nerves," the protagonist, a student, experiences a moral crisis after a visit to the brothel, and then stays up trying to solve the problem of prostitution:

> He recalled the history of the problem and its literature, and for a quarter of an hour paced from one end of the room to the other trying to remember all the methods for saving women employed at the present time. . . . Some, after buying the woman out of the brothel, took a room for her, bought her a sewing-machine, and she became a seamstress. And whether he wanted to or not, after having bought her out he made her his mistress; then when he had taken his degree, he went away and handed her into the keeping of some other decent man as though she were a thing. And the fallen woman remained a fallen woman. Others, after buying her out, took a lodging apart for her, bought the inevitable sewing-machine, and tried teaching her to read, preaching at her, and giving her books. The woman stayed and sewed as long as it was interesting and a novelty to her, then getting bored, began receiving men on the sly, or ran away and went back where she could sleep til three o'clock, drink coffee, and have good dinners.

It was on this class of women that underwear, as we think of it today, debuted. Unlike corsets, associated with respectability, historian Stuart Ewen has argued that panties were associated with prostitutes, and that "underpants on women sounded a strong erotic intonation—far greater than the absence of them." According to Anne Hollander, a historian of fashion and art, the French cancan was invented to "cater to this particular prurient interest" and display the lacy drawers of the dancers, and Victorian pornography often focused on displays of lace.

As the profession of prostitution itself implies, men were not expected to be chaste outside of marriage the way Victorian women were. No one illustrated this double standard quite like Isaac Singer. It was open knowledge within the company that Singer seduced the pretty girls he hired to demonstrate his machines.

In New York, at the height of his fortune, Singer was determined to flaunt his wealth. He designed a canary yellow carriage to take rides around Central Park. The vehicle could accommodate thirty-one people, with sixteen on the outside (a band, and guards). He kept three separate families, one in public and two in secret, under three different names.

This arrangement exploded in August 1860, when Mary Ann Spons-ler, the public Mrs. Springer and mother to ten of his children, was driving along Fifth Avenue in her carriage and came upon Singer driving in the opposite direction in an open vehicle with a young woman named Mary McGonigal. Mary Ann's intuitive response to this was to scream. "I used no language upon this occasion," she later recalled. This public eruption created a scandal that could not be suppressed. After her outburst, Singer beat her insensible. This was by no means the first time he had beaten her, but it was the first time she went to the police, informing them that he had attempted to choke her to death.

By this time, Mary McGonigal had known Singer for nine years and was the mother of five children by him. To avoid the ensuing scandal, Singer fled to Europe on September 19, 1860, bringing with him Mary McGonigal's nineteen-year-old sister, Kate. Mary, deeply ashamed at being disgraced publicly, moved herself and her children to San Francisco, where under the name of Matthews she made a paltry living by—what else?—taking in sewing.

The ready-to-wear clothing trade, like the fabric industry, had been fueled from the beginning by women's work. This was a force, as Alexander Hamilton had augured, as plentiful, cheap, and potent as the force of falling water. Within the new clothing trade, linen lost its centrality, and the labor of linen's historic producers—women— flowed into new and unfamiliar channels. But this alone would not have been enough to launch the global garment trade as we know it. That relied on two other crucial elements: the colonial domination of one part of the world by another, and the international slave trade. These two forces built the cotton trade.

Cotton

3

Texas Fields

Modern humanity's governing metaphor is that of the machine. Having placed ourselves in charge of creation, we began to mechanize both the creation itself and our conception of it. We began to see the whole creation merely as raw material, to be transformed by machines into a manufactured paradise.

—WENDELL BERRY

inen was swept away rapidly from the beds and bodies of Europeans and colonial North Americans with the advent of factory cotton. The plant before which the Europeans' ancient costume crumbled is an eerily beautiful one, and its soft boll can be spun and woven into cloth with a highly desirable softness. The cotton plant displays its fiber openly as its fruit, not buried cagily within its stalk, like linen. Looking at it, this soft, delicate plant, with a mind wiped clean of history, it would be difficult to imagine the truth: that those who have profited most from cotton in the last five hundred years have done so by displaying an unspeakable indifference to human suffering. Workers' lives have been held cheaply in its manufacture, while an equal measure of brutality has been visited upon the natural landscape. Unlike linen, cotton cultivation is not merely a feature of the United States' past, but part of its present, too.

In October 2012 I traveled to Lubbock, Texas, to watch the cotton harvest.

I sat in the front cabin of a cotton stripper with Dennis McGeehee, and looked down to see the white tufts of cotton being sucked up by the eight yellow two-pronged arms of the machine. Each of these arms pinched one perfectly straight row of cotton plants. The stripper was about twice the height of a military tank. It rolled across a flat field, piping the cotton into a cabin behind us. In the rearview mirror I saw a swath of bare brown stalks lying in our wake, defrocked and desolate. The plants up ahead of us had all been recently sprayed with ethephon. Their slim, desiccated stalks brandished big open bolls. Once a plant metabolizes ethephon, it becomes the potent hormone ethylene, which regulates ripeness. It is sprayed on fruit to "de-green" it, to make it ripe when the farmer decides, and it is sprayed on cotton bolls to make them all open at once.

The United States is the world's largest exporter of cotton, and it accounts for a third of the global trade in raw cotton. This is due largely to the fact that India and China, the world's two largest cotton producers, just ahead of the U.S., absorb their own raw cotton in massive domestic textile industries. The U.S., on the other hand, has jettisoned the mills that once transformed its cotton into denim and corduroy, canvas and flannel, but has clung stubbornly to its cotton fields.

Dennis McGeehee's hand rested on the steering wheel of the stripper lightly: the machine essentially ran on autopilot, down impeccably straight rows planted by GPS. This was the flattest place on earth, I thought. A Cartesian plane more than a place. A century and a half ago, at the close of the Comanche wars, white soldiers were so disoriented by the flatness of this region it gave them a disadvantage in battle against the native Comanche, who could register minute variegations in the flora in order to navigate.

It was late afternoon; the sun was about to set. An alarm went off inside the cab telling us that the stripper's storage was full. We had to idle in the field while we waited for the boll buggy, essentially a trough on wheels, to shuttle the cotton from the stripper to the edge of the field, where it was dumped into the module builder. With thousands of tons of hydraulic pressure, the module builder compacted the cotton into a freestanding loaf that stood on the field's edge until it was picked up in a semi and trucked to the cotton gin.

Dennis McGeehee was one of a cabal of Lubbock cotton titans. Cotton exists in the national imaginary as a southern crop, but after

1920 the development of large-scale industrial "cotton ranches" shifted cotton production from South to West. At the time of my visit, the area around Lubbock was growing more cotton than anywhere else in the U.S. The land in Lubbock is flat and well suited to the mechanical harvesting technology known as the cotton stripper, and the cotton farms in the area, like Dennis McGeehee's, stretch into the thousands of acres.

While we waited, Dennis explained to me that they didn't have to worry anymore about the boll weevil, an insect that can devastate a cotton crop. "Scientists have engineered the cottonseeds with a poison inside them that kills the bollworm." What they *did* still have a problem with, he said, were gophers. "They've got those big old teeth in front. One gopher can go down there and bite that tape twenty times." "Tape" referred, in Lubbock, to "drip tape": the underground irrigation pipes that deliver water to the cotton plants. "They don't believe you oughtta be killing them little beggars. *We* believe you should." I nodded gravely.

I n 1790, the United States grew 1.5 million pounds of cotton. In 1800, seven years after the invention of the cotton gin by Eli Whitney in 1793, it grew 36.5 million pounds. In 1820 it grew 167.5 million pounds. During the thirty years following the invention of the gin, the internal slave trade in the U.S. moved one million slaves to the Deep South to grow cotton, and by 1830, one thirteenth of all Americans, mostly slaves, were engaged in growing this single crop.

The transatlantic slave trade was abolished in 1807, but in the United States slavery flourished. Plantation owners treated their slaves with the same ruthlessness that they applied to the land itself. Monocropping cotton exhausts land. Over the course of America's history as a major cotton producer, wherever the land gave out, planters simply moved on: first to the South, and then the West. This need to find fertile land after the ravages of cotton helped drive the expansion of the newly formed United States. As each new region's soil was depleted, new territory had to be cleared of its indigenous occupants.

The Cherokee were removed from Georgia to make room for

cotton plantations in 1838. "I fought through the civil war and have seen men shot to pieces and slaughtered by thousands," wrote one Georgia volunteer who later became a Confederate soldier, "but the Cherokee removal was the cruelest work I ever knew." Men seized in the fields looked back to see their homes in flames. The pressure of fast-depleting land led cotton planters to Texas. The largest section of new cotton acreage was to be on land taken from Mexico in 1848.

The Civil War brought about the end of cotton agriculture's slave labor force. Planters and economists alike turned eagerly to the question of how to grow cotton cheaply, *without* slavery. In the spring of 1865 Georgia's *Macon Telegraph* wrote, "the great question now before our people is how to appropriate all the African labor of the country."

This "appropriation" was achieved, in the postwar period, by depriving the freed slaves of land and creating new restrictions against alternative means of subsistence like hunting, fishing, gathering fruits and nuts, and grazing animals on public lands, all to force them into sharecropping arrangements. Whatever could not be accomplished by this means was accomplished by Black Codes that allowed local authorities to arrest freed people for minor infractions and commit them to involuntary labor.

The effort to reestablish cotton growing in the American South by forcing freed slaves to grow cotton was so successful that it became a model the world over. Sharecropping, coercing tenants into growing commodity crops via a punishing system of perpetual debt, was the most common practice for growing cotton by 1900.

White sharecroppers as well as Black were immiserated by this system in the early twentieth century, and in the 1930s James Agee was sent south by *Fortune* magazine to write a feature on white sharecropper families. There he became embroiled in a moral panic that would ultimately yield his unwieldly masterpiece, *Let Us Now Praise Famous Men*. Midway through the project, seeing the desperate poverty of the farmer and the rapacious greed of the creditor, Agee wrote to his longtime friend and mentor, Father Flye, that the book was in "bad shape." The subject, as he saw it, "cannot be seriously looked at without intensifying itself toward a center which is beyond what I, or anyone else, is capable of writing of: the whole problem and nature of human existence."

The notion that a young farmhand could climb out of poverty, from hired hand, to sharecropper, to tenant farmer, to farm owner, was a fundamental tenet of American agriculture from the Civil War to the New Deal. To minds less probing than Agee's, the troubling spectacle of white sharecroppers who could not rise up a ladder was resolved by positing their innate racial inferiority. In Texas, bankers, landlords, and credit merchants claimed Mexican, Black, and "sorry white" tenants could not ascend the ladder to ownership because of their incompetence, and successful Texan whites racialized poor whites as the "scrubs and runts" of white civilization. "Race scientists" like Madison Grant and Lothrop Stoddard, influenced by eugenics, popularized the idea that the "Nordic" race was threatened not only by a "rising tide" of dark-skinned people but also by "defective" whites. While in urban areas of the East, immigrant Italians, Jews, Slavs, and Irish were in the process of "becoming white," historian Neil Foley argues, "Poor whites in Texas and elsewhere in the South were heading in the opposite direction—losing whiteness and the privileges it bestowed." In the 1930s, Edward Everett Davis, a researcher who wrote articles on cotton culture in Texas, was arguing that the only way to preserve the "racial hygiene" of the white race in the South was to abolish cotton agriculture, because it provided subsistence for "feeble-minded" whites. Regardless, by 1890, Texas had become the nation's leading cotton-producing state.

After I visited Dennis McGeehee's farm, I drove around Lubbock with Edwin Lewis, a friend of Dennis's and, like him, a third-generation cotton farmer. Edwin was retired, but he drove me out to see some of his son's cotton acreage. Oil pumpjacks dotted the land, on either side of the road, some rotating right over fields of cotton. Underground, a complex stratigraphy of oil, saltwater brine, and water lay one over the other. The water under the earth in Lubbock, Texas, is part of the vast Ogallala Aquifer, which stretches from Texas to South Dakota. It is the largest aquifer in the world.

A huge mass of water trapped in the pores between individual grains of sandstone, the Ogallala's water has been there since the end of the last Ice Age. Once, this now flat plane was mountainous and rocky. The sediment that lies over those ancient mountains and contains the water flew off the tops of the Rockies when the Laramide orogeny first thrust them into the air. Today, the underwater reservoir complies with the ancient topography. The water is deep where there was once a concavity, and shallow over the old mountains. This region, which was classed by an 1823 government survey following the Louisiana Purchase as "almost wholly unfit for cultivation, and of course, uninhabitable by a people depending upon agriculture for their subsistence," became, thanks to irrigation water from the Ogallala, America's breadbasket.

The Ogallala Aquifer is in grave risk. It was first tapped by diesel pumps installed in the mid-twentieth century. Kansas, the nation's leading wheat producer, and a region that produces one sixth of the world's grain, is entirely reliant on the Ogallala. A 2017 study found that in western Kansas, water levels have declined up to 60 percent, while declines in the aquifer in Texas, where the water is used to grow cotton, have been even more extreme.

We pulled over at a pump house and Edwin pointed out a large plastic cube containing nitrogen. He explained that water was pumped out of the ground, passed through a filtration system, dosed with liquid nitrogen, and sent out into the cotton field in subcutaneous tubes. These tubes were pricked by tiny holes through which water seeped out among the roots, injecting the cotton with water and nutrient at once.

The nitrogen that does not get sucked up into the roots of the cotton will join the agricultural run-off that flows downstream and into the Gulf of Mexico, where it causes the eutrophication of coastal waters. In other words, the excessive nitrogen in the water causes an overgrowth of algae. This excessive growth, or algal "bloom," prevents light from penetrating the water's surface, prevents oxygen from being absorbed by organisms beneath the algae, and creates zones in which most aquatic species cannot survive. The size of what is now simply called the "dead zone" in the Gulf of Mexico varies from year to year. In 2019, it comprised an area of approximately 6,952 square miles according to NOAA scientists, or about the size of New Jersey.

Before we got back in his truck, Edwin pointed out the barbed-wire fence running off in either direction from the pump house. "That fence was here when we bought the land," he said. "We just left it up. Now you can't see the bottom rung." He was right. The fence was half buried in sand. The desert was encroaching.

When I asked Edwin if he was worried about the Ogallala Aquifer running dry, he said he wasn't. "Reverse osmosis," he said calmly, knowingly. The wells had been producing as long as he was alive, and it was hard to imagine it could be otherwise. Edwin's grandfather bought property in Lubbock in 1913 from C. W. Post, who made a fortune selling vast tracts of West Texas land that was Comanche territory until their formal surrender to the U.S. Army in 1875. After his lucrative land deals C. W. Post moved back East and founded the breakfast cereal company for which he remains famous. Then, said Edwin, he shot himself.

"Why?" I asked.

After a reflective pause, Edwin replied, "I guess he ran out of things to do."

We drove past the house Edwin lived in when he and his wife were first married. It was a beautiful worn thing with a porch facing out onto a cotton field. We passed another worn ranch on the edge of a field of cotton. This one was the house where Edwin was raised, with no indoor plumbing and no electricity. "Spanish people," what he calls the laborers, live there now, he says.

Cotton farms consolidated as their technology mechanized in the twentieth century, and the Lubbock cotton elite moved up significantly. After our visit to his son's acreage, and our drive-by tour of the old homestead, Edwin and I headed over to the development where he and his wife, Linda, had since moved. Here, underground basketball courts were built into soil once threaded with the roots of pecan trees. Each of the houses was intended to look like it was from another time or place. There was a Tudor mansion, an Italian villa, a medieval castle. Edwin's house was a take on the Edwardian country estate. There was a new house under construction for an Arizona oil-man. Edwin stopped in front of it on the way in so that I could take a look. It would be seventy thousand square feet, with a driving range in the basement, and thirty-foot ceilings in the garage. Edwin seemed to relish these figures.

We took off our shoes before we entered Edwin's house. Outside, the world was full of dust and blowing cotton. Even the highway north of Lubbock was littered with cotton. Cotton that came off semis on its way to the gin, cotton from the fields after the stripper had run through, cotton from the modules that stood like enormous white bread loaves on the fields' edges. Inside Edwin and Linda's house, it was waxed and echoless as a funeral parlor.

Linda greeted us as we walked through the front door. She could not imagine I had much fun out there in the dust and heat. It was October, but Lubbock was in a record heat wave.

"No," I said, "I enjoyed it. I got to ride up in the cotton stripper!"

I mentioned to Linda that we had stopped by the old house that afternoon, where she and Edwin had lived when they were first married. "We were happy there," she said, with the face of one politely ignoring an offensive odor.

Linda went into a room adjoining the kitchen where there was a fridge just for beverages. It was spotless, with plastic embrasures that held up two parallel rows of bottled water and two of Bud Light. She brought Edwin and me each a bottled water and a napkin, placed the two napkins down on a coffee table in the living room, and then set the two plastic bottles on top.

In the fields that ran right up to the edge of the new development where Edwin and Linda's new house was, blue, brown, and white were the only visible colors. Blue sky, white clouds, white cotton, brown earth. There was no green in sight. There were no weeds, and not a single green leaf on the thousands of cotton plants that stretched to the horizon line. It was too early for a killing frost but the cotton had been recently sprayed with paraquat.

Paraquat, which kills green plant tissue on contact, is a widely used herbicide. In 2015, seven million pounds of it were used on fifteen million acres in the U.S. alone, according to its manufacturer, the

Swiss chemical giant Syngenta. Paraquat hit the American market in 1962, one year after a similar defoliant, Agent Orange, was dropped on the jungles of Vietnam. Defoliant was dumped from U.S. warplanes onto the forest canopy to rob the Vietcong of protection and food source. In Texas, paraquat withers the cotton plant so that when the stripper runs over it, green leaves won't gum up the machinery. Before paraquat, the farmers waited for a frost to kill the plants before they harvested. Now they make their own winter.

The use of paraquat was demonstrated by a 2007 National Institutes of Health study to be linked with Parkinson's disease in farmworkers, and has also been linked to leukemia in those exposed to it as children. It has been banned in the European Union since 2007, and even China, not known to be scrupulous in limiting toxicity, began to phase it out in 2012, but it continues to be widely used throughout the developing world, and rains down liberally on the fields of West Texas.

This is not the only point of disagreement between U.S. regulators and the international community over the use of toxic agricultural products. In 2015 the World Health Organization's International Agency for Research on Cancer (IARC) reviewed the existing scientific literature on glyphosate, the main ingredient in Roundup, a herbicide showered on Texas cotton, and declared the chemical to be "probably" carcinogenic to humans. Roundup was produced and sold by Missouri-based chemical giant Monsanto—famous for producing both pesticides and genetically engineered seeds. In June 2018, Bayer purchased Monsanto for $63 billion. They maintained, as did the Environmental Protection Agency (EPA) under Donald Trump, that glyphosate was not linked to cancer.

Bayer knew it had acquired a public relations nuisance along with Monsanto, and announced immediately after the purchase that it would retire the 117-year-old Monsanto name. By then the world's largest supplier of genetically modified seeds, "Monsanto" was a rallying point for the anti-GMO movement. Bayer ought to have known a thing or two about rebranding: the company itself was a spin-off of IG Farben, the chemical company that once produced Zyklon B for the Nazi death camps.

Nonetheless, even without the Monsanto name, Roundup would prove to be a huge liability to Bayer. In August 2018, a San Francisco jury unanimously found that Monsanto had failed to warn of the carcinogenic threats Roundup posed, and awarded the family of a school groundskeeper, Dewayne Johnson, who developed blood cancer in his forties, $289 million (later reduced to $78 million). This was the first victory against Roundup in a state court. In March of the following year, a federal jury ordered Monsanto to pay $80 million (later reduced to $25 million) in damages to Edwin Hardeman, saying Roundup had caused the man's non-Hodgkin's lymphoma.

By December 2019, Bayer was facing more than 42,700 cancer lawsuits concerning Roundup in the U.S. and its stock value had shrunk by 23 percent. The company went on a counteroffensive. Bayer asked a U.S. federal appeals court to throw out the $25 million Hardeman judgment, using as its evidence that the EPA had determined that glyphosate was not a carcinogen. Any warning label, Bayer argued, would have been in conflict with guidance from a federal agency. Bayer made perfectly clear that the Hardeman appeal had the potential to shape how every subsequent Roundup case would be litigated. The EPA and the Justice Department rushed to Bayer's defense, filing an amicus brief stating again that glyphosate, the weed killer's active ingredient, was not a carcinogen, and as a result a warning on the label was not required, echoing Bayer's exact line of argumentation. The brief stated: "It is unlawful for manufacturers and sellers to make claims on their labels that differ from what EPA approves."

The overwhelming burden of the toxic effects of agrochemicals falls upon a largely noncitizen agricultural labor force. Epidemiological studies conducted in France have shown the increased risk of Parkinson's disease in French farmers exposed to pesticides. In the U.S., these health risks are taken on by a labor force of farmworkers who are disproportionately Latino.

The demographics of cotton farms in Lubbock resemble those of the U.S. agriculture industry as a whole: the farm operators are older, white, and U.S.-born, while most hired farmworkers are younger, immigrant, and Latino. Estimates vary, but it is likely that 75 percent of the agricultural workforce is undocumented. Those charged with using Roundup on cotton are in an almost impossible position to seek legal redress when their work exposes them to known carcinogens.[*] The average life expectancy for Latino farmworkers in the United States is forty-nine, compared to seventy-three to seventy-nine for the rest of the population.

The particulars of cotton cultivation have changed almost beyond recognition but a rabid rapacity stalks the plant. In today's large-scale cotton ranches, weeds do not need to be chopped by hand laborers. Roundup now handles that task. But the deadly cost of this efficiency falls disproportionately on the shoulders of laborers who cannot in any real sense be considered free. Protected neither by the U.S. government nor any other, poisoned by agrochemicals, agricultural workers are threatened with being placed in the hands of ICE—U.S. Immigration and Customs Enforcement—if they attempt to unionize.

Nineteen nineties ads for Roundup showed a man wielding a hose that sprays the chemical like a gunslinger carries his pistol. In some of these, he speaks in a voice like a cowboy from an old western. When he sprays the hose the sound of a gun is heard as each weed in each crack in the pavement crumbles and turns brown. Weed control is sold as a glamorous expression of violent American masculinity, but in Texas the worker, not the owner, is asked to wield the gun and take the risks attached to it.

Out in the field the following day, Edwin told me about an optical phenomenon that occurs here sometimes on hot dawns. The earth was so flat, he said, that sometimes in the heat the horizon came up like the edges of a bowl. He said he didn't know why or how this happened. He told me about his older sister Cleta, who died of leukemia some years back. The old wound still throbs.

---

[*] U.S. agricultural workers are at higher risk of fatal injury than workers in any other industry in the United States, higher than mining, construction, warehousing. Studies indicate that between one and two thirds of agricultural injuries go unreported, and between 42 percent to 50 percent of Latino farmworkers do not seek medical treatment for their workplace injuries despite prolonged pain. (Snipes, " 'The Only Thing I Wish I Could Change.' ")

I was growing attached to Edwin, who had been a generous host. I wanted to believe everything Edwin said, and thought. Like when he told me the chemicals they used on the field were "environmentally friendly. We used to use arsenic acid but they won't let us do that anymore," he told me, and I nodded sympathetically.

As I stared out the window at the endless, perfect rows of cotton I thought about how in Navajo weaving, balance is essential but perfect symmetry is anathema, suggestive of death. In one Navajo myth, the trickster Coyote scatters stars randomly in the sky after the constellations have been carefully and neatly placed there. The story evokes a tension between entropy and its opposite that ought never be fully resolved, just as in nature the elements cannot be perfectly controlled. In Texas, a different cosmology was playing itself out. Man was the anti-entropic principle. The cottonseed itself—as Dennis had explained in the cotton stripper—was armed to kill. The type of seed planted here, Bt cotton, works by introducing into the cottonseed a gene from a soil bacterium called *Bacillus thuringiensis* (Bt), which has a natural poison called Bt toxin. The seed is also resistant to Roundup, so the pesticide can be dusted over the whole field, killing weeds but leaving the cotton standing. The Roundup, the boll opener, the synthetic frost by paraquat, all seemed to suggest that the goal here was not compromise but total extirpation.

Despite the Texan's tough guy facade, massive subsidies have kept Texas cotton afloat. In 2001, subsidies to U.S. cotton were worth more than all USAID to Africa. In 2017, total U.S. government subsidies to cotton farmers amounted to $1.1 billion. Critics have long argued that these subsidies allow the U.S. to export cheaply, depressing the price of cotton and hurting other cotton producers in some of the poorest regions of the world.

Edwin drove a little ways, then stopped the truck at the intersection of two dirt roads near his old childhood home. "I sat here once and watched a gun battle between a Black man and the Texas state troopers," he said.

Used to be, he told me, before ethephon was used to chemically auto-ripen the cotton boll, when farmers brought cotton in to the gin there were still some green bolls that hadn't opened yet, and those were set to one side to ripen. When they opened, they were ginned, and the proceeds from this late-ripening cotton were shared. The gin used these excess earnings to take its farmers fishing on the Rio Grande. One year they asked Will, a Black man who lived in a shack in the cotton field belonging to a farmer named J. O. Roberts, to go along to cook and do the dishes.

The farmers ran out of bait while they were fishing, and two of the boys were joking that they would just cut Will up, and use him for bait. Will overheard this and "he just went crazy. He took it literal." He ran off, and the Texas state troopers set out after him and brought him back home. When J.O. got back home, he went out to Will's shack to bring him some leftovers from dinner, and Will said "I don't want to see you anymore" and shot J.O. in the stomach. J.O. stumbled back to the house and called the troopers. The troopers came back out and had a gun battle with Will, in the field of cotton where Edwin and I were now sitting in his pickup. Edwin, a local kid who had come out from his house when he heard the commotion, had looked on. Will was shot dead, and J.O. died later of his wounds.

To me, it didn't sound like Will went crazy, so much as that he was completely sane. In *The Chicago Defender* of September 5, 1919: "Ekistman, GA, September 5 1919—Eli Cooper, an elderly field hand, was today hacked to death by 20 white men wielding axes. . . . Cooper had been attempting to organize local farm laborers *for the purpose of demanding better wages.*" An article in *The Birmingham Post*, October 27, 1934: "Photographers say they will soon have pictures of the body for sale at fifty cents each. Fingers and toes from Neal's body are being exhibited on street corners."

Across the South, in the years immediately following the Civil War, thousands of Black men were lynched, shot, dismembered, and tortured, while Black women were raped, disfigured, and murdered in extralegal terrorist violence sanctioned by authorities, who obligingly turned their backs. In Texas, according to the 1872 report of General William Reynolds, commander of the federal forces, "Murders of Negroes are so common as to render it impossible to keep an accurate account of them."

In the 1920s, the Klan was revived, part of a larger effort to enforce Jim Crow laws and enact new legislation specifically designed to keep Black Americans from the corridors of power and wealth, and segregated from white society. On October 11, 1921, witnesses before a congressional hearing testified that Texas towns were nearly entirely under Klan control. Robed Klan members frequently entered churches during Sunday morning or evening worship services, sometimes making a brief statement from the pulpit and earning the pastor's endorsement in response.

Recruiters relied upon an infantile obsession with resuscitated obscure rites and rituals, secret code names, Klan language (Klanguage), and most of all, costumes: gold-embroidered red robes for the officers, white cotton robes with red embroidery for the commoners. The first members in the revived Klan paid $10 to join and $6.50 for a Klan costume. By 1920, the costumes and other Klan memorabilia were mass-produced by the Gate City Manufacturing Company in Atlanta, producing significant profits for the Klan hierarchy.

Whether for Klan robes, church regalia, or simple white T-shirts, cotton clothed the country, an achievement wrested from the soil by violence. And D. W. Griffith's *The Birth of a Nation* helped to cement the Klan image and construct an imaginary origin story for the costume. The "inspiration" behind the costume in the film: in the 1860s, two white children hiding under a white sheet frighten four Black children, then the film cuts to two Klansmen in profile and the terrified faces of Black adults. "The sequence," writes cultural historian Tom Rice, "assigns an inherent power to the costume, as the African Americans (both children and then adults) respond in exaggerated terror to the image of largely motionless Klansmen rather than to any specific action or violence." Made invisible, the violence becomes a kind of total atmosphere.

At the cotton gin outside Lubbock, at night when I visited, cotton particulate hung in the air, illuminated by the headlights of semis as they pulled in and out of the parking lot every few minutes. Once, farmers brought cotton to the gin in trailers, and the limited number of trailers provided a bottleneck that kept the harvest season to a humane pace. The module builder had changed that. Now, work continued long after dark, with flood lights strapped to the top of the stripper, the gin was open until midnight, and the semis arrived nonstop from the fields.

Inside the building, cottonseed rained endlessly from the 222 teeth of the massive gin, which had not changed in any of its fundamentals since the time Eli Whitney invented it. Deseeded cotton lint was pneumatically piped into a machine that compressed it into bales ready to be shipped to China. After each bale was compacted a young Latino worker took a handful off of it to put in a small bag with a tag to send to the USDA classing office. There it would be classed for staple length, color, and micronaire, which indicates fineness of the fiber. The stronger the better, the finer the better, the whiter the better. A truck brought cottonseed from there to the compress, on the other side of town, where seed was piled in mountains seven stories tall. Cooling pipes ran through these piles so that under their own weight the orgy of seed would not spontaneously combust. At the compress the seeds were squeezed into oil, which would be sold to snack manufacturers and fast food chains to deep-fry potato chips and french fries. The hulls would be ground up for dog food and cattle feed, the elastins extruded for the filaments of flat-screen televisions.

Tired of haunting fields and factories, one evening I decided to visit the city's downtown. Downtown Lubbock, however, seemed not to exist, hollowed out like so many American downtowns by a move toward the car-centric suburbs. There was some life to be found on the ring road outside of town: some barbecue and big-box stores, a Hooters. Downtown, I walked for blocks without seeing a soul. The windows were boarded over with plywood that glowed orange in the twilight. The Cotton Club, where Buddy Holly's band used to play, was shut. Lubbock cotton now flows into the global supply chain with an eerie silence: no celebration amongst a community—no matter how flawed and blind to suffering—to see it off.

4

The Fabric Revolution

I claim that in losing the spinning wheel we lost our left lung.

—GANDHI, *YOUNG INDIA*, 1921

The endless rows of cotton that I witnessed in Lubbock, in their mechanized precision, neatness, and monotony, are a historic aberration. The vast majority of cotton, from its simultaneous emergence as a textile fiber in India and Peru around 3000 BC up until the nineteenth century, was raised in patches alongside vegetables and grains. New England farmers had intercropped linen with oats and peas, and similarly, farmers in Gujarat intercropped cotton with rice. In Africa, the Ewe interspersed cotton in yam and corn fields. For peasant communities, subsistence meant growing not just plants for food, but also for fiber. Historically, like linen, the majority of cotton was once processed within a few miles of where it was grown, spun and woven either at home or by local artisan networks, for the grower's own clothing, to raise currency to pay taxes, or in some cases *as* the currency in which taxes were paid. The story of how cotton *came* to be a monoculture crop is also the story of how subsistence fabric production was wrested from the agriculturalist. It begins in India.

To the extent that an intercontinental trade in cotton cloth existed before the nineteenth century, it was dominated by Indian weavers. Indian textiles were traded for Roman gold to the tune of a hundred million sesterces every year, according to the calculation of the first-century Roman historian Pliny, who complained that India, with its ultra-desirable cotton, was draining Rome of gold. The Arab trader Suleiman, who visited Calicut in 851, wrote in his diary: "garments are made in so extraordinary a manner that nowhere else are the like to be seen. These garments are woven to that degree of fineness that they may be drawn through a ring of middling size." In 1647, an Ottoman official complained that "so much cash treasury goes for Indian merchandise that . . . the world's wealth accumulates in India."

Meanwhile, as we have seen, in the England of Shakespeare's time Europeans knew little about cotton and were clothed in linen and wool, as they had been since the Bronze Age. Small amounts of cotton were imported during Greek and Roman times, but with childlike sincerity, and working from their own limited experience, medieval Europeans imagined and diagrammed the cotton plant as a plant that grew small sheep who bent down at night to drink water. When surer knowledge of the cotton plant arrived, it came via the same courier that brought knowledge of Indian textile innovations like the spinning wheel and the treadle loom: the spread of Islam.

Indian cloth reached medieval Europe only by being shipped across the Indian Ocean, transported by camel across Arabia by numerous middlemen, then shipped across the Mediterranean, until Vasco da Gama discovered a sea route to India in 1497, establishing direct trade. In 1498 da Gama received permission to trade in Calicut. The Portuguese established trading posts on India's west coast, most notably in Goa. By the end of the 1500s, both the British and the Dutch began to challenge Portugal's monopoly on the India trade. They decided, after a series of wars, to divide spheres of influence in Asia, with the Indian textile trade falling mostly into British hands. The British East India Company was established in 1600, and Dutch and Danish equivalents were formed soon after.

The British were delighted by Indian cloth. From 1604 to 1701, exports of cloth by the British East India Company grew more than seventy times, and half a century later cotton cloth represented 75 percent of the East India Company's total exports. The wild success of the fabric was not merely due, however, to European enthusiasm. It had largely to do with quite another project: the slave trade.

As colonial projects exhausted the mineral wealth they found in the New World, European powers turned to a new way of extracting value from their colonies: growing commodity crops, sugar in particular, using slave labor imported from Africa. Between 1500 and 1800, over eight million enslaved people were transported to the Americas from Africa. Spanish and Portuguese traders dominated the trade for the first century; then the British, French, Dutch, and Danish entered in. Meanwhile, African merchants and rulers nearly always demanded cotton cloth in return for slaves. A study of 1,308 barters of the British merchant Richard Miles between 1772 and 1780, for a total of 2,218 Gold Coast slaves, showed that cloth made up more than half the total value of all goods traded. African traders had, moreover, very specific demands in terms of Indian fabric. In a 1779 letter, Miles instructed his British suppliers to use the cloth from one Mr. Knipe, because those of Mr. Kershaw were not as good, "at least not in the eyes of the Black traders here, & it is them that are to be pleased."

Even while demand for cotton cloth continued to grow both among European consumers and as a currency by which to purchase slaves, the slave plantation itself became a market for Indian cotton fabric. The slave populations that labored on monocrop sugar plantations in the New World constituted a hitherto unknown phenomenon: a class of agriculturists who did not make their own cloth.

In response to ballooning demand, the European East India companies intensified their efforts to get cotton cloth from India. For the first two hundred years or so of its operations in India, until roughly 1800, the British East India Company bought fabric from weavers through local middlemen. They set up warehouses along the coast, where their agents placed orders eight to ten months out, advancing cash to middlemen, who in turn advanced it to weavers. Then, beginning in the eighteenth century, as the slave trade exploded and demand for cloth intensified, the British East India Company asserted more direct control over the weavers in India in an effort to drive down prices. The company began to use agents on its own payroll to contract with weavers, rendering them unable to sell cloth on the local market.

Weavers who worked for others were penalized. One witness recorded the fate of a worker caught selling to a private merchant: "The Company's Gumashta seized him and his son, flogged him severely, painted his face black and white, tied his hands behind his back and marched him through the town escorted by seapoys . . . announcing 'any weaver found working for private merchants should receive similar punishment.'" As part of this arrangement, weavers also lost the ability to set the price for their own cloth, and their incomes fell accordingly. The poverty among the weavers under the new system was such that in 1795 the British East India Company itself began to note an "unprecedented mortality among the weavers."

Meanwhile, cotton fabric poured into European markets, threatening local cloth manufacturers. Cotton textiles, as Daniel Defoe recorded, "crept into our Houses, our Closets and Bed Chambers, Curtains, Cushions, Chairs, and at last Beds themselves were nothing but Calicoes or Indian stuffs." English wool manufacturers protested. In 1701, printed calico was outlawed, and by the early 1770s selling Indian cottons in England had been criminalized. Following the ban, English merchants continued to do brisk business even with home markets closed, as the American and African markets were vast enough to support ever greater quantities of Indian cotton fabrics. This was, however, the bare beginning of a period of prosperity for the English, derived from controlling the world's flow of cotton cloth.

A series of mechanical developments in cloth manufacture ushered in the next phase of England's domination of the global cotton textile trade. The flying shuttle was patented by John Kay in 1733. The shuttle, which had a small spool of thread embedded in it, ran on a track through the warp threads on the loom, replacing an operation formerly done by hand. This sped up the pace of weaving to such a degree that hand spinners could not make thread fast enough to feed the looms.

Soon thereafter, an English Huguenot named Lewis Paul developed a machine that helped spin thread faster based on the principle that by passing cotton through sets of rollers moving at different speeds it was possible to stretch it thin. Paul was, like so many inventors, no businessman, and the invention was not put into use until decades later. Richard Arkwright, a wig dealer the Victorian intellectual Thomas Carlyle described as a "bag-cheeked, pot-bellied barber," capitalized on the new spinning technology. He hired a clockmaker, also named John Kay, to build a spinning machine using Lewis Paul's two-speed rollers, patented the machine himself, and gathered the investors necessary to build the first spinning mill on the River Derwent in Derbyshire in 1771. This mill was the first factory as we now conceive of them. Machines that could weave this thread into cloth followed soon after, beginning with Edmund Cartwright's invention of the power loom in 1784.

Mechanization raised productivity 370 times, with the effect that labor costs in England dropped below India's. The price of British-made cloth also fell. A length of muslin that had cost 116 shillings in the early 1780s cost 28 shillings fifty years later. Extraordinary social mobility occurred for some cotton mill owners in England who had begun as tinkerers or mechanics. In other cases, the rich became richer. In Liverpool, wealth derived from the slave trade was reinvested into the cotton industry.

The Industrial Revolution was a fabric revolution. The phrase "the industrial revolution" may conjure images of railroads and steam engines, but it was cloth, and the enormous burst of productivity that the new textile machinery allowed, that raised the capital to finance the railroads. The immense power in the mechanization of cloth lay in the fact that, while markets for other industrial products had yet to be created, the market for fabric was already vast by the time modern industry for it was formed. It was the most literal revolution: pertaining as it did to acts of *spin*.

Across the Atlantic, the invention of the cotton gin in 1793 made the short staple cotton that grew so well in the American South suddenly commercially viable. The U.S. emerged swiftly as a large-scale producer of raw cotton. British cotton manufacturers had suggested that India too could become a source of raw cotton, rather than textiles. But an East India Company official brought them up short: the export of raw materials would be no substitute for industry. To force Indian weavers to become cotton farmers would so impoverish the people as to lead to a drop in population and a loss in revenue. While land could be made conveniently "empty" in the U.S. by the forced removal and slaughter of the indigenous, and cheap labor readily supplied by slaves, in India labor was tied up in local craft networks and land was used for vegetables and cereal crops.

From the beginning of the industrial period, Europe's cotton fabric manufacturers relied on American cotton. In 1853 the *Bremer Handelsblatt* warned, the "material prosperity of Europe hangs on a thread of cotton. Would slavery suddenly be abolished, cotton production would fall." In March 1860, in a report to the Manchester Cotton Supply Association, James A. Mann warned, "While acknowledging [slavery's] terrible strength from its deep rooted vitality, we must all dread the severity of the revulsion which must sooner or later arrive."

Revulsion, after a fashion, arrived. Just as it had been feared, during the Civil War the American cotton supply was abruptly cut off. And when it was, Britain set about with a new resolve to transform the Indian countryside into a source of raw cotton. In the first year of the Civil War, money allocated to build infrastructure in India, to build railroads to move cotton out, and to move troops in case of rebellion, doubled.

India became a major cotton supplier to Britain and France through a series of state interventions in land use, taxation, and law. "Wasteland," land once open to the use of collective farmers, was turned to cotton. Lands were deforested, leading to changes in rainfall patterns. Private ownership replaced a system that had traditionally shared the harvest out among various castes. Large landowners and moneylenders profited, while small landholders and landless peasants became impoverished. Taxes were levied in cash, forcing peasants to produce cotton as a cash crop. Adulteration of cotton was made a crime punishable by imprisonment and hard labor.*

---

* Proponents of the free market and the "invisible hand" painstakingly justified making an exception in the case of Indian cotton. Although "we are strongly im-

British manufacturers considered the potential benefits of destroying the Indian weaving industry in order to force weavers into growing cotton early in the nineteenth century. "Nothing could be more natural than that the inhabitants, deprived of a market for their cloths, should be encouraged to cultivate the raw material," wrote a member of the Manchester Chamber of Commerce in 1838. Indeed, Indian spinners had already begun to show signs of distress. A letter to the editor of the *Samachar Darpan*, a Bengali weekly newspaper, showed the affliction caused to a widow woman by the influx of British yarn. The woman explained that while she was once able to support her family by her spinning, recently no one had been buying her thread, and she and her dependents had fallen into destitution. She had discovered the reason no one was buying: it was because of a flood of cheap foreign, or "bilati," yarn on the market.

The arrival of the railroad allowed British cloth to undersell native cloth, forcing spinners and weavers into agricultural labor. One British observer noted that what was happening in India reproduced what had occurred in England previously. In a letter to the Indian Finance Minister Sir Charles Trevelyan written in 1863, Secretary of State for India Charles Wood compared the situation in Berar to what had happened in his native Yorkshire:

> The Native weavers are exactly the class of people whom I remember in my early days on the Moor Edges in the West Riding. Every small farmer had 20 to 50 acres of land, and two or three looms in his house. The factories and mills destroyed all weaving of this kind, and now they are exclusively agriculturalists. Your Indian hybrids will end in the same way.

---

pressed with the belief, that, as a general rule, it is not judicious to interfere by legislative enactments in matters connected with trade," wrote the superintendent of the Cotton Gin Factory in the Dharwar Collectorate in 1862, in the matter of forcing Indian peasants to grow cotton for the world market, "we are forced to the conviction that exceptional and more stringent legislation is necessary."

Ultimately, in the words of historian Eric Hobsbawm, "India was systematically deindustrialized and became in turn a market for Lancashire cottons." In a huge and swift historic paradigm shift, India became a cloth *importer,* indeed the largest market for British cotton exports.

Millions of people gave up their spinning and weaving. In 1869 Henry Rivett-Carnac, the Berar cotton commissioner, observed that spinners and weavers of Berar had taken to work on roads, or as farm laborers. Just as the British East India Company had predicted in 1793, when the weavers' livelihoods were destroyed and they were forced to cultivate cotton for export, they became reliant on purchased grain, and thus vulnerable to famine.

Famine arrived. From 1861 to 1865 food prices went up more than 325 percent. Over the next decade, the price of a grain called jowar doubled, with respect to cotton. The colonial government of India observed in 1874, "The more the area's food stocks is diminished in favor of fibres, the greater the danger from any failure of the monsoon becomes, & the greater appears to be the necessity of some security against the consequences of such failure." Between six and ten million people died in famines in India in the late 1870s. In the 1890s, according to the British medical journal *The Lancet,* famine deaths in India totaled nineteen million, with the highest levels of fatality concentrated in the areas that had been transformed into cotton production for export.

The forced production of raw cotton proved to be disastrous in India, and it was only to be replicated elsewhere. From 1860 to 1920, across the world 55 million acres of cotton came into cultivation, mainly in colonial areas.

British colonial rule consciously and deliberately smashed Indian handloomed fabric. And precisely because of this, Mohandas Gandhi elevated traditional, handmade cloth into a symbol of resistance.

As mass nationalism burgeoned in colonial South Asia in the 1920s, Gandhi inaugurated a swadeshi, or indigenous goods, movement, which aimed to achieve swaraj, "home rule," by establishing India's economic self-sufficiency from Britain. The Indian subcontinent comprised a huge collection of distinct polities before it was forcibly united under British imperial rule, and had no common language. Gandhi therefore relied on a language of visual symbols. At the symbolic center of his campaign, he placed the spinning wheel, or charkha. His daily routine of spinning became internationally recognizable, and his costume, a white, handspun dhoti, an integral part of his message.

The Indian National Congress, founded in 1885, voted at Gandhi's urging to require its officers to spin and wear a handspun, handwoven cloth called khadi, and to boycott foreign fabrics. The National Congress selected the spinning wheel as its symbol, and emblazoned it in the center of the party's flag. The campaign to popularize this movement set up exhibitions that demonstrated cloth production and sold khadi goods. Gandhi explained in his weekly newspaper, *Young India,* in 1927, "[The exhibition] is designed to be really a study for those who want to understand what this khadi movement stands for, and what it has been able to do. . . . It is not a cinema. It is actually a nursery where a student, a lover of humanity, a lover of his own country may come and see things for himself."

By this time, India had also developed a class of homegrown industrial textile manufacturers, who naturally did not share Gandhi's commitment to handmade cloth. These industrialists fully supported the cause of Indian independence and threw considerable financial support behind it. Nationalist debates on economic policy pitted the commitments to heavy industrialization and self-sufficiency in capital goods touted by Nehru—another Indian independence activist and India's first prime minister—against a Gandhian vision of rural employment and small production. The debate bore some likeness to that between Alexander Hamilton, who favored rapid industrialization for the newly independent United States, and Thomas Jefferson, who wanted to preserve a nation of small farmers. In India, as in the U.S., it was to be the Nehruvian, pro-industrial strategy that won out.

Ultimately independent India would not see a massive regeneration in handweaving, but rather a massive wave of state-sponsored industrialization that drew millions of displaced rural cultivators into cotton factories. However, the handloom weaver still drew government support. Handweavers were to be provided with industrially spun yarn by setting quotas. This was the policy set in Coimbatore, a city in the southern state of Tamil Nadu, known as "the Manchester of India."

I visited Coimbatore in 2013 to look inside the cotton factories that produce so much of today's clothing. My companion was Ramesh Sivanpillai, a remote sensing expert—someone who uses data collected from aircraft and satellites in order to monitor and map natural resources—who had grown up in Coimbatore but was now a professor at the University of Wyoming. Using Coimbatore as our hub, Sivanpillai and I trekked out over the next ten days in various directions, charting an approximately seventy-five-kilometer region where the spinning, weaving, knitting, and dyeing units of Tamil Nadu were scattered. Sivanpillai was in his mid-forties, with a salt-and-pepper mustache, greenish eyes, and a mouth that was nearly always on the verge of smiling at some irony in human nature. Although Coimbatore was his hometown, he said that it was changing so fast, every time he came back it felt like returning to a different city.

In 1888, around the same time that the American textile industry moved from New England to the South in search of lower wages, the first spinning mills were built in Coimbatore. Coimbatore Spinning and Weaving Mills, popularly known as Stanes Mills after its owner, Sir Robert Stanes, was, like many of the first industrial textile operations in India, started by English investors, and later purchased by an Indian family. Cotton-spinning mills proliferated in the Coimbatore region after the Pykara hydroelectric power project, one of the oldest power plants in South India, was commissioned in 1932. Nine mills appeared in the region between 1931 and 1933. These textile mills introduced the colonial government into the economy in new ways. It granted industrial licensing, arbitrated in labor disputes, and controlled exports. In these capacities, the state intervened to ensure that Coimbatore's spinning mills provided thread to local handloom weavers rather than weaving it themselves on power looms, as did the "composite" mills of Bombay. It was a gesture toward maintaining a traditional vocation, but nearly a century later, Coimbatore was clearly defined more by its industrial output than its hand weavers.

A few days before our arrival the monsoon had set, tempering the pitiless June heat with clouds and wind. On the other side of the mountains, the eastern Ghats, the verdant earth was being lashed with rain. In Tamil Nadu, the sky was low and overcast, and the semiarid scrub stretched for dusty flat miles. Coconut trees kept green by drip irrigation tossed their heads in the wind over the reddish dirt. Narendra Modi had, at that time, just been chosen to head the BJP, one of the country's leading political parties, and his name was plastered across the front-page headlines of every newspaper. Critics pointed to his totalitarian rhetoric, and one of his own party's senior members had tendered his resignation upon the announcement. One editorial I read claimed that with Modi, the BJP had finally succumbed to the scourge of Indian politics from which it had until then remained aloof: the personality cult.

Once a prime cotton-growing region, noted by the British for its black soil, Coimbatore had grown from a cotton-producing region into a textile town, then into a major producer of textile machinery. Water pumps and aeronautical equipment were now made in and around Coimbatore, by firms ranging from large corporations to small family businesses. As Coimbatore has grown, it has pushed cotton cultivation farther from its center. Sivanpillai and I were to see a cotton auction, and we had to start out from the city early.

Although it is nicknamed the Manchester of India, neither Coimbatore nor its surrounding countryside evoked the North of England. Orange-flowering Gulmohar trees lined the road, along with spiky trees in the juniper family, full of thorns that the local goats cleverly ate around. Farther back from the road, the landscape was lousy with engineering colleges. The prospect of jobs in local BPOs (Business Process Outsourcing firms) incited parents here to sell their possessions in order to send their children to engineering schools, Sivanpillai said. In fact, the engineering colleges had become such a boom industry, and so many had been built, that the colleges had to send recruiters to other states to find students to fill their nearly empty classrooms. We passed lot after lot of failed real estate, where investors had bought up land from financially distressed farmers and put up tenantless cement buildings.

When we pulled in at the cotton auction, the farmers were loosely congregated in the courtyard. This was a big day for the farmers, some of whom had taken daylong bus trips to get here. This was the day when the farmer received his price for an entire year's crop. He would find out if it came above or below his debt.

Naturally our arrival caused a stir: strangers in a white Maruti Suzuki pulling in just when the tension was already pulled taut. The farmers surrounded me instantaneously. I was there to interview the participants and Sivanpillai was helping me by translating into Tamil. Getting the group to put forward one farmer to do the interview was a long, loud event. They chose sixty-five-year-old M. Ramasamy, who had traveled twenty kilometers to the auction from Dharapuram to sell his cotton, as their representative. Ramasamy owned three acres, and had been cultivating cotton there since 1976. He had planted many varietals in those years, and he began to list them one by one. Ramasamy, like the other farmers, grew only one cotton crop per year, as each crop required nine months. He planted in September. Ramasamy's cotton was irrigated weekly from well water supplied through small canals. Unlike the drip tape used in Texas, this is among the least efficient ways to irrigate, as much of the water evaporates on its way to the crop. It is also the cheapest. In the present year, he said, there was an extreme scarcity of water, and his production had been cut in half from its normal level of about twelve quintals to six.

Traditional Indian cotton varietals did not require irrigation. Though capable of producing incredibly fine fabric, the local *Gossypium arboreum* was unsuited to textile machinery, which was designed for the American *Gossypium hirsutum,* a stronger staple that was more fitted to the rigors of mechanical processing. The East India Company replaced the Indian varieties with American beginning in the 1840s. By 1947, when India gained its independence, India's own spinning and weaving mills demanded to be fed with American cotton varieties compatible with the machines.

In the late 1980s, under pressure from the International Monetary Fund, India opened its heavily protected economy and encouraged farmers to switch to "modern farming," urging them to use hybrid seeds, fertilizers, and pesticides, in a new effort to turn India into a major exporter of commodities including cotton. The hybrid American cotton made farmers still more reliant on groundwater, and chemicals. Irrigation increases humidity, which in turn encourages pests and fungus. A cocktail of fertilizer, pesticide, and fungicide had to be sprayed on the fields up to thirty times in one season. Cotton is grown on about 5 percent of the cultivated land, but accounts for 55 percent of all the pesticide used in India.

Production costs rose exponentially and many farmers got trapped in debt. They became desperate for a technical fix, and Bt cotton seemed to be the answer. Bt cotton entered the Indian market in 2002, the only genetically modified crop to be allowed in the country. In its first year of sales on the continent, Mahyco Monsanto, the company that holds the sub-license to sell Monsanto's Bt seeds in the Indian market, sold out of its entire stock. However, Bt cotton had been engineered to reduce pesticide use, not to increase yields, and yields were not high. Farmer debt exploded.

At the same time, animals were dying off en masse. In 2006, more than 1,800 sheep died in villages in Warangal district after grazing on post-harvest fields of Bt cotton. Thousands of cattle and goats also died after grazing in cotton fields, even as Monsanto insisted the deaths were unrelated to consumption of Bt plants. Hundreds of agricultural workers developed allergic symptoms when exposed to Bt cotton.

In January 2019, Bayer-owned Monsanto won a victory in a patent case that dealt with genetically modified (GM) cottonseeds in India. "The entire biotechnology space has been liberated," gloated Ram Kaundinya, director general of the Federation of Seed Industry of India, which represents foreign and local seed companies including Monsanto and Syngenta. Kaundinya was right to crow: in 2019, GM cottonseed sales were estimated to be worth $500 million annually, and Monsanto-developed seeds controlled 90 percent of India's cotton acreage.

For the last four years, Ramasamy told me, he had been planting Bt cotton, which was genetically engineered to be resistant to the white worms that formerly ate his crops, but not to insects, so he still applied pesticides as well as herbicides. He said he no longer used endosulfan, a cheap, off-patent pesticide, because it had been banned. The global ban was a response to endosulfan's incredible toxicity: in India it had killed hundreds and sickened thousands. Because bans of this kind tend to lag years behind clear evidence of harm, I wanted to know if farmers ever saw health problems from the pesticides and herbicides they use now. One of the nearby farmers cracked a joke that everybody laughed at. More farmers are injured from drinking accidents, he told me with bravado, than from pesticides. I asked Ramasamy about the cost of Bt cotton. Four hundred fifty grams cost 900 rupees while 400 grams of the old seed had cost 50 rupees. Besides this 1600 percent price hike, Ramasamy pointed out that farmers are not allowed to save Bt seeds, that was illegal, and had to purchase new cottonseed each year.

The auction was about to begin, and the men began to move away toward the low, stucco building at the back of the courtyard. Folding tables of the kind used in church craft bazaars lined the inside of the hall, piled with burlap sacks stuffed with cotton. The auction unfolded with silent intensity: the auctioneer barked the stats for each bag of cotton; then the buyers, who represented different cotton gins, placed bids by blinking their eyes. The auctioneer and the buyers moved down the rows together, from one burlap sack of cotton to the next. A few paces behind them, a woman was quietly stitching closed the slits in the burlap where the sacks had been slashed open so that buyers could inspect the product. She used thick scratchy twine, and a needle the length of my middle finger.

If a farmer like Edwin, in Lubbock, had a bad year, insurance and subsidy would make it up. For the farmers responsible for these bags of cotton, a bad year spells ruin.

The distress of Indian cotton farmers has led to stunning numbers of suicides. In 2004 in the state of Andhra Pradesh alone almost six hundred farmers, the majority of them cotton growers, ended their lives. Farmers purchase packages of seed, fertilizer, and pesticide on credit from middlemen, paying back the loan once the crop is harvested. Should a farmer lose a crop through bad weather, and become unable to repay, he gets caught in a debt trap. India's weather is variable, groundwater is fast depleting, and if the crop fails, the risks are the farmer's alone. On top of all the threats that arise from using Monsanto's seeds, in 2018 reports surfaced that the disastrous pink bollworm is becoming resistant to Bt cotton.

On a stone ledge outside the hall, waiting for the auction to end, a woman sat in an emerald green sari that stood out against the reddish dust. Selvi told me that in years with more abundant rainfall, she and other farmers could grow crops besides cotton, like corn, peanuts, and sunflowers, but this year the water was unusually low. If there was no rain, and the level continued to drop, they would not be able to plant at all. And what would they do then? Then they would have to take out a loan, Selvi said, and wait for the next year. With nothing growing on their own field they would hire themselves out to work.

Under normal circumstances, Selvi's husband would have brought the cotton to auction, but he was dead and her parents were too old. She started to cry softly. I could not bring myself to ask whether he was one of the thousands of cotton farmers who had committed suicide because of crushing debt.

Ironically, the suicide method of choice for many cotton farmers in India is by ingesting the chemical defoliant paraquat. "In early reports, accidental poisoning from drinking the dark brown concentrate, which resembles a cola drink after it has been decanted into soft drink bottles, was common," stated a laconic report released by a group of Indian doctors in 2009. "Recently, however, intentional suicidal deaths predominate."

After we left the auction, Sivanpillai and I visited a cotton gin in the countryside outside Tiruppur. About an hour east of Coimbatore, Tiruppur emerged in the late nineteenth century as an important railhead on the line between the provincial administrative center then called Madras, now Chennai, and industrial Coimbatore. We passed over a canal that used to bring water from a reservoir, now completely dry. As we got close, we stopped to ask an old woman in a pink sari combing her long hair on the side of the road where the gin was. She motioned silently to a dirt road, and we turned in, threading our way through coconut trees.

This gin, the manager told us, used to stand in the center of cotton country. But the landscape was shifting rapidly. Now his agents traveled far afield to find raw material. He was currently ginning a batch of Kumbakonam cotton. Kumbakonam is near the Kaveri River in eastern Tamil Nadu. Farmers there who traditionally planted two types of rice per year, with a gap in between during which the land lay fallow, now grow Bt cotton in that gap, he said. What the long-range effects will be on the soil is yet to be determined.

Outside of the gin, women loaded cotton into bushel baskets and stacked them on their heads, transporting them up a flight of stairs into the ginning room, with its rows and rows of American cast iron cotton gins from the 1930s, painted over in a soft lichen. The bushel baskets were dumped into the tops, like coffee into the grinder. The women were largely middle-aged, and wore saris and head scarves to keep the blowing cotton out of their hair. Only married women worked here, the female overseer told us. Unmarried girls went to the bigger factories to board: the women who worked here needed to go home at night to tend to their families.

In front, the ginned cotton piled up, and a woman pulled cotton off the giant mound with a two-pronged rake, while two other women lifted big armloads into a large metal compactor. The opening was at the level of their shoulders. All of this bending over, lifting, and heaving was quite awkward. Normally, the owner told me, the baling and packing is done by North Indian boys, but today they were away at a sister's wedding. A fourth woman stood inside the compactor, stomping down the cotton with her feet. When it was as full as they could make it with the woman inside, she got out, gingerly climbing down the side of the metal compactor door, and then all three women piled more cotton inside until it was completely full and the overseer pressed a lever that brought down pressure from above to make a bale. From here, the bales would be trucked to the spinning mills that fanned out around Coimbatore.

Work at cotton gins was formerly the only industrial work open to women in this region. For most of Tamil Nadu's industrial history, spinning mills employed men who were protected by a robust union. In the 1980s, India's textile industry reoriented toward exports, and spinning mills started to hire women laborers. The knitwear industry in Tiruppur took orders at any cost, even for a loss, in the hope of sustained contacts with foreign buyers, fueling fierce competition, forcing spinning mills to increasingly lower the price of yarn. The work now looks little like the desirable, unionized work it once was. By hiring rural women who were not integrated into the mostly male, non-Dalit* union culture, spinning mills increasingly found their way around union demands.

The day before, Sivanpillai and I had visited a spinning mill with Jagannathan, a Coimbatore industrialist who manufactured industrial shrink-wrapping machines. Early on in his career, Jagannathan installed and serviced textile machinery in the hundreds of textile factories in and around Coimbatore and later worked as a mill manager. He was curious to see how things had changed during the time he had been out of the mills. The three of us headed south out of Coimbatore.

To our right, mountains flashed in and out behind coconut groves. The cement walls of one-story houses bore brightly colored, hand-painted advertisements. *Ramco Cement. Krishna Plastics.* We narrowly missed a bicyclist balancing an enormous halo of plastic goods on his back.

As we drove through a massive field of wind turbines, Jagannathan told Sivanpillai and me that Coimbatore's factories are powered largely by wind, which can be unpredictable. Power outages had been so bad that some factories were moving to Gujarat—Modi's home state—for more dependable power sources. Air heats over the equator and moves up the west coast of India in the early summer, from the southern tip to Mumbai, causing the monsoon rains in Kerala, and winds in Tamil Nadu. The hot air hits the Himalayas and moves back down in October and November, when the eastern part of the country gets most of its rain. Tamil Nadu's rain-fed agriculture has traditionally been vulnerable to late monsoons, a problem that has

* Dalits are members of the lowest caste within India's traditional caste system.

only intensified in the face of greater water withdrawals for export cotton.

As we drove, I asked Jagannathan why he thought women had taken men's place in spinning mills. "Men say they are going to the bathroom and they go smoke," he said. "Women, they don't do that." Nodding, I asked whether he ever had to deal with unions when he was working as a manager in the spinning mills. Sure, he said. He used to have to work out a thing or two with them. Give them a bribe here and there.

We pulled up at the security gate of the mill we were visiting, and I saw in the courtyard a group of girls that I at first took to be the children of the textile employees. They looked about eight or nine, but later I was told they were teenagers, and just small for their age because of malnutrition. These were in fact the employees, tiny prioresses of the mill who spent their time off, like their time on, on the compound, where they also slept in a dormitory and ate in a dining hall.

We entered the factory, and walked into a room where the bales of cotton transported from the gin were being broken open and combed in a uniform direction. In traditional cotton processing this step was nonexistent, because the cotton bale is a relic of an imperial system that shipped Indian cotton to Lancashire mills. The machine that breaks the bales open and combs them is so costly that it creates an imperative for spinning mills to keep an enormous amount of spindles running. Spinning operations in India are huge, while gins, garment shops, and weaving mills are often small, family-run businesses. The cotton was combed into a loose thick tube of what is called "sliver," analogous to wool "roving," which was piped into the next room where it fell into a row of yellow barrels and coiled itself neatly there, ready to be strung on the plying machine. This room, with hospital blue walls, was the size of several professional basketball courts. I stood and watched a handful of women feeding fragile cotton worms through the metal loops of a machine that twisted eight of them together into one. The sliver was so delicate it broke like cotton candy as one woman threaded it through a metal ring. On the far side of the hall, the spinning machines were arranged in long aisles, with a woman pacing up and down each one.

The women employees were all wearing jewel-toned saris and shalwar kameez made from synthetic materials. Only the wealthy can afford to wear cotton saris in modern India. On top of the saris the millworkers wore hospital blue oxford T-shirts bearing the mill's company logo. On their ears, noses, fingers, and toes, they wore heavy chunks of gold. Its profusion reminded me of the Roman historian Pliny's complaint that India was *draining Rome of her gold,* and stood as proof that these women were heirs to the most paranormally sophisticated hand-spinning technique in the history of the world. Today, spinning barely rescues women from starvation. Boosters of industrialization celebrate factory jobs as saviors of indigent rural women, without acknowledging that their poverty is a direct result of the destruction of what was once a successful and sophisticated textile culture.

I turned and walked down the aisle of spindles. The power suddenly cut out. A little cluster of girls gathered in a pool in the aisle. No longer lit by fluorescent lights, the factory was dim, and almost peaceful. Then the lights flicked on, and the machines roared back to life.

Many spinning factories in Tamil Nadu relied on rural girls as a cheap labor force, recruited through a method known as the Sumangali scheme. The word "Sumangali" means "happily married woman," and via the scheme, young women are contracted to work in spinning mills in order to earn the money for their dowries. Dowries are technically illegal, but a practical necessity for the parents of young women in rural areas. Those who cannot come up with an adequate dowry face marrying their daughters off to bargain-basement husbands: extremely old or already married men.

While this scheme is not exclusive to Tamil Nadu, 80 percent of documented cases occur in the spinning sector, and Tamil Nadu accounts for over 65 percent of the total spinning units in India. Under it, girls from rural villages are recruited to work in spinning mills for a three-year "apprenticeship." On top of board and lodging at the mill, they receive a monthly stipend, with a lump payment at the end of their tenure. Many documented cases, however, show that workers are paid only part or none of this promised sum. Even when they are, labor advocates point out, the threat of losing years of wages prevents women from leaving the mills before the contract ends, even in the case of injury or abuse, both of which are rampant. They point out, also, that the total payment the girls receive works out to be vastly under the minimum wage. The courts have, upon examination, declared the scheme to constitute "bonded labor," an appellation the Southern Indian Mills Association is lobbying to have overturned.

From Coimbatore's spinning mills, thread is loaded onto trucks and driven east to Tiruppur. On our drive there later that week, we passed an orange Eicher truck stacked high with fabric, a bright yellow truck hauling giant sacks of yarn, and three buses that carried knitwear employees. All of them were plastered with pictures of the Swamiji, the religious leader to whom the local Tamil Nadu textile magnates were loyal. A major knitwear hub, Tiruppur is responsible for more than 60 percent of India's knitted garments. Knitwear has stretch: it is used to make underwear, T-shirts, leggings. It can be made with cotton or a cotton-polyester blend, but even pure cotton knits stretch, unlike wovens.

Tiruppur's first knitwear product was banyans, or men's undershirts. The first factories appeared there in the 1920s. Like in Coimbatore's spinning mills, an export boom in the 1980s prompted factories in Tiruppur to evade union demands by drawing in women, Dalits, and migrants from poorer southern districts of Tamil Nadu, using different definitions of work for these laborers, who were often treated as temporary hires, and paid piece rates and task rates.

The Indian government poured money into modernizing Tiruppur's knitwear machinery. The effort was not misplaced. In 2007, Tiruppur's exports of knitted garments amounted to over $2 billion US dollars and have been rising steadily since. Walmart, Target, Sears, H&M, and Mothercare are just some of the companies that source cheap cotton knit garments from there.

Unlike the cream-colored banyans produced for the home market, knitwear items destined for export are brightly colored. Thus, too, has been the Noyyal River, which runs from the Western Ghats through Coimbatore and Tiruppur before draining into the Kaveri

River. The river has served both as a dumping ground for the toxic waste involved in bleaching and dyeing fabric and thread, and as a source for the tremendous amount of water those processes require. Like the Newtown Creek in Greenpoint, Brooklyn, in the 1860s, or the Blackstone River in Lincoln, Rhode Island, in the 1830s, the Noyyal River in Tiruppur ran red, yellow, blue, and black by turns. Downstream from the dyeing units, farmers were forced to irrigate with a river full of dye and to produce food laden with toxic chemicals. Indigenous goats mutated. River fish and marine life in the bay carried a load of heavy metals in their organs.

In January 2011, the Madras High Court ordered the closure of all of Tiruppur's processing, dyeing, and bleaching units in response to unacceptable levels of pollution. More than 740 units, employing about forty to fifty thousand workers, shut down. Many of these dyers quietly moved operations over to the next county and resumed business as usual while local officials obligingly ignored their activities. According to Sivanpillai, whose father moved to Tamil Nadu as a young man to work in the textile-dyeing industry, the current administration in Tamil Nadu maintains its popularity through lax regulatory oversight and populist handouts, "freebies," like a table fan for every family, or bags of rice, or cheap meals at government-subsidized restaurants, to secure the blessing of the poor. "They turn a blind eye," he said, "like George W. Bush did for oil drilling in Wyoming. Like Dick Cheney said, the sage grouse doesn't need sagebrush, right? It's the same story."

Textile dyeing is a complex chemical process that demands real expertise. We visited one of Tiruppur's returning dyeing moguls at his new dyeing unit in the city, having decided it was worth the extra cost of effluent treatment to access skilled workers. An austere-looking man with excellent posture, he was dressed in a crisp white oxford shirt and a white dhoti. He was overseeing the installation of a huge new dye tank. He let me climb the metal ladder to the dye tank and peer through its round glass window into its depths. There were small holes in the stainless steel barrel for the water and chemical to shoot in, like the ones inside a washing machine.

Part of Tiruppur's appeal is that it boasts a dense fraternal network among producers. "Where in this urban landscape are the knitwear factories? Everywhere," writes ethnographer Sharad Chari. "The whole town was a decentralized factory." Garment accessories are produced in "the most temporary of shacks," with some contracted-out job work blurring distinctions between owner and worker, Chari argues. A family might have a pair of collar looms in the backyard, between the kitchen and bathing area.

Global markets for knitwear tend to be more volatile than those for wovens. The burden of this uncertainty is passed almost entirely to these small-scale producers and laborers. Work could dry up entirely for a month or two, forcing them to take out loans from moneylenders at monthly interest rates as high as 40 percent. During the height of an export season, on the other hand, the working day can last as long as twenty hours.

From the dyer's, Sivanpillai and I snaked the white Maruti Suzuki through a warren of one-story warehouses, until we arrived at a knit-wear factory, which housed about a dozen circular knitting machines. Inside, glass rooms arranged like cells in a honeycomb stretched on either side of a concrete corridor. Each one housed a whirling appa-ratus rimmed in blinking lights, and a control panel. In one of the bigger cells, a worker was instructed to shut down his machine and open it so that I could look inside. The machine turned slower and slower, making the sound of a plane landing. He opened the face of the machine and I peered at its mysterious innards, the tube of fabric raying out into its thousands of threads at the top, lit by a light at the base, so it glowed like a lava lamp. The walls and ceiling of the glass room were covered with spools of thread, and each spool fed a thread into the top of the machine. When it was switched back on, the machine turned and turned, mechanically tying the thousands of loops that constitute the fabric.

Knitting is the process of manipulating yarn into a series of inter-connected loops. Unlike woven fabrics, which are made with a warp and a weft crossing over and under at right angles, knitwear is made from knots, just like a hand-knit sweater would be. Unlike weaving, hand-knitting does not require a loom or any other large equipment, making it a valuable technique, historically, for nomadic peoples. Archeologists believe humans may have knit before they wove.

Mechanical knitting also predates mechanical weaving, although its commercial application lagged behind. A stocking frame, a machine for knitting socks that was famously smashed by Ned Ludd in 1779, provided a foundational moment and a name to the Luddites, disgruntled weavers and famous machine breakers who harassed capital in England between 1811 and 1817.

Adjacent to the knitwear building we visited was a small garment factory, where we headed next. The manager was busy, so his secretary seated me in a room lined with one-way mirrors that looked out onto the factory floor. From this perch, I watched two men stand at a long counter by the side wall folding stacks of peacock blue shirts with a fireworks scene printed on the front. Nearby, a man used a jigsaw to cut through dozens of layers of fabric at once, creating a large stack of shirt bodices. Three middle-aged women bent over sewing machines, and a young man ran an overlock machine, which seals the raw edge of a seam so it doesn't fray.

When the manager returned, he brought me through the factory, and we ended our tour in an adjacent room where a screen-printing machine with eight metal arms was inking the front of a shirt, and two women stood folding Snoopy T-shirts. Each of the arms of the screen-printing machine added another layer of color to the shirt, producing a scene of people fishing on a lake. Below the picture, the machine printed over and over, in cursive, "Wisconsin."

Clothing signals place. Like pride in a local dish, local cloth had historically been used to display hometown identity. This "Wisconsin" T-shirt might serve the same function for its wearer, but it is also a product of South India. It has left its residues there. It has taken its debt from there in the form of water.

It can be tempting to rely on notions of "globalization" that normalize the fiction that the origins of objects are simply too complex to understand. But while some things about the cotton trade are complex, others aren't: like the way it moves water across the globe. A 2005 UNESCO report on the water footprint of cotton consumption shows a map of the world with thick black arrows representing virtual water flows, in the form of cotton. From India and China and North Africa, the thick black arrows flow to the United States, England, the European Union, and Japan. Cotton is a thirsty crop. Although globally the land acreage planted in cotton has remained more or less constant since 1930, production of cotton has tripled since then. During this same period, water withdrawals increased more than six times. Reckless water withdrawals tend to point toward power imbalances, and to regions where the local population is being sacrificed for the benefit of some other party, who has less to lose when the aquifer, lake, or river disappears, or the oasis becomes a desert. More and more, this water is coming from an area of the world where a twenty-first-century colonizing process is under way: in the far western state of China, known as Xinjiang.

Drought

They filled that place
then lopped off the entire branch
And took the fruits away

——OMARJAN ALIM, UYGHUR SINGER, FROM THE SONG
"I BROUGHT HOME A GUEST"

_____

A raffishly handsome Tilvaldi Kurbanov, wearing a purple T-shirt with a camo vest over it and sporting a gray haircut in a youthful 1970s shag, smokes in front of the dark red shipping container that doubles as his storefront at a bazaar in Almaty, Kazakhstan. The year is 1994, and he is one of three Uyghurs featured in a documentary film by American cultural anthropologist Sean Roberts. Called _Waiting for Uighurstan,_ the film highlights the tribulations of a stateless people split between the Central Asian states of the Soviet Union and the People's Republic of China.

"This is new for me," Kurbanov tells the interviewer, gesturing to his stall, where cheap Chinese-made shoes line the floor. Kurbanov had migrated to Kazakhstan from Xinjiang in the early 1960s, before the border closed in 1963. In Kazakhstan, he had worked at a Soviet store as the head of inventory. "With the inflation during perestroika, my salary was no longer enough to survive. That's when I decided to start trading." He had used family networks, reestablished between Uyghurs on either side of the border who had been cut off from one another for two decades, to act as a middleman in a cross-border trade, selling goods produced in new southern Chinese Special Economic Zones. "The trade economy only really started in full force after the fall of the Soviet Union," he explains. When the border with China opened around the same time, many Uyghurs started buying and selling Chinese-made goods. "Now, why?" he says, looking with open contempt on his stock of cheap shoes. "Because nobody has money, and Chinese goods are cheap."

The fall of the Soviet Union brought the creation of the new Central Asian states. Living on either side of a border running between Kazakhstan and China, many Uyghurs hoped for their own. Xinjiang, or the Xinjiang Uyghur Autonomous Region, came into being in 1955. It was a political entity modeled on the Soviet Republic, as were the other Autonomous Regions Chinese communists established in Tibet, Guangxi, Ninxia, and Inner Mongolia, but there was one crucial difference. China's Autonomous Regions were expressly forbidden to secede in the constitution.

Xinjiang is about the size of Western Europe, and by far China's largest administrative region. Its strategic importance to China is perhaps best expressed by the fact that it shares borders with eight countries along 5,500 kilometers: Russia, Kazakhstan, Kyrgyzstan, Tajikistan, Mongolia, India, Pakistan, and Afghanistan, as well as, within China, bordering Qinghai, Tibet, and Gansu. Crucially, it also happens to be China's largest producer of cotton. This, in a country that exports more cotton garments than any other in the world.

Uyghurs are by far the largest ethnic group: 44 percent of its population according to the 2010 census, although the region is also home to many Uzbeks, Kyrgyz, Tajiks, Kazakhs, and Hui (Chinese Muslims). The Han ethnic majority that makes up 92 percent of China's population is a minority in Xinjiang. Uyghur culture is distinct from Han Chinese in many ways: Its food is based on soups, mutton, wheat noodles, nan, and savory pastries. Traditionally, Uyghurs have followed the Hanafi school of Islamic jurisprudence, one of four schools of thought within Sunni Islam, although as journalist Nick Holdstock notes, "the complex interplay of spiritual influences that have passed through Xinjiang during its history means that many Uyghur beliefs and customs . . . are leavened with influences from Sufism, Zoroastrianism, Buddhism and shamanism." The Uyghur language is part of the Turkic family, which also includes Kyrgyz, Kazakh, and Uzbek.

The aspiration for a nation-state that Sean Roberts captured on film in *Waiting for Uighurstan* did not slip past Beijing, which moved in the 1990s to set up extradition treaties with the new Central Asian states to ensure their cooperation in suppressing Uyghur nationalism. In 1995 President Nursultan Nazarbayev agreed that Kazakh security services would monitor Uyghurs in the country and share information with China. In 1996 China formed an intergovernmental organization known as the "Shanghai Five," which included China, Kazakhstan, Kyrgyzstan, Tajikistan, and Russia, to make clear that China's economic cooperation depended on the other countries' agreement to support its "security" concerns by giving no cover to Uyghur organizations.

The Uyghur diaspora in Central Asia today is vast. Approximately 220,000 Uyghurs live in Kazakhstan, 55,000 in Uzbekistan, and 49,000 in Kyrgyzstan. This reflects a time when borders were more porous, and also is the result of a people historically caught between disastrous and massive communist agrarian experiments. In the 1920s and 1930s, Uyghurs poured into Xinjiang to escape Soviet collectivization. In 1962, sixty thousand fled through the Ili region of Xinjiang into Kazakhstan, to escape the famine brought on by Mao's "Great Leap Forward."

Of the many man-made catastrophes that have plagued this region and these peoples in the twentieth and twenty-first centuries, the most extreme and protracted has been the story of cotton.

Russia's expansion into Central Asia began in the seventeenth century. Before its push into the Caucasus, "Russia" was a state of Eastern Slavs tied by Russian Orthodoxy living north of the Oka river. By 1650, the tsar's army had taken Siberia and extended the empire to the Pacific Ocean. By 1750 Russia had extended its control over the Kazakh steppe, and then moved into a contest with British

India over control of inner Asia, which British intelligence officer Arthur Conolly at the time dubbed "the Great Game."

From the early 1800s, Russian merchants and government bureaucrats imagined that Transcaucasia and Central Asia could become a source of raw cotton for Russia. The manufacturer Aleksandr Shipov argued that Central Asian cotton could "prevent all those negative consequences that might arise due to factory stoppages" should the raw materials run out. Russian commander in chief in the Caucasus Baron G. V. Rosen added enthusiastically in 1833 that if Central Asia was effectively colonized for cotton, its native people "would be our Negroes."

It was not, however, until cotton supply from America was abruptly cut off during the Civil War that Russia moved decisively forward. Between 1865 and 1876, Russian armies conquered Tashkent, then the rest of modern-day Central Asia. They moved quickly to achieve the goal of a secure cotton supply. In 1871, Russian colonial bureaucrat Shtaba L. Kostenko ordered: "the aim of all of our efforts has to be the striving to remove from our inner markets the American cotton and to replace it with our own, central Asian one." Toward this end the colonial government built railroads, linking the imperial center with a colonial territory that extended to the borders of Afghanistan, Iran, China, and British India. Russian manufacturing firms advanced credit for peasants to grow cotton for export, while government agencies imported and distributed American cottonseed. Like the British had done in India, the Russians succeeded within a few short decades in transforming a region where cotton had been intercropped with grain on family farms, and where textiles had been produced within the home, into a system that forced peasants to grow cotton for export and exist in a cycle of permanent debt.

The Soviets built on the cotton projects of imperial Russia, and extended their ecological stakes. As early as 1918, the newly installed Soviet planners decided to tap the Amu Darya and Syr Darya rivers to irrigate cotton. Lying between two of the world's largest deserts, the Karakum, or "Black Sand Desert," in the south, and the Kyzyl Kum, or "Red Sand Desert," in the north, Central Asian agriculture had traditionally been based around a series of self-contained oasis settlements whose inhabitants traded with passing caravans and local nomads. The water for these settlements came from two major rivers, both of which emptied into the Aral Sea. The Amu Darya, also known as the Oxus, originates in the Hindu Kush and flows along the borders of Iran and Afghanistan. When Alexander the Great conquered the region in 327 BC, Central Asia was called Transoxiana: "the land beyond the Oxus." The Syr Darya, or Jaxartes, begins in the Tien Shan mountains and passes through the Fergana Valley, once known to the Chinese as the home of the horses that sweat blood. The Soviets built massive dams and a web of irrigation channels to grow cotton between the two rivers, disrupting this traditional system of oasis agriculture. The resulting water shortages were acute, and the ancient settlements were swallowed by the desert.

Far more dramatic, however, was what happened to the Aral Sea itself. In 1960, the year that the series of diversions were completed, the Aral Sea was the fourth largest lake in the world. It was larger than the area of Belgium and the Netherlands combined, and its waters were teeming with fish. In the 1950s Soviet ships caught 48,000 tons of carp, bream, and sturgeon each year, the last of which was famous for its roe. With the completion of the diversions, fifty cubic kilometers of water that used to reach the Aral Sea went for irrigation. Cotton production doubled between 1960 and 1980, when 85 percent of the area's farms were devoted to this one crop. The sea level fell by twenty centimeters a year, and its area began to shrink.

Today, the once vast sea has been reduced to ten hypersaline pools that hold a tenth of the original water volume. Cities that once stood on its shore are now over ninety miles (150 kilometers) away from water, and the fisheries and communities that depended on them have collapsed. The sea had moderated the temperature in the area, and since its diminishment, summers have grown hotter and drier and winters colder. The wind blew dust up from the exposed lakebed. It was contaminated with agricultural chemicals, and produced both chronic lung disease and extremely high cancer rates in the surrounding populations.

. . .

Half the globe's population may face severe water stress by 2030, according to the United Nations Environment Programme. Freshwater supplies are threatened by population growth, climate change, and pollution. With all these risks, it seems we ought to be exquisitely selective in deciding what we use our water for. Our current water budget reflects something else.

Water consumption increased sixfold over the twentieth century: twice the population growth rate. Worldwide, agriculture uses more water than any other sector, well ahead of industrial and domestic consumption. But much of this agricultural water use isn't going toward food; it's going toward cotton. Cotton is the most widespread, profitable nonfood crop in the world, and it is demanding. It takes 8,500 liters to make 1 kg of cotton, compared to 3,000 liters to make 1 kg of rice, 1,350 liters to make that amount of maize, or 900 liters to make that much wheat. The water costs of cotton farming go far beyond those entailed in simply irrigating plants. Approximately 24 percent of the world's insecticide market is used for cotton farming, which pollutes water supply. About a fifth of the nitrogen fertilizer applied to cotton leaves the soil through the atmosphere, groundwater, or surface runoff. This nitrogen not only causes big fish kills in algal blooms, it also increases the cost of purifying local drinking water. It has been found that about one fifth of cotton's water footprint is in connection with the pollution it causes. And this is just for growing the cotton. When we account for the use of water used to process, dye, and finish the textile, it takes twenty thousand liters of water to make a pair of jeans, enough to grow the wheat a person would need to bake a loaf of bread each week for a year.

Political choices about water are as stark as deciding who lives and who dies. In the cotton trade, sacrifices are not spread equally. Certain territories become national sacrifice zones, while certain populations are consigned to watch their homes become uninhabitable. The story of the Aral Sea speaks unequivocally of the devastation caused by large-scale cotton projects in arid desert borderlands. And yet, as the

last of the Aral Sea vanished, the next major experiment in growing cotton in delicate Central Asian desert ecosystems was just then
ramping up: this time in Xinjiang.

The word "Xinjiang" dates back to 1884 and means "new territory"
or "new frontier" in Chinese, an etymology somewhat in conflict with the official communist position on the region as formulated
in 1959, and maintained as the official Communist Party line today:
"Xinjiang has since ancient times been an inseparable part of the
motherland." According to the historian James Millward, the idea
that Xinjiang is an essential part of China is something "no Chinese
would have argued before the 19th century."

Xinjiang is a frontier colony of China. In ruling Xinjiang, China
has relied upon one of its most ancient strategies for managing its
western frontier. This historic strategy, known as the tuntian system,
meant establishing military garrisons that doubled as farms so that
soldiers stationed on the frontier could raise enough food to support
their own presence. The modern-day heir to the old tuntian is an
institution called the Xinjiang Production and Construction Corps,
or XPCC. Like the soldiers of the tuntian, the soldiers of the XPCC
also engage in agriculture. Only they don't just grow grains and
vegetables. They grow cotton. The XPCC, so central to Xinjiang's
history of development, Han migration, and state control, can be, to
western eyes, a puzzling amalgam of a company and an army. However, as a "corporation whose purpose is to colonize," argues the
historian James Seymour, the XPCC bears marked similarities with
the British East India Company.

Xinjiang is divided into a north and a south by the Tian Shan
mountains, which bisect it horizontally. Most manufacturing is located
in the north. The southern region, the Tarim Basin, is mostly desert.
The Himalaya and Pamir mountain ranges cast what is known as a
"rain shadow" over the region, removing moisture from the tropical air that moves north from the Indian Ocean. Agriculture has
been practiced in the desert, the Taklamakan, for millennia, by using
snowmelt from the mountains. This region, home to 80 percent of

the world's Uyghur population, is where the Chinese government decided to establish the nation's new cotton-producing center.

When snow melts on the southern slopes of the Tian Shan, it forms many small streams, which merge to form the Tarim River, which means in Uyghur "converging of waters." The Tarim is China's longest inland river, and as it wends its way across the Taklimakan, China's largest, driest desert, it waters a forest of Hutong poplar that stabilizes the sand, and moderates the climate.

Han settlers began to cause severe changes in this ecosystem at mid-century. In the 1950s, the Xinjiang Production and Construction Corps sent two divisions to settle along the Tarim. By the 1980s, the Tarim River had been shortened by more than 320 kilometers. Population growth and the establishment of farms so dramatically reduced the volume and degraded the quality of water available downstream that severe desertification ensued. The inhabitants who lived nearby all fled. By the 1960s Lake Luobupo, China's largest, into which the Tarim had emptied, dried out and was buried under desert. In the late 1980s, another large lake fed by the Tarim, the Taitema, became a dry basin.

Uyghur farmers in southern Xinjiang were given both cotton and grain quotas in the 1980s and 1990s. Uyghur farmers had to grow cotton even if it would yield little or no profit. The small Uyghur farms were at a major disadvantage compared to the massive ones of the XPCC. XPCC farms had economies of scale, they received state subsidies, and they had better access to water, which was expensive.

At the beginning of the 1990s, China's grip on Xinjiang was stronger than it had ever been. But Beijing worried over the region's stability because of uneven development and the extreme poverty among the Uyghur population. An insurrection in April 1990 in Baren, a small township near Kashgar, that took three days to quell and during which thirty people were killed, was a turning point. Beijing suspected that it faced a separatist threat.

The government announced its intention to "open up Xinjiang to the world," and to transform the region into an economic powerhouse. Their strategy relied on massive investment to make Xinjiang into China's biggest cotton-producing region, which would in turn, they boasted, raise living standards for all. From 1991 to 1994, infrastructure investment more than doubled.

Following the campaign, the population in the Tarim River Basin rose rapidly. The river was depleted further as more land was converted into cotton fields: river water was used to flush salt from the soil so that it could be planted, and the salinated water then channeled back to the river. The more land that was thus "reclaimed," the more the downstream suffered. In Alagan, the proportion of desert reached 95 percent in 1996. The aquifer level dropped so dramatically that "almost all plants and animals, as well as human beings, were driven out completely from this area," found one scientific paper. Human settlements were abandoned, and the natural vegetation was stripped away. "Our investigation during the fieldtrips to Corp 31 and particularly Corp 35 in the far end of the Tarim River reveals that a large proportion of cultivated land and villages of the corps were abandoned due to water shortages, and then quickly desertified," reported the authors of a 2005 scientific paper that studied the dwindling water resources in the Tarim River Basin.

Anthropologist Agnieszka Joniak-Lüthi, doing fieldwork in Xinjiang in 2011–12, noted that "[Members of the XPCC] believe they have transformed it 'from a wasteland into a blooming garden.'" Notwithstanding the fact that the Uyghur population, as Joniak-Lüthi noted, strongly opposed the notion that their homeland was a "wasteland," scientific research also contradicts the idea that a wasteland was made to bloom. In fact the opposite was true. Scientists noted that, in comparison to areas managed by the local (Uyghur) populations, areas controlled by the XPCC "experienced enormous changes in land use and land cover in the period 1959–1999," stating that "the downstream of the Tarim River Basin had a serious problem of land degradation."

Xinjiang had been a crucial passageway for the Silk Road, and in oasis cities, like Hotan, coins had once circulated from the wealthy, multiethnic Kushan Empire that grew up and grew rich protecting the silk trade. So many cultures crossed paths there that Kushan gold, silver, and copper coins bore images of the Sumerian goddess Nana, the Persian gods Oado and Atash, the Hindu gods Vasudeva and Siva, and the Buddha. In a matter of mere decades, lands upon which traditional methods of oasis agriculture had successfully used the snowmelt as the exclusive water source for thousands of years had been made inhospitable to life. The ecological consequences of the cotton farms of the XPCC were, and continue to be, catastrophic.

On top of the destruction it caused to the land, the initiative failed to enrich Uyghurs. Their small farms became increasingly strapped for water. Meanwhile, the 600,000 seasonal laborers the XPCC hired to pick cotton every year generally came from outside Xinjiang. By the close of the 1990s, there was still a huge income disparity between north and south: in 1998 the average rural income for Xinjiang was 684 yuan, but only 200 yuan for southern Xinjiang.

The campaign was costly, and destructive to the ecosystem, but it succeeded in one way. It successfully encouraged the emigration of Han Chinese into the region. That had been the point. China scholar Nicholas Bequelin argues that the policies of the 1990s constituted "the comprehensive engineering of economic and social incentives to increase Han migration to Xinjiang in order to further alter the ethnic balance." The XPCC, as "the chief vehicle of the colonization of this borderland," had succeeded in its mission.

By 2019, Xinjiang became newsworthy in the West, and the headline was genocide. The Chinese state had been suppressing the practice of Islam as part of its Xinjiang policy since the mid-1990s. After 9/11, Islamophobic rhetoric had new purchase, and the United States had backed it fully. The U.S. offered the prototype for an Islamophobic "war on terror," as well as legitimation and logistical support. For instance, in November 2001 a Chinese Foreign Ministry spokesman gave a press briefing on Uyghur separatism, claiming that Xinjiang separatists had received training in Afghanistan, and that Osama bin Laden directed and supported an organization called the East Turkestan Islamic Movement (ETIM), which aimed for a theocratic Islamic state in Xinjiang. Both claims proved false, but the U.S. listed ETIM as a terrorist group the following year anyway. Eventually, though, a project the U.S. had largely supported began to make it a little queasy.

Beginning in 2016, when Communist Party Secretary Chen Quanguo relocated from the Tibet Autonomous Region to assume leadership of Xinjiang, the Chinese government subjected Uyghurs and other Turkic Muslims in Xinjiang to mass arbitrary detention. A 2019 Human Rights Watch report placed credible estimates of those held in what the Chinese government calls "vocational training centers," encircled by barbed wire, surveillance cameras, and armed guards, at one million people. A trickle and then, in 2019, a flood of reports emerged of massive detention centers, of Uyghurs forced to download an app that observes their telecommunications and monitors their use of electricity, of communities forced to give DNA samples, blood samples, and voice samples, to the police. Some reports stressed that Uyghurs were being used as a test run for new forms of optical control, and that what was being prototyped in Xinjiang were systems that police planned on implementing throughout China. One hundred sixty thousand cameras had been installed in the city of Urumqi by 2016. The surveillance would be used to justify the spiriting away of thousands of people into camps at the "vocational training centers" on charges of political subversion.

These "vocational training centers" happened to dovetail nicely with the Chinese Communist Party's desire to keep production costs down in China's garment sector. Garment production had largely been located on the east coast, and rising wages there were causing large global brands to move to places like Vietnam or Bangladesh. Central planners had felt since the nineties that China's textile industry could become more competitive by being moved closer to Xinjiang's cotton fields, and by making use of its cheaper rural workforce. By 2000, hundreds of thousands of spindles had been moved to Xinjiang from Shanghai and other textile centers. After 2016, textile and garment factories began using interned Uyghur inmates in reeducation camps, paying them a fraction of the minimum wage, while also enjoying subsidies for building facilities and shipping goods. In late 2018, the primary development ministry for the region circulated a statement announcing that the "vocational skills education and training centers" had become a "carrier" of the economy.

It was only a matter of time before the western brands quietly benefiting from this arrangement were faced with public scandal. The Associated Press revealed in late 2018 that North Carolina–

based Badger Sportswear was sourcing goods from a factory inside a Xinjiang internment camp. Several U.S. universities pulled Badger merchandise following the story, and in January Badger announced it was ending the partnership. But this was no aberration: the Badger revelations were merely the tip of the iceberg. *The Wall Street Journal* reported in May 2019 that Uyghurs processed through Chinese indoctrination camps were being channeled directly into work in the supply chain of western companies including Adidas, H&M, and The Gap.

In 2019 two Japanese brands, Muji and Uniqlo, came under fire for their ad campaign advertising the softness of the Xinjiang cotton in their flannel shirts. "What?! They're actually using that as a slogan?!" fumed Sophie Richardson of Human Rights Watch. One Twitter user declared, "Many Uyghurs love and idolize Japan, but this is a betrayal."

The truth was, however, that Xinjiang cotton had spread so deeply in the global supply chain that there were few global brands that could have accurately claimed their clothes did not contain it. Xinjiang was by then the source of an estimated 20 percent of the world's cotton. Because this cotton would be spun, knit, or sewn by an international web of producers, it was as likely to be present in a garment marked "Made in Vietnam" as in one marked "Made in China."

Xinjiang cotton appeared for a time to be guilty merely by association—with a region rife with human rights violations. It was soon revealed to be directly bound up in those violations. While it had already become clear that Uyghur forced labor was being used in garment production, in December 2020 German anthropologist Adrian Zenz released an intelligence briefing directly linking the Xinjiang's cotton harvest with the forced-labor regime, too.

Shortly after the release of Zenz's report, U.S. Customs and Border Protection issued a Withhold Release Order (WRO) on all Xinjiang cotton and tomato products. Since the Tariff Act of 1930, it had technically been illegal to import goods made with forced labor into the U.S., but until 2016 a loophole known as the Consumptive Demand

Clause allowed these goods entry if they were not produced domestically in sufficient quantities to satisfy consumer demand. Congress closed this loophole in 2016, and Customs had begun stepping up enforcement.

Uyghur forced labor emerged as a rare arena of bipartisan cooperation in the U.S. Congress. On his last day of office, outgoing U.S. secretary of state Mike Pompeo officially designated Beijing's actions in Xinjiang "genocide," and in February 2021 the bipartisan Uyghur Forced Labor Prevention Act was reintroduced in Congress. The act would create a "rebuttable presumption" that *any* goods made in the Xinjiang Uyghur Autonomous Region were made with forced labor. On March 22, the U.S., joined by the European Union, Britain, and Canada, imposed coordinated sanctions on Chinese officials involved in human rights abuses in Xinjiang.

China wasn't happy. The CCP's attitude toward being chastised by the U.S. for its Xinjiang policy was expressed succinctly in Alaska in March 2021, when U.S. secretary of state Antony Blinken met there with his Chinese counterpart, Yang Jiechi. Director Yang made a thinly veiled allusion to the history of slavery in the U.S., and suggested that with a record like that, the U.S. had no right to lecture China. "It's important that we manage our respective affairs well instead of deflecting the blame on somebody else in this world," he said.

The comment was cynical and self-serving. On the other hand, the similarities between America's history with slavery and China's practice of forced labor in Xinjiang are undeniable.

The past repeats, but with variations. In the annals of remaking land to grow cotton, what is occurring in Xinjiang does not precisely follow what had happened in America, where indigenous inhabitants were eliminated and replaced with vast numbers of slaves forced to grow cotton. Nor does it perfectly follow the model of the British in India, who forced the native inhabitants to grow cotton themselves. In Xinjiang, cotton agriculture is replacing native people with uninhabitable desert. Cotton is the means, rather than the ends, of elimination. The Uyghurs are being killed by cotton, rather than for it.

The United States bears grave responsibility for this situation, and not merely by virtue of parallel histories. The U.S. has been a monster consumer of Chinese cotton. Between 2002 and 2020, China was by far the largest source of garment imports into the U.S. Reciprocally, the U.S. has gobbled up far more Chinese garments and textiles than any other nation every year since 2006. In 2017, the United States bought up more than double that of the next-largest importer, Japan, taking in $42 billion worth: 16.5 percent of China's total garment and textile exports. Activists note that Customs and Border Protection's lack of transparency makes it impossible to see how, or whether, the Xinjiang cotton ban is being enforced. What can be safely said, however, is that regimes of genocide, forced labor, and environmental devastation in the service of growing cotton and producing garments made from cotton are not the stuff of history. These are the norms today in the world's largest producer of cotton.

The U.S. could not have become the world's largest importer of Chinese garments without eagerly overlooking human rights abuses. As China's policy in Xinjiang was ramping up, then–U.S. president Bill Clinton pressed for its entrance into the World Trade Organization. In 1992, Congress passed a bill that would have tied China's favorable tariff rates to efforts to improve its human rights record. Even before George H. W. Bush had vetoed the bill, a delegation of six retail executives arrived to urge Congress to sustain the veto, stressing that the China trade was vital in supplying cheap clothes to the U.S. market. The delegation was headed by Leslie Wexner, chief executive officer of The Limited and then the chair of a retail lobbying group called RITAC, and also included Kmart chair Joseph Antonini, Spiegel president John J. Shea, and Donald G. Fisher, chair of The Gap.

Before it became famous for its human rights abuses, Xinjiang was known to tourists mostly because of its Silk Road tours, which feature sightseeing in the Tarim Basin oasis cities like Khotan, Aksu, and Kucha. As China now moves to expand its Belt and Road Initiative, a colossal infrastructure project that aims to link China globally via railroads, shipping lanes, and gas pipelines with many of the central arteries crisscrossing Xinjiang, it invokes the silk route as a historic precedent. There are, however, major differences. Caravans along the silk route, which brought silks made by Chinese artisans to an eager market in the West, wended through a massive, extensive, and porous territory loosely governed by tolerant, multiethnic empires. Today, Uyghurs who flee to Kazakhstan are extradited back into Xinjiang like tethered birds. An object lesson of a paradigmatic fact of the new world order: while goods can easily and legally flow across borders, people cannot. However, if the Chinese state relies on the mythology of the Silk Road to boost a project that bears it little resemblance, the West has been doing something similar for centuries. The Silk Road is part of an orientalist fantasy that still pervades the West: one that invests the caravan route that once brought silk to the Mediterranean's eastern shores with nearly magical properties. It is still an integral component of the way the West defines luxury. Cotton may have provided the physical material for the arrival of a global garment trade. But the mythic material came from another place: from the story of silk.

Silk

6

Yangtze Silk

When you see the silkworms spinning their cocoons, you must attend to them day and night, picking mulberry leaves to feed them.

—SONG RUOZHAO, "ANALECTS FOR WOMEN"

The mulberry leaf is the sole food of the silkworm, the larva of the *Bombyx mori* or silk moth. The quality of the mulberry leaves it eats determines the quality of silk that a silkworm spins, so good silk begins with good mulberry. The fertile Yangtze River Delta, in southern China, is an ideal climate for mulberry trees. This is one reason why the region formed the center of Chinese silk production for thousands of years, and may even be the origin point of silk itself.

Compared to the first appearance of clothing made from animal skin, approximately 170,000 years ago, and linen cloth, 36,000 years ago, silk—which first appears in the archeological record between four and eight thousand years ago—is a relative newcomer. Silk cultivation emerged, and for a good deal of its history remained, exclusively in Asia.

Anatomically modern humans are believed to have arrived in Asia from Africa via a coastal route around fifty thousand years ago. These Paleolithic settlers lived a hunter-gatherer lifestyle until the beginning of the Neolithic, around 10,000 BC, when the gradual development of millet and rice cultivation began in the Yangtze and Yellow River Basins. The village-centered societies based on cooperative agriculture that evolved by the Yangtze spread to most of Asia by approximately 2000 BC. These agriculturalists also discovered silk. Between 5000 and 3500 BC silk industries sprang up within the farming settlements that had spread along the middle and lower Yangtze Valley. At an archeological site in Qianshanyang, a village in Zhejiang, pieces of silk cloth have been found estimated to be 4,500 years old. A 2016 study using mass spectrometry found biomolecular evidence of silk fibroin in soils obtained from 8,500-year-old tombs, indicating the possible presence of silk even earlier.

According to sinologist David Pankenier, by the early first millennium BC the language of silk fabric making had penetrated deep into Chinese conceptions of both the cosmos and the social order—two deeply interlinked fields in Chinese thought. By the Han Dynasty (206 BC–AD 220), the word for "warp thread" could be used as a noun to refer to canonical classics or societal norms, and as a verb to mean "to put in order, arrange, align, or govern." Ji of Lu, praised by Confucius for her wisdom, delivers a discourse in the 18 BC *Lienu zhuan* (*Biographies of Exemplary Women*) in which she says: "I will inform you of the essentials of governing a country: it is entirely in the *warp*." A crucial step in unwinding the silk strand from the cocoon is to find the head end of the thread. The Chinese word for this "filament lead-end" acquired the extended meaning of "to straighten out or to put in order" in pre-Qin literature. The *Book of Rites* states that the Rites are "the guiding threads of the masses. If the threads are scattered the masses are disorderly." According to the Chinese philosopher Mozi, active in the late fifth and early fourth centuries BC, "Just as a skein of silk has a lead-end and a net has a head-rope, [the Five Punishments] are what gather in commoners in the sub-celestial realm who fail to conform to their superiors."

The most famous Chinese star lore, mythical tales about the stars or constellations, is the story of the Weaving Maid, daughter of Heaven, and the Herdboy: lovers destined only to meet one night a year. The celestial pair appear in the *Shijing*, the oldest collection of Chinese poetry, dating from the eleventh to seventh centuries BC, where they are figured as the two bright stars Vega and Altair. The celestial Weaving Maid is the weaver not only of silk but of the galaxy itself. In a composition on the theme of the *Seventh Night*, a festival celebrating the lovers observed in China since at least the Han Dynasty, the Tang poet Liu Zongyuan (AD 773–819) described the Maiden like this:

> *Heaven's grandchild—*
> *Unique adept in the Sky,*
> *Interweaving by the Dipper*
> *Warp and woof of starry asterisms*

Pankenier believes that the silk loom was used to understand the complex movements of the stars because, in the Shang and early Zhou (roughly speaking, across the first and second millennium BC), the loom was the most complex mechanical device known, and had been since the Neolithic. Pure thread ranging from .70 mm down to .35 mm in thickness has survived from the Shang Dynasty, along with plain-weave silk fabric that has between fourteen and thirty individual threads per centimeter running across it. Threading these strands through individual heddles, devices that raise and lower the warp threads, is complex, precise work: as difficult, the ancients imagined, as arranging the motions of the stars.

According to one memoirist, during the Song Dynasty the lover's tryst on the seventh day of the seventh month was observed as "Entreating Artfulness Festival" and on that day, young girls would ask the celestial Weaving Maid to grant them skill in needlework, spinning, and weaving. That night, the girl would trap a spider in a box. If by the morning it had produced a neat web, it meant the plea had been answered.

In December 2018, I traveled to the Yangtze Delta region with Mrs. L., a retired fashion designer who came to the U.S. in 1988 from mainland China, graduated from the Fashion Institute of Technology as a fashion design major, and worked for an American jeanswear company that sourced goods in China.

Mrs. L. had contacts in manufacturing. One of these was Mr. S., the manager of a state-run silk-weaving plant that had come into semiprivate ownership in 1991, and was now a sprawling production complex that had diversified into garment manufacture, dyeing, and knitwear. Shortly before the western New Year, Mr. S. picked up Mrs. L. and me at our hotel in Jiaxing, in northern Zhejiang province, and drove us to visit a silk filature—where the strands of silk are unraveled from the silkworm's cocoon and wound onto spools. Mr. S. wore a brown polar fleece and a Yankees baseball cap. He was avuncular and laughed easily, his heavily lidded eyes twinkling under a boyish forehead.

Traveling through this region, south of Jiaxing, in June 1567, a man named Wang Zhideng had observed in his diary that "the area is rich with mulberry fields. The threads of the silkworms create a market, and great merchants from the four quarters come in the fifth month every year to buy up the thread, piling up hills of silver in the process." According to the county gazetteer published in 1624, "mulberry stocks cover the fields, and there isn't anyone who doesn't raise silkworms." Over the course of the late twentieth and early twenty-first centuries, however, all that had changed.

We entered the town of Gao Yang, and made our way to the filature, where we were met by Mr. Bo, the owner. The workers were sorting through late autumn cocoons. Mr. Bo explained that he bought silk cocoons from households with mulberry trees, and that the factory itself owned about 166 acres of mulberry trees a thirty-minute drive out of town. This was significant, Mr. S. said, because mulberry trees were increasingly rare in the region. Indeed, this filature was one of the last. Mr. S., who knew all the filatures because he bought up the spools of silk to weave, was one of their main buyers, and he said Mr. Bo's was the largest filature that remained in the region.

The women sorting were all over sixty, and sat on stools by a conveyer belt that moved white and yellowish cocoons past them. The white ones were allowed to go down to the end of the belt to drop into a large sack, the yellow ones were pulled aside, to be used for blanket fill. A hunched woman at the top of the line wore a black parka patterned with a smiley face skull and crossbones, and a facemask. She worked with her right hand gloved and her left ungloved, her hands wrinkled, deft, and sure. She reached out and grasped two or three cocoons, collecting bad ones under the pinky and ring finger of her right hand, and periodically dumping them into the sack, while keeping both hands free to work. They do a hundred bags a day, Mr. Bo said over my shoulder. He took obvious pride in his fiefdom.

Inside the factory, heat and moisture permeated the air. The cocoons passed through pipes where progressive stages of hot and even hotter water broke up the glue that held the long strands of silk together in a tightly wrapped cocoon. Silk is extruded in a continuous filament by silkworms, which wrap themselves up inside it to undergo metamorphosis.

In a large adjoining room were rows of reeling machines, which mechanically unwind the thread from a cocoon of silk and wind it onto a bobbin, with one young woman minding every eight. One of the workers looked up at me and smiled, and I felt that instant shame I feel whenever I go into a factory and watch women work. Phone in the front pocket of her puffer vest, leggings, ponytail, she passed back and forth along the channel of water that ran beneath the machines. Hundreds of cocoons bobbed in the water, shaking as the thread unwound off of them and into the spools above. The young woman stopped occasionally to catch a thread from the water and pull it up through a white ring, into a blue spool, then a red one, tying a knot between this filament and another. It was an odd thing to watch: like the performance of a deft mime, because the filament was so fine it was invisible to the naked eye. Well, to *my* eye. Mr. Bo said these women, who mostly came from north of the Yangtze, were all under twenty-five, and had very good eyesight.

Outside the reeling room, Mr. Bo showed me large buckets of silkworms. The cocoon is boiled with the silkworm inside it. If it were not, the moth would eat its way out, tearing a hole through the layers of silk, and ruining the long continuous thread. The worms, Mr. Bo said, would be sorted through. The bad ones would be sold to chicken farmers, the good ones canned and sent to South Korea, where silkworms were a popular delicacy. He pointed out the worker dormitories, said proudly that everyone had A/C and heat. A wood-pellet-fired furnace produced electricity for the factory.

Mr. Bo had opened the factory thirty years ago, in 1988, when the economy opened under Chairman Deng Xiaoping. Before that he was a math teacher at an elementary school, with an illegal side gig on his summer vacations, buying local vegetables and bringing them into Suzhou to sell.

After the factory tour ended, Mr. Bo took us out to eat at a restaurant downtown. As taro and sugarcane arrived at the table, specialties of the south, he told us about how from 1988 to 1998 business was great, but in 2000 it got harder. Development was happening too fast, he said, and it was massively disorganized. Plus, the futures trading market for silk cocoons had made the business into a casino: rather than focusing on the business of making silk, people were now speculating on the price of cocoons.

Mr. S. nodded. He too had weathered the exciting and chaotic decades of economic boom time in China after the economy opened at the close of the Cultural Revolution. Overproduction caused a drop in silk prices in the late 1990s. Silk factories undercut one another on the export market after years under strict government control. Meanwhile, industrial development had begun to threaten the mulberry trees that made the region famous for its silk. The Yangtze Delta region had been transformed. Sometimes referred to by locals as the "triangle region" for its shape, it was now what geographers call a "megalopolis," where multiple metropolitan areas bleed into one another with no clear line of demarcation.

The previous day, I visited Mr. S.'s silk plant, and watched the women laborers drop metal picks down over the threads and slide them one by one across the bar, creating the pattern. This was no Southern Song Dynasty brocade, but modern mass-produced silk in white, with a simple weave structure. In the back of the factory a massive tube, like a rocket, slowly spun, gathering thread from thousands of smaller spools to set the tension. The operation was being monitored by a woman in her thirties in green leggings, an orange sweater, and orange lipstick, who shifted back and forth on her feet. Only about 10 percent of the silk being woven here came from nearby, Mr. S.'s assistant told me. Most of it was coming from the south, near Vietnam, and the corporation was looking into buying land in

Guangxi in order to secure a steady supply of cocoons. I had asked Mr. S. if he was worried about whether the new silk cocoons coming from Guangxi would be as good as the traditional Yangtze Delta silk. "My heart is dying," he replied.

This was not at all what I had expected him to say. "The best in the world is from this triangle area," he said, "and now it is developing so fast. So many highways are being built. The best silk in this world disappeared because of industrial development." Not to mention, he went on, that most of the development had been in garments and textiles, and now buyers were looking for cheaper prices in places like Vietnam and Bangladesh. And as for the silk in Guangxi, Guangxi was still an undeveloped region, so what will happen when they inevitably begin industrializing *there*?

Today, however, Mr. S. was putting on a brave face. Filatures in this region and the cocoons they relied on might both be an endangered species in the Delta. But Mr. Bo had vision, and courage, Mr. S. insisted. There were maybe ten filatures left in the region, and Bo's was the biggest, and the last of that size. I asked Mr. S. what *could* threaten Bo's business. He thought about it and replied that *nothing* could. Bo's 166 acres were designated as agricultural land by the government. If the government wanted to build a highway through it, they would have to sign an agreement to give him an equal amount of land elsewhere.

I asked Mr. Bo if he made any effort to brand himself as the last producer of the world's most famous and ancient silk. On his third glass of Xinjiang wine, Mr. Bo tapped the lazy Susan with his middle finger, gestured with his upturned hand, and declared that *I* was the writer, and that he would not leave the table until I gave him a brand name. I suggested "Yangtze Silk." After all, I said, most Americans have never heard of the famous silk-making center of Suzhou, but everyone has heard of the Yangtze River. Cheeks flushed, he said he would go register it right away. It would take a while through all the red tape; a little change like that has to go through a chain all the way up to Beijing.

Mr. Bo wants his granddaughter to take over his silk-reeling business. His son ran a lucrative women's shoe factory in town, and wasn't interested. His granddaughter was learning about silk in school now, because all of the third graders had to raise silkworms. The children were tasked with bringing in mulberry to feed the worms. "It's killing the parents," Mr. Bo said, "trying to find the leaves." Mulberry trees were now in such short supply there wasn't enough to raise silkworms for a school project, let alone a silk industry.

After lunch, Mr. S. drove Mrs. L. and me to our hotel. The two of them sat up front, speaking in Mandarin. We crossed over the canal, past housing blocks, a Lego factory, Philips Manufacturing. ZH Automotive products. Cooling towers. Mansions, in a new style that features turrets shaped like mini–Berlin TV Towers. A few patches of field. Only after we had said goodbye to Mr. S. did Mrs. L. tell me what he said to her privately. He had told her that Mr. Bo was completely vulnerable. Mulberry trees are sensitive to pollution. Even though Mr. Bo would be able to keep his land, the quality of the trees and the worms, and the silk, are likely to suffer and he'd have no redress.

As its ancient silk region succumbs to high-rises and Lego factories, the end of an era of Chinese history is under way. And not just aesthetic, cultural, and economic history, but military and political history as well. Silk figured heavily in the contest between agricultural peoples on the southern arable lands and nomads on the northern steppe that has typified much of the Chinese past. Silk textiles would reach the rest of the globe as a result of this rivalry.

Before the creation of a unified Qin state in 221 BC, a collection of smaller states with vacillating boundaries populated what is now central China. In the 400s BC seven agricultural states were fighting one another for supremacy and subject to periodic raids from nomadic cavalry that looted millet, wheat, and silk. The steppe nomads to the north of agricultural China placed archers on horseback and devastated their neighbors. The leader of a warring state, King Wuling of Zhou, thus learned of and adopted the use of cavalry, and dressed his soldiers in the trousers and tight-sleeved robes that steppe nomads had found to be well suited for horseback. This reform dismayed his uncle, Prince Cheng, who wrote:

Now your majesty is giving up our high standards to follow the clothing style of outsiders, thereby changing the teachings of our ancestors and the ancient ways. This will upset your people and make scholars angry.

King Wuling's reforms proved so effective, however, that they were soon copied by the other Chinese states. The ensuing arms race for cavalry increased the need for horses, and good horses could only be bred on the wide, open spaces of the steppes. They began to trade silk for horses: agricultural states needed horses for war that could only be produced on the steppe, and the steppe nomads needed silk that could only be produced in settled agricultural states.

The trade was mutually beneficial in other ways too. Agricultural China gave tribute silk to nomads, to placate them and avoid their raids, while nomadic chieftains used silk to assert their status and clarify the political hierarchy of their clans. When the seven warring states were united under the first Qin emperor in 221, the emperor sent vast numbers of silk robes to the Xiongnu, a confederacy of steppe nomads that threatened from the north. The chieftain of the Xiongnu, in turn, distributed the silk robes among his followers, with the finest and most ornate robes going to his first in command.

In addition to granting these types of gifts to maintain a diplomatic balance, the first Qin emperor sought to keep out raiders by linking walls previously built by various states to form the Great Wall. Gates in the wall became sites for trade, where this exchange of silk for horses continued.

It was because of their dealings with nomadic raiders that the Chinese discovered a world beyond their known borders. The Qin (221–207 BC) exhausted itself quickly, not least because of unrest caused by the massive project of the Great Wall, and the Han Dynasty (206 BC–AD 220) replaced it. Around 140 BC the Han emperor Wudi sent out an envoy to try to form an alliance with the sworn enemies of a group of nomads who had been harassing his northern border. Before the envoy could reach them, however, he was captured by the northern raiders. The envoy, Zhang Qian, spent a decade among them. He finally made an escape. When Zhang Qian returned at last to the Han emperor, he brought news of a hitherto unknown world. In Zhang Qian's report on his thirteen years in the "Western Regions," Chinese leaders learned of a world that contained India, of Parthians living on the Iranian plateau, even of countries on the eastern shore of the Mediterranean. Silk, the Chinese rulers began to realize, a material so banal it was produced by the women of every farming household and was the currency (along with grain) in which taxes were paid, had huge allure and value on international markets. Although sericulture, or silk cultivation, had been practiced in China for millennia, it was utterly unknown elsewhere.

In order to capitalize on this vast demand for silk, Wudi extended the Han empire into the Western Regions, building garrison towns. Though Chinese control there would wane, oasis cities blossomed. Trade along the silk route would come to fall under the protection of a series of Central Asian dynasties, including the Yuezhi, the group Zhang Qian had been seeking, who relocated to what is now Afghanistan and founded the Kushan kingdom, a powerful and prosperous multiethnic state that grew rich protecting the silk trade. By the first century AD, caravan routes carrying silk connected China with the Mediterranean.

Until sea routes overshadowed and then supplanted the Eurasian land route at around the fifteenth century,[*] caravan traffic along the silk route encouraged the spread of Buddhism, and enriched a succession of Central Asian empires. It also gave rise to an unprecedented variety of textiles.

The Greek sun god Helios's image was transmitted from Greek pottery to Chinese Jin silk. A tree of life motif migrated into Chinese textiles from Sassanid Persia, transforming on its way from a dragon spruce into a mulberry. The technology for warp-faced compound brocade, developed in the pre-Qin period (before 221 BC) in China, moved westward. Textile historians have argued that the tensile strength of the naturally long silk fiber meant that the long silk warps

---

[*] From at least the sixteenth century onward, China's silk exports to the West were carried primarily along maritime routes in Portuguese, Spanish, and other European ships.

could withstand repeated manipulation, which led to the development of patterning in the silk warp. Wool, by contrast, has short strands that call for other strategies, like twill. The earliest twills were woven in short woolen fibers in the Anatolian highlands, and from there, knowledge of twill weaves may eventually have spread to China, and to silk, via Han Chinese living in oases or outposts along the Silk Road.

Within imperial China, silk was central to the theater of state. Public spectacles designed to display imperial might showcased silk as prominently as they showcased weapons. The Grand Carriage procession in Kaifeng, the capital of the Northern Song Dynasty (960–1126), was one of many such spectacles. On grand occasions of state, the number of people who paraded with the Grand Carriage hovered around twenty thousand throughout most of the dynasty. The memoir of a contemporary, Meng Yuanlao, describes the parade: "Each of the seven elephants is covered by a patterned damask cloth," he writes, and "a person in silk brocade straddles its neck." Next came "mounted officers in multi-colored jerkins. Some wear small hats over brocade or embroidered scarves, some black-lacquer round top scarf-caps. . . . Some wear garments of red and yellow fishnet-design brocades and embroideries. Some dress entirely in green or black, down to their shoes and socks, and wear cross-tailed scarf-caps. Some decorate themselves with silken cords wound like snakes around their bodies." Witnessing the Grand Carriage procession, the general public was given a lesson in political power. The entire retinue, the viewer would have understood—the musicians, astronomers, and eunuchs, the officials and guardsmen, and the supernatural forces depicted on flags—were forces at the command of the emperor.

Complex silk weaves, like *luo*-gauzes—transparent gauzes made by twisting together adjacent warp threads—and warp-faced polychrome-brocaded silks, were produced in state workshops, providing the emperor with luxurious fabrics to bestow upon the elite and for use in state payments. These required more advanced looms than the average slanted or horizontal treadle looms owned by peasant families. Only urban workshops operated by the state, or wealthy private patrons, had the necessary capital to invest in such advanced looms and the capacity to train weavers to operate them.

Farming families in China traditionally produced simple cloth for their own use, or to pay taxes. The rural ideal was one in which "women spun and wove, and men tended the crops," in the words of the Ming (1368–1644) civil servant Zhang Tao. During the mid-Ming, however, this classical model of men plowing and women weaving was beginning to be adapted to commercial conditions. Exports were pumping Japanese and Spanish silver into the Chinese market and helping lubricate the economy, and merchants were drawing producers and consumers into regional and national commercial networks.

Demand for silk skyrocketed in the 1470s and 1480s, breaking the urban monopoly on high-end silks and turning it into a predominantly rural industry. This meant that rural producers had to specialize. In the core of the silk regions of Jiangnan, women "only spin and do not know how to weave," noted a 1527 gazetteer. Specializing in thread production for export silks, they bought local "rough silk" to meet their own needs. Another local gazetteer from the Lake Tai region notes "in every village in reach of a town, residents were devoting their energies entirely to earning a living from silk," and purchasing rice, rather than raising it.

This commercial boom was not, however, a win for women. Historian and anthropologist of technology Francesca Bray has argued that in the late Ming, women began to be edged out of their position at the heart of textile production so that men could take their place. Men took over the work of weaving and left the more poorly paid steps such as silk reeling to women. Just as had occurred in Europe, the development of a money economy, which initially drew women into the cottage-based textile industry, in the longer term promoted the marginalization of their labor and reduced their place in production.

During the Ming, the center of the luxury trade was Suzhou, a 2,500-year-old city in the Yangtze Delta that first gained wealth when the Grand Canal was completed during the Sui Dynasty (581–618). The canal connected Beijing with Hangzhou and placed Suzhou on a major trade route. Suzhou was studded with the exquisite garden residences of the wealthy, some now UNESCO heritage sites, the warehouses of major merchants, and the workshops of craftsmen in the luxury trade. Canal bridges served as pickup spots for specialized day laborers. Spinners hoping to be hired for a day's work once gathered before dawn at the bridge by Guanghua monastery.

Suzhou was particularly noted for its embroidery. During the Ming (1368–1644) and Qing (1644–1912), it was one of three cities in the Yangtze River Delta—Suzhou, Nanjing, and Hangzhou—permitted to supply official textiles to the imperial court. Here, rank patches were embroidered, marking each level of military and civilian officialdom with a different bird or beast. One distressed scholar-official, Zhang Han (1511–94), noted how snobbish Suzhou's residents were: according to them, he complained, "If it isn't splendid Suzhou made clothing, it isn't refined."

In the Suzhou Embroidery Museum, I pored over a tenth-century embroidery depicting the dried husks of a lotus flower. Each of the contour lines, like those articulating the nine holes in the face of a lotus flower husk, were produced with the direction and the pattern of the monochrome stiches. This embroidery, along with others from the period, once served as sutra covers, or cloths that protected Buddhist scriptures. They had been discovered inside Suzhou's Huqiu Tower, an eight-sided pagoda constructed between 907 and 961.

Mrs. L. and I had arrived in Suzhou the evening before. The guidebooks and hotel leaflets all said Suzhou was a city of canals and delicate stone bridges, but from the moment I arrived I found it difficult to "see" the city they described. A bloated and indecipherable modern city was blocking my vision. Even the cab driver who picked us up at the train station wondered aloud where Suzhou had gone. It was a shame I could not see it as it really was, as it used to be, he said. This here all used to be rice and mulberry trees, he told me, gesturing to the sprawl that extended on all sides around the station.

Even as it swelled, and eviscerated its mulberry trees, Suzhou seemed determined to hold on to its reputation as the center of silk making. Brochures promised it. There was only *one* remaining place to see silk making in action in Suzhou: the Taihu Snow Silk Museum.

My tour guide and translator introduced herself as Tina. She wore nail tips, a plaid miniskirt, and a tight black mock turtleneck with gold buttons from wrist to elbow. I thought maybe it was due to some vagary of her English training and not a wish to be impolite when she pointed to a close-up image of silkworms eating and said softly, "Actually, this is the shit of the silkworms." I tried not to smile as she explained, "It can be made into medicine. Especially very good for the eyes."

In the center of the display that demonstrated the lifecycle of the silkworm, there was a white plastic mesh frame filled with live silkworms attaching themselves to a hold in the mesh and preparing to spin their cocoons. Their fat white bodies looked lethargic. I watched one that had begun to spin, its black mouth worked over a long strand of silk like hammers composing a long line of prose. I could just make out the sound of their spinning: a subtle hiss like that of Rice Krispies in milk. "Normally cocoons are white," said Tina, "but now we have yellow, pink, and light blue. That's because of . . ." She stopped to look something up, pointed to her phone. I looked down at the word brought up by her translation app: "transgenesis," or when a modified gene gets introduced into a recipient organism.

Tina deposited me in the Taihu Silk showroom, with bedding, pajamas, fake Louis Vuitton scarves, purses, and eye pillows on display. As I made my way back to the foyer, I passed a wall covered in photographs of Suzhou celebrities. Yao Ming, the Houston Rockets player. Ping-Pong gold medalist Zhang Yining, posing with Chairman Xi.

"I have been traveling around my whole life and I still think Zhen Ze is the best place," intoned the voice-over of a video playing on a loop in the foyer. Why, I wondered, was the Taihu Snow Silk Museum playing a booster film for the township of Zhen Ze? It wasn't until I saw the map in the foyer showing the future locations of a wedding resort and a senior center that it finally dawned on me that the museum wasn't just an elaborate ad for Taihu Snow Silk. It was an accessory designed to bring some local color, and some added value, to a high-end real estate development. Suzhou's acres might have been ideal for silkworms, but now they are far too valuable to be squandered on mere trees.

. . .

From Suzhou, Mrs. L. and I traveled farther south to Hangzhou to visit the China National Silk Museum, on New Year's Day 2019. The complex contained a "science of silk" hall with a six-foot-long plastic anatomical model of a silkworm. A bridge stretched to another building devoted to the history of silk. The lower lever established the Chinese silk industry's Neolithic bona fides, while a wall display put the technicalities on view: blown-up plastic versions of twill, damask, gauze, silk, tabby, satin, jin silk, weft-faced compound weave, velvet, brocade showed off their weave structure to anyone patient enough to try to understand. There were Qing Dynasty rank patches for civilian officials, each rank represented by a bird, from crane on down to egret.

South of the city, we drove toward the Eastern Sea to visit Shaoxing Industrial Zone. Many of the textile and garment factories that had boomed in this region were now struggling or going out of business, casualties of rising salaries on China's east coast, but fabric dyeing facilities—consolidated inside the Industrial Zone in order to provide wastewater treatment—were working at full tilt. Twenty minutes out from the Industrial Zone, we began to smell it. A huge row of factories faced out over the Cao'e River where it flowed into Hangzhou Bay. The Zone, at one hundred square kilometers, is nearly double the size of Manhattan. Inside one dyeing plant, navy fabric with white flowers was coming out of a softening treatment, and I was invited to feel it. "This will feed me for a year," joked the boss, "26,000 meters of this for H&M, just for this one color." A worker stood refilling the black paint into the dyeing machine from one of the blue plastic tubs the size of trash barrels that stood by, full of ink.

Hangzhou, like Suzhou, had once been a center of the luxury textile trade. The Hangzhou scholar Zhang Han noted in the 1580s "even the big merchants from Shaanxi, Shanxi, Shandong, and Henan don't consider several thousand li too long a journey" to buy textiles in Hangzhou. The story of how it went from being a center of handmade luxury silks to an exporter of machine-made polycotton knits is a story, in part, of imperial violence.

. . .

n the mid-eighteenth century, Chinese goods like silk, tea, and por-
celain were in great demand in Europe, but China was not interested
in importing British goods, and demanded sterling as payment. With
a well-developed textile tradition of its own, China certainly had
no interest in Britain's major export product: industrially produced
mill cloth. After repeated efforts to convince China to accept British
goods, the East India Company decided to offer up the one product
the Chinese would pay for: opium.

In 1839, William Jardine, a British East India Company surgeon
turned opium trader, traveled to London to organize a lobby of Midlands industrialists, London bankers, and merchants to pressure the
foreign office to use force against China in retaliation against local
Chinese leaders who made strident efforts to curb this trade. The two
wars that ensued culminated in the burning of the Qing emperor's
Summer Palace, in Beijing. Ordered by Lord Elgin in 1860, the event
was to remain a lasting symbol of Chinese humiliation. The entire
palace, stocked with libraries, ancient art, and artifacts, was looted
and then burned by British soldiers. One eyewitness wrote that he
saw looters using large bolts of silk like trash bags to carry off goods.

Following the first Opium War (1839–42), British merchants were
granted 140 acres of shoreline north of the Chinese walled city of
Shanghai. Shanghai's foreigners made a fortune exporting Yangtze
Delta cotton when the Civil War interrupted the American supply,
and another in the coolie trade, shipping unfree Chinese laborers to
Latin America from the 1840s to 1870s. They did not go into manufacturing until 1895 when the Treaty of Shimonoseki, which ended
the first Sino-Japanese War, gave the foreign powers in the treaty
ports—ports the Chinese had been pressured into opening to foreign
trade and residence—the right to open factories. British, American,
German, and Russian firms set up cotton mills and silk filatures, lining
both sides of Shanghai's Huangpu River.

Chinese silk making, at least five thousand years old, was industri-
alized in a matter of decades. But even before Shanghai's foreigners

opened mills on Chinese soil, foreign demand for Chinese raw silk upended traditional Chinese silk production. Between 1850 and 1930, raw silk became the leading export item for China and the demand starved domestic silk weavers for raw materials.

In 1881 South Chinese silk guilds organized a thousand weavers to attack a filature. They burned it, and looted expensive raw material, causing an estimated damage of 10,000 taels. Later that day, they gathered again in another village to attack Ch'en Ch'i-yuan's filature. The gentry in Ch'en's village organized a militia. The battle with the silk weavers lasted several days. Known as the Nan-hai silk weaver riot, this desperate effort to stop the spread of steam filatures came to little.

During and after World War I, as western businessmen left Shanghai for the front, Chinese businessmen stepped into textiles. The fortunes of Shanghai's silk mills followed the tumultuous events in twentieth-century China. In the early 1920s a communist-led strike of twenty thousand female employees at Shanghai silk factories was broken by police and soldiers. The communists' labor headquarters was closed down, and the party was forced underground.

During the Cultural Revolution, silk was condemned as a symbol of the old order. On August 18, 1966, Lin Bao, standing beside Chairman Mao at the rostrum, told students to set forth and destroy "all the old ideas, old culture, old customs and old habits of the exploiting classes." Books were one main target, clothes were another. The uniform of the orthodox revolutionary was a blue worker's costume. Silk, velvet, cosmetics, and fashionable clothes were confiscated and destroyed by eager, self-deputized students, and condemned as bourgeois luxuries. Nonetheless, the export of raw silk remained a crucial earner of foreign dollars for China.

When China opened for business again after the formal end of the Cultural Revolution in 1978, Shanghai was the first place to explode as a major center of export garment manufacturing, owing to its history as an industrial textile center. This country's rise as a garment exporter helped catalyze truly fabulous levels of wealth. The center of the world textile economy returned east. But the days of the artisanal, luxury silk once prized the world over had come to an end.

I went to Shanghai's New World Mall to ogle its fashionable citizens. An old woman in tasteful gray draped slacks and a loose cream-colored boiled wool jacket and black boots tried on a 1930s-style mustard-colored hat at Hermès and examined herself in the mirror. She put on her pillowed black leather Chanel purse, and tried it on again, this time for a friend. On a leather chair, a thin young woman in a black pollution mask and a black ballcap that said "Not a Rapper" slouched as a salesman brought her a Hermès belt. Along the wall curved a long line of people waiting to go into the Louis Vuitton. A young couple was let in: they unclipped the red velvet cord, like at a nightclub.

From there, I went to visit Shanghai's Donghua University, which is the oldest textile institute in China. Founded in 1951, its textile museum contains careful and exact replicas of ancient silk constructions for its design students to study. Outside, there were yellow gingko and red maples on campus. In the university museum I peered at replicas of dizzying brocade from the Eastern Han (AD 25–220). They reminded me of the Magic Eye books I scrutinized as a child. In the costume of a priest in Sichuan from the Shang Dynasty (1766–1122 BC), I was tempted to perceive occult messages written in the weave structure. In the pattern of a Warring States Period (475–221 BC) silk, with its large interlocking lozenges, symmetry was suggested but never completed: a design that tantalized by the satisfactions it foreclosed. In a brocade with mountain, bird, and forest motif on white ground from the Eastern Han Dynasty (or around the time that the silk route began to open), fat, amorphous birds skitter down the sides of parallel craggy rocks with a tree growing up between them. In between this repeating pattern was what looked like a tree sprouting nine mushrooms. Or were they flying saucers? Or fried eggs? A Song Dynasty patterned weave was subtlety itself. Green on green, ovalesque diamonds. A repository for five thousand years of design history, it was hard to believe that handwoven Chinese silks had really come to an end.

7

Costume Drama

I'll be at charges for a looking-glass;
And entertain some score or two of tailors,
To study fashions to adorn my body:
Since I am crept in favour with myself,
I will maintain it with some little cost.

—SHAKESPEARE, *RICHARD III*

n the 1130s, in the wake of the fall of the Northern Song Dynasty, a Chinese government official from Jiangan named Lou Shou painted a pair of scrolls depicting the twenty-four different steps in the production of silk, and the twenty-one steps in the cultivation of rice. On the silk scrolls, women plucked mulberry leaves and sorted silkworm eggs, fed and cleaned the larvae. On the rice scrolls, men irrigated, planted, sowed, and threshed rice. The scrolls, called the *Gengzhi Tu* (Pictures of Tilling and Weaving), became a wildly popular motif in Chinese art, recurrent right through the nineteenth century. In them, the praxis of a whole civilization became transparent. From the seventeenth century, the *Gengzhi Tu* also gained a wide European audience in the form of "chinoiserie."

From the later 1600s to the early 1800s, chinoiserie was in vogue in Europe. Decorating ceramics, prints, and textiles, chinoiserie was a European art comprised of Chinese or pseudo-Chinese ornamental motifs. Fed by the rise of trade with East Asia in this period, chinoiserie followed a long orientalist tradition within Europe. The trend was fueled by books like Marco Polo's account of his travels and his stay at Kublai Khan's court, published in Venice in 1295, or *The Travels of Sir John Mandeville,* published in Lyon in 1480 and translated into every European language, with its fairy-tale description of East Asia.

During Roman times, Chinese silk that traveled across Central Asia defined the luxury of the imperial court. Sericulture began in Byzantium under Justinian, and had reached the Arab world by the ninth century. The Crusades acquainted Western Europe with sericulture, and the first mulberry tree was brought to France from Syria in 1147. In the early thirteenth century, silk began to be processed in Lyon and Tours.

European adaptations of Chinese styles sprang up to meet the popular taste that genuine Chinese silks had provoked. The French artist Antoine Watteau (1684–1721) is credited with producing the earliest examples of rococo chinoiserie, replete with elements such as priests, pagodas, and parasols, generating textile designs in France and throughout Europe. In the mid-1750s Lyonais landscape painter and designer Jean-Baptiste Pillement engraved chinoiserie designs in pieces he called "One Hundred and Thirty Figures and Ornaments" and "Some Flowers in the Chinese Style."

Despite prohibitions against the trade erected to guard domestic industry, Chinese silks continued to be smuggled into England and France. The estates of the English and French gentry contain numerous examples of eighteenth-century Chinese painted silks. Textile historians encounter puzzling questions of provenance for silks of this period, particularly when both western and Chinese artisans copied one another. With demand so high, the East India Company officials sent samples of western chinoiserie designs for Chinese artisans to copy, prompting Chinese designers to create fabrics for export that featured people with Asian features in eighteenth-century European dress and hairstyles.

What most concerned commentators in France during the period of chinoiserie's great vogue was not, however, the imitation of foreign fabrics. It was a different kind of mimesis that perturbed them: French citizens of lower social stations began to imitate the fashions of the nobility. In 1670, the playwright Molière lambasted the upstart bourgeois Monsieur Jourdain, and his aspiration to dress like an aristocrat, in the play *Le Bourgeois Gentilhomme*:

> MONSIEUR JOURDAIN: What's this? You've put the flowers upside down.
>
> MASTER TAILOR: You didn't tell me you wanted them right side up.
>
> MONSIEUR JOURDAIN: Did I have to tell you that?
>
> MASTER TAILOR: Yes, surely. All the people of quality wear them this way.
>
> MONSIEUR JOURDAIN: The people of quality wear flowers upside down?
>
> MASTER TAILOR: Yes, Sir.
>
> MONSIEUR JOURDAIN: Oh! It's alright then.
>
> MASTER TAILOR: If you like, I'll put them right side up.
>
> MONSIEUR JOURDAIN: No, no.
>
> MASTER TAILOR: You have only to say so.
>
> MONSIEUR JOURDAIN: No, I tell you. You've made it very well. Do you think the suit is going to look good on me?
>
> MASTER TAILOR: What a question! I defy a painter with his brush to do anything that would fit you better.

This scene was first performed on October 14, 1670, before the court of Louis XIV at the Château of Chambord, a hunting lodge in the Loire Valley where the king entertained a few weeks out of the year. Molière was comedically illustrating one of the great anxieties of the age: that people dressed outside of their station.

According to Molière, the nobleman was copied by the rich bourgeois, and hot on his heels was his own tailor, who is discovered later in the scene to have cut himself a suit out of his master's cloth. The same phenomenon was described in 1672 in *Le Mercure Galant*, a magazine that reported on court society. It reported that fashions passed "from the ladies of the town to rich bourgeois women, and from them to milliners." Dutch philosopher Erasmus had proclaimed that clothing was "the body's body, and from [it] one may infer the state of a man's character." This reflected the values of a feudal society according to which a person's rank was immutable. Clothing signaled a man or woman's station, but a new Enlightenment perspective increasingly challenged that belief, and justified promotion by wealth and its expression in appearances.

The aristocratic audience members that attended the premiere of *Bourgeois Gentilhomme* at the Château of Chambord were costumed scrupulously according to rules set down by Louis XIV himself. Beginning in 1660 the king, alongside his finance minister, Jean-Baptiste Colbert, took charge of the minute details of French clothing, just as he had of all else.

When Louis came to power in 1643, Spain, not France, dictated European fashion. Early-seventeenth-century aristocratic style, with its starched ruffs, rigidity, and overwhelming use of black, was a Spanish export. Black dye was very expensive. Made from Mexican logwood, it displayed the extent of the Spanish wealth and empire.

Louis XIV made France the fashion capital of Europe. The king wielded clothing to enhance the prestige of the monarchy and the French court. Colbert, meanwhile, monetized the king's considerable genius as a fashion director by ensuring that, as thirst for French fashion and lifestyle spread, the profits were benefiting local French artisans. The revenue gained from the burgeoning French luxury goods industries would then be reinvested in the military, funding Louis XIV's many wars. This was a phenomenon noted by clothing historian Daniel Roche: "the real and the imaginary are imbricated in the history of clothing." For Louis XIV the image of power produced power.

Louis XIV sought out and hired ministers from bourgeois backgrounds, believing that nobles promoted to high office could become powerful enough to attack him. His trusted finance minister Colbert had been born in Rheims in 1619 to a respectable, bourgeois family. His father was likely a cloth merchant. In 1665, Colbert was made comptroller general of finance, and in 1667 he was able to furnish proofs of nobility in order to enable his son to be admitted to l'Ordre de Malte, a prestigious Catholic military order. These papers were probably not scrutinized because of the station that Colbert had achieved. In fact, some speculated that Colbert himself was the inspiration for Monsieur Jourdain in Molière's *Bourgeois Gentilhomme.*

Together, Louis XIV and Colbert reinvented the luxury goods industry. Louis XIV took the throne at five years old, and early in his reign French aristocrats bought luxury goods abroad: lace and mirrors in Venice, silk in Milan, tapestries in Brussels. France's luxury industry was not yet capable of producing items of comparable quality. But heavy import duties were imposed on foreign items while foreign lace, cloth, and trimmings were banned outright. In another policy intended to support French artisans, Colbert mandated that new textiles appear seasonally twice a year, so that on November 1 promptly, the court was required to put aside lightweight silks and don velvet and satin. Thus, the fashion season was born. Colbert's calendar provided a predictable cycle for the textile industry in Lyon. To ensure that people bought plenty of cloth, Colbert mandated that textile patterns change each year so that it would be obvious if anyone was wearing last year's fabric. In 1668 Louis demanded by edict that his courtiers "remain fashionable," and instituted a strict dress code.

Court dress as codified by Louis in the 1670s, particularly the *grand habit* for women, with its tight bodice, low décolleté, and vast skirt, still constitutes the image we have of the French court, and indeed of the ancien régime. Clothing historian Kimberly Chrisman-Campbell has noted that the *grand habit* was Louis's deliberate riposte to the more comfortable and informal "mantua," a looser gown that had been gaining popularity among aristocratic women. The *grand habit* was not designed to make women look beautiful, or young, she argues. Rather, "it was designed to make them look rich." It was the splendor of the French court, after all, that Louis wished to exhibit. Each noble body was an opportunity for this display of wealth. Chrisman-Campbell has noted that, although Louis has been accused of trying to bankrupt the nobility by demanding they seasonally update their expensive wardrobes, in fact he subsidized their clothing expenses.

In the newly invented fashion press, the court became a showpiece for French luxury. Renaissance printers developed the etching plate, and with that technology, the *Mercure Galant* launched in 1672.

Its pages depicted the newest fashions, while detailed captions told readers what to wear and how to wear it. Fashion plates were also distributed as stand-alones, or issued in series, like the "Collection of the Fashion of the Court of France" published from 1678 to 1693, which consisted of 361 plates by renowned Parisian engravers, all subsidized by the crown.

In the eighteenth century, these magazines were dispatched monthly around the world, along with mannequins of wax or wood, to spread French fashion and style abroad. The mission of these dummies was taken extremely seriously. The dolls enjoyed diplomatic immunity and were even escorted by cavalry in times of war. Particularly after 1750, French fashion publications reshaped the dress of European elites. Parisian style "was inseparable from the Enlightenment," Daniel Roche has argued, "from Saint Petersburg to Botany Bay."

Louis XIV and Colbert's policies precipitated a lasting and spectacular economic success. During Louis's reign, from 1643 to 1715, the fashion industry employed a third of the workers in Paris. Over the course of the seventeenth century, and especially in its last decades, Paris doubled in size, coming to be tied with London as the world's fourth largest city after Constantinople, Edo, and Beijing. "Fashions were to France," Finance Minister Colbert said, "what the mines of Peru were to Spain." This was a huge boon to the silk industry in Lyon. Enriched by state sponsorship, Lyon became the preeminent European silk-manufacturing city in the eighteenth century.

One hundred years after Louis made France the center of fashion, its sway remained absolute. John Adams wrote in 1782:

The first thing to be done, in Paris, is always to send for a Taylor, a Peruke maker and Shoemaker, for this nation has established such a domination over the Fashion, that neither Cloaths, Wigs, nor Shoes made in any other Place will do in Paris. This is one of the Ways, in which France taxes all Europe, and will tax America. It is a great Branch of the Policy of the Court, to preserve and increase this national Influence over the Mode.

While these economic achievements were vast, Louis XIV and Colbert's policies also served internal political needs. Louis used costume as an elaborate and ingenious method of control. Certain garments served as a mark of particular favor. For instance, the *just-aucorps à brevet*, a blue silk jacket embroidered in silver and gold and designed by the king himself, was permitted to be worn by only fifty nobles at a time, and only those wearing it were permitted to follow the king on his hunt, a rare opportunity to get the king's ear. Personal access to the king was important to nobles.

Louis himself was the center of the costume drama. A lover of ballet, he received the moniker "The Sun King" for playing the role of Apollo in a court ballet, and continued to dance the lead role in court performances, a chance to display the excellent pair of calves about which he was reportedly very vain. Shoes, rather than boots, showed calves to the greatest effect, leading to their vogue under Louis XIV, red high heels in particular.

Ultimately, the greatest role Louis performed was the role of himself, which he played the way Marilyn Monroe performed the role of *herself*, with great virtuosity and precision. In fact, the king's dressing became the most elaborately scripted ritual of the court. During what became known as the King's "levee," six rounds of entrances occurred, indicative of very fine and subtle variegations in rank and favor. Attendance at the levee, with its intimate and coveted access, was the highest mark of favor a courtier could hope to attain.

The first two entrances occurred while the king was still in bed: the *entrée familiale*, with his legitimate and illegitimate children, and then with his most favored nobles. Once he had risen, and the Lord Chamberlain, with the first Gentleman of the Bedchamber, had laid out his robe, the next group was brought in. When he had put on his shoes, the next. The *maître de la garderobe* pulled his nightshirt off by the right sleeve, while the first servant of the wardrobe pulled it off by the left. His day shirt was pulled on with just as much care. It was brought in by the Lord Chamberlain. The first valet pulled on his right sleeve, and the first servant of the wardrobe the left. So it continued, through the fastening of his boots, dagger, and coat. One is reminded of the tale of Inanna, Sumerian goddess of love and fertility, who decided to pay a visit to her sister Erishkigal in the underworld and had to pass through eight gates on the way in, removing an article of clothing at each gate in order to pass.

Although the king devised and codified these elaborate rituals, the courtiers upheld them, even after the king's death.

The anxiety over appearances and class mobility present during the reign of Louis XIV was by no means new. In fact, it had been codified in legal terms from the fifteenth century onward in a series of sumptuary laws. Eighteen decrees were passed between 1485 and 1660 attempting to control the use of French clothing and ornament. The preamble to the decree of 1514, for example, announced: "Prohibiting absolutely categorically all persons, commoners, non-nobles . . . from assuming the title of nobility either in their style or in their clothes." In these two centuries, the monarchy attempted to restrict silk to the nobility, prevent gold and silver from being used in fabrics, which diverted precious metals from state coffers and circulation, and to create a hierarchy of colors. Sermons between the reign of Henry IV and Louis XIV reinforced the logic of the sumptuary laws, insisting that each person should dress according to their rank.

Sumptuary laws had dubious efficacy. Philosopher and essayist Montaigne believed they backfired: "The way in which our laws try to regulate the foolish and vain expenses of the table and dress is self-defeating," he wrote, because they merely served to "increase in everyone the desire to adopt them." However, when the sumptuary laws fell into disuse at the death of Louis XIV in 1715, the sluice was opened in earnest.

Sumptuous fabrics were no longer the preserve of aristocrats. In the absence of assurances with regard to fabric type the aristocracy relied upon ever-changing nuances of style. In the words of Saint-Preux, the central character of Jean-Jacques Rousseau's 1761 novel *The New Eloise:* "You see the same fabrics at all levels and one could scarcely distinguish a duchess from a woman of the bourgeoisie were it not for the fact that the former possessed the art of finding distinctions which the latter would not dare to imitate." This "art of finding distinctions" caused an acceleration of change in clothing forms in eighteenth-century France. It is to this accelerating cycle that we can trace the birth of fashion as we know it.

Every social class was hot on the heels of the one above it. Fashion was commented upon with a particular intensity as the dispute over clothes became a kind of proxy war for the debate about increasing social mobility that was replacing an ancien régime of fixed stations. The new plasticity in social rank was upsetting to some, and clothing was made a scapegoat. In dramatist Edme Boursault's 1690 *Les Fables d'Esope:*

> *The sergeant's wife, if she could afford,*
> *Would wear clothes just like a bawd;*
> *The pimp's wife wants, in order to impress,*
> *To equal the wife of the lawyer in her dress;*
> *The lawyer's wife even dares*
> *To copy the wife of the councilor's airs;*
> *The councilor's wife is then not hesitant*
> *Even to vie with the wife of the president.*

Where ordinances on fabric use do persist in the records after Louis XIV, they merely demonstrate the ways in which conspicuous consumption was spiraling out of control. Aristocrats used the uniforms of their servants to advertise their own prestige. Status wars between these aristocrats ultimately resulted in a 1724 ordinance that prohibited liveried servants from wearing silk stockings that were literally decorated with gold or silver pieces.

In an exhaustive study of Parisian property records, Daniel Roche determined that over the course of the eighteenth century, consumption of clothing grew among the Parisian nobility, men of the professions, artisans and shopkeepers, wage earners, and domestic servants: "every social category was caught up in the acceleration of the rate of change and replacement." The fashion press that had emerged under Louis XIV blossomed: from 1700 to 1800 fifty distinct French periodicals were in circulation. Books on clothes exploded also, with over five times as many published in the second half of the century than in the first. Perhaps it is no surprise that this period saw the popularity of Charles Perrault's retelling of Cinderella, published in 1697, in which a girl changes from a kitchen drudge to a queen by the intervention of an elegant gown and a fine pair of slippers. The pull of what new clothes could do exerted a powerful draw, and theft of clothing escalated. Between 1760 and 1769, over 900 (52 percent) of Paris's 1,700 trials addressed thefts of clothing and linen. Clothing rental was a bustling trade. However, if Cinderella could be rocketed out of a life of drudgery and obscurity with the loan of just one gown, the actual underclass was far less fortunate. One M. Lafontaine complained that he had lost 4,500 livres on clothes rented to "women of the world" (prostitutes) who had died in them, in hospitals or prisons.

One of the greatest transformations in clothing that took place in the last quarter of the eighteenth century, the consequences of which remain with us today, occurred not in women's clothes, but men's. These decades witnessed a paradigm shift that the British psychoanalyst John Carl Flügel dubbed "the great renunciation." Men began to wear more somber, subdued clothing in dark, plain fabrics. To women were left the silks, high heels, makeup, lace cuffs, bright colors, and ornamentation hitherto enjoyed equally by the nobility of both genders. Flügel notes that this occurred as centers of power shifted out of the court, and the households of the noblemen, and into professional offices. For women, whose juridical and social status was eroding, clothes became more ornate as they were tasked with becoming shop windows for their husband's wealth.

Flügel believed that for men at this time, the narcissism involved in self-adornment was transformed into scopophilia, the pleasure of seeing. A simpler explanation is that men gained in real power what they were losing in finery. Men's clothing emphasized their role as active subjects, while women's clothing defined them as passive objects. By the time Simone de Beauvoir theorized women's oppression in 1949 in *The Second Sex*, the effects of the logic of the Great Renunciation were cemented, brutal, and clear:

A man's clothes, like his body, should indicate his transcendence and not attract attention; for him neither elegance nor good looks calls for his setting himself up as object; moreover, he does not normally consider his appearance as a reflection of his ego.

Woman, on the contrary, is even required by society to make herself an erotic object. The purpose of the fashions to which she is enslaved is not to reveal her as an independent individual, but rather to cut her off from her transcendence in order to offer her as prey to male desires: thus society is not seeking to further her projects but to thwart them.

While fashion increasingly became a woman's concern, women also began to carve new niches for themselves as producers of high-end clothing.

Prerevolutionary clothing was produced by the members of guilds, whose legal personality and statutes were approved by the crown. They drafted regulations for their craft and set criteria for admission, effectively holding monopolies over a carefully defined economic sector. Guilds regulated the various steps in garment production minutely. For instance, the statutes of the thirteenth-century Parisian tailors' guild reserved cutting cloth for established masters, leaving sewing to subordinate workers called *valets cousturiers*. Cloth was so expensive that cutting it was a high-risk operation. A faulty stitch can be removed, but a faulty cut can ruin an entire piece of fabric. *Couturier*, which comes from *coudre*, to sew, was thus enshrined as a lower-status occupation than *tailleur*, or tailor, which derives from *tailler*, to cut. Indeed, it was not until the end of the nineteenth century, when the mass production of clothing rendered the bespoke trade glamorous, that the word "couturier" shook off its humble medieval connotations.

The female form of the word, *couturière*, was to have a different fate. Even in the late twentieth century it was used to refer to a modest female artisan mending and doing alterations for a neighborhood clientele. However, in the closing years of the ancien régime, women were responsible for some of the most sumptuous garments to be found at court. During the seventeenth century, women carved out a

niche for themselves by making the argument that it was inappropri-
ate for women to be fitted for clothes by men, and in 1675 seamstresses
in Rouen and Paris acquired independent, exclusively female guilds.

Another class of female guildswomen who carved out a niche
within the highly regulated French guild system were the *marchandes
de modes*. These were late-eighteenth-century stylists who made sure
that the gloves, the mantle, the trim, the lining, the shoes—a noble-
woman's whole look—lined up. The most famous was Mademoiselle
Bertin, a self-made millionaire who sent her last bill to Marie Antoinette for 40,000 livres three days before the queen's wardrobe was
scattered to the winds during the sack of the Tuileries on August 10,
1792.

Marchandes de modes generally got their start as the wives of mer-
cers who themselves dealt in clothing. They expanded their legal
range of operations from trimmings and caps and were entitled to
produce full *grand habit*—the court dress mandated by Louis XIV.
Marchandes excelled in inventing novelty items, which served them
well as new items wouldn't yet fall under another guild's monopoly.
This practice also helped them to devise subtle nuances that could
help differentiate the elite from their imitators.

Susan Sontag noted that "the French have never shared the Anglo-
American conviction that makes the fashionable the opposite of
the serious." Never was this more true than in the eighteenth century,
when serious people spoke about fashion, just as fashion remarked on
serious subjects.

Marchandes de modes used clothes to make political commentary in
the language of puns. For instance, in 1784 the celebrated courtesan
Rosalie Duthé was seen out at Longchamp in one of Mademoiselle
Bertin's confections: a black hat of flimsy gauze dubbed *à la caisse
d'escompte* to make reference to the floundering French national bank,
the Caisse d'Escompte. The hat had no "fond," or crown, as the bank
had no "fond," or funds. Other styles were more direct: the first fashion plate issued by the *Gallerie des modes* in 1778 depicted a *bonnet à
la Victoire* to celebrate France's entry into the American Revolution.

Another hat celebrating a naval victory featured an entire miniature ship floating above the wearer's head. Fashions regularly commented on the politics of the moment, like the 1774 *pouf à l'inoculation*, a headpiece that celebrated the vaccination of the king, and helped promote the idea of vaccination.

The most famous, and famously irreconcilable, philosophers of the Age of Enlightenment, Voltaire and Rousseau, dueled on the subject of fashion, and in particular over whether fashion-fueled consumption was of any benefit to the public. Voltaire's philosophical poem "Mondain" served as an apologia for luxury: "This profane age was made for my habits. / I love luxury, and even softness, / All the pleasures, the arts of every sort." Rousseau, in turn, had some choice words for Voltaire: "Tell me, celebrated Arouet [Voltaire], how many strong, masculine Beauties you have sacrificed to our false Delicacy, and how many great and noble Designs our Taste for Show and Finery, so fertile in Trifles, has cost you?" Rousseau was skeptical of the economic miracles that could be achieved by luxury and warned of the dangers of consumer society. He wrote:

> Granting that Luxury is a certain Sign of Riches, or, if you please, that it even serves to multiply them: What Conclusion must we draw from this Paradox, which is so worthy of being produced in our Days; and what will become of virtue, if we must acquire Wealth at any Rate?

And yet Rousseau, not Voltaire, sparked the next big fashion movement, following the vogue for orientalist dress that swept the aristocracy in the last decades of the eighteenth century.

Rousseau became extremely influential on the reform of French dress, especially for children. French children were dressed exactly like adults until Rousseau suggested that children be given more room to move. Parents starting dressing their children in comfortable sailor suits. Rousseau himself had produced a spectacle by eschewing the wig, breeches, and waistcoat of court fashion for the long loose robe and round cap of his Ottoman "Armenian" suit that made him the laughingstock of the salons. After his death, Rousseau's arguments for rustic simplicity would, through the unlikely figure of Marie Antoinette, remake the aristocratic wardrobe.

In the last quarter of the eighteenth century, Marie Antoinette was France's major fashion icon. Traditionally, this position had been held by the king and his mistresses, but Louis XVI had neither an interest in fashion, nor a mistress. At Marie Antoinette's side was the celebrated Marchande de Modes, Mademoiselle Bertin.

Marie Antoinette and Mme Bertin were blamed, together, for the intensification of fashion worship, even for families' financial ruin caused by overspending wives of noblemen. Upon the queen was also pinned, of course, responsibility for famine and the French debt itself. Historians have noted that her expenditures on clothes, while large, essentially represented her keeping up with what was expected of her. Symbolically, however, she was luxury personified.

None of Marie Antoinette's famous excesses, however, evoked more fury than her turn to simplicity. Never one to miss out on a fad, Marie Antoinette read Rousseau during his great vogue, and personally made the popular pilgrimage to his tomb. She then remade herself after his vision of "simplicity."

Marie Antoinette's pastoral period corresponded with the construction of the Hameau de la Reine, the Queen's rustic retreat in Versailles, in 1783, as well as her thirtieth birthday, after which youthful styles no longer seemed appropriate. The dress of the French peasantry became a fetish in French high society. Having run through an orientalist streak, with dresses à la Chinoise and à la Turque, the exoticism of the French provinces was evoked, no doubt, as a last source of zest for the jaded palate. The nobility started wearing elements of peasant dress like aprons, straw hats, bonnets, and lappets. In the September 1788 *Magasin des Modes Nouvelles* the caption beneath a fashion plate of a "woman dressed as a court peasant" announced, "This get-up is almost the only one that our ladies find acceptable for morning walks."

Had these gestures only been tasteless, perhaps they would not have been so detested. But in fact, the queen's turn in the 1780s to muslin "chemise gowns," and the general vogue for imported muslins and gauzes, had disastrous implications for Lyon silk. "The superb manufacture of fabrics of silk, gold and silver which French commerce prided itself on, which furnished all of Europe, and provided subsistence for thousands of men, has been ruined by the fashion for cottons, muslins, gauzes, and linen," wrote the journalist Proudhomme. Silk gowns were no longer wanted in private life, and kept only for holidays and formal occasions. In 1786, there were twelve thousand silk looms in Lyon. By 1789 that number dropped to just 7,500. Honoré de Balzac once described the French Revolution as "a debate between silk and broadcloth," but the popularity of the muslin chemise gown, almost a decade before the Revolution, had already dealt a blow to Lyon and to silk.

The Revolution demanded another costume change. A mob ripped Marie Antoinette's wardrobe to shreds after storming the Palais de Tuileries, the royal palace in Paris. "All the rich suits of clothes were pulled to tatters, and every one sought to decorate his or her person with some fragment of the devastation," one spectator recalled. "How many curious women visited her wardrobe! How many bonnets, elegant hats, pink petticoats . . . flew from the room!" In the spring of 1793, the Revolutionary government put on a sale of items appropriated from the palace, including the remaining wardrobe of the king and queen. One spectator remarked: "I saw a suit embroidered with peacock tails that had cost 15,000 livres sold for 110 livres." Decadent clothes and fabrics such as these were anathema. Simple wool sold for more.

The Revolutionaries insisted on not only destruction of the old costume, but the positing of a new one. Trousers became the totem of the lower-class sans-culottes, a term which literally translates to "those without breeches." An article in the 1792 *Encyclopédie méthodique* about shirt collars argued that "we ought to make this part of our manners, our customs and our costumes, the same changes we are now making to our Constitution and our laws."

The Reign of Terror that followed the removal of French royalty also destroyed existing professional and patronage systems, and devastated Parisian workers in the luxury trades. One woman recorded:

My mother makes accessories and anything to do with fashion; my sister can make lace and gowns, I can sew and embroider. . . . The embroiderers are going bankrupt, the fashion merchants are closing their shops, the dressmakers have sacked three-quarters of their workers. . . . We are dying of hunger.

In Paris, the fashion for simplicity in dress turned out to be just that: a fashion, and conspicuous consumption came into vogue again by 1799. Still, the French luxury trades had been altered. Years after the Revolution, the duchess d'Abrantès wrote with notable bitterness that the so-called "equality" of the post-Revolutionary period came in the form of a universal cheapening:

It has been alleged that every thing has been simplified, that every article has been placed more within the reach of persons of all classes. That is true in one sense; that is to say, our grocer shall have muslin curtains and gilt rods to his windows, and his wife shall have a silk cloak like ours, because that silk is become so slight and so cheap that everybody can afford it. . . . You will have bad taffeta, bad satin, bad velvet, and that is all.

In the span of a few short years, guilds, artisans, and the traditional patronage system of Parisian fashion were lost. Their mythos, however, was to prove more durable. Many contemporary goods are designed for obsolescence, but with clothing, rapid turnover can draw upon a much deeper well of fantasy than can, say, a refrigerator. An article of clothing can evoke a period before the birth of industrial capitalism, when cloth was handmade and clothes made to measure, and a time when dressing in the silk formerly reserved for the elite became accessible to all members of society. In America, clothing manufacturers learned early on that in a trade based on fantasy as much as it is on necessity, they weren't simply in the business of selling fabric, cut and sewn. Rather, they were selling glamour, and the glamour of Parisian fashion had no equal.

8

The Rise of Mass Fashion

*As they have no understanding of the value of objects, they
go by the labels only.*

—PAUL POIRET

Paris still reigns in American conceptions of high culture. "I got expensive fabrics. I got expensive habits," Beyoncé sings, sitting beneath the statue of Nike, Greek goddess of victory, in the Louvre, wearing a Stephane Rolland couture dress, in her 2018 video "Apeshit." In another shot, she dances in a matching Burberry crop top and pants under the Jacques-Louis David painting *The Consecration of the Emperor Napoléon and the Coronation of Empress Joséphine,* a nod to her own queendom. Expensive fabrics, however, have been increasingly displaced in the popular understanding of what constitutes luxury clothing, by a different marker of exclusivity: the brand name.

In 2015 I went to visit and interview Shannon O'Hara, a Brooklyn-based seamstress who tailors Beyoncé's clothes for concerts, fashion shoots, and red carpet events. O'Hara was tall, blond, tattooed, and calm. On the wall of her apartment was a gravity anomaly map, which showed variations in the strength of the gravitational force over the surface of the earth. Her father was a cartographer, she told me when I asked her about it. I reflected that, perhaps, the tailor's art and the cartographer's are not dissimilar. The tailor transforms two-dimensional forms into a three-dimensional object, while the cartographer maps a three-dimensional landscape onto a two-dimensional form. There were once thousands of tailors in New York, O'Hara was telling me. By this, she did not mean tailors who do basic alterations at the dry cleaners, but the kinds of highly trained artisans who once created perfectly fitting custom garments for their clientele from scratch. The heirs to this tradition, in O'Hara's view, now work for fashion conglomerates or stars who can afford the type of virtuosic service they provide, and there are a mere handful.

O'Hara works as part of the luxury brand marketing apparatus that is centered, like garment manufacture *used* to be, in New York. Before a new item goes into mass production, a designer will produce a garment in a single size, called a sample. At red carpet events, photo shoots, and fashion shows, O'Hara transforms a sample into something that fits the model or actress who is to wear it. "It doesn't matter if it's not her size, I have to make it fit," she said. There is no such thing as a uniform sample size: each brand has a different one, depending on its demographic and aesthetic. For example, O'Hara often does work for Pucci, "and his sample is *a model*. So if I'm trying to put it on an actress I've got to figure out how to make it fit a real woman." On the other hand, when she does work for Jones of New York, the problem is reversed. "Their sample size is a size 8 because they're marketing to midwestern women, office women." From the tailor's perspective, the bodies of the model, the actress, and the office woman form a frenetic constellation. This is where the money is: in the space between what a woman is and what she can be made to believe about herself.

O'Hara's work is done at the point where fantasy confronts reality. Although the triumph of ready-made clothing is near total, which has by definition meant the end of garments made to measure by a tailor, clothing manufacturers still rely on tailors to project the fantasy that these mass-produced clothes will fit real bodies perfectly. Ready-made garments fit wrong in real life, but behind the scenes on television shows, movies, and advertisements, someone like O'Hara is fitting the clothing so that it appears to perfectly hug and shape its wearers on-screen, online, and in print.

O'Hara's work brings her into contact with idiosyncratic bodies, different bodies. Ready-to-wear garments produce the fraudulent concept of a uniform figure when in reality, O'Hara said, "I've never met anybody who's perfectly symmetric. Almost everybody has something that's messed up about them, like one shoulder—one of my shoulders is an inch shorter than the other, and I'm sure yours is, and one of your legs is probably longer, and you definitely have one bigger biceps." These aberrations are what make her work interesting. When tailoring for Sean Penn, O'Hara had to find a way to disguise the fact that "one of his shoulders is three inches taller than the other." Different people's bodies need different fit. Notoriously, Hitler instructed his tailor to make his garments loose so that he could make elaborate gestures with his right shoulder. His left shoulder was stiff after the November 1923 putsch, when he fell on the pavement, dislocated it, and refused to have it X-rayed for fear of being assassinated at the hospital.

Ready-to-wear garments have become ubiquitous, but before the late nineteenth and early twentieth centuries, ready-made clothing practically didn't exist in the United States. Most people wore clothing made at home, while those who could afford it dressed in clothes made by a tailor or a seamstress. A government report issued in 1811 found that "two-thirds of all garments worn by inhabitants of the United States" were homemade.

During the course of the nineteenth century, clothing was to become mass-manufactured. These changes came in slow increments. As we have seen, undershirts and pantaloons made by impoverished pieceworkers were the first mass-produced garments after the rise of textile mills, followed by corsets at mid-century. Before the Civil War, the only ready-to-wear outer garments available were made for sailors, and slaves. The very first off-the-rack clothing was sold at "slop-shops," which sprang up on the streets adjoining wharves in the early nineteenth century in Boston, New York, Philadelphia, Baltimore, and smaller cities with whaling or fishing trades. This clothing was produced in only one size, to be modified by a sailor heading out to sea as best he could.

Mass-manufactured garments for enslaved peoples developed as an industry in 1840–60. By buying cheap, mass-produced clothes, planters discovered, they could avoid using valuable slave labor in stitching. Trade routes between New York and other eastern cities and the port of New Orleans were established to ship ready-made clothing of cheap, coarse fabric to large plantations. The New Orleans dealer Folger and Blake Company claimed in one advertisement that planters would "find it greatly to their advantage to purchase their clothing ready-made" for slaves, while numerous New York firms specialized in what was known as "Negro clothing." Seamstresses in northern cities were an economical option, with opportunity costs of labor lower than those of slaves. Unsurprisingly, the clothing firms demanded high productivity from home or factory workers, in oppressive conditions, for low pay.

Sewing machine advertisements traced the landscape of clothes making as it evolved. In its first advertisement, on November 7, 1850, Singer addressed the promise of "SEWING BY MACHINERY" to "Journeyman Tailors, Sempstresses, Employers, and all others interested in Sewing of any description." Later in the 1850s, the I. M. Singer Company advertised a "new, improved sewing machine especially adapted to the making up of Negro clothing."

For the broader consumer market, the major leap forward for the ready-to-wear industry came with the advent of standard sizing. During the Civil War, conscripts were measured for their uniforms. This mass of body measurement data allowed for the creation of a range of generic sizes. Although these were later refined during the Spanish-American War and then the First World War, the standard sizing of garments was generally adopted for the production of ready-to-wear by the end of the 1860s. It was adopted even sooner for home dressmaking. In 1863 printed paper patterns in standard sizes became commercially available, developed by a New England tailor named Ebenezer Butterick.

After the Civil War, factories that had produced uniforms transitioned to producing men's suits. Cloaks and jackets for women soon followed. These were at first little-known garments in the United States, where the masses wore shawls, and what few cloaks were seen were worn by wealthy women, and imported from Germany. Even in these early days, mass-produced clothes promised to make elite fashion available to an underclass who could never before have afforded it.

By the 1880s women's clothing was being mass-produced in distribution networks organized initially by German-Jewish immigrants. The ready-to-wear garment industry grew dramatically. The value of production more than doubled between 1880 and 1889. Capital investment went from $8 million to over $22 million, and the number of manufacturers doubled: from 562 to 1,224. The number of workers increased by the thousands, and the majority lived and worked in New York City. Although ready-to-wear for men had come before women's wear, women's fashion comprised 76 percent of the industry by 1920. Clothes were produced according to seasonal patterns in a system directed by "jobbers." Twice a year, jobbers outlined a merchandising plan. They acquired patterns through various means: designing them in-house, copying them from others, or buying precut patterns. The jobber bought cloth directly from textile mills, sold the materials on consignment to a sub-manufacturer, and then bought back finished goods. Within this system, exploitation was virtually ensured.

The American advertising industry was born in the 1920s also, and it played a critical role in developing the fantasy of ready-to-wear. Helen Woodward, a 1920s ad copywriter, instructed those in the advertising business, "Never see the factory in which it was made . . . don't watch the people at work. . . . Because, you see, when you know the truth about anything, the real, inner truth—it is very hard to write the surface fluff that sells it."

New ways of purchasing clothes concealed the realities of factory life from consumers. Department stores rose up in American cities in the 1880s, and by 1915 ready-to-wear departments had become regular features in these stores. Here, industrially produced products could be displayed in palatial settings, showing no hint that they were made in sweatshops. For those who lived in the country, as most Americans still did, ready-made clothes became available with the founding of the United Parcel Service in 1907 and the arrival of mail-order catalogs from Montgomery Ward and Sears, Roebuck & Company, among others.

In the early decades of the twentieth century, as women's dresses became mass-produced commodities, yardage decreased, and simpler styles began to appear. In 1913 an average woman's outfit required nineteen yards of fabric. By 1928 the average outfit consumed only seven. Manufacturers understood that styles that consumed less fabric were cheaper to produce. Not only did clothes become lighter, but their market became younger. By 1922, the primary market for nearly every category of garment was people under thirty.

Despite the advertising dictum that consumers ought not to be told the origins of their garments, some of the first consumers of mass-produced women's fashions surely knew the origins of the clothes, because they were the garment workers themselves.

Poor shopgirls and garment workers were enthusiastic consumers of mass fashion. In 1913, home economist Bertha June Richardson complained that New York City's poor shopgirls dressed "beyond their station." In tenement neighborhoods, she observed women who earned five or six dollars a week, at most, with "plumes on their hats, a rustle of silk petticoats, everything about them in the latest style."

Buying mass-produced clothes was touted as a way to "Americanize" immigrants. "I'd like them better if they didn't wear such queer clothes," said an alleged *American* housewife "of her foreign neighbors" in a study carried out by consumer economist Elizabeth Hoyt in 1928. However, when immigrants espoused mass fashion zealously, a moralizing middle class referred to these fashionable poor as a "Monkey's Parade." To them it was unthinkable to see "shop apprentices, the young work girls, the boy clerks, and so forth, stirred by mysterious intimations, spending their first-earned money upon collars and ties, chiffon hats, smart lace collars, walking-sticks, sunshades." Bertha June Richardson, in her 1913 study of "the woman who spends," attempted to explain to her audience of middle-class social reformers why immigrant girls in city settlement houses cared so much about clothes:

> Did you ever go down to one of our city settlements full of the desire to help and lift up the poor shop girl? . . . There must be some mistake, you thought. These could not be poor girls, earning five or six dollars a week. They looked better dressed than you did! . . . In time you learned that it was only an attempt "to bridge the difference" between themselves and those with larger opportunities by imitating all they could see.

Inequality was great and growing in the 1920s, and clothes offered a form of satisfaction to the poor. This was not without political implications. Historian Stuart Ewen has argued that "mass fashion provided a means by which poor people could develop an appearance of upward mobility, construct a presentable, public self by which that mobility might in fact be actualized." The existence of this fashionably dressed working class served a critical role to combat a growing challenge from socialism, Ewen argues. "Where working people had once looked as poor as they were, now they were able to take on the appearance of abundance," he wrote.

Consumer culture in this period was an explicit response to the threat of communism. These were the years immediately following more direct forms of political repression: the Red Scare, the Palmer Raids, and the massive deportation of immigrant workers. If those were the stick, consumerism was the carrot. Capitalists promised that consumerism would bring more good to people than socialism or communism. "Mass production," wrote the merchant Edward Filene, "holds possibilities of accomplishing for mankind all of the good that theoretical reformers or irrational radicals hope to secure by revolutionary means." Filene's version of consumption could not only displace revolution, but democracy. "The masses of America have elected Henry Ford. They have elected General Motors. They have elected the General Electric Company, and Woolworth's and all the other great industrial and business leaders of the day."

American advertising worked explicitly to transmute the dissatisfaction of the working class away from social reform, and toward consumerism. Gratification that used to come from meaningful work could now be purchased. With the rise of assembly-line-style manufacture, work itself became a dull, monotonous task. Business economist Paul Nystrom argued that the monotony of industrial work had produced a widespread sense of "disappointment with achievements" and a widespread *philosophy of futility.*" Advertisers, he argued, should use this to their advantage. By closing off avenues for political change, fatigue with the boredom of industrial life could be transformed into "fatigue . . . with apparel and goods used in one's immediate surroundings."

Helen Woodward certainly agreed. Personal frustrations of all kinds could be redirected toward purchases, not politics. "To those who cannot change their whole lives or occupations," she began, "even a new line in a dress is often a relief. The woman who is tired of her husband or her home or a job feels some lifting of the weight of life from seeing a straight line change into a bouffant, or a grey pass into beige."

Advertisers of the 1920s boldly appropriated the language of the suffrage movement. One Toastmaster ad touted "The *Toaster* that FREED 465,000 HOMES . . . From ever watching, turning or burning toast." At the same time, they reminded women endlessly that if they did not take care of their appearance, they would not be able to keep a husband, along with the wage he brought home, threatening their security. "A man expects to find daintiness, charm, refinement in the woman he knows," Woodbury Soap reminded readers in 1922. "And when some unpleasant little detail mars this conception of what a woman should be—nothing quite effaces his involuntary disappointment."

H and tailoring and seamstresses became obsolete, along with all their careful measurement, handwork, and artisanry. But with the rise of mass and accessible fashion came the veneration of a new class of celebrity, the "designer," and with it the designer label, was just beginning.

At the turn of the twentieth century, Parisian designers turned, of necessity, to the American market, which was irresistibly vast and a distasteful, but unavoidable, economic imperative.

Paul Poiret, the Parisian designer responsible for what came to be known as the "flapper look," made his first trip to Manhattan by steamer in 1913. As soon as the ship docked, the press swarmed the boat and rushed to photograph Denise Boulet, Poiret's wife and muse, whose flat-chestedness had launched a new silhouette, in the yellow Russian leather boots he had designed for her.

In New York, Poiret was courted by garment manufacturers. "How many of them made me magnificent offers, in order to be able to give the name of Poiret to their merchandise," he recorded in his memoirs. To Poiret, it was obvious the American manufacturers wished to use the cachet of a famous designer to compensate for an absence of quality. "To sell common merchandise under the name of Poiret seems to them a happy and fortunate notion."

Poiret saw superficiality everywhere he went in New York. Seeing Americans in the art museum gave him the impression "that in America what is acquired by the eye is not woven on a very active mental loom, for so many seemed content with a superficial receptivity." He signed a contract with an American ladies-handbag company, but found the company could not keep the contract:

> on the pretext that it could not understand my designs. An American has to see an article manufactured, completed, solid in front of him, so that he can copy it servilely. Their absolute lack of imagination prevents them from conceiving the unforeseen and the hypothetical. Like St. Thomas, they only believe what they have seen.

If the Parisian was unsparing, he was probably correct when he noted that the "propensity of all their manufacturers to enter into contracts with famous men in order to be able to appropriate their names and profit by them is an American characteristic." After all, Americans loved their celebrities, and Paris had long been cemented as the epicenter of fashion in the American imagination. Henry David

Thoreau had written despairingly in 1854, "The head monkey at Paris puts on a traveler's cap, and all the monkeys in America do the same."

In the ensuing decades, designers formalized relationships with mass manufacturers. In 1947 Christian Dior entered into a partnership with a French manufacturer of cotton textiles to produce a line of mass-produced clothing in various levels of quality. The partners arranged a system by which Christian Dior sold models twice a year at fashion shows. Overseas buyers had three options: they could purchase a paper pattern of the model, but not be allowed to label it Christian Dior; they could buy a canvas copy and change it to suit their purposes, labeling it "Original-Christian-Dior-Copy"; or they could buy the original model in material, the most expensive option, and would then be permitted to label it "Christian Dior." This basic model persists today: designers give their franchise to manufacturers of garments whose factories may be anywhere in the world.

Parisian designers did not just travel to the West to produce prototypes for mass manufacture. In the 1930s Elsa Schiaparelli, great rival to Coco Chanel and a collaborator of Salvador Dali's (and, unlike Chanel, *not* a future collaborator with the Nazis), ventured to the Soviet Union with a delegation from the French Ministry of Commerce. She had been commissioned to design a dress "for the average Soviet woman." The designer recalled in her memoirs that on this occasion she shocked the public by departing from her typically flamboyant designs:

> Contrary to all expectation I had designed a very plain black dress typically "Schiap," a dress that was high in the neck and could be worn both to the office and the theater, the sort of dress I wear all day myself. Over it was a loose red coat lined with black which fastened with large, simple buttons.

The novelty of a Parisian designer producing a dress for the Soviet housewife may have been more than anything a gag for the western press. As Schiaparelli recalled, "Newspapers carried the sensational news that I had made a dress forty million women would wear." The idea of forty million women in the same dress would have been consistent with American ideas of communist Russia. In the West, mass production of dresses was just as real, but the language of advertising insisted instead that the garment was a singularity, like the woman who wore it. Though garments were mass-manufactured, it was critical that the buyer feel unique. "One of the most important points in selling fashion goods is the necessity of individualizing every sale and of avoiding any attempt to handle either merchandise or customers in a mass way," business economist Paul Nystrom wrote in 1932.

When Schiaparelli was in Moscow, through the intervention of the British ambassador, she was allowed into a Kremlin vault that held treasures from Russia's imperial past. "The robes were specially beautiful. I fell in love with one of stiff apricot velvet completely embroidered in emeralds and huge pearls." The luxurious handmade garments gave pause even to a designer who would specialize in ready-mades. "All this, I reflected, may be useless but it gives so much pleasure and so much work to so many people. And who will ever make such things again?"

In the 1850s, as the birth of ready-to-wear was taking place, the British art critic John Ruskin had noted the trend toward diminishing opportunities for creative expression on the part of the worker. He extolled the medieval European cathedral, in whose asymmetries and idiosyncrasies he claimed it was possible to read a generous sharing of creative control among many artisans. In the perfect symmetries of a classical Greek temple, by contrast, Ruskin saw proof of a system of slave labor perfectly executing the design of a single architect, all the more galling because the structure symbolized the democratic sharing of political power. Mass fashion was likewise marketed to consumers as opportunity for self-expression, while its actual mode of production revealed a vast diminution in the opportunities for expression on the part of the worker.

Along with the tailor, a whole class of artisans who had served aristocracies was disappearing. Despite the avowed ideological oppositions between the types of governments replacing feudal aristocratic societies, mass production on either side of the communist-capitalist divide gave birth to twin monotonies. Perhaps still more disturbing, in both fascist Germany and democratic America, mass-produced forms looked eerily similar. In Leni Riefenstahl's elaborately choreographed crowd scenes of 1934, the visual effect is nearly identical to that produced in the five back-to-back blockbuster musicals choreographed by Busby Berkeley for Warner Brothers in 1933–34: *42nd Street, Footlight Parade, Gold Diggers of 1933, Dames, Fashions of 1934*. Berkeley, like Riefenstahl, used the individual body as a minute pixel in an enormous geometric diagram. Identical sewing machines yielded identical clothes that yielded identical-looking bodies.

The political implications of various kinds of clothing have long been of interest to historians and philosophers. Clothing historian Cecil Saint-Laurent argued that there are two types of clothing: the draped and the sewn. Laurent saw these two types as symbolic of, respectively, Athenian freedom and Spartan fascism, and came down decisively on the side of draped garments. In this position he was preceded by Hegel, who in 1820 declared the aesthetic superiority of draped Athenian garments to sewn German ones:

> Our modern clothing is wholly inartistic: this is because what we really see in it . . . is not the fine, free, and living contours of the body in their delicate and flowing development, but stretched out sacks with stiff folds . . . something cut, sewn together over here, folded over there. Elsewhere fixed, and, in short, purely unfree forms.

His critique anticipated the legacy of ready-made clothing of the type that would dominate not only the West, but the entire world. These "purely unfree forms" were now produced by workers whose creative freedoms had been stripped. As the pleasures of artisanship disappeared advertisers seized the chance to transmute dissatisfaction with stultifying production line or piecework into excessive purchasing of new ready-made styles. But the painful loss of expression was undeniable.

. . .

n the 1920s, advertisers found ways to channel political discontent into consumerism. In the late 1960s and the 1970s, corporate fashion flagrantly copied and commodified the clothing of the counterculture.

By the 1970s, it was clear that the western fashion industry could absorb and defang any political gesture made with clothing, even the uniform of the Maoist cadre. In 1975, *Time* magazine reported on a new fad:

> Starting last spring, when the first Chinese-inspired fashions swept Paris, European and American designers have been having a collective field day redecorating workers' uniforms and baggy pants, overblouses and quilted jackets. The style might be called Mao à la mode. Now, with the fall collections, American couturiers have gone from paddy to palace, digging deep into the treasure chest of Imperial China. Result: high-collared mandarin robes, silk jacquard jackets, sable-lined evening coats of old damask and golden-scrolled pajamas, all done up in poesies of color pirated from the Orient.

Orientalism wasn't new, nor was the titillation in turning to poverty for a source of exclusivity: a gesture at least as old as Marie Antoinette in her shepherdess apron and bonnet. What is notable, perhaps, is the completely unselfconscious manner with which political implications are readily flattened, reabsorbed, and offered to the consumer, who is given the chance to play the part of the Maoist cadre by day, and wear sable-lined damask by night.

In October 1986 an article in *Vogue* called "What's in a Name? The Big Business of European Style" offered readers a romantic origin story of the relationship between the European designer and American mass fashion. "Once upon a time," wrote the author, "the pioneers among them, the French couturiers, were content with the chance to create beautiful things as the talented servants of the very few. Their beginnings now seem shockingly feudal." These words are expressive of the self-congratulatory, nearly messianic pretensions of the fashion industry: what once brought pleasure only to the very few now brings pleasure to the many. The implication is that the story of fashion has been that of a great humanitarian success. Ruskin might have noted, however, that an artisan tailor had more respect accorded to his humanity and more opportunity for creative expression than a 1980s sweatshop worker.

The *Vogue* article insists on fashion as art rather than as business, and points out that although the designers of the 1980s "have taken on the power of financial magnates, they still live, like rock stars, for their performances. Each has his own style and is totally committed to *it,* the thing he does, his own expression."

Fashion magazines participate zealously in constructing the fantasy of brand names. They must, because of how deeply invested they are, themselves, in brand-name profits. Lucinda Chambers, fashion director of *British Vogue* for twenty-five years, gave a candid interview in 2018 in which she alluded to the ways in which magazines serve paid advertisers. "The June cover with Alexa Chung in a stupid Michael Kors T-shirt is crap," she admitted. "He's a big advertiser so I knew why I had to do it."

f there *is* a corrosive that can break down some of what the branding apparatus would like us to believe about the magic of the brand name, it is the prodigious production of fakes.

In the autumn of 2018, before we took our trip to China together, Mrs. L. and I went shopping for knockoff bags in New York's Chinatown.

The police had been getting tougher lately at the behest of the large brands, she told me, as we walked down bustling Canal Street, at the heart of Chinatown. She spun around midstream, like a mackerel at the touch of some subtle shift in the current, so I did the same. I followed her glance to see who we were trailing: a Chinese woman in a white ballcap, leading a woman with bleached hair and dark roots and skintight heather gray sweats and her hapless boyfriend to a quieter part of the street. We walked into the huddle. Acknowledging us, the woman in the ballcap handed us a laminated sheet with photographs of different bags. My eye went to a red patent leather Chanel bag with hard sides rounded at the top, like an old-fashioned doctor's case.

Mrs. L. noticed it too, and pointed at it. "That's the one I want," I said to the woman in the ballcap. Okay, she said, and made a call on her cell.

"Can't we go to the warehouse?" Mrs. L. asked. "It would be easier to go through them all together."

"I can't," the woman said, "that would be easier for me too, believe me."

The bag arrived, wrapped in black plastic. Mrs. L. and I opened the top, touched it. So bright, Mrs. L. said. I agreed: it was too red. It looked darker red in the picture, the woman admitted resignedly.

These bags, which can be surreptitiously purchased in Manhattan, or quite openly from a stall at the Ben Thanh Market in Ho Chi Minh City, radiate out from the commodity market in Yiwu, in Zhejiang province, about an hour and a half's drive south from Hangzhou. While in China that winter, Mrs. L. and I paid a visit.

We arrived at the Yiwu market at about two, on a cloudy New Year's Day. A vast structure, the market was comprised of five buildings attached to one another with walkways, reminiscent of an international space station. Each floor was laid out as an indoor city, with lettered and numbered streets. Building 5 held the floors with bags and shoes on which "Bally" became "Baisty." The word "Dasfour" looked like "Barbour" when it was typeset in the Barbour font, and like "Dickies" when set in Dickies font. Swiss Army became "Soldierknife." "Versace" became "Falani," Gucci, "Guigi." The Tory Burch cross was emblazoned willy-nilly over the Gucci logo. Dior became "Dor." Moschino became "Moschicno." "Supreme" became "Superem," white sneakers said "Givenchv," but the "c" looked like the Champion logo. Many of these could have passed for the real thing if it weren't for the garbled lettering: after all, the brand name is often nothing more than a magic word setting apart an object that could have been, and sometimes was, produced in the very same factory as the knockoff.

An ancient civilization that had defined luxury in the West since antiquity in the form of rich silk brocade, now produced overwhelming numbers of Falbnoagaiga and Auexahder Mqlene.

. . .

Paul Poiret had remarked on his trip to America that "American traders" tended to "pack mediocre merchandise under a distinguished
label." Indeed, the language of the label has far outstripped all other
kinds of language in the common parlance around clothing. Before
the triumph of ready-to-wear, press coverage of fashion commented
on the quality and appearance of materials. For example, at one major
society event in 1888, the marriage of sewing machine mogul Isaac
Singer's daughter Blanche in Paris, *The New York Herald Tribune* gave
the following account of the affair. The bride:

> wore a superb costume of white peau-de-soie, said to have cost
> 30,000 f. . . . The Duchesse de Camposelice wore a pearl gray
> brocade silk, with tassels of the same color, and a bonnet of lace
> and feathers glittering with diamonds. The Princesse de Scey-
> Montbéliard wore pale rose. Princess Philip of Saxe-Coburg-
> Gotha appeared in pale blue silk, with demi train, trimmed
> with lace, and a bonnet of lace, pearls, feathers, and old rose
> ribbon. Queen Isabella wore a striped old rose silk, pearls and
> a Persian mantle.

Conspicuous in this account is the complete absence of brand names.
In any contemporary gossip sheet covering a high-society affair, fabric types like "peau-de-soie" give way to descriptors like "Givenchy"
or "Dior."

Not only have words that rely on a basic knowledge of cloth construction disappeared from magazines, so too have words that refer
to garment construction. Words like selvedge, darts, drape, pleats,
basting, pocket facing, placket, or bodice are rarely mentioned before
consumers who are not expected to understand the way clothing is
made. This is natural for a clientele that doesn't sew, or visit the tailor.

I had a shirt tailored to me once. I visited a tailor while in Ho Chi
Minh City. The tailor told me how many yards of fabric I needed to
buy, and I went to a store that sold silk by the bolt. I examined each
fabric, and the attendant helped me unspool some of my favorites
from the big bolts so that I could hold a length of cloth over my torso
and look in the mirror to see if the color suited. I was reminded of the

scene in *West Side Story* when Maria holds her new dress up against her body expectantly. This is a gesture that has almost gone extinct. In it, care for the cloth and care for the person are expressed. It is something like matchmaking.

Internally I did calculations for the cost of a shirt in the white silk, versus the green silk with little diamond patterns in the weave. I felt like I was shopping for ingredients for a dinner. It suddenly occurred to me that in America, where we go neither to the tailor nor to the fabric store, we rarely have a chance to be in touch with our clothes' ingredients. This seemed suddenly just as odd to me as never going to the grocery store might be, as if I had eaten *out* at fast food chains for every meal of my life. There was so much pleasure in my encounter with these rolls of cloth.

After I returned with fabric to the tailor's, two women took my measurements. One of them wielded the tape measure, the other took down numbers. Together they mapped my body, first by measuring a series of hoops around my chest above the breast, at the breast, just below the breast, at the waist, the upper hip, the butt, and then by measuring a cross-section down through them, marking down the distance between each hoop, making up a map of my body. Tailoring is intelligent, intimate work. A few days later, I returned for my shirt. When I put it on, I could sense that it was designed for my shape, and for some reason this transmitted to me a sense of dignity. How vast the difference between a shirt that is made for one body, my body, and one that is made for anybody, and nobody in particular.

In the twentieth century marketers learned how to transform every dissatisfaction into the desire to purchase. This manipulation can work on a particularly deep level when it comes to clothing, which carries ancient connections to self-expression, self-protection, self-esteem, and group belonging. Intimations of the court of Louis XIV and the ancient Silk Road are brandished to sell goods, along with the promise of personal value they might bestow.

The old Chinese silk route brought goods to the wealthy, while the new international trade routes would bring them to the poor, and indeed would become instruments in maintaining the poverty of workers across the world. But the powerful myths of advertising did not accomplish this alone. Fantasy wouldn't have been enough without the powerful aid given to capitalist expansion by U.S. government policy. Over the course of the twentieth century, the trade arrangements and labor conditions needed to expand and perpetuate the global circulation of cheap fashion clothing would be hammered out alongside a new material type: synthetics.

Synthetics

9

Rayon

It's no crime in the South to kill a mill worker.

——FRED E. BEAL

Rayon, also known as viscose, is a fabric made from trees. Wood is pulped, then liquefied, then extruded into thin filaments that can be woven into a fabric that imitates silk. Rayon opened the miraculous possibility of mass-producing fiber in countries that grew no cotton. As Dmitri Mendeleev wrote in 1900, "Russia with its heartland of forests and grasses could, with the production of viscose, provide the entire world with a colossal amount of fiber."

In the early twentieth century, rayon was essentially a start-up industry based in small manufacturing units, many carried out on a prototype scale. By the late 1920s, it had become big business: a staple fabric for women's dresses and hose in the new ready-to-wear garment industry. Such was the demand for it, that not even the Great Depression slowed the industry meaningfully. In the United States there was but a light and brief downturn in rayon filament production from 1931 to 1932, followed by steady growth through 1936. In Italy and Germany, production increased every year after 1933. In Japan, it shot up even more dramatically, passing the United States as the leading producer by 1935.

The development of a new viscose product, a short-cut rayon staple, allowed rayon to be mixed with other fabrics to produce cotton-rayon or wool-rayon blends beginning in 1931. It also allowed rayon to be used in nonwoven, feltlike materials. Rayon was poised to threaten the use not only of silk, but other fibers as well. In Australia, the Adelaide *Advertiser* sounded the alarm: "there is too much reason to regard artificial silk, or rayon, as Australia's 'Public Enemy No. 1' in the markets of the world." The advent of this short-cut staple led to even more dramatic growth for the industry, and there were hundredfold increases in production worldwide.

In the 1930s, Europe's new fascist states turned to rayon to fulfill dreams of autarky: Italy and Germany both pursued rayon as a means to textile independence, having previously relied on cotton imports. In Germany, the Nazi-era rayon conglomerate Phrix, which used slave labor from the Neuengamme concentration camp, opened a facility in 1938 called Phrix Wittenberge that used straw, rather than wood, to make rayon. Wood pulp was a limited resource for Germany in 1938, and Phrix's achievement, evoking Rumpelstiltskin in its ability to spin cloth out of straw, was a propaganda coup. A short film shot and edited by UFA (Universum Film AG), under the close oversight of the regime, celebrated the achievement. Italy built an entire city solely to produce it: Torviscosa. Both the factory and city were inaugurated in 1938 with a visit from Mussolini and a dedicatory ode by the futurist poet Filippo Tommaso Marinetti: "So let alkaline cellulose wed the carbon bisulfide to which it was betrothed to liquify in a xanthate orange- and rust-colored like a bloody weapon amidst the festive drumbeat of belts that fearlessly stretch between lower and upper wheels."

The Nazis aspired not only to achieve textile independence with rayon made from straw, but to produce an alternative edible protein with yeast grown on by-products of rayon production. The ersatz sausage made from yeast, named Biosyn-Vegetabil-Wurst, was tested at the Mauthausen concentration camp, where inmates suffered severe adverse gastrointestinal effects, and hundreds died, as a result of the artificial diet.

In the U.S., rayon was celebrated as a feat of human ingenuity.

"The chemist is fast becoming master in his own house," wrote a *Scientific American* reporter in 1926. She continued:

> Everywhere about us are manifestations of the part he has played in making this world a safer, saner, and better place in which to live. Yet how many pause to consider that the chemist is a very real and dominating factor in contributing to our modern-day conveniences and comforts? Let us take, for example, but one achievement of the chemist—the manufacture of artificial silk, now called rayon, in which he has triumphed over Nature.

Artificial silk was also lauded as a populist achievement. One 1936 American advertising prospectus proclaimed that rayon had "given to women to-day wardrobes that only a few years ago were reserved for the exclusive few." Rayon was modern: the name "rayon" itself was chosen for its allusion to ultramodern "radon." Aldous Huxley's 1932 *Brave New World* made sardonic allusion to its newfangled proletarian glamour: "He was thinking of Lenina, of an angel in bottle-green viscose, lustrous with youth and skin food."

Rayon was one of the first truly multinational corporate enterprises, a status it achieved in the period just before World War 1. Grace Hutchins pointed to the rayon industry as the period's preeminent industrial cartel in her 1929 *Labor and Silk*, published by International Publishers, a press aligned with the Communist Party. The book diagrammed the complex interrelations between international corporate entities and their subsidiaries with an intricate network of circles and dotted lines. Rayon workers, Hutchins wrote, worked long hours for low wages and were under-unionized compared to the overall rates in textile manufacturing.

In August 1931 Harvard economist Frank William Taussig and future senior U.S. treasury official Harry Dexter White published *Rayon and the Tariff: The Nature of an Industrial Prodigy*, a study that features one of the first uses of the term "duopoly." The term refers to a market with only two sellers, and was coined in part to deal with the nature of the viscose industry. In the U.S. DuPont and American Viscose, itself the U.S. subsidiary of the British megalith Courtaulds, carved up the industry between them.

Concentrated corporate power was axiomatic not just in the U.S., but worldwide. When workers went on strike at a rayon plant in Hopewell, Virginia, in 1934 as part of a mass walkout that year, the plant shut down and shipped its machinery to Brazil, having merged with an Italian company with Brazilian interests in 1930.

Corporate power bought political power, or tried to. DuPont funded reactionary politics in the 1930s through the American Liberty League, an anti–New Deal organization that produced pamphlets, radio addresses, and speeches to discredit FDR and his progressive policies.

Rayon was good business, and textile executives were living well. A July 1937 *Fortune* article on Samuel Salvage, former president of the American Viscose Company, who had retired to become its chairman of the board, reported that he split his time between his apartment at the Sherry-Netherland hotel in Manhattan, a country estate at Glen Head, Long Island, where he raised prize tulips and entertained 1,500 Englishmen on Empire Day 1928, and his 150-foot yacht, *Colleen II*, which he kept for "short weekend cruises."

For the workers who made rayon, this thriving business did not prove to be such a blessing. Viscose is used to make both rayon and cellophane, and both processes rely on a highly neurotoxic solvent called carbon disulfide. The process begins by mixing wood pulp with caustic soda, then adding carbon disulfide. This cocktail is churned and allowed to "ripen," then more caustics are added to yield a syrupy substance known as viscose. If this syrup is pressed through a long thin slit, it becomes cellophane. If it is pushed through spinning nozzles submerged in a bath of sulfuric acid, it forms filaments that can be spun into the thread that makes rayon.

Carbon disulfide's potent toxicity had been clearly recognized since the 1850s. Despite this knowledge, throughout most of the twentieth century viscose manufacturing was allowed to proliferate even as it caused widespread, severe, and often lethal illness among workers. Carbon disulfide exposure poisoning is a dramatic sickness, because it causes acute insanity in those it afflicts. The chemical induces degenerative brain disease by damaging the sensory capacity of nerves, including those responsible for vision. Long-term, low-level exposure causes even more insidious damage in the form of increased risk of heart disease and stroke.

While scientists worked to carefully track the chemical and its effects on the human frame in the nineteenth and twentieth centuries, advocates for the health and safety of the workers forced to use carbon disulfide on the job struggled to put these scientific findings to use in policies that could protect workers. Rayon might have been celebrated as a victory for science and a "triumph over nature," but would scientists be heeded when their findings threatened profits?

Carbon disulfide was first synthesized in 1796 by a German mining and metallurgical chemist named Wilhelm August Lampadius. In the 1840s, chemists discovered its use as a potent solvent, which soon led to its use in cold-process vulcanization. Without vulcanization of one sort or another, natural rubber becomes too gooey or too brittle to use for most commercial applications. Chemists discovered that by dissolving sulfur in carbon disulfide and then immersing the rubber in this solution, rubber could be stabilized and transformed into a huge variety of products, from bathing caps and infant pacifiers, to condoms and playing balls.

French workers making balloons and condoms using cold-process vulcanization were the first industrial workers to experience the devastating effects of carbon disulfide poisoning: sexual excitation followed by impotence, eye trouble, and psychosis. Exposure often led to depression and to suicide, hallucinations, rage, and a murderous impulse. From the beginning of its use, carbon disulfide victims often landed in prisons, mental hospitals, or the grave, before they could possibly identify, let alone protest, the workings of an invisible gas on their bodies and brains. In the 1850s the Parisian physician Auguste Delpech studied the carbon disulfide exposure among vulcanization workers. His report illustrated twenty-four cases with devastating neurological symptoms akin to end-stage syphilis, only more severe.

The twenty-fifth member of the cohort had died before being examined: she had become progressively deranged until she intentionally self-asphyxiated with carbon disulfide vapor.

Carbon disulfide arrived in the U.S. in the 1870s as a premier poison for farmers to use against gophers, which can damage crops. Not long after, its deadly psychoactive effects began to make themselves felt. In 1882 a French immigrant named Alois Albrecht, hitherto known as an upright citizen of Ventura, California, walked to his neighbor's house, accused him of trying to poison his brother and himself, and shot him. When he was taken to the sheriff, Albrecht said he had seen the poison in the man's hands but that it would be pointless for them to search the body for it, because he had also seen the devil carry it away. Only later did it emerge that in the room adjoining Albrecht's bedroom was a fifty-pound can of carbon disulfide with a small leak that had been filling his log cabin with fumes. Nonetheless, an 1883 ad in the *Los Angeles Times,* just one year later, assured consumers: "Read and Foster's Bisulphide is safe, cheap and effective, and can be applied at any time without the least danger. . . . A boy can use it without danger."

After an 1887 outbreak of insanity among rubber industry factory workers treated at the Hudson River State Hospital for the Insane, the physician Dr. Frederick Peterson began to investigate. Peterson, the chief of clinic of the Nervous Department of the College of Physicians and Surgeons in New York, learned that the rubber factory jobs exposed the workers to carbon disulfide. In his report in the *Boston Medical and Surgical Journal* (later renamed the *New England Journal of Medicine*), Peterson made clear that his efforts had been blocked repeatedly by industry:

> I have delayed in publishing these cases for some years, thinking that I might hear of other similar ones, or that I might acquire more information from the owners of the factory or from doctors in attendance upon their employees, but it is astonishing what a large amount of ignorance and secretiveness develops among the authorities connected with any factory, when

questions arise as to the unhealthful conditions under which the operatives pursue their vocations.

Meanwhile, vulcanization had opened up a huge range of possibilities for the use of rubber in everyday life. One that seemed particularly promising to manufacturers was in clothing.

Manufacturers dreamed about a way to get around sewing altogether by designing clothes and shoes cast in one piece, or stuck together with a rubber emulsion. Thanks to carbon disulfide, rubber might eliminate the most cost-intensive part of making clothes: the seamstress. As for mending, all "you have to do to repair it is to glue a new piece of gutta-percha onto the worn area," wrote Charles Dupin in his enthusiasm about the rubber goods exhibited in The Great Exhibition in 1851. In thread form, rubber produced elastic fabrics, and chemists, mechanical engineers, and industrial tailors dreamed about mass-producing clothes in fixed sizes that would be able to fit all body types because of their elasticity. From the end of the 1840s onward, companies in England, France, and the U.S. marketed rubber shoes that imitated leather: French advertising agencies described them as "Cinderella's rubber slippers."

When it first became available in the 1850s, rubber clothing was high fashion. In 1858 a journalist announced, "In Cherbourg, all of the beautiful Parisian and foreign women . . . are distinguished from the uniformity of costumes by silky and smart rubber clothes . . . that reproduce Scottish patterns and taffetas." In 1862, affordable waterproof rubber raincoats came on the market, along with white rubber, paper, and celluloid straps, collars, and cuffs that allowed poor clerks and working-class people dressed in their Sunday best to possess that white "linen" look that had been so long venerated and so difficult to achieve. But by the end of the nineteenth century, rubber clothing had decidedly shed its elite status and became symbolic of the democratization and standardization of garments by the ready-to-wear industry. Rubber, paper, and celluloid became the symbol of popular, industrial clothing, and the new name for rubber clothing in France and the U.K. became "linge américain," or American underwear. "American" being synonymous in Europe with democratic, cheap, and vulgar goods. From 1855, rubber shoes were called "American shoes" even if they were made in Europe. Rubber had found a handful of applications in shoes and clothing, but failed to launch in a major way.

Manufacturers may have been disappointed in their dreams for rubber clothing, but they would not have long to wait before another novel fabric took off in earnest: rayon.

The process to make rayon using carbon disulfide was discovered and patented in 1892. Although various methods for making artificial silk *without* this chemical compound were being prototyped during the same period, carbon disulfide was prized for its unique ability to liquefy cellulose without fundamentally changing its structure. It was also more efficient and far cheaper than the rival methods.

As carbon disulfide found increasingly lucrative new application in rayon manufacture, concerned toxicologists tracked the havoc wreaked by the poison in its new milieu. In Europe, the chemical received extensive medical attention in the second half of the nineteenth century. By 1930 carbon disulfide poisoning was linked irrefutably to psychological illness via central nervous system poisoning, and in the 1930s Italian medical papers linked carbon disulfide with Parkinsonism and psychosis. However, the scientific research followed "a curious pattern," wrote professor of medicine Paul David Blanc, a scholar of the history of medical research into carbon disulfide poisoning. "The path was not linear but ran almost in circles. . . . Each time, the neophyte seemed to rediscover the problem all over again, going back to square one. It was as if a kind of cyclical amnesia had come into play in which all that had been learned was soon forgotten, or nearly so, and the knowledge had to be reconstructed." This was especially true, Blanc notes, as the use of carbon disulfide fell off in the rubber industry and began to pick up again in the new technology of viscose.

As scientists fought to catch and keep the trail of carbon disulfide toxicity research, the huge market incentives created by viscose posed grave new risks for workers. The cultivation of cotton takes a sharp

Rayon | 161

toll on the bodies of the laborers, and taxes the land. The machinery for manufacturing cloth is often harmful to workers. But with the rise of viscose, the production of the fiber itself ravaged the bodies of those who worked it in insidious, invisible ways.

Labor protections for workplace injury were being worked out in the period of rayon's rise, part of a much broader struggle over the rights of workers. Rayon workers, and other textile and garment laborers, were front and center in the battle for better pay and safer conditions.

"We have very good sanitary conditions but there is something in the air that makes the girls faint," wrote Ida Heaton, a female employee in the inspection department at the Glanzstoff rayon factory in Elizabethton, Tennessee. "I have known as many as 27 to faint in one day." Another employee, Christy Gallaher, noted, "about half a dozen girls faint everyday [sic]. I know several girls that have fainted and fallen on the concrete floor and hurt themselves very badly."

The employees at Glanzstoff, like other rayon workers, were non-union. Indeed, that was part of why the owners of Glanzstoff had opted to build their factory in Tennessee. In the 1920s, civic and business elites in small towns and cities throughout the American South aggressively courted industries to take advantage of its cheap labor. By the 1930s, rayon factories were located in a narrow band that swooped east, then north from Old Hickory, outside Nashville, to Elizabethton, Tennessee, to Parkersburg, West Virginia, to Covington, Roanoke, and Richmond, Virginia, up into Lewiston, Pennslyvania and, at the easternmost end, Marcus Hook.

Southern plants had two distinct advantages. While northern factories had been set up for wool and cotton, and had to be retrofitted to weave rayon fabric, southern plants were newly constructed with rayon manufacture in mind. Second, northern textile factories were becoming increasingly unionized. Plants relocated to the South from higher-waged, unionized New England, as well as from farther afield. In 1925 Elizabethton, a town of 2,749 inhabitants located in rural Carter County in the northeastern corner of Tennessee, lured one of Europe's leading rayon manufacturers, the German corporate giant J. P. Bemberg, to open a plant just outside its city limits. American Bemberg Corporation opened in 1926 and the second plant, American Glanzstoff, began production in 1928. Bemberg's employment manager, J. R. Gardner, wrote in a labor survey he conducted in the region that the Appalachian laborers ought to be a safe bet for Bemberg, because they were desperate for work and free from radical European labor union influences.

> We believe the employment of native labor will greatly lessen the danger of strikes and labor disturbances. In the main these people know nothing of unions or labor organizations; they appreciate the opportunity for steady employment and advancement and will be loyal to the industry.

Gardner was wrong. Days were long and wages low even by the standards of the southern textile industry. One employee, Flossie Cole, worked fifty-six hours in her first week and took home $8.16, a modern equivalent of about $120.[*] This, combined with dangerous conditions, including the mysterious fumes that caused so many employed in the spinning rooms to faint, convinced workers to pay attention to the legacy of union struggles in the North.[†]

In 1912, the massive "Bread and Roses Strike" had rocked Lawrence, Massachusetts. Led by the International Workers of the World or IWW, immigrants from fifty-one countries had joined together and, following months of bitter struggle, gained a 15 percent pay raise for millworkers. Fearing strikes of similar intensity, mill owners across New England raised their workers' pay, so that all told 300,000

---

[*] Glanzstoff's and Bemberg's average wage of $9.20 for a fifty-six-hour week. (Draper, "Gastonia Revisited," 6.)

[†] The workers may also have been emboldened by the fact that, on August 18, 1920, Tennessee had become the thirty-sixth state to ratify the Nineteenth Amendment, which granted women's suffrage, making it into law.

workers saw raises as a result of the strike. In 1926, a massive strike had erupted among textile workers in Passaic, New Jersey.

Less than five years after the plant in Elizabethton, Tennessee, was established, in response to low wages and "speed-ups," an industrial strategy whereby workers were given increased production quotas for the same, and sometimes even less, pay, Elizabethton's workers asserted themselves. In 1927 and 1928 they walked off the job in wild-cat strikes, and in 1929 they walked out in a concerted effort backed by the United Textile Workers Union of America.[*]

These events received widespread attention in the press. The Women's Trade Union League (WTUL), which had been founded by an alliance of settlement workers, including the famous activist Jane Addams, after a 1903 Boston meeting of the American Federation of Labor that made it clear that the AFL had no intention of including women, quickly sent its representative Matilda Lindsay to cover the strike. In her report in the April 1929 issue of the WTUL's *Life and Labor Bulletin*, Lindsay seemed keen to emphasize the striking workers' homegrown bona fides. "Working in these two plants are approximately 5000 natives, 100% Americans, the majority of whom are women and girls." The developments seemed optimistic: Lindsay reported that an initial agreement had been reached with the support of a local sheriff and General Boyd of the Tennessee National Guard. Documentary footage shows the strikers in orderly contingents. The men first, wearing neckties, or overalls over ironed white shirts, followed by women in drop waist dresses, side-parted bobs, cloche hats, high heels: their Sunday best. The women leading their contingents were draped in American flags.

Conditions, however, quickly soured. The two plants were jointly managed by a German organic chemist named Dr. Arthur Franz Felix Mothwurf. The July issue of *Life and Labor Bulletin* reports that Mothwurf had reneged on their agreement by blacklisting all the union

[*] The United Textile Workers of America (UTWA) was founded in 1901 as an affiliate of the American Federation of Labor (AFL). It was less radical than the communist IWW, and admitted only white men.

leaders. The strike resumed, and the National Guard was called in. Machine guns were mounted on the road and on the factory roof. Mass arrests ensued.

From Elizabethton, the unrest spread across the textile towns of the Carolina Piedmont. As *Time* magazine reported in an April 15, 1929, article entitled "Southern Stirrings": "Textile mill strikes flared up last week like fire in broom straw across the face of the industrial South. . . . Though their causes were not directly related, they were all symptomatic of larger stirrings in that rapidly developing region."

Compared to the previous decade, the 1920s were a relatively quiet period for the U.S. labor movement. More than three thousand strikes had occurred, on average, each year between 1914 and 1920, and 1919 had set a twentieth-century record when over four million workers, or 21 percent of the workforce, went on strike. Nineteen twenty-eight, by contrast, saw a mere 604 strikes, the fewest on record since 1884. Nineteen twenty-nine saw only nine hundred, involving 289,000 strikers, or just 1.2 percent of the labor force. Violent and heavy-handed anti-union tactics at the close of the 1910s, like the 1919 Palmer Raids, had worked to suppress strike activity. So had rising wages. Average worker wages had grown almost 40 percent between 1914 and 1929. This was the same period in which ad copywriter Helen Woodward averred that most women didn't have the courage to make deeper changes to their lives than to the line of their dress. There were some exceptions to this spell of relative quiet. One was the Great Railroad Strike of 1922. Another was the strike of southern textile workers.

For textile workers in the South, conditions deteriorated steadily after World War I, and dissatisfaction was enormous and widespread. During the war, government defense orders for uniforms, tents, and war matériel had brought prosperity to southern mill towns, and the war years were marked both by higher wages and more jobs. When the wartime boom ended, and throughout the 1920s, overproduction led to the adoption of the "stretch-out." By assigning more looms to each worker, curtailing break times, paying workers by-piece rates, and increasing the number of supervisors to keep workers from slowing down or talking, management doubled employees' work while reducing their wages. Unsurprisingly, it was a universally reviled practice.

In the spring of 1929 union organizers Fred Beal and Ellen Dawson, from the New York City–based, communist National Textile Workers' Union (NTWU), traveled to Gastonia, North Carolina, drawn by reports of merciless stretch-outs and notoriously dirty and dangerous conditions in the city's Loray Mill. The pair arrived to find millworkers who needed very little persuasion to gear up for militant action. Two days after the union held its first public meeting in Gastonia, 1,800 millworkers from the Loray Mill walked off their jobs, demanding a forty-hour workweek, a $20 a week minimum wage, union recognition, and the abolition of the stretch-out system. It was just two and a half weeks since the rayon workers' strike had begun in Elizabethton, Tennessee: the spark among the Southern textile workers had become a fire.

Within just forty-eight hours, North Carolina governor Max Gardner sent in five companies of National Guardsmen to confront the unarmed strikers, mostly teenaged girls and mothers. Gardner himself owned a textile mill in the adjoining Cleveland County, and was unsurprisingly not sympathetic to the cause. The *Gastonia Daily Gazette* published full-page paid advertisements penned by a group that referred to itself as "Citizens of Gaston County" declaring that the NTWU "seeks the overthrow of capital, business, and all of the established social order. . . . It has no religion, it has no color line, it believes in free love—it advocates the destruction of all those things which the people of the South and of the United States hold sacred." Accounts like these inflamed private citizens, who formed armed militias. When Governor Gardner pulled out some of the state troops, a vigilante group called the "Committee of One Hundred," organized by mill owners and civic leaders, moved in to patrol the strike zone.

As the conflict escalated, it became perfectly clear that the strikers and union organizers were not just facing off against their employers, but against the combined strength of industrialists, civic leaders, local law enforcement, the press, National Guardsmen, and the terrors of extralegal violence. In the tent city where workers moved after they were evicted from mill housing, bands of hired mill thugs arrived nightly, destroying union property, beating and kidnapping union organizers, and terrorizing the three hundred strikers and their families who held out until the bitter end.

Against this onslaught of incredible violence, the one potent weapon the workers had was the power of song. "From experience, I knew the tremendous value of singing the right songs on a picket line," wrote Fred Beal. "These workers knew none of the union's strike songs. To overcome this, I typed a number of copies of Solidarity and told them to sing it to the tune of Glory, Glory Hallelujah." Before long, Gastonia's striking workers were composing their own music. Daisy McDonald, a Loray Mill spinner whose $12.90 salary supported seven children and a tubercular husband, wrote a nine-stanza ballad that chronicled the strike's main events. An eleven-year-old "spare hand" named Odell Corley set "Up in Old Loray" to the tune of "On Top of Old Smoky," replacing the faithless lover in the song with a rapacious capitalist:

> *The bosses will starve you,*
> *They'll tell you more lies*
> *Than there's crossties on the railroads,*
> *Or stars in the skies.*

Of all Gastonia's songstresses, none was as prolific as Ella May Wiggins. Between April and September 1929, she composed at least twenty-one songs intended to keep the fire burning in strikers' hearts. She wrote songs with titles like "The Big Fat Boss and the Workers," "Two Little Strikers," "Come and Join the I.L.D.," to melodies based on mountain ballads she had learned as a child of the western Carolina Blue Ridge Mountains. "No evening passed," Fred Beal would later write,

> without getting a new song from our Ella May, the minstrel of our strike. She would stand somewhere in a corner, chewing tobacco or snuff and fumbling over notes of a new poem

scribbled on the back of a union leaflet. Suddenly someone would call for her to sing and other voices would take up the suggestion.

As labor organizer Vera Buch later recalled, "Her rather gaunt face would light up and soften as she sang. Her hazel eyes would shine; she became for the moment beautiful."

Ella May Wiggins didn't just sing, she also gave public talks. In both mediums, she spoke as a mother.[*] In one speech, she clearly laid out the impossibility of the task of raising a family on her salary: "I never made no more than nine dollars a week, and you can't do for a family on such money," Wiggins told the crowd.

> I'm the mother of nine. Four died with the whooping cough. I was working nights, and I asked the super to put me on days, so's I could tend 'em when they had their bad spells. But he wouldn't. . . . So I had to quit, and then there wasn't no money for medicine, and they just died. I couldn't do for my children any more than you women on the money we git. That's why I come out for the union, and why we all got to stand for the union, so's we can do better for our children, and they won't have lives like we got.

Mothers like Wiggins, along with teenaged girls, planted themselves in the front lines of public protests, and faced off against police officers and National Guardsmen on the picket lines. "One woman carried a baby in one arm and a big knotted stick in the other," reported a *Charlotte Observer* correspondent of one such confrontation.

Ella's most celebrated song was called "Mill Mother's Lament,"

---

[*] From the beginning, as labor historian Alice Kessler-Harris has noted, women's low wages in textile work were justified with the theory that they would be supported by men. This had only ever been marginally true, and in the case of Wiggins and other North Carolina women workers like her it wasn't true at all: they were breadwinners earning less than a living wage. Among the demands of the strikers was equal pay for women.

and spoke to the particular pains that mothers face working at the plant:

> *We leave our home in the morning,*
> *We kiss our children good-bye,*
> *While we slave for the bosses,*
> *Our children scream and cry.*
>
> *And when we draw our money,*
> *Our grocery bills to pay,*
> *Not a cent to spend for clothing,*
> *Not a cent to lay away.*

Wiggins had been raised in the timber camps of the Blue Ridge Mountains, an itinerant life in a series of converted boxcars. The introduction of machine logging by lumber companies after 1910, and the arrival of Champion Fiber Company and other pulp mills, which supplied the new rayon factories, provided a market for even the smallest trees, which meant entire mountains were clear-cut and left to erode. Streambeds and the reproductive capacity of the lands were destroyed, including the bottomlands that had once been desirable for farming. By 1919, the Appalachian hardwoods were diminishing. Ella's father, James May, was crushed to death by a log while cutting timber for the Champion Fiber Company near Andrews, North Carolina. In the early 1920s, when the western North Carolina lumber industry collapsed, thousands of mountain families headed into the industrializing Carolina Piedmont to find jobs, the Wigginses among them. Around 1926 John Wiggins, a logger that Ella May had married at fourteen years old, abandoned the family, and she was left on her own to raise nine children.

When the union arrived in Gastonia, Ella May Wiggins was working in a factory that made automobile tire cord. She threw herself into the struggle with the fearless energy of one who has nothing to lose. She handed out relief, joined committees, and helped organize the imprisoned strikers' defense. She kept "neat and accurate account books," Vera Buch recalled, of which she was proud. Ella had chosen to live in a small cottage outside of town, within the African American hamlet nicknamed "Stumptown," rather than in company housing. Confronting prejudice within the union itself, Wiggins advocated for organizing Black laborers along with whites, and in a close vote her local union branch voted to admit African Americans.

In May, Wiggins traveled with a delegation of eleven strikers to Washington to testify before a U.S. Senate committee tasked with investigating labor conditions in the southern mills. Before she could testify, however, the committee abruptly adjourned. She made national news anyway, when during a chance run-in with North Carolina's junior senator, Lee Slater Overman, in the hallway of the U.S. Capitol, she confronted him over the fact that her wages were so low, she couldn't dress her children decently enough to send them to school.

But her music was what Ella May Wiggins was most known for, and it was her music that marked her as a target. "The bosses hated Ella May," claimed one striker, "because she made up songs." On September 14, 1929, traveling to a union rally in South Gastonia with a truckload of other strikers, Ella May Wiggins, pregnant with her tenth child, was shot in the chest by a band of armed thugs. Shortly after her murder, the Gastonia strike collapsed.

On March 6, 1930, disregarding the testimony of over fifty eyewitnesses, the five Loray Mill employees indicted for her murder were acquitted after thirty minutes of deliberation. "We knew no one would be punished," Fred Beal later wrote. "It's no crime in the South to kill a mill worker." Her songs lived on. "Mill Mother's Lament" was later recorded by Pete Seeger, who claimed her as an inspiration for his own songs, as did Woody Guthrie. Ella May Wiggins and the events surrounding the strike inspired six novels: Mary Heaton Vorse's *Strike!* (1930), Grace Lumpkin's *To Make My Bread* (1932), Dorothy Myra Page's *Gathering Storm: A Story of the Black Belt* (1932), Fielding Burke's *Call Home the Heart* (1932), Sherwood Anderson's *Beyond Desire* (1932), and William Rollins's *The Shadow Before* (1934).

Tragically, despite producing a rich cache of poetry and lore, the strike had failed to win any concessions for the workers.

. . .

Just before the strike in Gastonia crumbled, and as textile workers across the South were holding the line against hostile plant owners, a different kind of battle was being waged at rayon factories up north. That year, an industrial toxicologist named Alice Hamilton, who had been publishing her findings for decades in scientific journals and government reports, decided to turn to the popular press to get her urgent message public attention. In an article in *Harper's* magazine, Hamilton decried the practice of using harmful chemicals in industrial processes without first testing safe exposure limits: or, as she put it, creating a situation where "the workers will serve as experimental animals."

Born in 1869, Dr. Alice Hamilton was by that time a leading U.S. expert on the toxicity of carbon disulfide. In 1915, in a report for the federal Bureau of Labor Statistics, *Industrial Poisons Used in the Rubber Industry*, she devoted six full pages to carbon disulfide. Her 1915 report remarked presciently that "it is certainly possible that the insane asylums have received cases of unrecognized carbon disulfide psychosis, since insane rubber workers are committed from these towns without any inquiry being made as to the exact occupation of the patient and the possible industrial source of his disease."

Misdiagnosing carbon disulfide poisoning was in fact common practice both in the U.S. and abroad. In Italy, an outbreak of nervous diseases suffered by rayon factory workers in 1915 was diagnosed by some physicians as "collective hysteria." Hamilton knew from her own experience that afflicted workers were themselves sometimes uniquely unable to help doctors draw the connection between the chemical and the illness. One Hungarian-born rubber worker sent to the doctor in 1915 insisted he was not a rubber worker. When the doctor asked him about his work, Hamilton noted, "he told a rambling tale of lumbering down a river, and could not be convinced that he had ever worked in a rubber factory." In her ongoing work on the poison, Dr. Hamilton found that male pride could also militate against the disclosure of psychiatric illness. In one case report in 1924 she noted:

He did not wish to talk about his symptoms but to be left alone. Only unwillingly would he admit that he had been much depressed, and that he slept heavily, but his wife said that he jumped and jerked all night, that he was always drowsy and that latterly he had had queer things happen, for instance that when he was looking at a thermometer it seemed to leave the wall and come towards him.

In 1935, Hamilton spearheaded the most ambitious study of carbon disulfide yet. Since 1920, Hamilton had been affiliated with Bryn Mawr College in Pennsylvania, teaching as a special lecturer in industrial poisons at the Carola Woerishoffer Graduate Department of Social Economy and Social Research. This department was a nexus where a number of progressive, women-led efforts to improve worker conditions intersected: the Women's Trade Union League, the industrial sections of the YMCA, the National Consumers League, and the Summer Schools for Labor all had affiliations with the department. The department's founding chair, Dr. Susan Kingsbury, wrote in February to the dean of Bryn Mawr to arrange a research assistant appointment for Adele Cohn MD to undertake "an investigation of industrial disease in eastern Pennsylvania." Pennsylvania was the one northern state with a major rayon industry. Alice Hamilton was to oversee the study.

For three months in the spring of 1935, Cohn, assisted by three of Dr. Kingsbury's graduate students, tracked down cases identified to them by union referrals. There were no known cases of carbon disulfide poisoning in hospital records, as the disease was not usually recognized by general physicians. Cohn found another important source of information on a visit to the county clerk's. The clerk commented, Cohn wrote, "that for some unknown reason there had been much more Insanity in the county since the rayon factory had come there."

Hamilton resolved to broaden the scope of the study. In 1937, she secured a commitment of support from the U.S. Department of Labor for a multistate assessment of the viscose industry, to begin in Pennsylvania. Hamilton assembled an impressive research team. On the ground, she relied on industrial hygienist and occupational health expert Lillian Erskine, a special agent for the division of labor standards who was lent to Pennsylvania for the purpose.

Whereas the Bryn Mawr study had lacked direct on-site access to the rayon workers through their employers, who were openly antagonistic, the multistate study found a way around this. Participants were recruited by word of mouth and interviewed with a questionnaire. Then they were brought to off-site locations to be examined by a medical team. Transportation had to be done in unmarked state cars supplied by the office of Ralph Bashore, Pennsylvania's secretary of labor and industry. One hundred fifty-nine workers were interviewed, from two rayon factories, and 120 were directly examined. The results were astounding. Seventy-five percent reported mood or personality changes. Thirty percent reported hallucinations, about a third reported loss of libido, and 10 percent reported ideas of persecution. In the direct physical examinations, three fourths of workers were found to have evidence of peripheral nerve damage, and almost the same proportion showed abnormal findings on a psychiatric assessment. One seventh showed evidence of Parkinsonism and, overall, one in four of the workers was determined to have severe carbon-disulfide-related intoxication.

The Erskine-Hamilton study, though dogged by resistance at every step, was released in 1938 in the *Journal of the American Medical Association*. In the report, Erskine emphasized the cost to taxpayers of institutionalizing the insane: the high number of commitments for insanity was "convincing proof that industrial exposure to carbon disulfide . . . has been responsible for direct expense (for the institutional care) to the taxpayers of Pennsylvania."*

Despite the conclusive nature of the report, the legal apparatus that would have been needed to address the problem of carbon disulfide exposure did not exist in 1939. This would wait another three

---

* This gross "externalization of costs" is chilling, but perhaps even more chilling is a 1950s Polish medical report that describes a rayon factory that had taken upon itself the cost of this kind of care: a "Night sanitorium" had been organized for workers exposed to carbon disulfide where they could "spend all their free time at night hours under the best possible conditions for the treatment of their maladies."

decades for the creation of the Occupational Safety and Health Administration, or OSHA.

Hamilton's testimony did have some effect on the recommendations given by the American Standards Association, which voted, in the June 1939 meeting of its Sectional Committee on Standard Allowable Concentrations of Toxic Dusts and Gases to adopt the target for carbon disulfide exposure of 20 parts per million. This was much lower than what had been proposed by the American Viscose Corporation's consultant, Philip Drinker (30 ppm). It was, however, far higher than what was proposed by Hamilton, and far too high to keep workers safe.* Gallingly, it was made clear that concrete scientific knowledge wasn't going to fix anything.

While the fight to unionize textile workers hit insurmountable obstacles and the fight to protect rayon workers from workplace poisoning stalled, victory was won in garment manufacture.

Unlike the textile industry, which had its historical roots first in New England and then the American South, the U.S. garment industry as it had evolved since the invention of the sewing machine was largely centered in New York City.

In the early 1900s, a wave of Jewish immigration from the Russian Pale brought teenaged girls with a potent and particular combination of qualities to the Lower East Side en masse. These women were hungry for education, forced into sweatshops, and on fire with Marxism. The latter they had picked up in the Old Country, where "behind every other volume of Talmud, in those years, there was a volume of Marx." Some historians call these women, like Clara Lemlich, Pauline Newman, and Rose Schneiderman, "industrial feminists," a name coined in 1915 by Mildred Moore, although I fondly think of them as hustler-scholars, because of how aggressively they educated themselves.

---

* DuPont's own in-house limit was half as high as that adopted by the American Standards Association, and the limit in the USSR was 3.2 ppm, less than a fifth the U.S. limit.

Clara Lemlich, who helped ignite a massive garment workers' uprising in 1909, was born in the Ukrainian village of Gorodok in 1886. As a girl in a Jewish family, she was denied a formal textual religious education, and as a Jew in the Russian Empire she was denied entry into the only public school in Gorodok. Her parents banned the speaking of Russian in the house in protest. Lemlich befriended non-Jewish peasant children who taught her Russian folksongs, and then taught the folksongs to older Jewish girls, who, in exchange, taught her how to read Russian and lent her volumes of Tolstoy, Gorky, and Turgenev. When she had exhausted that library, she started sewing buttonholes on shirts and writing letters in Yiddish for illiterate mothers to send to their children in America in order to earn money with which she could buy more books. She hid these under a meat pan in the kitchen. When her father discovered her library and burned it, she simply started her collection over. She was sixteen when the Kishinev pogrom prompted her family to move from Ukraine to the Lower East Side.

Lemlich arrived hoping to find in the American public school system what had been denied her in Russia: a formal education, and she was bitterly disappointed when the family's circumstances demanded she work in a sweatshop sewing clothes.

There, however, Lemlich met like-minded workers, with whom she would revolutionize the politics of garment manufacture. By day, they toiled in the sweatshop, and by night they organized the garment workers of the Lower East Side, forging a radical theory of labor: they demanded the right to art. Industrial feminism called for educational and cultural access for workers. According to Rose Schneiderman, "What the woman who labors wants is the right to live, not simply exist—the right to life as the rich woman has the right to life, and the sun and music and art. . . . The worker must have bread, but she must have roses, too."

On November 22, 1909, there was an overflow audience crowded in Cooper Union's Great Hall. In late September, three hundred women workers from the Triangle Shirtwaist Factory had gone on strike, and were holding the picket line daily in the cold. While cops turned their backs, paid off with a hundred-dollar bill slipped in a cigar case, according to labor organizers' accounts, the blows of company thugs rained down on strikers. Defying expectations of established unionists, who did not think either women or immigrant workers could be organized, these three hundred–some Italian and Jewish girls had been conducting an orderly strike for weeks. Now, thousands of other workers at the city's other shirtwaist shops were considering following their example.

Samuel Gompers had just finished speaking to the packed house, and the next scheduled speaker was about to be introduced, when a slim young girl, who had recently been beaten on the Triangle picket line, stood up and asked for permission to address the gathering. When this was granted, Clara Lemlich got up and called for a vote to authorize a general strike. The vote passed, and twenty thousand garment workers walked out.

During the strike she helped foment, Clara Lemlich had six ribs broken by company guards' and policemen's clubs and was arrested seventeen times. The eventual arrival to Washington Square Park of the so-called Mink Brigades, wealthy women who came downtown to join the striking seamstresses, helped turn the tide of public opinion by bringing attention to the brutality occurring daily in the park. When the strike ended in February 1910, union contracts had been signed at nearly every shop, although not at the Triangle Shirtwaist Company. The International Ladies' Garment Workers' Union (ILGWU), which had been formed in 1900, but whose membership had languished, exploded in size and strength. Two years later, the Triangle Shirtwaist Factory burst into flames, killing 146 garment workers. This ushered in a new and triumphant era in the battle against sweatshops.

Three months after the fire, New York's governor, under pressure from activists, created a commission that would investigate factories across the state. The following year, the state's labor laws were rewritten. Frances Perkins and Robert Wagner, who headed the factory commission, would later help to create the nation's most sweeping worker protections through the New Deal, in the National Labor

Relations Act, guaranteeing federal protection for workers' right to unionize. More radical still, however, was what the International Ladies' Garment Workers' Union would accomplish.

The ILGWU gained in size and stature after the Triangle Shirt-waist Factory fire, and it adopted a strategy that would give responsibility for factory conditions to those who designed, purchased, and sold the garments produced by the small contract shops. About 70 percent of all women's apparel workers in America were represented by the ILGWU by 1935. By the late 1940s, weekly wages in the garment industry had reached almost 85 percent of those in manufacturing overall. In the post–World War II prosperity, the ILGWU and the Amalgamated Clothing Workers of America would reap the benefits of their decades of hard work. By the 1950s, allied with the New Deal and the Democratic Party, apparel unions in New York, New Jersey, and Pennsylvania had organized the entire East Coast.

The ILGWU made good on the utopian visions of its early theorists. It opened up a resort in the Poconos for union workers. Its educational department offered courses in economics, history, literature, philosophy, and union leadership skills. Its health centers provided medical care for union members and their families. It offered opportunities in the arts, drama, music, and sports.

Through its cultural arm, the union helped advertise its message and gain support for the cause of workers, while helping workers access high culture. The inaugural broadcast for WFDR, its radio station in New York (the union also owned radio stations in Los Angeles and Chattanooga), featured "Verdi arias and Rooseveltian folksongs" side by side, reported *Time* in June 1949. In 1937–40 union members staged the musical *Pins and Needles,* still one of the longest-running shows on Broadway. With songs like "Sing Me a Song with Social Significance" and "It's Better with a Union Man," the musical portrayed a world populated by young people as taken up by political consciousness as they are by romance. One of the songs asks: "Are you ready to learn your lesson for today? Are you ready to hear what history has to say?" Then comes the chorus, sung in turn by Thomas Paine, George Washington, Paul Revere, and finally, by the garment worker:

You can't stand still on freedom's track,
if you don't go forward you go back.

While the ILGWU began to make concrete gains in the North, the fight in the South to organize textile workers was still gearing up. The 1929 strike that killed Ella May had not defeated hopes for a textile union in the South. It helped set the stage for another, even larger strike.

The largest textile workers' strike in U.S. history, and one of the largest strikes in any industry, kicked off on September 1, 1934. Led by the United Textile Workers of America, almost half a million workers from New Hampshire to Mississippi walked off the job. Forty-three thousand people in South Carolina alone joined the protest. In 1933, on FDR's ninety-ninth day in office, Congress passed the National Industrial Recovery Act, which workers had interpreted as a victory for the right to unionize. South Carolina workers carried signs on the picket lines that read, "Roosevelt, Our Greatest Leader."

On September 6, in Honea Path, a town just south of Greenville, where two thirds of the state's mills were shut down by the strikers, around three hundred people stood outside Chiquola Mill waiting for the whistle to blow. Across from them stood deputized townspeople and anti-union millworkers armed with shotguns, rifles, and pistols. Dan Beacham, the mill superintendent (also the town mayor and town judge), had mounted a World War I machine gun to the roof of the four-story mill. When the whistle blew, strikers moved forward to block the mill gate. Strikebreakers headed for the entrance. A fight broke out, and then the shooting began. A pistol was fired, then the machine gun. The gunfire lasted three minutes. Seven strikers were killed, most shot in the back while fleeing, dozens more were wounded. The strike collapsed soon after.

A mediation panel appointed by President Roosevelt concluded weakly that the textile workers' grievances called for further study, urged the creation of a Textile Labor Relations Board to hear workers' complaints, and toothlessly suggested that employers not discriminate against strikers. Roosevelt announced his support for the panel's findings, and in late September 1934 personally appealed to employees to return to work and to the manufacturers to accept the recommendations. The United Textile Workers of America declared victory and held a number of parades to celebrate the end of the strike.

The outcome was a complete failure. Mill owners refused to recognize the union or meet any of its economic demands. The backlash was to be most intense in the South, where many employers refused to reinstate strikers, leaving behind a legacy of bitterness.

drove south to Gastonia, where Ella May Wiggins was shot, in the spring of 2016. Mist rose in the early evening light, and the green countryside was beautiful. As night fell I rode through the outskirts of Charlotte and saw it gleaming in the distance. I arrived in Gastonia at a big yellow house with a well-manicured lawn. When I told my Airbnb hostess, Lynn, that I was tracing the history of the 1929 textile strike, she told me she had never heard of it, despite having grown up in Gastonia. All she knew, she said, was that her grandmother had come down out of the hills to work in the Loray Mill, and vowed that no child of hers would ever do the same. When I visited the Loray Mill the next day, there was no hint of a marker to commemorate the strike.

From Gastonia I headed to Greenville, South Carolina, just north of Honea Path, where the most violent moments of the 1934 strike had occurred. Perhaps, at its epicenter, some memory of the strike was being kept alive? There was one local history organization in Greenville that seemed likely to have kept the records, the Textile History Society. One of its members, Marshall Williams, agreed to meet with me.

I pulled into the parking lot beneath the letters, each held in its separate, inviolate yellow square, W-a-f-f-l-e H-o-u-s-e. Marshall Williams turned out to be a blue-eyed Baptist minister. He had written a volume about the mill village in which he grew up. He bought me coffee. We were the only customers. He laid out a stack of self-published booklets held together with plastic binding combs with names like *The Story of Textile Greenville* and *Greenville's Textile Giants.*

Marshall grew up in the Dunean Mill community. His parents arrived in Greenville in 1934. I pointed out the synchronicity of their arrival with the strike. "That was the year," he answered slowly, "that the northern unions tried to come into the South. There was a lot of controversy in some of the plants. Didn't last very long because they were not welcome. And the unions could not organize here. 'Course everybody knows the story of Chiquola Mill where some folks, you know, had gotten killed. Some people did want to unite but most of 'em didn't. As far as I know very few of the mills have ever unionized. They closed labor organizing." The union organizer was remembered as a carpetbagger, a notable victory for the southern capitalist.

That afternoon I went to the South Carolina room in the Hughes Main Library. I searched for references to the 1934 strike and found a 1974 doctoral thesis entitled "Greenville, Unionism, and the General Strike in the Textile Industry, 1934," by Stan Langston. It was in Langston's own typewritten keystrokes, mimeographed, with some handwritten corrections. Langston's introduction reported that "if one mentions . . . the General Textile Strike of 1934" to a Greenvillian, "he will very likely discover that it is a subject many Greenvillians prefer to avoid. . . . In fact, very few young Greenvillians know of the strike because of their older relatives' reluctance to talk about it."

A clipping from *The Greenville News,* September 6, 2014, on the eightieth anniversary of the killings at Chiquola Mill pointed to the longevity of this conspiracy of silence. "This day will slip by quietly in the little town of Honea Path," the journalist wrote. She told the story of the attempt of the seventy-seven-year-old then-mayor of Honea Path, Earl Lollis Meyers, to get his mother to talk about the strike of 1934. "You shut your mouth," said the mother when Meyers asked her about the union one Sunday dinner. Despite his repeated requests, Mary Lollis Meyers refused to talk until she was on her deathbed. She had been a young girl in 1934, and she had been playing in the yard when the shooting started. Her father, an overseer in the cloth room, gathered the family inside the house and then put them on the P&L Railroad to Greenville to wait out the violence. Then he went up to the mill, recalled Meyers, "and turned over the ones who were shot with his cane so their noses wouldn't be flat."

Children of the murdered workers were met with the same amnesiac response as the children of the killers. Sue Cannon Hill, whose father, Claude, was among the murdered millworkers, grew up watching her mother go to work each day in the mill her father died in front of.

"More than anything, though," wrote journalist Peter Applebome, "she remembers the communal conspiracy of silence, how the most important event in her young life and in the life of everyone in the little mill village where they lived was never mentioned, as if the shots had never been fired, the men had never died, the union had never existed, the whole thing had never happened at all."

In Honea Path, as elsewhere, when the strike ended, those who had been involved in the union were either fired and kicked out of their mill housing, or made to promise they would never organize again, and never talk about the events that had transpired.

The labor struggles of the early twentieth century met with mixed success. Northern garment workers succeeded in achieving quality working conditions, while textile workers in the South faced insurmountable odds when attempting the same. U.S. rayon manufacture relied on weak worker protections from the time it was established in the early twentieth century until the industry was offshored in the 1970s. Conditions in rayon factories may have continued to be deadly, but the workers didn't give up without a fight. While many organized strike actions against their employers, one worker in Delaware tried another avenue.

Between January and February 1934, months before the general strike, a young woman named Emily Bowing worked in the reeling room of a rayon factory in New Castle. Bowing suffered from neurological and psychological symptoms: "Irrationality, unconscious spells, lack of self-control, nightmares, crying spells, headaches, weakened eyesight, and a loss of libido," all classic symptoms of carbon disulfide poisoning. Bowing decided to do what very few other employees had dared to: she brought a negligence suit against Delaware Rayon.

The company adroitly responded with a full range of gendered character defamation. Delaware Rayon requested that Bowing be examined by five physicians of their own choosing, and the court agreed. Their physicians rendered the opinion that Bowing suffered from endocervicitis and a retroverted uterus with adhesions—in other words, hysteria as it had been medically defined in the fifth century BC. They also cited, as causes for her perceived distress, her marital and—gallingly—her economic conditions. The court decided for Delaware Rayon.

Although Bowing was the only one to file suit, numberless others were poisoned at Delaware Rayon. In 1933, toxicologist Dr. Alice Hamilton received a telegram at the Harvard medical school: "RAYON FACTORY HAVING EPIDEMIC OF MENTAL CASES LAID TO CARBON DISULFIDE POISONING PHYSICIANS ANXIOUS TO GET GENERAL SYMPTOM OF DISEASE STOP BEST PROBABLE TREATMENT STOP CAUSES OF DISEASE PLEASE ANSWER QUICKLY." Hamilton would later report that although she responded immediately, her telegram was never answered, and the case was quickly hushed up.

It was beyond doubt that carbon disulfide was toxic. Indeed, it was such an effective nerve agent that rayon specialists moonlighted as war criminals. Walter Scheiber, who had been deeply involved with the Nazi yeast protein project (Biosyn-Vegetabil-Wurst), had worked on nerve agents at IG Farben before moving into rayon. After the war, Scheiber was recruited to work for the American postwar chemical weapons effort, Operation Paperclip. Rayon production was closely linked, via carbon disulfide, to poison gas and munitions manufacture. In Hungary, rayon plants were converted to munitions factories at the beginning of World War II. Munitions plants in New Castle, Delaware, had been repurposed by Delaware Rayon after the war.

Science had shown conclusively that carbon disulfide was a powerful neurotoxin, and that anyone working near it needed comprehensive protections. But getting these worker protections enshrined in policy was another story.

When OSHA was first established in 1970, carbon disulfide was one of many chemicals whose old exposure limits were grandfathered in, and the inadequate ASA standard of 20 ppm became the law. Today, the standard of 20 parts per million is still the law of the land in the United States. More important, however, it is also the standard in India, Indonesia, and Thailand, three of the big four Asian rayon producers. China's official target is much lower, at 2 ppm. The target, however, is not always the reality: eight workers in China's northern Shanxi province were killed in May 2015 by a carbon disulfide "leak." Not much biomedical data exists for these workers, but one anthropological study of rayon workers in Nagda, Madhya Pradesh, reports that the locals complain of impotence, mental illness, paralysis, and heart attack, all classic manifestations of carbon disulfide poisoning.

Rayon fabric had promised the luxe of silk to the ordinary woman. But its story shows the hollowness of the twentieth-century promise of luxury for all: that it has too often substituted the image of well-dressed workers for the reality of safe and well-paid ones. Despite the inadequate government protections offered to U.S. workers in the cloth and clothing trades, in some areas they made significant strides during the first half of the twentieth century, the International Ladies' Garment Workers' Union in particular. However, in the years following World War II decisions made by the U.S. State Department would make it increasingly easy to move clothing manufacturing overseas, erasing those gains that had been won. These developments took place alongside the arrival of a whole new type of fabric: one that was made entirely from oil but could take on many forms and appearances. Like other totems of progress of the postwar era, it was a shape-shifter that many times promised to liberate, and as many times worked to entrap.

10

Nylons

When nylon stockings debuted on October 24, 1939, in Wilmington, Delaware, four thousand pairs sold out in three hours. DuPont chemist Wallace Hume Carothers created the synthetic in 1935 and committed suicide two years later, before witnessing its remarkable success. Nylon, which has since become a generic name for polyamide, was the brand name of DuPont's "hexamethylene diamine—adipic acid condensation product" or nylon 6, 6 for short. Nylon soon found commercial application in toothbrush bristles, and then in women's hose. Unlike rayon, nylon is synthesized entirely from petroleum products. At the 1939 New York World's Fair, nylon was advertised as being made from just "carbon, water and air." The product promised to shape a woman's legs in such a way that she would satisfy the desire of men. The novel hosiery became all the rage. On May 16, 1940, four million pairs of nylons arrived in U.S. department stores, and sold out in two days.

When the U.S. entered World War II, nylon was rationed, and funneled into matériel: parachutes, tire cords, ropes, mosquito netting, hammocks. Without their stockings, women painted nylons onto their legs with nude-colored makeup, drawing seams up the back of their calves with eyebrow pencil. In 1945, nylons returned, and riots broke out across the United States when too many women lined up for too few pairs. The most famous of these "nylon riots" took place in Pittsburgh, where forty thousand people vied for thirteen thousand pairs of stockings.

For American women, the end of the war meant the return of nylons and the end of high-paying jobs. From 1942 to 1944, American women streamed into the labor force. Pushed by the Women's Bureau and organized women's groups, U.S. employers hired women to do jobs previously only done by men: operating forklifts, welding, digging ditches, and working in steel mills, shipyards, and munitions factories. Some women entered the labor force for the first time to perform this work, while others upgraded from lower-paying jobs. Nurseries and hot lunches were set up to support women who were both workers and mothers.

"They are the women," reporter Lucy Greenbam wrote, "who feel that if they are good enough to serve in a crisis they deserve a chance to earn a living in peacetime." Nonetheless, even before the end of the war, trade unions and the War Manpower Commission encouraged women to give up their jobs. Funding for day care disappeared. Union seniority rules dictated that returning veterans replace war workers. A massive propaganda campaign was launched to urge women to relinquish their jobs to returning vets, and return to the home.

The frenzied fight for nylons, perhaps, canalized the anger that many women felt over their shrinking life choices. Ironically, this newly awakened passion for synthetics and the good things they seemed to promise would help precipitate the demise of American garment manufacture.

On August 6, 1945, the Reverend Mr. Kiyoshi Tanimoto, pastor of Hiroshima Methodist Church, was helping his neighbor Matsuo bring a large Japanese cabinet filled with his daughter's clothes out to the relative safety of a rayon manufacturer's home two miles out of town, when a strange and brilliant flash of light crossed the sky. Both men reacted immediately. Matsuo ran into the house and dove among some cushions, while Mr. Tanimoto wedged himself between two large rocks in the garden. There, he felt an enormous pulse of air, and tiny fragments of tile and wood rain down on him. When he stood up the house lay in splinters. The atomic bomb had been dropped on Hiroshima.

Over the course of the war, 80 percent of Japanese textile machinery had been wiped out: either destroyed, shipped to overseas territories, or repurposed. After Japan's defeat, the country was occupied by American troops under General Douglas MacArthur (whose formal title was Supreme Commander for the Allied Powers, or SCAP). An immediate postwar priority was the rebuilding of the Japanese textile industry. Particularly after Mao's victory in China in 1949, the U.S. State Department wanted to make Japan the bulwark of democracy in Asia by reindustrializing it as rapidly as possible.

Initially, a five-year plan to revive Japanese textile production centered on silk. In the 1930s Japan had exported silk to the United States and Europe, but with nylon as the new stocking fabric of choice, in 1947 the value of silk exports fell dramatically. State Department strategists, with some encouragement of southern lawmakers, looked to another material: cotton.

Coincidentally, ten million bales of raw cotton were sitting in storage in the U.S. Subsidies had increased cotton acreage during the war, and now it had nowhere to go. In 1948 Senator James Eastland, a Mississippi cotton planter, introduced what became known as the Eastland Bill, which authorized U.S. foreign aid appropriations to finance the sale of U.S. cotton to Japan, and soon the country became the largest importer of U.S. cotton. In the 1953–54 season Japan took 25.7 percent of the U.S.'s total cotton exports. And, in turn, Congress opened America's markets to Japanese textiles, creating a major source of competition with U.S. cloth.

Textile interests had strong representation in Congress, and they attempted to block the deluge of imports. However, Congress found its hands were tied. Although it had originally been granted the right to set tariffs by the Constitution, Congress had temporarily ceded this power to FDR in response to accusations of political corruption in a big tariff bill of the mid-1930s. This represented a serious loss of

its power, so Congress limited the handover—called the Recipro-
cal Trade Agreements Act—to three years. The renewal of the act
became a perennial flashpoint, the occasion for conflict between pro-
tectionist forces in Congress who wanted to save American textiles,
and hardliners in the State Department who believed it was essential
to subordinate the needs of the textile industry to the need to fight
communism. For these hardliners, if Asian countries weren't offered
an opportunity to make and export cloth, they would be more likely
to "fall" to communism. The communist bogeyman was powerful.
Just as Congress was about to take back its right to set textile tariffs in
1954, key members were pulled aside to be dramatically briefed on the
communist victory at Dien Bien Phu in Vietnam, and they changed
their votes, which allowed the rise of imports to grow unchecked.

In 1956, Japanese textile shipments to the United States were at
seven times their level in the years after the war. U.S. textile producers were hit hard. While U.S. foreign aid had enabled Asian mills to
purchase the newest technology, 65 percent of the machinery in use
by U.S. textile producers was obsolete. Between 1947 and 1957, U.S.
textile workers' wages dropped from being 16 percent lower than the
wages of other U.S. industrial workers, to 30 percent lower.

As the U.S. textile industry was made a sacrificial lamb for the
Cold War cause, they raged against what they perceived to be a historic injustice. "Isn't this the first time," Nevada senator George
Malone demanded in a 1958 hearing, "that we have ever given the
executive the right to trade an industry to further the foreign policy?"
In another 1958 hearing, a textile executive acknowledged that while,
certainly, "our allies need to be buttressed against the economic programs of Russia and its satellites," it would be counterproductive if
these tactics ended up "undermining . . . a sector of American industry." By 1960, the rhetoric was still more desperate. The outgoing
president of the American Cotton Manufacturers Institute, asking for
quota protections, said: "Must there be closed mills and breadlines
before the Administration in Washington concedes the possibility
of irreparable damage to our industry?" They were right to panic.
Even when in 1957 Japan committed to voluntary export restraints on
clothing and textiles in response to pressure from U.S. congressional

textile protectionists, it was clear that the State Department's policy of welcoming Asian imports spelled the beginning of the end for the U.S. garment and textile industries.

The United States never occupied South Korea or Taiwan, like it did Japan. However, it did militarily intervene to prevent both countries from becoming communist, and provided massive payouts in military defense funds. Between 1945 and 1958, the U.S. provided $2.6 billion worth of economic aid to South Korea, according to one U.N. estimate. Economic aid meanwhile went to building infrastructure: paved roads, modern harbors, electrical capacity. The U.S. also channeled large-scale funding into industrial revitalization in Taiwan and South Korea, as it did in Hong Kong, Malaysia, Thailand, the Philippines, Indonesia, and Singapore. All this was intended to link these countries with Japan, and through Japan to western trade and investment networks. The rapid economic growth in these countries would lead them to be called "Asian Miracles," and it also set them up to become major competitors to U.S. textile and garment producers. For the U.S. garment workers who had fought a successful battle to unionize, the approaching influx of impossibly cheap garments was to be a disaster.

The first cotton blouses arrived in 1947. By 1954, with the end of the Korean War, 171,000 cotton blouses were imported from Japan. A year later, it was four million. Between 1947 and 1960 the amount of apparel imports increased twelvefold. In the 1960s, Hong Kong and Taiwan had also begun to produce low-cost women's and children's clothing for export to the U.S. Unions were now competing with offshore producers who could work at a fraction of U.S. costs.

Japan could undersell U.S.-made garments not merely because by the mid-1950s they enjoyed annual tariff reductions, U.S. foreign aid, cheap cotton, and modern technology. Their low price tags also came thanks to an extreme gender wage gap. Modernization of textile equipment can increase efficiency and lower costs for manufacturers, but in garment production no technology is more efficient than human hands. Just like manufacturers in the U.S. had done, Japan relied on a heavy gender wage gap to lower costs. In Hong Kong, Taiwan, and South Korea, also, young women received alarmingly low wages.

When the U.S. State Department created industries in East Asia and opened the U.S. market to their products, it allowed the high gender wage gap overseas to erode the progress made against the U.S. wage gap by American women unionists. Indeed, the greatest women's labor success story of the twentieth-century U.S., the International Ladies' Garment Workers' Union, was about to be blown apart.

President John F. Kennedy eventually conceded to pressure from U.S. cotton textile manufacturers to offer at least some protection, and capped the import growth rate for cotton textiles and apparel at 6 percent each year. Kennedy also provided tax breaks to southern textile producers to help them upgrade equipment, and established funds to provide for job training and assistance for displaced workers, which remained in effect until Ronald Reagan cut these programs in the 1980s. But these programs were designed to help the U.S. industries fade less slowly, not to keep them alive. Trade liberalization became the new paradigm. And Kennedy's quota was to have unexpected consequences.

Kennedy's quota regime had been set at the behest of the American Cotton Manufacturers Institute, and thus it only regulated cotton fabric and clothing made from cotton fabric. Increasingly, however, the important industry story in the postwar period was taking place in the realm of synthetics like nylon.

In the decades after the end of World War II, synthetics had grown fast. Worldwide, the total production of textile fibers nearly doubled between 1950 and 1966,* and the share of those textile fibers that were made from petroleum doubled also.† Much of this increased production was gobbled up by the United States.

---

* From 9.4 million tons to 17.7 million tons.

† Although cotton production increased in this period also, it declined as a percentage of world fibers. In 1940–41 cotton had made up 75 percent of world fiber, whereas in 1976–77 it had dropped to 49 percent. In the same period, the share claimed by wool dropped from 12.4 percent to 5.7 percent, even while output remained the same, in terms of quantity. Silk had already, by this time, lost market share to rayon and nylon.

DuPont dominated the synthetics business. The discovery of nylon had given it a strong patent position initially. Nylon quickly became DuPont's most profitable product, and in 1962 it was the leading firm in the $19.1 billion U.S. chemical industry.

The panoply of fabrics that could be made from oil blossomed. Immediately after World War II, DuPont's "Rayon Department" oversaw four product lines: rayon, acetate, cellophane, and nylon. In January 1952, anticipating more fibers, executives at DuPont reorganized the Rayon Department's 24,300 employees into the Textile Fibers Department. By the 1960s, DuPont produced seven different families of fibers: rayon, acetate, nylon, acrylic, polyester, spandex, and fluorocarbon, with three thousand varieties within the seven fiber families. By 1969, DuPont had invented thirty-one Dacrons and seventy nylons. Each of these was a molecular chain to which the DuPont marketers would need to join a name, like Adam naming the animals.

DuPont was quickly joined by domestic competitors. In 1955, DuPont controlled 70 percent of the nation's capacity for synthetic fibers, but by 1960 its market share had dropped to 50 percent in the face of competitors such as Allied Chemical, American Cyanamid, American Enka, Celanese, Dow Chemical, Eastman Kodak, Monsanto, and Union Carbide. Five U.S. firms produced nylon fiber in 1960, ten by 1965.

Because nylon required twice the capital investment of rayon, the major players to emerge in the petroleum-based synthetics market were highly concentrated. Of the five hundred largest companies in the world in 1972, thirty-two were synthetic fiber manufacturers. Three fifths of the world supply was produced by just thirteen massive firms. In this oligopolistic framework, product differentiation and patenting were crucial. Nylon was the first fabric to be engineered exclusively from petroleum derivatives, and its emergence tempted manufacturers to see what other petro-fabrics they could concoct. In 1965, U.S. synthetics manufacturers spent $135 million on research aimed at developing new fibers.

Synthetics producers didn't just invest heavily in the science of polymers, but the emerging science of marketing as well. In the 1960s, the handful of huge companies that dominated synthetics in the U.S.

spent $70 million on promotion, compared with $4 million spent by the cotton fiber industry. They also advanced credit to retailers, subsidized their advertising, and financed the installation of faster knitting and weaving machines for the factories that wove and knit their fibers.

DuPont was at the vanguard of this surge, boasting the largest marketing program in the fiber industry. To give their products a high-fashion sheen, DuPont set out to win the imprimatur of Parisian designers. Beginning in the early 1950s, DuPont established a mutually beneficial relationship with France's Chambre Syndicale de la Haute Couture, a trade organization for elite designers. French dressmakers would integrate synthetic fibers into their Paris collections, and in return DuPont would buy models of the couture originals, hire famous photographers to take pictures of them, and create enormous amounts of publicity. In 1952, the French designer Christian Dior traveled to Delaware to meet DuPont managers, study new synthetics, and tour laboratories. In 1953, DuPont hosted Givenchy. Givenchy, who got his start as a boutique designer for the avant-garde couturière Elsa Schiaparelli, borrowed the idea of "separates" from American sportswear and introduced it into evening wear. If Dior linked DuPont to high society, Givenchy's inclusion of Orlon acrylic in its February 1954 collection worked to link the brand to younger consumers. To the female consumer in the U.S. the message was clear: if DuPont's synthetics were good enough for haute couture, they were good enough for her.

During the mid-1950s, polymer chemists created Lycra spandex prototypes, and in 1964 DuPont inaugurated the Stretch Corps, a group of 120 men and women who traveled around the country to promote the fiber. The Stretch Corps visited stores and interacted with shoppers to show the salesclerks how to explain Lycra's features, dressed in uniforms made from blended fabrics of cotton, Dacron, and Lycra.

The boom in synthetics prompted a rage for a new, informal type of clothing: sportswear. In 1958, there were seven hundred companies producing sportswear in the U.S., worth $2 billion in sales. This was largely fed by a new market of buyers with leisure time and disposable income: teenagers. By the second half of the 1960s, nearly half of all outerwear purchased in America was bought by shoppers fifteen to nineteen years of age.

Synthetics also found a home in lightweight Orlon spring sweaters in vivid colors, which became popular with young women. By 1959, 100 million Orlon sweaters were sold annually. By the decade's end, half of all women's sweaters in the U.S. were made from Orlon.

Synthetics were appealing in part because of how easy they were to care for. As the Los Angeles writer Ellen Melinkoff recalls in her social history of postwar U.S. women's fashion, when Dacron-ruffled blouses first appeared in 1956, they attracted instant converts because they dried fast and required so little ironing. "We were so charmed by synthetics," Melinkoff wrote, "that we turned up our noses at cotton . . . weeded it out of our wardrobes as quickly as possible." Previously, laundry had been arduous, Melinkoff recalls. Most of Monday had to be set aside for washing. Prior to the advent of steam irons, women sprinkled line-dried clothes with water and stored them rolled up in the refrigerator's vegetable bin to stay moist, but not mildewed, until there was time to starch and iron them.

Synthetics, however, were not just easy to care for; they were vividly colored. Because of the way petroleum-based fabrics interact with synthetic dyestuffs, they can be dyed fluorescent tones.

The discovery of aniline dye was an accident. In 1856, an eighteen-year-old chemist attempting to synthesize quinine from coal tar found that the inside of his beaker had turned a deep mauve. This first color, marketed as Perkin's mauve, was soon followed by a bright fuchsia, and then by a whole range of other colors. These dyes were the first commercial products of the synthetic chemical industry, out of which the pharmaceutical industry would one day be born.

Like coal tar itself, aniline dyes are fantastically toxic, and textile dyeing is among the most polluting industries in the world, responsible for about 20 percent of global wastewater according to the World Bank. Textile dyeing relies on chromium, lead, cadmium, sulfur, nitrates, chlorine compounds, arsenic, mercury, nickel and cobalt, formaldehyde-based dye fixing agents, chlorinated stain removers. Dangerous on their own, these dye materials can also react with the disinfectant used to process fabric, particularly chlorine, and form by-products that are frequently carcinogenic. Dye effluent can clog the pores of the soil, crippling its productivity. Dumped into waterways, it can pollute drinking water and soil, impacting entire ecosystems, creating serious public health problems.

At the very outset of the chemical dye industry, textile designer and social theorist William Morris denounced aniline colors as "crude, livid—and cheap" and warned that they were on their way to "destroying all beauty." Eighteen hundred years earlier Pliny had mourned the degradation of the Roman aesthetic as a result of the flood of imported pigments. "Now that purple is being put to use on our walls and India contributes with the mud of her rivers and with the gore of her snakes and her elephants, there is no longer noble painting." Morris's eye had grown accustomed to the color palette of global trade that Pliny decried, but was shocked at the spectrum unleashed by chemistry.

Color used to carry very specific significance in clothing. Saffron yellow once signified maidenhood because it was a young woman's job to collect it. The purple from the murex shell could only be worn by royalty because of its rarity. But aniline dyes all exploded from the same test tube of tar, just as each of the new synthetic fabrics emerged from the same single ingredient—petroleum—in the DuPont chemists' laboratories.

From Orlon sweaters to polyester jersey dresses and Italian-style acrylic striped tops, synthetics evolved, and by 1960, manufacturers upgraded knitting technology to make flat knits—or "double knit"—heavy enough to be used to make both men's and women's pants and suits.

These new fashions made with synthetics were celebrated for transcending old distinctions of class. British designer Mary Quant, who helped loosen the grip of Parisian couturiers on European and American fashion with the iconic miniskirts on offer at her shop at the King's Road Bazaar in Chelsea, wrote in her autobiography, "Once only the Rich, the Establishment, set fashion. Now it is the inexpensive little dress seen on girls on High Street. . . . They may be dukes' daughters, doctors' daughters, dockers' daughters. They are not interested in status symbols. They don't worry about their accents or class. . . . They represent a whole new spirit . . . they are mods."

The immense popularity and versatility of the new petro-fabrics seemed, for a time, a boon to many American garment and textile manufacturers. But trouble was on the horizon.

In the 1960s, Japan reconstituted its chemical cartels and began to increase production of man-made fibers. By 1970, Japan was the world's second largest producer of synthetic fiber behind the U.S. Japan became a major textile supplier to apparel industries in Hong Kong, Taiwan, and South Korea, who in turn assembled and exported clothing to U.S. contractors, importers, and retailers. Kennedy's quotas had only covered cotton cloth, remember, so these passed into the U.S. market unhindered.

Although U.S. manufacturers faced a flood of low-priced fiber and apparel imports from Japan, Hong Kong, Taiwan, and Korea in the mid-1960s, the rapid expansion of the global market as a whole enabled DuPont's gross sales of fiber to grow as well, from $741 million in 1960 to $1.36 billion in 1970. But the apparently bottomless demand soon hit a wall.

As competition from Asia escalated, firms in the United States increased their output of synthetics. To keep up with the pace, companies built and rebuilt facilities to process the newest noncellulosic man-made fibers, and to do so—they consolidated. Meanwhile, natural fiber producers, which tended to be smaller, suffered.

The result was vast overproduction. In the 1970s there was a glut of economical polyester clothes in the market, and the fabrics came to be perceived as cheap. So much of the value of the petro-fabrics had been granted to them by the mystique of advertising: they were really just recombinations of oil, after all. When synthetics lost the cachet that came with being cutting-edge, the backlash against them was swift. After 1973, consumers increasingly viewed them with contempt, and synthetics as a proportion of their clothing purchases steeply declined. In 1985 an entire issue of *American Fabrics and Fashions* was dedicated to polyester, bewailing the fact that double-knit had become a byword for bad taste, tarnishing polyester's name.

When President Richard Nixon negotiated the Multifiber Arrangement in 1974, quotas were imposed for the first time on textiles and clothes made of man-made fibers. The scope of the Multifiber Arrangement, or MFA, to restrict imports was limited, however. It reduced quota *increases* for the coming year, but did little to stabilize or reduce the volume of imports. These quotas, like Kennedy's, would have unexpected consequences.

Foreign manufacturers, faced with per-piece quotas, looked for new opportunities to increase the value of their exports by making more expensive "fashion products." They began to produce products that targeted the large numbers of American women who were entering the workforce in the 1970s. "Career wear" was born.

In 1945, women had brawled for nylons: rabid with desire to secure a product that they had been told could secure them men's affection as they were abruptly shoved from the job market. In the early 1970s, they marched back to work, now draped in polyester. The quintessential "career wear" item of the 1970s was the pantsuit. Although designers, including Elsa Schiaparelli, had produced pantsuits before World War II, Yves Saint Laurent is generally credited with launching them into the mainstream with his "Le Smoking Suit" in August 1966. The first tuxedo designed specifically for women, "Le Smoking" was a bold statement: Manhattan socialite Nan Kempner was turned away from La Côte Basque in 1969 when she showed up wearing one. After being denied service, Kempner returned wearing just the jacket as a minidress. Women wearing pants for formal occasions was far from acceptable. Girls would not be granted the legal right to wear pants in public schools until 1972.

The pantsuits that began with Le Smoking defined the look of the "career woman," and women turned to them in the 1970s as a way to assert their right to exist in masculine workplaces. Business consultant John T. Malloy's 1977 best-seller *The Woman's Dress for Success Book* pleaded with his readers to abandon them: "In most business offices, the pantsuit is often a failure outfit. . . . If you have to deal with men, even as subordinates, you are putting on trouble. . . . If you want to be a liberated woman, burn your polyester pantsuit, not your bra."

But women had bigger problems on their hands than unsolicited fashion advice. Although they could dress the part of the upwardly mobile, self-determining woman, there was a worm in the bud: American women were moving back into the job market just as well-paying manufacturing jobs were moving overseas.

American women streamed into jobs that paid the minimum wage. According to one estimate, 70 percent of the new private sector jobs created between 1973 and 1980 in the U.S. were in the low-paid retail and service areas. The employment "boom" for women in the late 1960s and 1970s was chimerical: the media might have linked it to "women's liberation," but the reality was that these jobs offered little in earnings or upward mobility. "We may be approaching a situation like that in some industrializing third world countries," one economist declared, "where there has been a big increase in jobs for women . . . but the jobs don't lead anywhere, they don't lift women out of poverty." Indeed these decades witnessed the rapid acceleration of what has been termed the "feminization of poverty" in the U.S.

For the U.S. garment industry, the problems compounded. The new quota regime under the Multifiber Arrangement ironically seeded even more competitors to the U.S. garment industry. Under it, countries who had reached their export limit were incentivized to outsource production to countries who were new exporters. New exporters were permitted to trade with no quotas at first. Firms in Hong Kong, Taiwan, and South Korea subcontracted production to Association of Southeast Asian Nations (ASEAN) countries like Singapore, Vietnam, and the Philippines, where quota limits could be evaded, and labor costs were lower. Between 1960 and 1980, apparel production for export to the U.S. spread to countries around the world. By the early 1980s, more than one hundred countries were exporting garments to the U.S. market. By 1981, the U.S. trade deficit in apparel reached $7 billion.

In 1984, the trade magazine *American Fabrics and Fashions* released a special issue on "the import crisis." Fifteen percent of the rising U.S. trade deficit was because of apparel imports, they announced. The country now imported fifty-three yards of cloth and clothing for every one hundred yards made in the U.S. The nation's third largest industry, one that had contributed $45 billion to the GNP in 1983 compared to the automotive industry's $40 billion, was in danger. Trade liberalization had already caused massive job loss in the 1970s: 210,000 people worked in New York City's garment sector in 1970. By 1981, this figure had almost halved. Now, they warned, the 2.3 million workers who worked in fiber, textiles, and clothing manufacture were at risk.

Between 1972 and 1991, the number of workers in U.S. manufacturing is estimated to have dropped by 7 percent, with the textile and apparel industry accounting for just over three fifths of this decline. Organizing became more difficult, and working conditions deteriorated. Although textile workers in the U.S. had been largely thwarted in their efforts to unionize even before the imports began, garment workers had enjoyed quality, union work for two mid-century generations. Now, sweatshops reemerged.

In 1995, a raid by California and federal authorities on an apartment complex in El Monte, east of Los Angeles, revealed seventy trafficked Thai nationals being held against their will, producing garments for American name brands. By 2000, an estimated one half of all garment producers in the U.S. employed their workers in sweatshop conditions: that is to say, firms employed women immigrants and paid them wages that violated federally mandated minimum wage standards and other employment standards set in the Fair Labor Standards Act.

Carol Malony, who produced a line of lingerie in Los Angeles in the 1980s, and helped introduce American women to the lacy and luxurious lines of French undergarments through her work with Victoria's Secret, used to manufacture her own "Carol Malony" line in a Los Angeles factory. "It just got harder and harder," she said.

"Believe me, I wanted to find a way to keep producing in the U.S. I looked." Ultimately, though, Malony had to join the exodus, and moved production of her underwear to a factory in Pakistan. Now, she lives in Ho Chi Minh City, where she is an in-house lingerie designer for Fashion Garments Limited, a Sri Lankan–owned facility inside the Bien Hoa Industrial Zone.

In-house designers for factories are rare, but Fashion Garments hired Carol because they wanted to expand into intimates, and the strategy worked: H&M placed a huge order for her designs. Malony remembered when, in the 1990s, retail chains such as Macy's, JCPenney, Kmart, and Sears maintained full-time offices in Seoul, Taipei, and Hong Kong. They were soon joined by specialty chains like The Limited, The Gap, Esprit, and L. L. Bean. In these Asian cities, companies could contract more quickly with factories. Today, the internet has made these buying offices unnecessary. Designs can be produced in New York using software that makes it simple to send detailed manufacturing specifications across the ocean.

Export processing zones, EPZs, like Bien Hoa, where Carol works, have proliferated in the past half century. These zones are legal entities apart: sovereign space allowing unlimited, duty-free imports of raw inputs and capital goods necessary to produce exports. They are advertised to manufacturers as offering "less governmental red tape" and "more flexibility with labor laws for the firms in the zone than in the domestic market." They offer generous and long-term tax holidays and concessions to firms, along with communications services and infrastructure often superior to that in the host country. If in the immediate postwar period, American military umbrellas and infrastructure funds helped turn South Korea, Taiwan, and Hong Kong into major clothing exporters, today the export processing zone offers a miniaturized version of this kind of bubble: private security, private generators, and enhanced access to ports.

Just as high-flown anticommunist rhetoric helped build the Asian garment export industries, EPZ rhetoric insists they help national development and boost local economies. Critics point out that the lack of backward linkages into the host country—imported raw materials arrive, untaxed, to be processed, then leave without export taxes—make this improbable. What they *do* provide is easy access to low-wage-labor foreign multinationals.

Exiting the highway that ran north out of Ho Chi Minh City toward Hanoi, and passing through the toll to get on the road to the Bien Hoa Industrial Zone, my taxi was the only passenger vehicle among the eighteen-wheelers. We entered Bien Hoa though a manila brick arch, planted on either side with palms and white flowering magnolias, and circled past Racino Plast, Lucky Starplast, Boramtek Vietnam, the Taiwan Business Association, and Vingal Vnsteel. Lost, we pulled into a Peugeot factory to ask directions. On the showroom walls were blown-up images of the Eiffel Tower, a blond woman with her face pressed close to a brunet man with a five o'clock shadow. I called James Poleski, Carol's husband, who told me to wait, and I did under the shade of a tree on the corner of 15A and 3A. A Filipina who checked shipping at the aluminum factory chatted with me through the metal bars of her factory's compound. Every once in a while, a truck or a motorcycle buzzed by the otherwise empty streets. The Zone was uncanny: as large as a city, with wide pedestrian sidewalks, only the streets and sidewalks were both completely empty.

Jim came to meet me, and we walked the fifteen minutes up 3A to Fashion Garments Limited. At the security gate, Jim had them print me out a pass. Once inside, we walked through the production floor, first down a row of sewing machine operators producing Nike Golf polos in a gray performance fiber. Each of the factory's large aisles had a sign hanging over it with a company name and logo. Under Armour. Victoria's Secret PINK. In the Victoria's Secret aisle, the workers were making pink jersey zip-ups with the word "Pink" across the chest. Jim explained that companies basically committed to keeping a certain amount of factory space running full-time for a year, or for the length of a contract. This was a state-of-the-art facility: more convenient to big companies than the many much smaller units and webs of subcontracting that often characterize overseas production. A small entrepreneur who can afford space and sewing machines, but not shipping insurance, might do subcontracting work for a larger operation in direct contact with the buying agent for the brand. This facility did it all, and made it easy for the western buyer to come and contract for production. As we walked through the factory's sample room, where prototype versions of each design are fabricated to be approved by the buyer before going into production, Jim leaned over and said that this sample room alone was "bigger than a lot of *factories* I've worked in."

We walked up to the design room, which had glass walls overlooking the production floor. A big table lined with folded Adidas and Carhartt shirts had been set up at the entrance, put out by the factory for the Adidas Kids design team, who were visiting that day, so that they could see the various printing technologies available to them at Fashion Garments Limited. Three white women sat around a table with MacBook Pros and cups of tea. Another long table held the remains of complimentary snacks: long white ceramic trays of now cold french fries. One of the women, with frosted blond highlights and wire-rim glasses, was telling the others her method for making Baked Alaska. Through the plate glass that lined the room, you could see down to the production floor below. The workers, in a line, bent over their machines, were stitching the same seam over and over without break or pause in automatic movements, skilled movements, the movements of people trained to understand the difference a fraction of a second makes. No one was speaking, and only the sound of the machines was audible. This was a clean, new, LEED certified facility, the kind that bragged about itself in pamphlets to investors. But something about it was bothering me.

Jim and Carol had big desks at the rear of the glass-lined loft, surrounded by mannequins in lingerie. Carol was in her sixties, well put together, and had the air of a woman who had been well put together for decades. As we started talking about her early days as a lingerie manufacturer, my eyes drifted over to the women in front of their MacBooks. Their glass-walled studio perched over the sea of workers reminded me of a *New York Times* Sunday Styles section piece I had read about Natalie Massenet, founder of a company called Net-a-Porter. In the profile photograph, Massenet was at her headquarters, standing on a balcony looking out over hundreds of drones at desks arranged in parallel lines that stretched almost to the vanishing point.

It was as if, the photographer wished to suggest, Massenet had risen above. She stood in the pose adopted whenever the press wants to christen a new female titan: arms crossed, with a facial expression suggestive of amicable domination.

I had seen a similar profile of Tory Burch, put on the *Forbes* billionaires list in 2013. Burch made her fortune peddling the costume of the Upper East Side to a nation of women in middle management. Massenet and Burch were the emblems of a neoliberal feminism determined to frame exploitation in terms of opportunity and advancing freedoms. Burch's taglines were #EmbraceAmbition and "Feminism is about equality." This kind of "feminism" celebrates the upward mobility of a few women capitalists. It props up the narrative of steady progress for American women, and swallows minor inconveniences like the endemic and structural impoverishment of foreign and immigrant women laborers.

As the garment industry left the United States, it undid the work of industrial feminists like Clara Lemlich and Rose Schneiderman, who had the audacity to demand that intellectual satisfaction was the birthright of every sewing machine operator. This new brand of feminism didn't care to protect sewing work as good work; rather it scoured the earth to find the cheapest new sources of exploitable, female labor.

Working-class immigrants like Clara Lemlich had only managed to gain the public's sympathy in their strike of 1909–10 when they were joined by their bourgeois women sympathizers, the "Mink Brigades." But wealthy "feminists" like Massenet don't seem interested in standing shoulder to shoulder with working-class women. Rather, they looked out over them, in their insignificant multiplicity, through glass. And if these Vietnamese workers wanted to demand the same rights that Clara Lemlich had demanded, they would have to face off against employers who were literally a world away. The ILGWU had fought hard to organize the whole East Coast; the workers here would have to organize whole continents. And even that wouldn't be enough.

The language of anticommunism in Asia had trumped all other

concerns of the postwar era, and garment and textile industries had slipped away from the U.S. When this Cold War rhetoric was reprised by Reagan in the 1980s in Central America, it would usher in a new, and disturbing, chapter of the globalization of the U.S. garment industry.

11

Export Processing Zones

I see America spreading disaster. I see America as a black curse upon the world. I see a long night settling in and that mushroom which has poisoned the world withering at the roots.

—HENRY MILLER, "THIRD OR FOURTH DAY OF SPRING," FROM *BLACK SPRING*

It's like a little Puerto Rico, we're basically run by the U.S.," said Allan nonchalantly, as we drove around San Pedro Sula, the second largest city in Honduras and the country's largest manufacturing center. "Here there is more 'freedom,'" he added, with air quotes.

Allan had spent most of his adult life working as a production manager for companies like Gildan and Hanes, making socks and underwear for American bargain shoppers. All of this garment manufacture now takes place behind the gates of Honduras's export processing zones, known locally as "ZIPS." When export processing zones proliferated in the 1980s and 1990s, boosters of these zones claimed that the employment opportunities inside them would lift up local economies. If anything could refute that argument, it was Allan's story. After all, he wasn't just a low-paid garment worker: he was management. He had done everything right. And now, he said, he was moving to Canada.

Allan was born in 1986. His mother worked as a pharmacist and his stepdad in sales. Allan had been sent to private schools by his family. The public schools are so dramatically underfunded that the teachers have to teach students sitting on the floor, he said. He enrolled in UNITEC, in San Pedro Sula, in 2003 and graduated in 2009, majoring in industrial engineering. He got his first job in 2010 at Gildan, as a process engineer. He made and maintained a manual for all of the processes of the production floor, trained the workers, and audited the production floor. Allan started in knitting, moved to dyeing, and then to boarding, which is a process like ironing that removes wrinkles from fabric by using heat. After ten months he moved to product development. He went to work at Hanes, and for Grupo Kattan, a manufacturer for companies like Nike. Then he hit a pay ceiling earning $700 a month.

When Allan talks on the phone to his wife, who had gone ahead of him to Ontario to start her studies in a Canadian university, they compare grocery prices over the phone. Often, he said, items like grapes cost less in Canada. That $700 a month salary didn't go far in Honduras, he said, where his family of three typically spent $70 to $85 a week on groceries, "and that's *just* for what you need."

He said it was difficult to imagine how the textile and garment workers that he used to manage, managed. At the high end, minimum wage paid $465 a month, at the low end $263. Many of these workers have three to four kids. And besides, he said, it was only the really big companies that actually *paid* the legal minimum wage.

The only other job his college degree could get him in Honduras, Allan said, was work in a call center, but that work paid $500 a month at most. Unless, he said bitterly, you were the president of the Central Bank of Honduras, Rina María Oliva Brizzio, daughter of the president of Congress, who makes $8,300 a month even without a degree in finance.

I asked if his parents were going to be sad to be so far from Allan's daughter, who is three. Allan said his mom died a few years ago of diabetes. "She made bad decisions in her youth," he said. Then again, he added, "in Honduras, Pepsi costs less than water."

n scouring the globe for cheap labor, U.S. clothing brands are not merely opportunistic, they are also sometimes actively parasitic. Honduras is a case study: one in which U.S. corporations and the

U.S. State Department have worked together over decades to bring cheap garments to American consumers, framing job creation as a blessing for the Honduran economy while simultaneously engaging in political interventions that keep Honduran citizens poor. The story of Honduras's emergence as a garment exporter began in the 1980s, when Ronald Reagan moved to confront what he saw as a rising threat to U.S. interests—a communist drift in the Caribbean Basin. His two-pronged strategy was to consolidate U.S. military hegemony over the region, and to encourage the growth of export processing. He launched the Caribbean Basin Initiative (CBI), which granted military aid and one-way duty-free access to the U.S. market for a designated range of products.

U.S. garment and textile interests sensed an opportunity. In the early 1980s, many U.S. garment producers were struggling to compete with cheap imports from Asia. The Caribbean Basin offered companies both cheap labor and geographical proximity, a manufacturing annex where they could make goods at more competitive prices. Textile firms in the U.S., meanwhile, saw that garment factories in the region could absorb their cloth at a time when struggling U.S. garment manufacturers were buying less and less. Asian garment manufacturers certainly weren't going to purchase American textiles when they had such a vast textile industry in their own backyard.

In 1984, the year the Caribbean Basin Initiative first went into effect, United States textile corporations, apparel firms, importers, and retailers began lobbying to loosen import quotas and reduce tariffs in the Caribbean Basin. They added an important caveat: if U.S. markets were to be thrown open to clothing sewn in the Caribbean Basin, they had to be made with U.S. cloth. In the early 1980s, the "Big Three" Asian suppliers of garments to the U.S. market—Hong Kong, South Korea, and Taiwan—began subcontracting in the Caribbean to get around the quota restrictions limiting their access to the U.S. market. U.S. textile lobbyists wanted to make sure that in raising quotas, they weren't inadvertently helping Asian producers. The result of these lobbying efforts was the 1986 Special Access Program (SAP), which allowed clothes made of U.S. fabric and sewn in the Caribbean Basin to enter the U.S. with low or no tariffs.

Reagan implemented SAP unilaterally and it went into effect in 1987. Under this program, apparel exports to the United States assembled in the Caribbean more than doubled in only four years, from $1.1 billion in 1987 to $2.4 billion in 1991. "The Caribbean," declared *Forbes* magazine in 1990, "is becoming America's garment district."

The Special Access Program for apparel enticed investment by making export to the U.S. easier, and supplied funding for the development of local infrastructure. Offshore production in low-wage areas demands more than cheap labor. It requires water supply, transport, telephone and other communications services, tax holidays, rental subsidies, and training grants. Export processing zones in the Caribbean Basin Initiative countries offered all these features, sponsored by the World Bank, the International Monetary Fund, and the United States Agency for International Development (USAID).

USAID had been in existence since the early postwar period, funding programs to support the infrastructure and social programs of developing countries. Under Reagan it began to move money through business promotion organizations rather than recipient governments. When funding was channeled to apparel production in the Caribbean Basin, the USAID drew criticism, most notably from the National Labor Committee (NLC). A 1992 report put together by the NLC, "Paying to Lose Our Jobs," charged that U.S. taxpayers' money was being used to subsidize job flight under the guise of foreign assistance.

Even more absurd, the National Labor Committee pointed out, was the fact that Asian garment producers were reaping benefits from American taxpayers' support to the Caribbean. By the mid-1990s South Korea was the largest Asian investor in the region. Most of Guatemala's assembly industry was Korean-owned. In the free trade zones of Kingston, Jamaica, the majority of investors were from Hong Kong. Taiwan, too, was well entrenched in Central America.

Although the U.S. put pressure on Caribbean governments to limit the entry of Far East firms, these efforts proved largely unsuccessful, complicated by the fact that the Asian firms were often contractors making goods for American brands. Even without manufacturing, American retailers monopolized control of the most lucrative aspect of the garment trade: design and merchandising. Large U.S. retailers moved to bypass domestic manufacturers by launching lower-cost private-label lines, like JCPenney's Arizona, Saks Fifth Avenue's The Works, or Federated Department Stores' Inc. They relied on firms based in Hong Kong, Korea, and Taiwan to coordinate the actual manufacture, and these firms subcontracted the garment making to the Caribbean Basin.

Although the Caribbean Basin Initiative was intended to spur economic growth, in practice, apparel brands used the Caribbean as a source of cheap labor while scrupulously curtailing any independent production that might benefit local competition. U.S. companies brought little technology and low-skill and low-wage work. At the same time, quotas made it almost impossible for local companies to develop their own export products for the American market.

In some places, local garment manufacturers were thriving before the Caribbean Basin Initiative crippled them. This pattern first played out in Jamaica. Even before the CBI was enshrined in law, Jamaica's prime minister Edward Seaga had enthusiastically supported its underlying logic of trade liberalization and structural adjustment, and set out to transform his country into a garment exporter. Seaga's handling of the Jamaican economy met with Reagan's frequent and vocal approval. Seaga became a crucial consultant to Reagan in forming the Caribbean Basin Initiative's policies, and, in turn, Reagan held up Jamaica as an example of the type of development that the CBI would reward. In Seaga's first three years, U.S. assistance amounted to $500 million, compared to $56 million in the last three years of the previous government. Jamaica became the second-largest per capita recipient of American aid. Loans from USAID, the Inter-American Development Bank, and commercial banks moved cash into the country, along with multilateral aid.

In the ensuing years, the Jamaican garment industry was transformed. Small and medium-sized local enterprises gave way to a group of large-scale firms, most of which were foreign-owned, and almost entirely export-oriented. In 1980, 85 percent of the clothing worn by Jamaicans came from domestic manufacturers. The industry exported only about a quarter of its products, and most firms were

Jamaican-owned. In 1992, by contrast, just 15 percent of the domestic market was supplied by the local industry. Upward of 97 percent of apparel exports were produced in free zones, and Jamaican ownership had fallen off precipitously. Jamaica became one of the most indebted nations in the world.

The story of Jamaica's rapid rise as a garment assembler for the U.S. was to repeat throughout the Basin. The "Three Jaguars"—El Salvador, Honduras, and Guatemala—surpassed Jamaica in the sheer quantity of clothing they exported to the U.S. Exports from El Salvador rose 3,800 percent between 1985 and 1994. At the same time, the real wages of workers were slashed. In 1998, a garment worker in the export processing zone made an average of 56 cents an hour or $4.50 a day, which was nowhere near enough to provide for a family's basic needs.

Practically all the major American clothing retailers had arrangements in the region. The list of those found operating in El Salvador, Honduras, and Guatemala under the Caribbean Basin Initiative included Walmart, Kmart, JCPenney, Sears, Saks Fifth Avenue, Calvin Klein, Christian Dior, Victoria's Secret, Spiegel, Liz Claiborne, The Limited, and The Gap.

Hiding behind anonymous subcontracting arrangements, these companies benefited from the most exploitative working conditions in the Americas. Asian factories in Central America and the Caribbean were notorious for brutal labor practices and anti-union tactics. A National Labor Committee–facilitated cross-border campaign in 1995 against Mandarin International, a Taiwanese-owned plant in the San Marcos Free Trade Zone in El Salvador, uncovered stories of abuse involving the employment of minors, death threats, physical violence, forced overtime, starvation wages, and mass firings of workers who joined unions. Mandarin subcontracted for a variety of U.S. companies, including JCPenney, Eddie Bauer, Liz Claiborne, J. Crew, Casual Corner, and The Gap. Asian companies gained a reputation for brutality, but they were operating on behalf of American retailers. In the words of sociologist Cecilia Green: "the most successful and 'advanced' fractions of capital do not appear to get their hands dirty."

Occasionally, a public relations storm would connect a western brand to the exploitative conditions. "You can say I'm ugly, you can say I'm not talented, but when you say that I don't care about children . . . How dare you?" said Kathie Lee Gifford tearfully on her TV talk show, *Live with Regis and Kathie Lee,* in 1996. She pleaded with the American public after an investigator in Choloma, Honduras, discovered that the workers producing her $300 million private label clothing line for Walmart, a brand which promised a portion of sales to children's charities, were Honduran children.

Later that year, in a Rose Garden press conference, Bill Clinton announced the creation of a task force that would look into conditions in sweatshops. Kathie Lee stood by in a pastel skirt suit. "As long as there is greed in the world, the problems will remain," she intoned philosophically. "As long as there is one dollar to be made by somebody on the back of somebody else's work, somebody will make it. But that's what we're all here [to talk] about today, to make sure that there's a watchdog organization in place. That we can find these people, and weed them out, and restore the good name to this industry." Kathie Lee had engineered a remarkable turnaround. In a matter of months, she had gone from being a national villain to a heroic crusader. Little, however, was to change for the industry.

Twenty years after Kathie Lee's public relations fiasco, Allan and I drove out to Choloma to visit the factories. In Vietnam, I'd had no trouble gaining access to an export processing zone by introducing myself as an interested investor.* In Honduras, the act hadn't worked.

The reason no one returned my emails, I learned, was that Honduran EPZs and factories played inside baseball. In Honduras, these zones are commonly owned and operated by the same small group that runs manufacturing facilities. They rent space in EPZs to themselves through a web of various alias companies. For instance, Grupo Kattan owns INHDELVA, one of the main duty-free zones in Choloma.

---

* I toured Linh Trung EPZ on this pretense. I visited the Bien Hoa Industrial Zone 1 as the guest of James Poleski.

Grupo Kattan also owns multiple manufacturing facilities, producing 720,000 garments monthly for companies like Jos. A. Bank, Stitch Fix, Pronto Uomo, Kenneth Cole, Vanity Fair, Ministry of Supply, Dickies, VF Corporations, Van Heusen, and Men's Wearhouse.

Shut out of the zones themselves, I took in the perimeter. Laborers were clearing out of work at one of the export processing zones owned by Grupo Lovable as Allan and I drove down a side road, past guards with big guns and a wall topped with razor wire. A metal gate swung open to let out a Crowley truck. Stalls on the street, right by the exit, sold shoes, melon slices and mangoes, cell phone cases, leggings, Barbie and Snow White towels. One couple came out of the factory gates, leaving together on a motorcycle. Three girls stopped to chat with a friend who owned a stall. There were a few women who looked older, but for the most part these workers were teenagers. Decommissioned American orange school buses loaded up with employees who would take the buses back to their homes in San Pedro Sula, ten miles to the south. One girl who passed us in red leggings, pearl earrings, and with her hair pulled back in a headband was thwacking the back of her wrist against her palm rhythmically as she walked. She did it so casually, but this sore wrist she was trying to tend was the banal price of a twelve-hour day spent at a sewing machine.

The day before, Allan and I had driven to a squatter encampment by a riverbank on San Pedro Sula's northern edge. Chickens pecked while milling about, and a kid climbed a pile of trash. Many of the people here work as house cleaners, Allan said. A lucky few get jobs in the ZIPs. At another settlement of squatters by the nearly dried-up Río Blanco, a cow wandered the riverbed, while women with plastic bowls headed down to the water. White stones jutted like bones from the rolling green grass grown over dried-up riverbed. Another boy swung a rock tied to string over his head. The mountains in the north appeared tinted in blue as dusk fell at around 6 p.m., as it always does this near to the equator.

The riverbank was lined with shanties with sides stitched together of corrugated metal and cast-off plywood. A few more durable cinder block structures were scattered among them. Settlements like this have become an uncertain refuge for thousands of Hondurans pushed off their lands in recent years, like those evicted from their farms when businessman Miguel Facussé acquired a 22,000-acre palm oil plantation in the Aguán through a series of purchases from farmer cooperatives. Locals say these "purchases" were made through intimidation and coercion.

When the river rises, which happens increasingly often as tropical storms grow in intensity, Allan said, the people living on its bank lose everything. Every time, they are flooded. The smell of burning plastic hung in the air. Allan pointed out the cable that the community uses to siphon electricity off the grid. Sometimes houses have dishes for satellite TV. Sometimes they have TVs, he said. "At every single river in the city you will see people like that."

The poverty on display here is of the kind used to boast of the "opportunity" provided by the ZIPs. The Caribbean Basin Initiative didn't create wealth for workers, but in Honduras, it did lead to the rise of a class of oligarchs who would exert a powerful right-leaning force on the nation's politics. Many of the elite families like the Canahuatis and Facussés rose up in the 1980s on the business enabled by the Caribbean Basin Initiative. They made their wealth from the foreign investment that flowed through the garment export processing sector. So when the Honduran government attempted to improve conditions for workers, these elites were the people who had the most to lose, and they intervened.

Former Honduran president Manuel Zelaya was a member of one of the two traditional conservative parties that ruled Honduras for decades on behalf of a handful of oligarchic families who controlled, along with the U.S. and transnational corporations, the vast majority of the Honduran economy. Zelaya was elected in 2006, and espoused progressive positions, taking his cue from the left and center-left governments that had arisen in the 1990s and early 2000s in El Salvador, Venezuela, Argentina, Bolivia, Brazil, Ecuador, Uruguay, and elsewhere. Zelaya supported a 50 percent increase to the minimum wage and urged the government to restore the land rights of small farmers. He blocked attempts to privatize the publicly owned ports, education system, and electrical system. As a result, wealthy business owners who had backed Zelaya during his election withdrew their support, and his power began to slip.

In April 2009, Zelaya announced he was asking voters to decide on a nonbinding survey question on June 28: Should the November presidential election also include the election of delegates to a constitutional convention, or *constituyente,* to be held at some undetermined point in 2010 or 2011? Seeking representation, Honduran grassroots social justice activists had demanded the formation of a *constituyente.* Such constitutional conventions were newly implemented in Venezuela, Ecuador, and Bolivia, expanding democratic rights for traditionally disenfranchised groups like indigenous peoples, women, and small farmers.

On the eve of the June 28 elections, the military refused to distribute the ballots, although, under the Honduran constitution, they were legally required to do so. At 5:30 a.m. on June 28, 2009, in the first successful Latin American coup in two decades, the Honduran military, acting on behalf of the oligarchs, deposed Zelaya, installing in his place Roberto Micheletti. In the midst of international outcry, and as Hondurans flooded the streets in protest, the Barack Obama administration moved quickly to stabilize the situation, helping the new regime buy time until an already scheduled election in November could take place. The election was to be fraudulent—opposing candidates withdrew from the race. The U.S., however, quickly recognized the results, and congratulated the new president, Porfirio Lobo, on his victory.

Honduras had long held strategic importance to the U.S. imperial project. In 1954 the United States used Honduras as the base from which to launch a CIA-led coup that overthrew the democratically elected socialist president of Guatemala, Jacobo Árbenz, an act that initiated decades of state-sponsored genocide against Guatemala's Mayan indigenous population. In the 1980s, the U.S. used Soto Cano Air Base at Palmerola, operated jointly with the Honduran government, in the contra war against the left-wing Sandinista government of Nicaragua. Soto Cano, staffed by six hundred U.S. troops, retained strategic significance for U.S. military interests in Latin America on the eve of the coup in Honduras. It was one of very few places in Latin America that the U.S. could land large planes.

If the desire to keep Soto Cano was one factor that motivated the Obama administration to protect the coup, the blandishments of the Honduran business community, its garment and textile industry in particular, were another. Weeks after Zelaya's ouster, in July 2009, Lanny Davis, who is best known as the lawyer who defended President Clinton during the impeachment proceedings, was on Capitol Hill. He was testifying against exiled president Manuel Zelaya before the House Foreign Relations Committee. Davis, a partner at the law firm Orrick, Herrington & Sutcliffe, had been hired by those responsible for overthrowing Zelaya's rule. "My clients represent the CEAL, the [Honduras chapter of the] Business Council of Latin America," Davis told a journalist. "I do not represent the government and do not talk to President [Roberto] Micheletti . . . I'm proud to represent businessmen who are committed to the rule of law."

Juan Canahuati, who has been identified as one of the main intellectual authors of the coup, was from one of Honduras's largest garment manufacturing clans. The Canahuatis own Grupo Lovable, which owns three export processing zones in Choloma and makes products for Costco, Hanes, Russell Athletic, Foot Locker, JCPenney, and Sara Lee. It is one of the largest industrial groups in Central America. In 2010, another member of the Canahuati clan, Mario, was President Porfirio Lobo's foreign minister, even while he remained the director of Grupo Lovable. Jacobo Kattan, president of Grupo Kattan, is another of the oligarchs named by Honduran sociologist and economist Leticia Salomón as one of the chief proponents of the coup. The pro-business oligarchy was eager to keep U.S. aid dollars flowing in, and it seemed the feeling was mutual.

U.S. law demands that funding to a foreign government be immediately suspended in the case of a coup with "substantial military involvement." On July 24, 2009, a cable came in to Secretary of State Hillary Clinton from the U.S. ambassador to Honduras that stated, "There is no doubt that the military, Supreme Court and National Congress conspired on June 28 in what constituted an illegal and unconstitutional coup against the Executive Branch." Yet Clinton and Obama both scrupulously avoided the use of the phrase "military coup." Money continued to flow into Honduras.

Conditions for average Hondurans on the eve of the coup were by no means idyllic, or even particularly bearable. They were overwhelmingly poor. Major newspapers were owned and controlled by oligarchs. However, Honduras did have the strongest labor movement in Central America. Grassroots social movements, particularly among women and indigenous peoples, were flourishing. Some newspapers, particularly San Pedro Sula's *El Tiempo*, allowed for political dialogue. Independent publications were published openly and community-owned radio stations were not harassed. After the coup, all that changed.

During President Lobo's first six months in office, eight journalists were murdered, according to Reporters Without Borders. Lobo oversaw a near total disintegration of Honduran criminal justice, and the rule of law along with it. Assassinations, rapes, kidnapping, and drug trafficking proliferated without consequence. The welfare state was gutted. This withdrawal of basic services paved the way for the free reign of organized crime. The murder rate shot up, becoming the world's highest. In response to the devastation, thousands of Hondurans fled to the United States.

The Honduran elite framed this implosion to their advantage. In late September 2011, as Honduras was devastated by chaos, President Lobo flew north for a speech at the United Nations, where he warned that gangs and drug traffickers were on the rise, and that there were now "serious threats" to the lives of Honduran people. This rhetorical framing was so successful, labor historian Dana Frank argues, that in 2014, when 57,000 undocumented and unaccompanied minors from Central America crossed over the Mexican border on the way to the U.S., fleeing for their lives, neither the Honduran regime who had taken power in the coup, nor the American backing that made that possible, was assigned responsibility. To the American right-wing press, the Honduran children were simply taking advantage of soft border enforcement. The liberal papers, meanwhile, reported that gangs and drug traffickers had made Honduras so violent that children were forced to flee for their safety. Neither version hinted at the reality that, as Sarah Chayes put it in a report for the Carnegie Endowment for International Peace, "Urban violence and out-migration are by-products of the corruption of the very government that enjoys US (and European Union) support."

Honduras first appeared on my radar in 2012. I noticed that the tag on my brother's college hoodie read, "Made in Honduras." On the same day, I read an article in *The New York Times* that reported four Afro-Indigenous Honduran civilians, two of them pregnant women, had been mistakenly shot and killed by a pair of State Department helicopters carrying Honduran security forces and U.S. advisors. Four more were injured. How could our ordinary sweatshirts, I wondered, be made in places so apparently chaotic that innocent women were mistaken for drug traffickers and shot down out of helicopters? This was flawed thinking, the same kind as that displayed by a journalist for *The Guardian* when he wrote, in 2013, that in San Pedro Sula the export processing zones "churn out New Balance T-shirts and Fruit of the Loom boxer shorts for markets abroad. It should be a bustling place, but there is little movement on the streets and the air is tense." The writer's assertion that "it should be a bustling place" belies the reality that the violence in Honduras and the country's export processing industry are inseparable: one necessitates the other. EPZs provide islands of security and infrastructure to companies so that they can avail themselves of advantageous labor rates. Meanwhile, average citizens struggle to find safety or security, and extralegal violence is sponsored by the police. The EPZ does not make a city "bustle." It is an extraction unit, just like the banana plantation, bauxite mine, and sugar plantation it replaced.

The office of the Honduran Manufacturers Association is located on the Altia tower's eighth floor, inside the Altia "Smart City," a gated enclave just around a bend in the highway from a squatter settlement on the Río Blanco. The glittering glass tower forms a marked contrast to the appearance of the rest of the city. The tower houses call centers rented out to businesses by the owner, Yusuf Amdani, the president of Grupo Karim's, a major presence in textiles and real estate in Honduras. A young Honduran like Allan could spend his entire life within Amdani's suzerainty. Indeed, Allan almost had.

Amdani owns UNITEC, Allan's alma mater, which gives a discount to students who work in the call centers of the tower he also owns. Students and call center workers on their lunch break can shop at Altera, a mall within the Smart City, also owned by Amdani. When they graduate, they can find full-time work at the call centers, or in one of his many manufacturing facilities in Choloma. There, his holdings include spinning mills, fabric plants, and garment factories. Past the Altia tower, Yusuf Amdani's own house is easily recognizable from a distance because it is built higher up in the hills than any other structure in the city, set flagrantly above the line above which it is technically illegal to build.

I stopped at the tower on my way to the major port in San Pedro Sula. With the help of my translator, Gustavo, I explained to the receptionist at the Honduran Manufacturers Association that I was writing a book and needed access to the port to understand how export processing zones helped the Honduran economy. Astrid dropped three glossy pamphlets in my hand, one featuring a photograph of a Honduran woman in reading glasses and red lipstick sitting at a sewing machine, with the title "We are ready" printed across it. She told me to ask for Carla Johnson.

When we arrived, Gustavo called through the metal gate at the armed guards, and gave Carla Johnson's name. The guards slid open the gate and then slid it shut behind us, searched the car, and motioned us through. Carla Johnson wore heels, sweeping dark eye shadow, a blond wig, and large hoops threaded with white plastic beads. She deposited us in the conference room. Portraits of Lobo's successor, President Juan Orlando Hernández and First Lady Ana García Carías, hung on the wall beside a hash of flags and a wooden ship's steering wheel. The manager came to meet us there. Alfredo Alvarado was a product of an expensive private school, funneled into this job through family connections from his former job at Gildan, where he oversaw quality control. I understood suddenly Allan's sense that only with the right connections could he have risen any further in Honduras than Gildan management, something Alvarado had accomplished with ease.

This port received goods from EPZs in Choloma, Villanueva, Progreso, La Lima, Bufalo, Dos Caminos, Naco, and El Polvorín. Almost all of it, Alvarado said, went to the United States. He was about my age, holding two phones in his hands. A busy man.

We chatted about the main imports—Texas cotton shipped from Houston, grain, fuel, and textile machinery. The port is open twenty-four hours a day, he said. It's three days by ship from here to Point Everglades, Florida, or to Houston, or Miami.

Not everybody was so thrilled about the port's recent boom time, facilitated by President Orlando in lockstep with exporters' business interests, or so eager to assist in the smooth functioning of the transport system. I asked about the protesters who blocked the bridge in Choloma by burning tires recently, the teachers who protested the government's attempt to privatize the education system, and the doctors who demonstrated against plans to privatize healthcare. Yes, he said, shaking his head, like a wounded lover. "And not everybody wants to take the risk of trying to ship into this port when there are protests going on. *That*," he said, looking at me with earnest eyes, "that's like terrorism."

After the interview, Gustavo and I drove to the beach. From under the thatched roof of El Sapo Enamorado, "The Toad in Love," a beachfront restaurant in Puerto Cortés that caters to locals and working-class weekend tourists from San Pedro Sula, I watched the tiny Caribbean waves, grateful for the breeze. Two teenaged girls waded out into the ocean, twisting, bending, the way bodies become languorous and free when they are close to the sea. Across the inlet, a container ship slipped out of the harbor and started its slow procession across the horizon.

When the container ships arrived on U.S. shores, they would carry no visible signs of the country, or the history, they are so entangled in. Buyers of the Hanes boxer briefs wouldn't be able to see the squatters who had to cope not only with flooding, but with drinking water polluted with textile dye effluent, nor would they know the names of the murdered journalists and environmental activists. But as hard as the garment industry works to keep out of consumers' sight the lives and lands it touches, there is a part of the trade that literally touches every shore on earth.

Clothing pollution is not just a plague on the ecosystems of developing countries. There is a new kind of water pollution coming from clothing production that is pervasive, invisible, and devastating. Rivers running red with dye are a dramatic symbol of the environmental toll of the garment industry. But this pollutant is too tiny to be seen by the naked eye: the minuscule man-made plastics called microfibers that are now used to make synthetic fabrics.

In the 1990s, polyester gained popularity once more, thanks to the advent of microfiber. "Micro" was "the fashion message of the 1990s," DuPont representatives announced triumphantly, "with the company's own 'micromattique' poised to take the lead." Under five millimeters in length, and with diameters measured in one thousandths of a millimeter, microfibers are vastly more versatile in producing different fabric feels. However, because the fibers are so tiny, no filter inside washing machines can catch them, and they pass through the sewage to treatment plants, most of which also lack filters fine enough to catch them. Treated wastewater is then dumped into rivers or seas, bringing the plastic fibers with it.

Once the tiny plastics are in the ocean, there is no way to remove them. There, they enter "the diets of marine animals and accumulate throughout the food chain," writes journalist Brian Resnick. The plastic pieces are "toxic to wildlife on their own, but they can also act like sponges, soaking up other toxins in the water." A 2018 study showed microplastics in the stomachs of three quarters of fish caught at mid-ocean depths in the northwest Atlantic. Even animals in the Mariana Trench, where the Pacific Ocean sinks to its deepest reaches, have been found to be ingesting microfibers.

Microfibers represent the dominant source of plastic pollution in the ocean. They have been found in the sediment surrounding beaches, in mangrove groves, in Arctic ice, and in products for human consumption. "The average person ingests over 5,800 particles of synthetic debris" a year, a 2018 paper looking at contamination in beer, tap water, and sea salt found, and "most of those particles are plastic fibers." Every year, half a million tons of plastic microfibers seep into the ocean, the equivalent of fifty billion plastic bottles. Microplastics are a dramatic new problem for the world's water, even while older ones persist, now magnified by the sheer scale of garment production.

Garments made from microfibers are increasingly sold by fast fashion retailers like Zara, Forever 21, and H&M—retailers that found a way around the dwindling fortune of the department store by producing both more and increasingly faster changes to their offerings. Traditionally, department stores had an average of approximately three "turns" or seasonal deliveries of merchandise a year. In 2000, retailers were getting deliveries up to once a month, which then seemed an outlandish pace. Today, that pace is quaint.

In 2010, JCPenney joined the fast fashion model, partnering with Italian company Mango, which is capable of moving new styles from design studio to store in a month. According to JCPenney's CEO, "If you only deliver four times a year, there's only a reason to come to the store four times a year." Zara, founded in 1975 and based in A Coruña, in the northwest corner of Spain, helped create this paradigm. Zara stocked new fashions in stores every two weeks. In 2014, the company invested in four warehouses close to the Madrid airport, from which they began to ship almost 500,000 garments every day, making deliveries to each of the company's stores twice a week. Inditex, the group that owns Zara, became Spain's biggest company, and Zara the world's largest fashion retailer.

But not even Zara's manic unveiling of novelty items could have achieved the explosion of garment production that took place in the first decades of the twentieth century without the rewriting of global trade rules.

In the 1980s, bankruptcies and declining profit margins prompted the retail industry to push hard to further liberalize trade, removing quota restrictions and tariffs on imports. In 1984 Sears, JCPenney, and seventeen other retailers and a host of retail associations formed the Retail Industry Trade Action Coalition (RITAC) to lobby for global sourcing. They had lobbied for lower tariffs from Caribbean

Basin countries; they would go on to lobby for NAFTA—which allowed for the unrestricted flow of textiles and garments into the U.S. market from Mexico, seriously damaging American fabric and clothes manufacturers—expanded trade with China, and finally, for the elimination of the Multifiber Arrangement, which had controlled the flow of garments around the globe since 1974. When the Multifiber Arrangement quotas were phased out in 2005, the cost per unit of imports declined steadily. The U.S. garment industry was finally dealt its mortal blow.

As recently as 1997, over 40 percent of all apparel purchased in the U.S. had been produced domestically. In 2012 that figure was less than 3 percent. The abandonment of quota limits eliminated all impediments to buyers, leaving them free to source from whatever country gives them the best price. Countries competed on price alone. Honduras is doing well as an exporter under this new paradigm simply because its workers are desperate.

As clothes get cheaper, people buy more. In 1984, 6.2 percent of the average household's expenditure was on clothing; in 2011 it was 2.8 percent. Even as the outlay declined as a percentage of paycheck, American closets expanded: garment purchases per capita grew 60 percent between 2000 and 2014. The proportion of these garments made from synthetics expanded also. In 2013, polyester, nylon, acrylic, and other synthetic fibers made up 60 percent of all clothes worldwide.

Increasing wealth inequality and the abundance of cheap clothes have gone hand in hand. In addition to the disappearance of manufacturing, poverty in the United States has also been fed by the dramatic decline of salaries paid for retail jobs. According to the Bureau of Labor Statistics, the 2018 median pay for retail sales workers was $23,340 a year.

Retail workers are not only lower paid, they are also more minutely monitored. In 2007 Ann Taylor rolled out the Ann Taylor Labor Allocation System, or ATLAS, to monitor each employee's sales per hour and dollars per transaction. With this data, the most productive employees could be made to work during the busiest hours, and unproductive salespeople would see their hours cut. The name was important, one executive said, "because it gave a personality to the system, so [employees] hate the system and not us."

The global supply chain that brings us our clothing can seem intimidatingly complex. But what if it isn't? Clothing brands farm out the making of goods to whomever in the world can do it most cheaply, and then divorce themselves in the eyes of customers from the facts on the ground. That's pretty simple. The complexity only comes in when brands really need it to: to prove how many layers removed they are from the human lives being touched—sometimes lost—as a direct result of their purchase orders.

Western brands have come to prefer a model for ethical commitment, commonly enshrined in the "Corporate Responsibility Code" or the "Code of Conduct." These codes proliferated in the early 2000s as a PR response to the revelations of labor abuse overseas. But studies conducted by sociologists on the ground suggest these codes make no fundamental difference to the way big retailers go about purchasing goods or in the way contractors and subcontractors go about making them.

The effectiveness of such codes is demonstrated as follows: in Bangladesh, 256 factory fires occurred in the apparel industry between 1990 and 2012, resulting in the deaths of 1,300 workers and hundreds more injuries. In a study conducted of the six largest fires during these years, researchers found that in all cases "exits were blocked, fire-fighting equipment was deficient or absent, and training was nonexistent or minimal." In every case, the companies sourcing from the factories were major European and North American brands. Each of these brands had codes of conduct with "specific references to safety standards and expectations of compliance among their contractors."

Clearly, these codes do little to protect workers. This became spectacularly clear on April 24, 2013, at Dhaka's Rana Plaza, a complex that produces garments for Bon Marché, Primark, Carrefour, Benetton, Inditex, JCPenney, Walmart, Store Twenty-One, C&A, The Children's Place, DressBarn, Essenza, FTA International, Iconix Brand, and Mango among others. That morning, a government engineer warned workers gathered outside the building that visible cracks in support columns showed that the building was not safe. Still, managers insisted that laborers enter the building to work. Virtually every brand and retailer that sourced from the complex administered their own code of conduct. The building had been built without full permits and floors had been added on top beyond original permissions. At 8:45 a.m., as the workday began, the building collapsed. More than 1,100 workers were killed, and over 2,500 were injured.

In the wake of the collapse, momentum was great enough to lead to the May 2013 Accord on Fire and Building Safety, currently signed by more than 150 global brands and retailers, by the powerful Bangladesh Garment Manufacturers and Exporters Association, and by two international union federations, IndustriALL and UNI. The accord was the product of a multiyear series of negotiations that only reached resolution in the immediate wake of the collapse in Rana Plaza. The accord rejected the voluntary Corporate Social Responsibility codes of conduct model and demanded, rather, that all signatories sign contracts that ensured joint financial responsibility between Bangladeshi manufacturers and the global brands and retailers that use them. Just like the contracts that the International Ladies' Garment Workers' Union had jointly signed with jobbers and manufacturers, ensuring that the former could not shunt responsibility for worker conditions to the latter, these were legally binding obligations. Their enforcement could take place in the court of the home country of the signatory party.

Although American retailers represent 22 percent of Bangladesh's apparel export market, all of its biggest firms refused to join the accord. The Gap, Walmart, and at least fifteen other companies that source products in Bangladesh instead established a rival "Alliance for Bangladesh Worker Safety." The most important feature of the American "Alliance" is that it legally liberates American brands from ever being held accountable.

The same forces that had driven the rise of the industrial fabric trade at its point of origin: willingness to exploit women, willingness to exploit nature, and colonial violence, had reasserted themselves with a vengeance to build the global garment trade of the twenty-first century. It is a fearsome beast. But it isn't all-powerful.

The capital-intensive synthetics industry, like the fast fashion system with which it is entwined, must metastasize in order to survive. That fact makes it voracious, but it also makes it weak. Meanwhile, even as the fast fashion system has been hurtling toward achieving its grotesque proportions, another kind of production has been quietly taking hold, driven by people interested in creating more intelligent, humane ways of working. They work with many materials, although there is one fiber that has generated a particular passion among them. It is a fiber that, although it can be made compatible with vast industrial scales, can also work well on very small ones. It is an ancient fiber, historically associated with the common people, the poor, and the humble: wool. Its story demonstrates that sometimes when an industry grows to the point where it hits a dead end, it can reconstitute itself on a more modest, sustainable scale.

Wool

12

Army of the Small

Do not be afraid, little flock, for your Father has been pleased to give you the kingdom.

—LUKE 12:32

Outside the Buckhorn Bar & Parlor in Laramie, Wyoming, one evening in February 2013, a couple of guys from a North Dakota fracking crew complimented me on my Woolrich blanket coat. I loved this coat, although I felt self-conscious wearing it sometimes, because of the blithe way Woolrich had co-opted Navajo iconography. I had bought it in a thrift store in Laramie, which contains a higher concentration of thrift-store Woolrich than any other place I know of.

The air is thin in Laramie, which, at around seven thousand feet, stands at a higher elevation than Denver, the "Mile High City," by a good two thousand feet. It was 20 below outside, a cold made more bearable on the High Plains because of the dryness. Inside the Buckhorn Bar, the walls are plated with taxidermied elk. A weekly open mic night provides one of the few entertainments on offer in this part of southeast Wyoming. Despite its vast territory, Wyoming contains the smallest population of any state in America. Mule deer still far outnumber people.

I thanked the guys for the compliment on my blanket coat and asked them why *they* weren't wearing any wool.

"This is all regulation gear," one of them said, gesturing toward the black synthetic jacket and pants combination he was wearing, complete with reflective strips. "We have to wear it on the rig. It's supposedly fireproof."

"You think that stuff would protect you if a rig exploded?"

"Definitely not," one of them said, and laughed. "I ashed on one of these once by accident and it burned right through."

What an irony, I thought, that these men were not allowed to wear wool up on a rig in subzero temperatures, in the very part of the country where wool had once been produced for a vast American fabric industry.

Right here in Laramie, the University of Wyoming had at one point been the only university in the country to offer a PhD in wool. The university's Wool Department was created in 1907—when the state of Wyoming was just seventeen years old, and home to more than six million sheep and fewer than 150,000 people, a ratio of about 41 to 1—with the goal of improving the quality of western fleeces.

In the late 1930s, the USDA tasked the UW Wool Department with using its Wool Laboratory—a small pilot plant for scouring wool that would grow into a semicommercial operation—to develop federal standards for wool fiber, particularly as they pertained to fiber diameter, length, and shrinkage. The ones they developed would determine labels we see on wool products, so that fabrics marked "Super 100's" were comprised of wool fibers with an average width of 18.75 microns or finer; while "Super 250's" indicated 11.25 microns or finer.

Access to plentiful grass on the open range alongside strong wool and lamb prices created Wyoming's first major sheep boom in the 1880s. Wyoming sheepherders competed for grass with cattle ranchers, and "away from the settlements the shotgun is the only law, and sheep and cattlemen are engaged in constant warfare," Wyoming banker Edward Smith testified before Congress in the early 1880s. An 1897 tariff on Australian wool started a second boom, and by 1900 Wyoming had more than five million sheep. As grass became scarcer, conflicts escalated. These conflicts were brutal. In 1905 masked riders rode into a sheep camp in Big Horn County and shot, dynamited, or clubbed to death four thousand sheep, burning the herder's sheepdogs alive. Nevertheless, sheep herds kept expanding. By 1908, Wyoming led the U.S. in wool production.

In addition to performing scouring and research services, the UW Wool Laboratory became a hub of research, a place to work out the best diet for minimal wool shrinkage, and breeding protocols to maximize wool production. Further research ventures of the Wool Department extended throughout the world, and faculty traveled internationally on USDA and USAID programs. They published research carried out in Afghanistan, Iraq, Iran, Europe, Australia, New Zealand, and China. A career in wool might look like that of Robert Homer Burns, onetime head of the Wool Department, who worked from 1937 to 1939 with the U.S. Department of Agriculture as a wool shrinkage researcher and marketing specialist. He traveled to China to study carpet wool in 1946, and went on to serve as consultant to the Iranian government in New York.

From its inception, the Wool Department sought to improve the quality of Wyoming wool, through careful testing and breeding recommendations. By mid-century, the project had succeeded: it increased both the quality and quantity of Wyoming wool. Wyoming sheep alone produced almost 17.5 million pounds of wool in 1950.

Like many American projects, the work of the Wool Department and the industry it supported were vastly productive, and destined to last only a few decades. By the mid-1970s, trade liberalization and competition from cutting-edge acrylic fibers caused the price of wool to tank. Some years, the price of wool was so low that sacks of wool were left to rot in warehouses and barns. Wyoming's sheep producers had to adapt, and they started breeding their sheep to optimize the meat, letting wool quality slip. And all the work done by the Wool Department to increase the quality of American wool was rapidly undone.

In February of 1977, in the midst of an energy crisis precipitated by a global shortage of petroleum, Jimmy Carter famously appeared in a televised fireside chat wearing an oatmeal-colored wool cardigan to dramatize the fact that he had turned down the heat in the White House in an effort to conserve energy, imploring Americans to likewise turn down their thermostats. But the energy crisis was not resolved, as Carter quaintly proposed, by Americans who turned down their thermostats and bundled up in wool cardigans. Rather, it was resolved by finding bigger stores of hydrocarbons, commonly know as coal, in the American West, a rich supply to be exploited in new and novel ways.

At Black Thunder, a coal mine in the Powder River Basin, which stretches between northeast Wyoming and southeast Montana, I watched a train pull out of a loading dock. "To me, that's a beautiful sight," the tour guide told me, "having that train go out loaded with coal, going where it needs to go."

The Powder River Basin is huge: about 120 miles east to west and 200 miles north to south. It holds a deposit of coal large "enough to light the United States almost into the 23rd century," in the words of environmental writer Gary Braasch. Up to one hundred coal trains left the Powder River Basin daily, bound for power plants to the east and south. Some went west toward Vancouver, then by ship to China.

Black Thunder Mine opened in 1977, the year of Carter's oatmeal sweater, and for years it was the largest coal operation in the world. All the mine's processes were computer-controlled, and in a darkened room back at headquarters, we tracked the blinking lights representing the trucks as they moved through the mine, picking up thousands of tons of coal and snaking their way back like so many Pac-Man ghosts. Outside, the coal was loaded into massive silos via conveyor belt. The mine had storage capacity of more than 100,000 tons, so in the chance of an unforeseen stoppage, the coal trains scheduled to pick up would not have to leave empty.

The other members of the tour and I piled into a Suburban to move out into the coal field. I sat next to Mike, an MBA student from the University of Wyoming. Every time we stopped for gas on the drive up from Laramie, Mike bought a Red Bull. He told me that when he was stationed in Iraq, he drank Red Bull all the time. Another soldier's mother was an employee at Red Bull and she would send cases of it. He remembered the feeling of his heart pounding out of his chest when he was on watch, from the combination of adrenaline and caffeine. He told me about how he used to shoot out speakers on the streets when the Imam sang the call to prayer.

"Why?" I asked.

"Because it was annoying," he said.

Sending young men like Mike to the Middle East to achieve political stability appeared to me about as sane, in that moment, as it had been to send Wyoming wool specialists to Iraq to provide local Iraqis with advice on how to raise sheep.

Zawi Chemi Shanidar, in northeastern Iraq, is home to the earliest known site for the domestication of sheep. A comparative analysis of the faunal material from the proto-Neolithic site shows that sheep were domesticated there at the beginning of the ninth millennium BC, although it's possible domestication may have occurred earlier among nomads, who then would have transferred knowledge of shepherding to settled peoples.

In what is now Syria, Israel, and Turkey, a warming postglacial climate from about 10,000 BC caused huge stands of wild grain to flourish in the regions, supporting the rise of humanity's first permanent settlements. Purposeful planting began between 10,000 and 7,000 BC—something paleontologists can tell from changing seed forms—and animals, too, began to be domesticated. Humans, who used to hunt animals and drag them home, now rounded them up alive to store them, with fodder, to be individually slaughtered as needed. This event in mankind's history is stored in fossil records. Domestication selects for greater docility, so in the period when it first arose, skeletal remains show animals with weaker necks, shorter muzzles, and less prominent incisors.

The second phase in the domestication of animals arrived at around 4,000 BC, when people in Mesopotamia realized they could extract materials from their animals other than meat and hides. Kept alive, they could provide secondary products: milk, wool, and strength to pull the plow. As people discovered they could get a steady supply of cloth from live sheep, the wool on these sheep's backs changed in character. Wild sheep, and the earliest domesticated sheep, were hairy, but by selective breeding practices early domesticators created breeds that were woolly.

At this juncture, wool joined the plant fibers, linen and cotton, to become a staple of human clothing. Another animal-based fabric, silk, arrived at roughly the same time. Unlike silk, which can only be produced by a settled agricultural society, wool was the cloth favored by nomads, or seminomadic pastoralists. Taken together, plant and animal fibers—linen, cotton, silk, and wool—formed the basis of human clothing until the advent of rayon, and then petro-fabrics, in the twentieth century. Fossil fuels, however, crept into our closets long before the advent of polyester.

Beginning in the 1820s, coal became a critical component in the making of clothing. Like the steam-powered cotton mills of industrial England, electric-powered denim mills in Xinjiang today consume thousands of tons of coal each year. That was why I was visiting the Powder River Basin.

The Bucyrus 257 WS Dragline, which was at work dragging coal when we drove up in the Suburban, is just as crucial to the production of clothing as the spinning frame and the loom. Among the world's largest machines, the Bucyrus, our guide said, "could build an Olympic size swimming pool in a couple of hours." Mining here in Thunder Basin was a two-part process. The earth on top of a coal seam was first scraped away, and then the coal seam was blasted with dynamite. The Bucyrus dragged a huge shovel across this blasted coal in order to load it into massive trucks. "Beautiful piece of equipment," the guide remarked.

Once, he said, a Japanese company set up a small structure here at the mine to test how well it would do under seismic stress waves, since the explosions that are set off daily create waves as big as earthquakes. When I blew my nose, I realized my snot had turned black. We drove next to an area of the mine that had been blasted, but not yet stripped, so we could experience what it was like to walk right over a coal deposit. As we picked our way over the black rubble underfoot, the tour guided explained that "this used to be an inland sea. And then climate changed. So, what that says to me is that the climate is always changing."

"I think I'm gonna stop here," he said. "Any questions?" Nobody had any. "COAL IS GOOD," he said, by way of conclusion.

Wyoming was, in fact, once an inland sea, and also once a rainforest. A good portion of the world's extant dinosaur fossil record comes from here. And it is true that earth's climate has vacillated greatly over time. What our guide had not mentioned, however, was that these big fluctuations in temperature correspond to moments when big loads of carbon pass in and out of the atmosphere. For instance, after two tectonic plates crashed into each other to form the Himalayas, the temperature of the earth plummeted. This is because, scientists believe, the rapid breakdown of rock caused by the collision accelerated a phenomenon called silicate weathering, which draws carbon out of the atmosphere, and locks it away in the calcium carbonate released from the rocks.

Textile production is one of the most energy-intensive industries there is, responsible for one tenth of all global carbon emissions. The vast amount of labor that was once poured into spinning and weaving by human hands has not been erased: it has been replaced by electricity, which is to say, by carbon.

World War II brought the last big boom for Wyoming's sheep industry, and its numbers declined steadily. In 1984, Wyoming's sheep population fell below one million. In 2011 the U.S. Department of Agriculture counted just 275,000.

Falling profits induced sheep ranchers to cut costs, and like others, the sheep industry of the West evolved in the postwar period to become reliant on an exploited workforce. More than three thousand people from Peru's central highlands have migrated northward on H-2A visas to work as shepherds for American ranchers since the late 1960s, their three-year contracts facilitated by the Western Range Association. Peruvian shepherds legally earn $650–$750 a month to herd sheep 24/7, for three years, on Wyoming's High Plains. The position of the H-2A sheepherder entails an unparalleled brutality among legal forms of exploitation in the United States, with perhaps the exception of the United States' population of incarcerated workers. A report produced by the Migrant Farm Worker Division of Colorado Legal Services identified such practices on behalf of employers as withholding documents, coercion, control of movements, and lack of access to church or medical attention. Although legal, the arrangement bears all the hallmarks of human trafficking as defined by the Polaris Project, an NGO that works to combat modern-day slavery.

The carefree life of a shepherd guarding his flock is a central image in the fantasy of the pastoral. And this is indeed fantasy.

Sheepherding can be, and often is, carried out on an industrial scale. However, sheep and wool are also eminently compatible with small-scale production. And they have become central to a widespread turn toward local fiber production in the late twentieth and early twenty-first centuries.

Rather than relying on high doses of coal and petroleum to fire large machinery and transport materials across continents, there is an increasing interest among environmentalists and people with a longing for handcraft, in the U.S. and elsewhere, in working with materials that can be found close at hand. Often, for the fabrication of garments, that has meant working with wool.

When American wool fell behind in quality in the 1970s, scouring facilities across the United States disappeared, making it more difficult to process wool locally. When they returned, they would be geared toward cleaning much smaller quantities of wool. Small-scale fiber production, ranging from hobby farms to full-time businesses, have grown up alongside the burgeoning fiber craft movement. This has stimulated the rebuilding of infrastructure on a new, modified scale, resulting in the creative reuse of earlier machines and processes. Smaller farms engendered smaller mills.

In 2012, I visited Fingerlakes Woolen Mill, in Genoa, New York. I don't know what I was expecting to see, only whatever it was, I drove right by it. I stopped and turned around. On my second pass, I noticed a small oval sign and pulled in the driveway of a buttercup yellow farmhouse with an old red barn beside it. Perhaps I had been looking for something more industrial.

Jay Ardai greeted me in the driveway. He was mostly bald, but wore a salt-and-pepper beard. We stepped into a low-slung gray outbuilding that had eluded my attention as I pulled in. Inside, it smelled profoundly of lanolin, a wax secreted by sheep. Fluorescent light fell through stainless steel drying racks onto green and gray cast iron machines. All of the technology in the mill dated from between 1925 and World War II. The wool carding machine was about my height, with long cylindrical drums coated in metal teeth that rotated to pass wool between them.

To assemble his mill, Jay Ardai purchased one of each of the machines that an early-twentieth-century woolen mill would have used to transform just-clipped, still-dirty wool into yarn. In their original setting, each would have been placed on a factory floor among dozens or hundreds of identical machines, sometimes filling a whole building. For Ardai's purposes, one of each was plenty. Fingerlakes Woolen Mill mostly did custom work, which meant people sent fleeces to Ardai to be processed. Some wanted their wool washed—the most time-consuming aspect of wool processing—while some wanted it carded, and some wanted finished yarn.

Small mills like Ardai's depend on a proprietary instinct among fiber enthusiasts, Ardai explained. They did not simply want roving, a cloud of combed wool that is ready to be spun, or yarn; they wanted roving or yarn from *their* sheep. Ardai also had some clients who visited fiber fairs to pick out a perfect fleece for their project, and sent it to him for processing. "They'll see the slightest difference between this fleece and that fleece and they'll home in on it like a laser." Ardai himself was still a relative newcomer on the fiber scene, which is, he assured me, a *scene*.

Hand spinning has achieved a large, passionate following in the United States in recent years, sustained by community guilds, festivals, online groups, national yearly events, and regular local gatherings. It is a community large enough to support several active manufacturers of spinning wheels along with a handful of custom wheel builders.

According to American folklorist Mathilde Frances Lind, the hand spinning revival of the 1970s associated spinning with "idealized historical narratives of self-sufficient pastoralism." But the newer crop of spinning enthusiasts seek satisfactions that "are more direct and personal than symbolic." Commenters on message boards devoted to spinning speak of RPMs and wheel specs, rather than romantic justifications for hand spinning in the machine age. They just like doing it. Fortunately for these pragmatic-minded enthusiasts, after the utopian fires that fueled the 1970s spinning revivals cooled, dedicated spinners continued on, building up infrastructure that is still prevalent: festivals, publications, schools, supply businesses.

The recent revival of fiber crafts extends to encompass knitters, weavers, felters, dyers, and embroiderers. Socially and politically, this movement has a very broad range. Mainstream forms can be found in publications like *Martha Stewart Living*. Some fiber craft communities carry strong ties to the anarchist milieu, sharing with them a dedication to nonhierarchical organizational forms and a politicized practice of resourcefulness.

Scholars have argued that fiber handcrafts grew in popularity alongside increasing exposure and scrutiny of global sweatshop practices in the 1990s, and that craft culture, by emphasizing slow production, can be seen as an explicit rejection of mass production and its exploitative tendencies. Fiber culture also rose up alongside the internet, and has a strong presence online. As business professors Stella Minahan and Julie Wolfram Cox have argued, the fiber craft scene presents a way to connect online that is "based on material production using traditional craft skills," and cultural theorists sometimes speak about the fiber scene within the frame of New Media Studies. Participants at the Digital Politics and Poetics Summer Institute, held at Queen's University in Ontario in August 2004, "set out to explore the surprisingly plentiful interconnections between knitting as a form of activism and computer viruses."

Before Ardai bought Fingerlakes Woolen Mill in 2001 together with his wife, he designed and built oceanographic instruments while she mapped the seafloor in polar regions. With more and more PhDs competing for a stagnant amount of government grant money, the couple decided to try something else. She was already a fiber enthusiast. Ardai himself had no particular interest in wool. However, "a machine's a machine, and I'm kind of a gearhead," as he puts it.

Ardai was "a super technician who could fix almost anything," according to oceanographer Stan Jacobs, and a critical crew member to have aboard if something went wrong, mechanically, while a ship was in an Arctic ice floe. In the search for the *Titanic* in the early 1980s, Ardai constructed delicate parts for deep-sea cameras and a huge winch capable of holding up to ten kilometers of electro-mechanical cable while staying perfectly level. In the 1990s, he had orchestrated supply drops onto drifting ice. With textile machinery, he would discover new engineering challenges.

Ardai showed me his Bramwell feeder, a component of his carding machine. He explained the historical developments that had led to its invention. Carding is the process of combing out wool fibers so that they can be spun. Mechanical carding, he said, preceded the advent of mechanical spinning by at least a half century. When the carder was first developed, it did not need to produce roving of a consistent volume or density, because the spinner was a human being, and she adjusted for these qualities by eye. The advent of mechanical spinning necessitated a way to ensure that wool emerged from the carder at a consistent thickness. At first, people stood by the carder and fed it handfuls of wool at regular intervals. Then, an English minister named Bramwell invented this feeder, essentially a long trough which also worked as a scale. The wool rode up a conveyor belt and into the trough, and when it reached a certain weight, the bin tipped over, spilling the wool onto another conveyor belt leading to the carder. The action of the trough tipping, Ardai explained with obvious relish, "throws out the clutch that drives the belt," which temporarily stops more wool from traveling up into the trough.

Ardai had made small modifications to the machines to engineer them to do things they weren't meant to do. Yarn is plied by twisting two strands together to make a stronger yarn, and Ardai adapted his spinning frame to ply his yarn for him, by looping it overhead and doubling it back through the frame. Like a reader who had come to live with the authors he loved, Ardai was clearly working in dialogue with the original inventors of these machines. "You're looking at one hundred fifty years of thought that went into this," he said, gazing at a detail in the spinning frame, "little increments along the way." His inventions and improvisations were a continuation of a ritual performed across time, in the language of design.

Even without Ardai's mechanical understanding, it was difficult to remain insensible to the beauty of these machines. I had to remind myself that I was seeing them when they were quiet and still. Immense power and danger were implicit in their hulk. Dozens of iron cylinders spiked with rows of sharp metal teeth. The external belts—which, as Ardai pointed out, clearly dated the machines to before the formation of OSHA—could easily rip off a human scalp. "You have to keep your wits about you when you work on this stuff," he said.

Ardai's wife arrived home then from a library book sale where she had been volunteering. She wore a long, loose floral skirt and a baggy denim shirt with small appliquéd images of horses, squirrels, houses, trees, card decks, and bouquets scattered across the front. Together, the three of us walked out behind the barn to see the sheep.

Goats gamboled up eagerly to the couple to have their ears twisted, something they were quite fond of. But the sheep did not budge, sprawling in the shade of their lean-tos like hungover teenagers, wisely avoiding the hot August sun. These were Hog Island sheep, a breed that evolved when a group of domesticated sheep were abandoned on an island off the coast of Virginia. As a result, they were highly self-sufficient animals capable, for example, of lambing alone. They are what is known as a critical breed. On the spectrum of endangeredness, the appellation "critical" is code red. Ardai said that every year he could sell the fleece of one of these sheep for as much or more than the sheep had originally cost.

Ardai estimated that he spent about half of his time in the shop and half on his farm. In a sense, his lifestyle was a cartoonish amalgam of the Jeffersonian and Hamiltonian ideals: a country gentleman with a small industrial operation on the side. The operation at Fingerlakes Woolen Mill was by no means aiding in the national aggrandizement Hamilton imagined would come from industrial power. It was not "growing the economy" in the sense of the term when it is fetishistically incanted in the press and by politicians. It had no employees, and ideally, it helped its customers to buy less and make more for themselves.

Fingerlakes Woolen Mill demonstrated that there were ways industrial machinery could be used other than to generate huge pyramidal structures of power and wealth. They could, instead, be used to take on the most arduous aspects of textile processing, while leaving both the materials and the creative control in the hands of producers themselves.

In 1978, as the world worried over what it called an "energy crisis," the Croatian-Austrian social critic Ivan Illich took aim at this term, asserting a crisis of another kind. For Illich, the problem wasn't running out of carbon, but what reliance on it was doing to humans. To him, "high quanta of energy degrade social relations just as inevitably as they destroy the physical milieu." Wyoming's scarred landscape, with its earth-rattling Bucyrus Dragline, and its shepherds enduring solitary confinement on subarctic plains, seem to validate Illich's assessment. As the warming climate became undeniable, Illich's voice became more insistent. "Preindustrial ethics," he argued in 1989, had held that "technology was a measured tribute to necessity, not the implement to facilitate mankind's chosen action." Reversing that relationship had unleashed disaster. By 1989, the warming atmosphere made it "intolerable to think of industrial growth as progress," he wrote. It was in fact "aggression against the human condition." The solution, Illich believed, lay in a radical reorientation of men and machines, one that would provide a universal outlet for the one resource evenly distributed among people: individual genius.

Like Illich, many of the people reenvisioning fabric are interested not in throwing out the machine and abandoning technology, but revising its use, and adjusting its scale. This group includes among its ranks many sheep and wool enthusiasts. It also includes another American subculture engaged in small-scale clothing production, and the resuscitation and reinvention of old technologies: denimheads. These are young (mostly) men (mostly) who developed an interest in narrow shuttle looms made by heritage American companies like

Crompton and Knowles or Draper, because of their love for Japanese selvedge denim.

The "selvedge" refers to the long, neat edge along both sides of a bolt of cloth. To weave, threads are strung taut in a row, parallel to one another. These parallel threads, which remain still during the weaving process, are called the *warp*. The thread that is woven under and over these threads at a perpendicular is called the *weft*. To move the weft thread through the warp, for nearly all the history of weaving, you needed a *shuttle*. The motion of the shuttle creates the selvedge, in the multitudinous moments when the weft thread reaches the edge, and turns around.

The power loom, which was first used in the late eighteenth century, is essentially a handloom with a motor strapped on. It throws a wooden shuttle back and forth carrying a little supply of thread wound on a quill. Then, in the 1960s, a Swiss company called Sulzer developed a machine that did away with the shuttle. Instead of using one continuous weft, the Sulzer loom shot individual threads across, one by one, using pneumatic pressure. The wider, shuttle-less loom ran much faster and with fewer technical challenges than the clattering cast iron power looms. Only one thing was lost when the Swiss looms were adopted by manufacturers: the selvedge.

The selvedge is a valuable thing for making a garment, because it doesn't need to be hemmed. It will never fray on its own. With denim, the selvedge had found an unlikely fame. When denim looms were designed, they were made to produce a bolt of cloth just wide enough to allow the leg pieces for trousers to be cut along the selvedge, leaving enough space in between to cut extras like the pockets, the fly cover, and the waistband. Newer looms dispensed with this practice. They also eliminated the selvedge down the outside seam of both trouser legs. Instead, the raw edges would be gone over with a kind of zigzag stitch to keep them from fraying.

The selvedge, however, is beautiful. There is a thoughtful economy to the way it connects weaving fabric with sewing it into a garment. This alone could account for nostalgia for selvedge denim, and the narrow shuttle loom. But selvedge denim's rise in the late nineteenth century and fade beginning in the 1960s, alongside the myth of American exceptionalism also tracked the rise and fall of American industrial engineering and labor.

By the end of the 1980s, selvedge denim had disappeared from America. Denim became wider, paler, shoddier. Virtuosity on the part of the Japanese would ultimately rehabilitate it. In postwar Japan, a fascination with American youth culture had prompted fashions that took the form of facsimiles more ingenious than the originals. As denim factories in the American South transitioned to wider-style looms that allowed them to weave more material and cut costs as they faced dire threats from Asian manufacturers, Japanese producers developed the process of weaving selvedge denim on narrow looms into a high art. Fixated on the minutiae of American menswear, they developed "slow" manufacturing processes that imitated the errors produced originally by the rocking of a cast iron loom on a wooden factory floor in North Carolina. Magazines like *Popeye*, launched in Tokyo in 1976, minutely documented L.A. fashion and particularly the clothing on the UCLA campus in their inaugural issue.

Moreover, the Japanese brought to selvedge a centuries-old indigo dyeing tradition. To achieve the effect, dyers extract indigo from the plant *Indigofera tinctoria*, a legume. Natural indigo did not appear in Europe until the sixteenth century, mainly from India (hence its name), but has been used as a dye for many thousands of years. Japanese dyers achieved subtleties in color and patterning that yielded green and violet undertones shimmering within and underneath a deep indigo blue so rich and mesmerizing that, when Japanese denim began to trickle into America in the 1990s, it would elevate many young American denimheads to a state of near-religious ecstasy.

An urban legend persists that the Japanese "bought up" American looms to develop their selvedge, but in fact Japanese denim was made on looms made by Toyota, which made looms before it made autos. Most Drapers were smashed up and discarded or sold for scrap, and those that remain are now highly prized. Eventually, interest in Japanese selvedge denim ran strong enough among a certain type of young American man that its production was reintroduced at Cone Mills, in Greensboro, to cater to the dozens, and then hundreds of small jeans-making companies springing up across the U.S.

. . .

The first denimhead I met was Luke Davis. I had been friends with his older brother, Cooper, first. Soon after Luke arrived in Cooper's kitchen in December 2008 with a couple of his college friends, the four boys retreated into a bedroom where Luke spread a pair of jeans made of Japanese denim on a twin bed, unrolling them as one might unwrap a relic retrieved from a secret cave, or a jewel brought up from a well. For a moment they sat in rapturous silence and then they all began talking at once, marveling over the tonalities in the indigo dye: the purples, emeralds, flecks of yellow that appeared in certain light.

Luke dropped out of Penn State a year later and moved back to West Hartford, where he had grown up. He began making jeans in his mother's driveway with two of his high school friends who had never left Hartford. One had been working as a pizza delivery boy and the other as a builder. Both were eager to join Luke's mission. Before long, they had moved into a warehouse in downtown Hartford and were doing a brisk business under the name Hartford Denim Company.

Luke was a person whose interests unfolded like a perpetual motion machine. Getting into jeans got him interested in vintage sewing machines, which got him interested in machining. If you want to run vintage sewing machines, you have to be able to get your own parts made since replacements are not commercially available. On the Fourth of July 2016, on a visit to Hartford, Luke explained to me a new theory of his, that man was someone who made tools, and that this was fundamentally what made him human. What about clothes, the fact that people wear clothes? I contested. "Clothes are a tool," Luke said adamantly, meaning, I suppose, that they can serve to expand the range of possible human actions.

The young American denimhead could have gone to developer boot camp and moved to Austin or San Francisco to try to make the next Uber. He could, in short, have become a member of the tech elite who form a major market for the jeans he makes. Although the denimhead's métier and personal style derive cachet from the 1940s

American worker that he decidedly is not, the app developer's attempt to absorb this same cachet by way of workman's boots and selvedge jeans is unjustifiable to another degree. The denimhead values both the analog world and physical labor.

Another thing to note about the American denimhead is a tendency to commit to the hollowed-out postindustrial city in which he was raised. It is critical to his identity and he becomes a booster of this city. He becomes a kind of organic intellectual, organizing labor along new and semi-utopian lines. The small city reciprocates with feature pieces in the calendar section and together the group of artisans ride a wave of local prestige that helps buoy their spirits and mitigate their sense of living outside of time. As idyllic as this sounds, it is not, however, an easy life.

Small-scale clothing production in the U.S. is no easier a thing to make a living at than small farming.

Jack Roche, owner of Old North, a clothing store in downtown Asheville, North Carolina, carries jeans made by the Hartford Denim Company, as well as many other small American jeansmakers. Roche is evidence that a person can be into denim without being a utopian. "Levi Strauss stole Jacob Davis's idea, and Davis died in a ditch in Reno, and that's how the story always goes," he said, giving me an informal history of denim when I interviewed him in 2016. Roche said that since he opened his store in 2012, he'd seen the number of small denim companies explode, and he thought very few of them would make it. Every little town had a guy, or a group of guys, making jeans, he said, and he thought it was only the brands with investors and marketers who would survive and last.

Some people got into the scene for the cachet, Roche complained. There were kids with big inheritances who could afford to lose money on a business making selvedge jeans. They crowded the market, making it harder for other small makers to break through. Roche's time as a retailer of American-made clothes had rendered him somewhat cynical about the whole concept. He told me that people come into the store and ask, "Is this American-made?" When he shows them the section with the American-made jeans, "they say 'good,' and go to Walmart, like they were just doing their duty to make sure I was carrying it." The biggest buyers of American-made aren't Americans, he said, but the Chinese. Roche ships to Taiwan and to mainland China weekly, as well as to Indonesia: Indonesians, he said, "they can't get enough."

Denim aficionados know about Greensboro, both as the historic center of American denim production, and as the home of the Cone Denim Company's White Oak Mills, which made selvedge denim using cast iron Draper looms from mid-century. I toured their factory in 2016.

Past huge spindles full of white and blue thread, wide indigo vats through which thread was towed via a vast pulley, I was brought through the rows of the old 1940s Draper looms, their solid cast iron bodies clattering away, and then shepherded over to the clean, modern Nissan X3 looms weaving wide. "Thank goodness our forefathers had the foresight to put some aside," I was told in the boardroom after, in a meeting with one of Cone Mills' publicists. As selvedge denim grew more popular, the Cone Denim Company had pulled out whatever selvedge looms they had saved from their past operations, then had to go searching for more. At the time of my visit they were planning to expand the selvedge program, but not long after all that would be scuttled.

Cone Mills was at the time of my visit owned by a conglomerate called ITG (International Textile Group), which was formed from the merger of Burlington and Cone. The group also owned mills overseas: in China, Vietnam, South America. Its American plants made fabric for airbags. ITG would be bought up at the end of 2016 by a capital fund, at which point, a few months after my visit, the White Oak selvedge denim looms were shut down.

Cone Mills was not the only one in Greensboro interested in reviving some of the city's denim legacy. There, I also met a vintage loom aficionado named Evan Morrison, whom I knew about through Luke of Hartford Denim. Evan had been raised in Greensboro, and grew up going to secondhand stores, estate sales, and exploring abandoned houses, amassing a unique archive of American denim history.

He received a scholarship to attend a luxury brand marketing MBA program in Paris. When he returned home in 2012, he interviewed with Wrangler, which was owned by the Greensboro-based megalith VF Corp., which also owns Lee, Rustler, Eastpak, JanSport, The North Face, Reef, Vans, SmartWool, Timberland, Nautica, and over twenty other brands.

At his interview, Evan was asked what he'd do in a dream scenario. "I said," Evan recalled, "'I want to launch a made-in-USA category of well-made clothing that pays homage to the original items that were made by Blue Bell Wrangler and I want to do it *exact*. And I want to do it here in the U.S., and I want to push it to the marketplace.'" At the time, VF Corp. was not interested.

Evan went his own way, and opened a storefront in downtown Greensboro to sell custom and vintage jeans. He also set himself up as a go-between, making purchases from Cone Mills on behalf of small jeans-makers who couldn't meet minimum fabric orders on their own. Ultimately, though, Evan didn't want to just buy denim manufactured at Cone: he wanted to make his own fabric. He noticed that there was a hole in the market for shirting material. Selvedge jeans were wildly popular, but the market was crowded, while the supply of heritage shirting was nonexistent. Besides, the average consumer purchased five shirts for each pair of pants.

Evan's dream was to build a factory that could also function as a museum: a place to keep vintage shuttle looms running that would allow the public to view them at work. Having a museum that runs its looms is also the best way to care for the machines. Like cars, old looms are best preserved by being used.

At the time that I visited, Evan had his eyes trained on a huge cache of vintage textile equipment sitting in a warehouse in Asheboro, just south of Greensboro. We drove down together to look at the machinery, along with a man named Ralph Tharpe, who had been the design engineer at Cone Mills throughout the 1970s. Evan and I rode in Ralph's rental car. I gazed out the window at the passing lush, green trees swaying in the warmth.

Ralph was tall, with a leonine face, brown eyes, dark eyebrows, and white-gray hair brushed straight back. His accent, he said, embarrassed him: it was a mountain accent—he was from the foothills of western North Carolina. Ralph said he was a poor student, but his SATs were good enough to get him into the engineering program at NC State University, in Raleigh. It was 1967, and he wanted to be an aeronautical engineer. He found he didn't have the math for it, and switched over to NC State's Wilson College of Textiles. When he graduated in 1971, he was chosen to work on the Sulzer weaving project. He attended the Sulzer technician school in Spartanburg, South Carolina, in 1972 to learn how to operate the cutting-edge, shuttleless loom that was about to permanently alter the landscape of American fabric production.

When Ralph finished his training, he started work as a supervisor in a Cone Mills plant that was essentially an experimental facility working on developing different kinds of fabric with the Sulzer. When Levi's made the decision to start making their signature 501 fabric on a wide loom instead of a narrow one, Ralph worked with the Product Quality Department to help set the standards for the wide fabric.

By the time the White Oak plant's narrow shuttle looms were powered down to make way for wide looms in 1985, Ralph had been relocated south to work on corduroy finishing. "And I was glad that I was away because that would have made me sick," he said. Despite having presided over a degradation he felt keenly, Ralph had erected small retaining walls whenever and wherever he could. For example, throughout the 1970s, 1980s, and 1990s he was continually pressured to put cheaper, less durable open-end thread in the warp. He had already been forced to put it in the weft, and he said, "Well there are just some things I won't do."

Unfortunately, it would be Ralph's fate to watch the decline of corduroy also. "One could make the argument that we cheapened the fabric so much that it became no longer what it was and people didn't want to buy it," he told me. When he started in 1972, Ralph said, "we were making the lightweight, 14 wale with 140-some picks. It was a very fine, tight, nice, beautiful fabric. And then when we shut down, some of those styles were down to 112 picks. Some even lower." With the lower pick count, "the little tuft that makes that corduroy edge comes out easily, so you have to put a bunch of glue in the back. The fabric doesn't feel good anymore. It doesn't drape the same way that it did."

Ralph's father and his grandfather before him sold overalls in a little company store attached to their gristmill, called "Tharpe's Mill." Pre-Depression, Ralph says, they were selling overalls for around a dollar and forty cents. Local people bought the overalls, and the wage for a farmhand at that time, Ralph said, was around 20 cents an hour. "So that means that the jean cost minimum, *minimum* seven hours of work." When we take that into consideration, Ralph reasons, "The very least expensive jean we should find would cost forty bucks. The *least* expensive. But you can buy them in Walmart now for fourteen. But it's not a jean that's gonna last very long," he says, with his eyebrows raised, "and they're spun with open loom." "Open loom" refers to a type of yarn that is fatter, and easier to break. Why had the price of jeans stayed the same since 1960, he wanted to know, while the price of a truck had gone up by a factor of ten?

Ralph and Evan got on the subject of napping, which was the process by which multitudinous thread ends, left protruding from the surface of a flannel, are fluffed up to achieve a soft, fuzzy surface. Evan was currently making a line of flannel shirts woven on vintage looms in traditional Cone Mills plaids, but he still needed to find a domestic napper. He had gotten thread spun for samples in North Carolina and dyed to reproduce the traditional colors. The samples were woven by a woman named Rabbit Goody, one of the only remaining people in America who make cloth on looms old enough to have made the original Cone flannels. While Rabbit was working on the prototypes, Evan was trying to find someone to nap the flannel, and trying to get his hands on the old machines being stored at the warehouse in Asheboro.

It was partly because of Ralph Tharpe's nostalgia for old shuttle looms that Evan Morrison wanted to bring him down to Asheboro with us to see the machines. But he also hoped that, with Ralph's imprimatur, it would be easier for him to convince an investor that getting the old machines running was a feasible plan.

The machinery we were on our way to see was in the process of being deaccessioned from the American Textile History Museum in Lowell, Massachusetts, which was going bankrupt.

In 2006, the museum packed up thirty-nine 18-wheeler Schneider trucks with the extant record of American industrial textile history, and drove it south to Asheboro, North Carolina, to sit in a state of limbo. The machinery was deposited in no particular order into the lichen-scented chambers of the former Cedar Falls Mill, which had closed for Easter in 1978 and never reopened again.

"So, that's why it looks like it does," said Mac Whatley, a small-town Asheboro lawyer and affiliate of the American Textile History Museum, who had overseen the shipment of the collection, as we entered the warehouse. It was blessedly cool after the hot sun. "Nothing makes any sense. There's looms, spinning frames here, there, and everywhere."

It was musky and damp in the warehouse. Filthy pipes ran overhead. Peeling paint curled out from the wall. Broken-off warp threads still hung from the looms, dust clinging to them.

"Kid in a candy store," Evan whispered in my ear, as he passed by me watching Ralph looking ecstatically over the old machines.

"C and K's most hated loom," Ralph said fondly, gesturing at a Crompton and Knowles number 12 loom. Ralph paused next before a horsehair loom. Mac came over to point out a pincers that fed horse hairs individually in between the warp threads. Ralph looked really tickled. "You learn something new every day," he drawled. "I never heard of such a thing." As he wandered from one to the next, Ralph assessed the machines and selected the ones he "wanted" for an imaginal water-powered denim operation on his NC homestead, which has a waterfall on it that was once the site of the family's gristmill.

"I was a little bit disappointed in the condition of those machines. They've not been taken care of," Ralph said to Evan and me on our drive back up to Greensboro.

Evan agreed, but was undeterred. Ralph asked if he knew how much it would cost to refurbish one of those old looms.

Evan floated the number: $20,000.

"Where'd you get that figure?" Ralph asked, acknowledging it was correct. "It's just a looooot of work," Ralph added. It was clear that Ralph recognized Evan's dream and his drive, wanted to help him, and also exert some fatherly restraint.

Ralph dropped us back at the storefront. Evan went up to work on some jeans, and I went upstairs with him. He told me he was sick of old men telling him the things he was trying to do were impossible. "They're bitter," he said. "They did everything they were supposed to do. They followed all the rules." And they still lost. The industry had just picked up and left.

At Thistle Hill Weavers, Rabbit Goody's custom and commission weaving business in Cherry Valley, New York, the red, black, and white plaid shirting from Evan's project was still on the loom. Goody said she hadn't actually made a profit on the job: she just did it because she believed in it. I asked her whether Evan knew that. She said she didn't think so. She had short hair in front and a long red auburn braid, Keen sandals, wool socks, army green cargo shorts, and a merlot-colored T-shirt with a Coelophysis on it.

"Weaving," Goody said, taking a spoonful of honey, "is math, it's not creative. I am a weaver *by trade*, I believe in trades. I'm very good at it, but it's a trade." Like most of those deeply involved in mechanical weaving and the resurrection of American textile equipment, Goody said, "I don't really have an attachment to cloth, I have an attachment to *machinery.*"

Goody specializes in weaving reproductions. She turned on her computer to show me something she was producing for the Cleveland Museum of Art, a new fabric for a nineteenth-century Shah's tent. By using images of ancient scraps of tent fabric, Goody could identify the weave structure, which she would then warp onto one of her late-nineteenth- and early-twentieth-century industrial shuttle looms. With her tinkerer's knack, she made her machines work like short-order cooks. "I make them do things they were never intended to do." All of her looms are Crompton and Knowles, one of the most celebrated makers in the United States. Her shuttle looms were far slower than the Swiss-designed shuttle-less looms and other air jet looms used in modern manufacture, but they produced fabric with a selvedge, which allowed her to do work that most factories couldn't.

Goody was like many people who got into handweaving in the 1970s, when weaving kits could be purchased from the *Whole Earth Catalog* alongside agricultural equipment for back-to-the-land projects. In some ways, she was a hippie. Goody became a Quaker, and got involved in nonviolence and the antiwar movement. During the protests against the Vietnam War, she said, "I marched with the communists because they sang better songs." When her friends started advocating for the political use of violence, she went back to the land. "I felt like I had to do something legitimate. The only thing I could do was farming." She was given land by a woman who wanted to populate Cherry Valley with like-minded young people, and Goody has been there since. She started growing organic vegetables.

Unlike many people from the crafting scene of the 1970s, Rabbit stuck with weaving. Handweaving only whetted her appetite for mechanical weaving. She began buying up machinery from mills that were going out of business or scrapping old looms that were obsolete by modern standards. I asked whether it was disappointing to watch the enthusiasm for weaving fade out. No, she said, weaving revivals have always been cyclical: there had been revivals both before and since the 1970s.

In America, the first revival in the interest for weaving happened in the 1870s in connection with Colonial Revival more broadly, at which time handweaving was already an anomaly. The next big revival came in the 1920s, this one attached to an interest in Appalachia. In programs initiated by settlement schools, Appalachian women sold coverlets, baby blankets, and tea towels to support their families. After the Bicentennial, in 1976, there was another revival. This one emphasized the Scandinavian tradition, Goody told me, which is a tradition that continues to this day.

Ironically, Goody said, although newer handweavers based their practice on the Scandinavian weaving tradition because of its unbroken line, the handweaving traditions of New England had also never really vanished: they had been passed on to mechanical looms. If you wanted to be in direct contact with an ancient weaving tradition, she said, you had to get to know the cast iron Crompton and Knowles.

In Goody's mind, weaving evolves according to the tools at hand: it is a plastic art that meets the various exigencies of the time. Innovation, she believed, was an essential human behavior. "Human beings in every culture come up with the solution to the problems of food, shelter, and clothing." This includes discovering weaving. Goody was prone to looking toward the big, panoramic picture, and to her, "The breadth of textile knowledge that existed in the world is unfathomable."

Growing up in Tenafly, New Jersey, Goody spent summers at a socialist Jewish camp called Camp Northwood in Remsen, New York. Her father was a famous electrical engineer. She considered herself privileged enough to have had an inheritance from him, and she never took a paycheck from Thistle Hill Weavers. She had seven employees here in the shop and three on the farm, which provides boarding and training for dressage horses. She does all the warping herself. "I work hard, but this is a privilege. I am a socialist. The employees come first. I run it like a nineteenth-century trade shop." One of her employees, a middle-aged woman in plaid, came in to say goodbye for the day, and shared the news of a death in the community. "I wonder whether Mary is able to stay on the farm," Rabbit murmured. A man in his sixties with a heavy build, brown mustache splashed with gray, came over to say goodbye as well. Goody offered him some tomatoes: "I am *overrun*."

Mammoth structural forces built the modern clothing system: a willingness to violently exploit the earth's natural resources, devalue women's labor, and build neocolonial trade regimes on old colonial foundations. These Goliaths are not only being stared down by scholars, activists, and politicians. They are also directly confronted by individual people insisting on simply doing something they really enjoy. This is the army of the small.

"I get more thrill out of pulling that handle," Goody said, "and having eight, ten yards come off the loom. That is *pure*, producing something real."

13

Woolfest

Sympathy nowadays is dispensed chiefly by the laggards and failures, women for the most part . . . who, having dropped out of the race, have time to spend upon fantastic and unprofitable excursions.

—VIRGINIA WOOLF, "ON BEING ILL"

Spinners, knitters, weavers, felters, and other wool enthusiasts who have increasingly turned to the pleasures of the handmade in the twenty-first century are not merely returning to older models of craft. They are engaged in the critical work of helping preserve the diversity of sheep.

The Cumbrian fells, in northern England, just south of the border with Scotland, were crucial to sheep biodiversity in Britain, and to the whole system of livestock raising. Changes in agriculture after World War II, including the rapid and widespread adoption of Continental meat breeds, threatened the richness of Britain's sheep varieties. By the 1970s, the Bampton Nott, the Berkshire Nott, the primitive Mendip, and twenty-four other native British breeds had become extinct. In response to this crisis in local sheep biodiversity, the Rare Breeds Survival Trust was formed in Britain in 1973. To date, the work of this organization has helped prevent any other native breed from slipping into extinction.

Maintaining the biodiversity of sheep is not just important for knitters and spinners, but for the health of the environment. Essentially, a sheep functions like a carbon sequestration system. Atmospheric carbon makes up 50 percent of wool's weight, and, unlike synthetic fabrics, wool is naturally biodegradable. When disposed of, wool acts like a fertilizer, slowly releasing valuable nutrients and carbon back into the soil. Wool fixes carbon in the topsoil rather than releasing it into the atmosphere. This process can help regenerate pastures, which sheep will graze. And sheep can help answer the problem of how to avoid far-flung fiber supply chains. Because sheep do well in such an extraordinary range of terrains, wool is a natural choice for people interested in rebuilding local systems of cloth manufacture. Certain breeds are more suited to certain atmospheric and geologic conditions than others, so preserving diversity also means preserving the geographic range in which sheep can flourish.

In 2001, an outbreak of foot-and-mouth disease among populations led to enormous culls of British sheep. By the time the last case was identified at Whygill Head Farm in Appleby, Cumbria, over six million sheep, pigs, and cattle had been culled. In the wake of this slaughter, government funds became available to help support British sheep, and the Wool Clip was formed in Cumbria. The Wool Clip, a cooperative of wool artisans, launched an annual festival, "Woolfest," in 2005 to help support and promote the work of the Rare Breeds Survival Trust, and to publicize the importance of British wool. In 2019, I decided to attend the fifteenth annual Woolfest, held in the Cattle Mart in the Cumbrian town of Cockermouth.

When I was a child, in Vermont, my family kept a small flock of sheep, to help keep the grass down. There were a handful of gentle ewes and a ram I was terrified of. We sent the wool to be processed by a small mill on Prince Edward Island and I remember it returning as yarn, dyed yellow, red, and green. My mother did not often have time to knit, but while she was pregnant with my younger brother, I remember that she made him a small green hat and matching sweater. Perhaps because of witnessing these transformations, which I registered as a sort of magic, I felt a residual affection for sheep and wool. I was looking forward to Woolfest.

When I arrived in England, I spent a day in London before traveling north to Cumbria. From my vantage there, I considered the irony of a movement toward localism being nurtured in the bosom of a country that did so much to help dismantle localism the world over. Inside the British Museum, sheep called up not so much the homely face of the olde English rustic as the height of British imperial reach. I examined an Assyrian relief carving of a flock of sheep and goats, being driven back to camp after being captured in a campaign against the Arabs. The artist had even hatched the lines in the sheep's wool into the stone, and captured the gentleness in their lidded eyes, and the twists in their horns. The carving, from about 728 BC, once decorated the palace of King Tiglath-Pileser III. It was taken from Nimrud, an ancient Assyrian city located twenty miles south of what is now Mosul, in Iraq, by Austin Henry Layard. He supervised excavations at Nimrud from 1845 to 1851 and was granted a permit allowing him to take to England "such stones as he may find useful." The following morning, I boarded the train for Cumbria.

Sheep were not domesticated in Europe; rather, they were brought there by Neolithic people who migrated from the Near East. While early civilizations around the Mediterranean were flourishing, primitive farmers gradually spread through Europe, and sheep arrived in Britain when Neolithic settlers crossed the English Channel at about 3000 BC. The region was too densely forested at first for many sheep to be kept, so pigs and cattle were more common. The early pastoralists in the hills of the Lake District and the Pennines were nomadic, and the wandering of herders with their livestock helped stimulate sheep breeding in Europe, as it had done in the Middle East. In the Bronze Age, woodland gradually decreased and sheep became more numerous.

One of the most ancient surviving specimens of woolen cloth in Britain was discovered at a burial site inside an Early Bronze Age barrow at Rylstone, Yorkshire, tucked inside a dug-out oak coffin. The Urn People of the Middle Bronze Age seem to have been even more skilled at textile manufacture than their Early Bronze Age ancestors, but most of the material record of wool textiles from that period comes from contemporary people of Denmark, who also buried their dead in oak coffins. Because some of these burials were in peaty and waterlogged soil, entire bodies complete with clothing have been pre-served. The first workers to examine these ancient textiles assumed they were made from a mixture of sheep's wool and deer hair. What the workers thought were "deer hair" were really the kemp hairs, the outer layer of the fleeces of wild sheep, typical of the fleeces of primi-tive domestic sheep.

New breeds arrived with new waves of migrants. When the Deverel-Rimbury people reached Britain in the Late Bronze Age, about 750 BC, migrating from the alpine region in Central Europe to set up dwellings on the banks of the Thames, they are believed to have brought with them the larger horned *studeri* sheep.

The Romans had a well-organized wool textile industry in Britain, and poet and historian Dionysius Periegetes made reference, about AD 300, to British wool so fine that it was comparable to a spider's web. A letter from Charlemagne to Offa, king of Mercia—a kingdom of Anglo-Saxon England—in 796 suggested a revival, or continu-ance, of the Roman export trade in wool goods. Charlemagne wrote that his subjects wanted cloaks of the same pattern "as used to come to us in the old times." Saxon place names like Shepley, Shepton Mal-let, Shipley, and Skipton point to the ubiquity of sheep in the period.

After the Norman Conquest, Britain contained more sheep than all other livestock put together, and their most important product was milk. Wool came second, followed by manure, then meat. Wool, however, became increasingly important, first as a raw export, and later for the medieval cloth industry.

Wool was of major importance to the medieval English economy. Indeed, English barons sitting in Parliament in 1297 declared that wool represented "half the value of the whole land." In 1280 about 25,000 sacks of wool were exported from England. The exchange of raw wool moved around 40,000–45,000 sacks per year, at its peak. Exports of woven woolen fabric rose on the shoulders of the raw wool industry. In the mid-fourteenth century, 10,000 cloths were being exported per year. Exports had increased by a factor of six a century later, and they more than doubled again by 1539–40, when 140,000 cloths were exported. The wealth of the British islands was built up by its wool industry, and the monasteries that owned much of the Lake

District in Cumbria during the Middle Ages owed their fortunes to wool. In honor of wool's importance, a British parliamentary tradition dating from the fourteenth century demanded the Lord Chancellor sit on a woolsack, and today the Lord Speaker has this honor.

Ironically, the excellent quality of medieval British wool was the result of poor grazing. The more nutriment a sheep receives, the larger it becomes, and its fiber diameter grows proportionally as well. In the Middle Ages, the richest grazing area in England, the great Midland clay plain, was largely under the plow, devoted to growing grain. Sheep grazed on common wastes and on corn-stubble after the harvest. In the mid-fifteenth century, enclosures for pasture farming, driven by the demand for wool, provided improved grassland feeding for sheep, and as a result the short and fine medieval wool of the Midlands and Lincolnshire was slowly replaced by a longer and coarser staple. As the quality of English fleece deteriorated, losing its fineness, Spanish wool became desirable. By the early sixteenth century, English wool was losing its reputation for fineness to merino, and, by the end of the Tudor period, merino was considered superior.

Meanwhile, enclosures displaced traditional systems of communal agriculture. The struggles against enclosure began in the late fifteenth century and persisted through the sixteenth and seventeenth. The hedgerows that were planted to enclose fields were dug up, and the act became symbolic of the rebellion. Riots often included women and sometimes were entirely female, as in 1608 when forty women went to "cast down and fence the hedges" of an enclosure in Waddingham (today's Lincolnshire), or when in 1609 on a manor of Dunchurch (Warwickshire) "fifteen women including wives, widows, spinsters, unmarried daughters, and servants, took it upon themselves to assemble at night to dig up the hedges and level the ditches." At York, in May 1624, a group of women were jailed for destroying an enclosure, and then "enjoyed tobacco and ale after their feat."

In the 1780s, the British economy entered a period of unprecedented growth and turbulence, perhaps faster than any economy had ever experienced. One of the first results was a huge growth in demand for and consumption of textiles. Wool prices shot up and rural entrepreneurs led a massive expansion of pastoral production.

The Scottish Highlands were recognized as a region that could easily be converted for the use of large-scale sheep farming. The Highland Clearances, mainly contained in the period between 1780 and 1855, were a series of forcible removals of the population of the Scottish Highlands and the northern Scottish islands. Many thousands of commoners were pushed out of ancestral homes in the Highlands' straths and glens to make way for vast sheep farms. By about 1840, 85 percent of Sutherland, 61 percent of Ross and Cromarty, 60 percent of Inverness, and 35 percent of Argyll were made up of these farms.

Agrarian peasant society in the Highlands had looked stranger and stranger to its industrializing neighbors on the plains. In the Highlands, as in England formerly, most local production was consumed within the community. Barter was widespread, and rents were, at least partially, paid in kind and in services. Adam Smith used the Highlands prior to the Clearances as an example of the poverty of nations tied by antiquated restrictions and organization. It was a victim of the poor division of labor, he believed, consuming its products, absurdly, "in rustic hospitality at home."

Karl Marx, too, tried to distill the experience of the Highlands into theoretical material. As the Clearances moved forward, Marx made them the centerpiece in his account of the ways in which capitalist agriculture recklessly displaced feudalism. For Marx, the Clearances signified a moment when the breaking up of feudal bonds created a mass of proletarians forced suddenly into the labor market, a process that entailed "thefts, outrages and popular misery . . . [when it] accompanied the forcible expropriation of the people."

Impoverished Highlanders were drawn toward the towns and villages of central Scotland both before and during the great influx of sheep. Many were specifically recruited to work in the new mills that arose in the region to spin and weave cotton from the American South.

The Highlanders had traditionally kept their own breeds of native sheep, called *seana chaorich cheaga* or "little old sheep," which they would take inside their cottages in the winter. The new Cheviot sheep that were being moved onto the land by the end of the eighteenth century were reviled. The poor Cheviot sheep were not at all to blame, but their passage across the Great Glen became symbolic of the acceleration of capitalist sheep farming in the 1790s and the displacement it caused.

The British leisure class discovered Cumbria as a tourist destination when the Napoleonic Wars cut them off from vacationing in the Alps. The Lake District poets like William Wordsworth and Samuel Coleridge made it a fetish: a pastoral idyll for a rapidly industrializing country. And indeed, even while British imperialism ended the communal life of subsistence agriculturalists around the world, and industrialism displaced the British peasant, Cumbrian commoners continued to raise sheep according to a tradition a thousand years old, in part because the spare and steep hillsides, or fells, of the region made it unamenable to the type of agricultural "improvement" transforming the countryside in lower, lusher grounds.

My train was now passing an old Lancashire factory, as we traveled up through the cradle of the Industrial Revolution. Soon after, rolling hills appeared out the window. Cumbria is just south of Scotland, and we were not far from the Roman wall built to keep out the Scots. I looked out on the sheep in Technicolor-green fields. It was just past midsummer; big rounds of hay stood ready to be brought into the barns. As a child in Vermont, we mercilessly mocked the tourists rubbernecking at cows, and ogling an agricultural lifestyle. Now I was one of those tourists. I wanted to romanticize this place, hearing the occasional low of a cow, the sounds of birds at dusk, the gentle pulse of nature which somehow always seems to stand both within and apart from the awful yoke of history.

On the first day of Woolfest, tea was flowing liberally in the cafeteria. There were well over a hundred exhibitor stalls, including those from spinning wheel and loom manufacturers, small flock owners selling fleeces, little mills selling yarn and roving, weavers selling tweed. Each of the two days was filled with demonstrations and talks, and special events like the Rare Breeds Parade, which put the sheep themselves onstage. Beside me at a table, a woman ate a heap of cottage pie. Her daughter went back up to douse hers with more gravy. One might be forgiven for mistaking this cafeteria for the cafeteria in a retirement home. I had to admit it: Woolfest was a gathering of old women.

My first stop, after tea, was the stall of the Hebridean Sheep Society, where a rack of scratchy brown wool sweaters with elbow patches and flat caps displayed some of the uses to which the deep, chocolaty brown wool of this breed can be put. The society's main role is to authenticate members of the breed, which the Rare Breeds Survival Trust recognized in 1974 as being in danger of extinction. The Hebridean, explained a stately volunteer named Helen, crossed from a "rare breed" to a "minority breed" when it reached a threshold of three thousand ewes. "It's a success story." The Hebridean sheep had been preserved, like many of the breeds that escaped extinction in the postwar years, on the Scottish islands. "They do well on very little," Helen told me. Conservation lands in the U.K. often keep a flock because they keep down weeds and invasive species without altering the land, she said.

I rushed to take a seat at the tapestry-weaving demonstration, which was about to commence. In tapestry weaving, warp threads are covered up, and the weft threads change color to form a pattern or an image. The most famous tapestry in the West, the Bayeux Tapestry, is not a true tapestry. It is an embroidery, made with stitches of wool thread on linen cloth. True tapestry produces an image by weaving it in with the weft, not by decorating the surface of an already woven cloth. Embroidered images often mimicked tapestries and served as lower-cost replicas.

The Bayeux Tapestry was made in the eleventh century and depicts the Norman Conquest of England in seventy-five discrete scenes with Latin inscriptions. It is believed to have been commissioned shortly after the occupation, and stitched in England by nuns at St. Augustine's Abbey. Incredibly large, measuring seventy meters long, and well preserved, the tapestry was displayed yearly in Bayeux and served as a propaganda tool celebrating the glories of the French army. Napoleon put it on display in Paris in 1804. Tapestries, real or impersonated, were ways of telling stories, often the tales of famous battles. In Homer, Helen of Troy is seen producing a tapestry:

> . . . *she was weaving a great web,*
> *A red folding robe, and working into it the numerous*
> *struggles*
> *Of Trojans, breakers of horses, and bronze-armoured*
> *Achaians,*
> *Struggles that they endured for her sake at the hands of*
> *the war god.*

Textiles like these were the epic product of female historians, and they have modern analogues. In the 1980s and 1990s Hmong women embroidered picture cloths depicting the events of the Secret War in Laos, during the Vietnam War era. One such cloth depicts a village bombarded by aircraft dropping a chemical agent called T-2 mycotoxin, commonly known as "yellow rain." Pile rugs knotted in Afghanistan showed Stinger missiles shooting down Soviet helicopters.

Tapestry, said our instructor, beginning the class, "was the way they kept the draft out. It was their central heating. But also, because they didn't read, they had pictures woven in. It is storytelling as well."

Pairs of women in the audience kept a running commentary up as the instructor demonstrated. "Keeping it steady, keeping it the same distance," the sisters beside me murmured. The teacher had put in a row of colored weft, and now she pushed it down with a thick wooden comb to form the next line in the picture.

There are two ways to build an image in tapestry. One is to work across the line, row by row, changing colors along the way. The other is to work up a block of color. The instructor called this second method "meet and separate," because the threads of different-colored string work toward and then away from one another.

"But won't there be a gap?" one woman in the audience asked, noticing that when the two colors met, a slit formed, as each thread doubled back on itself and moved toward opposite edges of the loom.

"Yes, exactly. You have a slit, and slits are an important part of tapestry. The important thing is not to be afraid of slits, because you can play with slits. They can make a shadow. You can pull it tight and make it a hole. If you want, you can sew them up later."

"Most important thing is not to panic," she said. "There is no rushing tapestry weaving." This advice was strangely soothing. So was it, later in the day, when the instructor at the spinning demonstration said, "That's the great thing about fiber, you can repair it." My spindle had dropped as I attempted to spin. She picked it up, got the two ends, removed some of the twist in the roving, fanned them out, and joined the two ends together with a twist.

Things can be mended, they must not be rushed, and their imperfections are an intrinsic part of their value: these were the messages that I kept hearing reiterated at Woolfest. They were messages, it seemed, issuing forth from an agricultural time that was forgiving of idiosyncrasy and error.

The Cockermouth Cattlemart building where Woolfest was held was about the size and shape of a factory. The height of the ceilings, the corrugated metal roof, and cement floor were reminiscent of many of the factories I had been in over the course of my research. Like nearly every factory I had visited, it was full of women. Like them, it was a fabulously productive space, where women knit, spun, and wove while sheep chomped hay in their pens. But the rhythm was easier. In a factory, errors mean that money will be lost, or perhaps a person's health endangered. Work *must* be rushed, and imperfections have no place. At Woolfest, meanwhile, mothers and daughters strolled together. People who were strangers a moment before talked to one another about carding brushes and the looms they used. This hall was a celebration of everything society teaches us to scoff at and devalue. Here, production was compatible with nurture rather than domination, and most important—this labor did not belong to anyone but the artisans and craftspeople at work.

The spinners and weavers I spoke to told me stories about how careers had interrupted, but not ended, their handicraft. Joy Exeter learned to weave in Bethesda, Maryland, while her husband was working as the economist for the embassy. She wasn't supposed to be employed in her role as his wife, so she learned how to weave. Later she became a nurse. She picked up weaving again after she retired. Now she helps run an old mill building that has been repurposed as an arts center.

Marilyn, who was manning the table for the local fiber guild, moved up from Surrey to Cumbria with her husband. She had three kids, and they bought a small fell farm with sheep, goats, and no running water. "I learned how to spin in the eighties, then I went back to work after I'd raised my children," she said. She used to work in sales but now she was spinning her own sheep's wool. For many if not most of the participants of Woolfest, their craft activities were a source of supplemental income and pleasure rather than a real means of earning a living. But that doesn't diminish the significance of what they do.

The resurgence of craft is a profoundly collective phenomenon. Although it can take overtly political forms, like the knitting of protest signs or "yarn bombing" public spaces, craft is also inherently political because it is collective, and because it is slow. Scholars have argued that the communal nature of "craftivism" makes it an antidote to alienation within an information society. They note too that in protests where knitters are present, they serve to remind us of the intrinsic value of building a cooperative project. Scholars describe this as a " 'prefigurative politics,' one that creates collaborative relations now as if the world to come has already arrived."

The labels on the goods for sale in the stalls at Woolfest looked like goods one might see in some version of a utopian "world to come." Some green yarn at the North Devon–based John Arbon Textiles stand was marked, "60% exmoor blue face, 20% corriedale, 10% zwartbies, 10% nylon." The paper tags on a rack of sweaters listed, rather than a price, instructions to make the sweater oneself, in terse statements like, "Size small/medium. 9 balls main. Two balls contrast." These tags assumed a knowledge of sheep, a competency and intimacy with the materials.

At another table, a hand spinner could buy the fleeces of a blue-faced Leicester crossed with Swaledale, no chemicals or dips used, for £15. The fleeces were stacked on tables in feed bags. One was stuffed in a Lactovis bag: "the ultimate free flow milk for lambs/made using British milk." I remembered mixing powder like this to feed a lamb rejected by his mother when I was a child. I pored over the Hebridean fleece being sold from Plumland, a Ouessant fleece from Eaglesfield, and a big bag of Polworth and Corriedale from Thropton, Northumberland. Hand spinners carefully choose a fleece with the types of coloration they desire for a particular project. Indeed, the rise in hand spinning has created more room in the market for colored fleeces. Sheep have been largely bred for whiteness to make dyeing wool easier, and renewed interest in coloration is a relatively recent phenomenon.[*]

At the Rare Breeds Parade, held in the ring that serves as the Cattlemart's auction stage the rest of the year, sheep were displayed whose breeds had been preserved from extinction. In the 1830s, when islands in Scotland were cleared of their traditional sheep, and larger sheep breeds like Cheviots and Leicesters were brought in, some of the native species disappeared entirely. But on North Ronaldsay, the northernmost island in the Orkney archipelago, which lies off the north coast of Scotland, a drystone wall was constructed around the circumference, above the high-water line. The wall, which became known as a "sheep dike," was completed in 1832, and it confined the local sheep to the beach. There, local sheep adapted to a diet of seaweed. And there they remain for all but a few months each year, when the ewes and lambs are brought inland to graze. These little sheep—the top of the back of one of the sheep reached just to a woman's knee—resemble the fossil remains of sheep from the Iron Age, and indeed dental traces of seaweed have been found on these four-thousand-year-old sheep.

Another little group of survivors who muddled through the mid-century on the Orkney Islands were the Shetland sheep, as shaggy and small as Shetland ponies. Once endangered, their numbers are now secured. Shetlands were selected to be small, the announcer told us, because they were often carried on rowboats, and larger species might have upset the boat.

---

[*] Celtic references to white sheep during the Saxon period suggest they were an exception.

A smug-looking Beaumont sheep was displayed next. A recent creation, this breed is the result of a Shetland crossed with a Saxon Merino. Part of the impetus for preserving the genetic diversity of sheep is that, without them, new crossbreeds like this are not possible. "If we had let them all drop off the planet in the fifties, we wouldn't have been able to do that," said the announcer.

The next batch of sheep provided a little history of Merrie Olde England. Perhaps the platonic ideal of "sheep," the Portland sheep, native to the southern end of Britain, had a cream-colored wool that matched the color of the stone quarried in Portland that was used to build London. The chubby brown Ryeland sheep, from Hertford-shire, an area bordering England and Wales, provided the brown wool out of which monastic garments were made. Ryeland sheep got their name from the fact that they were turned out on the rye crop, where they would nip buds off of the grain, encouraging its growth, even while their feet stimulated the roots of the rye, and their manure fertilized the plants. The white Leicester sheep with its ridiculous great ears, like a rabbit's, came next. The Wensleydale Longwool, of Yorkshire, had ringlets dripping nearly to the floor. This wool was once used to make undergarments for the gentry, and linings for cloaks.

The Rare Breeds Parade drew to its close, and I thought about the fact that these sheep, who had fed and clothed kings and com-moners alike down through the centuries, were a testament to a kind of human intervention that works over long periods of time rather than in short, exhausting bursts. Breeding these sheep had been a multigenerational project.

"They're grown over centuries to be able to survive," Cumbrian shepherd Simon Bland told me. Bland, a native of the area, raised Cheviot crossed with a Texil, originally from Norway, and kept a flock of white-faced Woodlands, a rare breed, only 1,100 of which remained after hoof-and-mouth. Bland's knowledge of Cumbrian geology and of the way different terrains could support different sheep was profound. The white-faced Woodlands, he said, "they're a limestone sheep." Swaledale and Herdwicks, by contrast, "they're better suited to wetter ground. A lot of uplands have peaty soil. You'll have sheep that will do well on one hill, they won't do well on another. Rough Fell was dominant in the lakes, you don't see many in the lakes anymore though," he said. I asked him how to spell "Rough Fell." He looked at me pointedly and said, after a beat, "You're talking to a dyslexic shepherd."

In addition to sheepherding, Bland had a business producing a commercial fertilizer from wool and bracken, a kind of fern. Plummeting wool prices had led, in recent years, to shepherds burning their wool when the cost of transporting it for wholesale outweighed the price it would fetch. Events like Woolfest are one way to help sheep farmers, because specialty, high-quality wool and direct marketing to craftspeople tends to be more profitable than bulk wool sales. But Bland thinks it is important to think in terms of scale too, and of what can be done with the large quantities of wool, with no commercial use, that exist now that the wool market is globalized.

He hit upon the fertilizer idea because he kept losing his own sheep in bracken six feet high. Bland's wife, who has a PhD in environmental science, knew that bracken, like comfrey and seaweed, is high in potassium, and the two began to experiment with using the plant in combination with wool, which is a protein, to make fertilizer. Bland's growing medium has become extremely popular with gardeners. Meanwhile, he helps support sheep farmers not only by buying up and transporting their wool, but offering free bracken control. It helps ensure that, rather than going up in smoke, the carbon-rich wool improves the soil.

Much of the work to make the Cumbrian landscape farmable was carried out in the twelfth and thirteenth centuries: fields were cleared, valley bottoms were drained, and land was made arable by the application of lime, and other treatments. An old ditty, quoted as early as 1603, shows how the British farmer tended to the long-range health of the soil. "A man doth *sand* for himself; *lyme* for his sonne; and *marle* [add clay to soil] for his graunde childe."

Bland calls the type of animal husbandry practiced in the Cumbrian fells "hill farming." Intrinsic to "hill farming," by Bland's definition, is taking a long view: making breeding choices that will work out well not just in the coming season, but over many yearly cycles,

and many generations. In addition to his sheep and his fertilizer business, Bland does work in peat bog restoration, which to him is merely
an extension of the same kind of long-range thinking. Carbon stored
in trees, Bland said, will last maybe fifty years. But if you're storing
carbon in a peat bog, "it can be here forever." To him, "*That's* hill
farming because you are always thinking about your next crop, your
next breed of ewes, it's all intertwined, isn't it."

The Herdwick sheep native to Cumbria are notable for how they
"heft" to a particular part of the fell. A hefted sheep has a strong
and unshakable sense of where it belongs. It becomes so attached to
its pasture that, although it can be sold down to the lowlands, it can
never be moved onto another part of the fell: it will simply walk back
home. Ninety-five percent of the world's Herdwick sheep exist within
twenty miles of Coniston, a village in the Furness region of Cumbria,
which placed them at grave risk of being wiped out during the culls
that marked the government's response to foot-and-mouth.

Almost as tenuously held as this precious and ancient breed of
sheep is the expertise that has been passed down here: the competencies of a way of life that is centuries old.

At the sheep-shearing demonstration, Paul Lorrey, who looked
barely eighteen, had his sheep sitting on its rear, his hand on the
sheep's muzzle pushing its head back. Then he had it by the horn,
occasionally using his skinny knees to jog it up and down, like one
would bounce a fussy baby. He clipped it just up to the nape of the
sheep's neck, with sharp, foot-long handheld clippers. Then he laid
out the fleece all in one piece, as though he had peeled an orange.
He made it look easy, but a less expert shearer could easily have
left the wool too long on the sheep's back, or worse, nicked the
sheep with the clippers. He took off the little scraps, and rolled the
rest up.

Now Paul was shearing a Portland. Her under chin was pressed
up against his knee. When she kicked, he readjusted her, pressing her
nose down to the side, and she calmed. He knew the holds that made
the sheep relax: with her head tucked between his knees, or under his

armpit, the sheep stopped fussing, and allowed herself to be sheared by his deft, precise clips.

Paul pointed out there were no double cuts, which meant that there would be no "short bits." Paul wore a buzz cut, he was ash blond, and his ears stuck way out. He was tall and lean and strong. He had wide cheekbones and was very pale. He looked like you could find him smoking menthols outside a gas station. Only something illuminated him subtly from within. It flashed when he paused just for a half second, clippers suspended, to give himself time to orient them just right. It was the same brief second of charged, intelligent stillness that Lynn, a man selling traditional Taras tweed, took right before he cut a meter of his own cloth. It was the pleasure of mastery. Now Paul was clipping a Shetland. The pile of soft wool lay beside him—deep, velvety, and black.

As Paul clipped, an announcer talked about how sheep sense emotion, so that "there is no place for anger in handling sheep. They don't go together." Scientists call this "kinopsitic behavior": a social adaptation for detecting and avoiding predators that involves learning signals. Sheep are highly attuned to rapid movements of group members. The announcer's statement made me think, however, not so much about sheep, as about people. If weaving calms, and spinning soothes, and anger has no place in handling sheep, no wonder a culture robbed of its sheep goes mad.

Sheep are mentioned more than 550 times in the Bible, more than any other animal. This is partly because they were central to the lives of the nomadic peoples whose lives the Bible chronicles. Abraham, Moses, and King David were all shepherds. Shepherds were the first people to see the newborn Christ. The Prophet Mohammad worked as a shepherd when he was eight years old. Shepherding, however, is also an irreplaceable metaphor for a certain kind of unswerving service and care. The flock has complete trust in and reliance on the shepherd. Conversely the shepherd has to be utterly attuned to his flock. No wonder this relationship, then, has been emblematic of care, vulnerability, and trust in civilizations for millennia.

. . .

The greatest protection a sheep has is the flock itself. By grouping together, the probability of any single individual succumbing to the attack of a predator is minimized. But it also means more eyes, ears, and noses are available to sense the arrival of predators. Scientists speculate that animals can devote more time and energy to foraging when they have to devote less to scanning the perimeter. This was how I felt inside of Woolfest, knitted in, surrounded by old women and pens of sheep. When I returned to Woolfest for the second day, I felt a great surge of relief. I felt I was within a system of mutual and collective care, and it allowed me to relax.

I knelt by a little North Ronaldsay lamb eating hay from a metal basket that looked like a shopping cart. The ewe, his mother, was at her tallest up to my knee. People who walked by them paused, it seemed to me, responding to the tug of their sweetness. Cat, who taught me how to use a Turkish spindle the day before, came over to admire them too. The lamb used his tender little nose to get at the hay, sidling up next to his mother so their fleeces were abreast.

I spent the morning speaking to women with flocks of sheep, each of whom seemed to have come into her flock by some accident of fate. Sarah had Portland sheep. It was her son who wanted them, when he was eight years old. She had about fifteen now. They were called by name, she said, and they came when they were called.

Jane Dryden lived in the Cotswolds, where she and her husband had bought a derelict farm. A couple of sheep wandered over from a neighboring farm. It looked to her as though they were starving, and so she patched a wall and kept them. Her neighbor let a ram in as a joke. "I guess he thought, if 'you're going to keep my sheep? Then you will lamb them.'" Soon, she said, she was "all in." She went to an agricultural college for a year to study sheep. Now she has five hundred: Wensleydale and Blue Faced Leicesters. She sells yarn and roving to customers in Norway, Finland, Japan, the United States, and China. It was satisfying, she said, birthing lambs. "It's really gruesome and horrible and then they come out and they're okay."

I went to one of the few stalls I hadn't yet examined, with heaps of vintage wool blankets, marked "Made in Britain, all wool" or "Made in Scotland, all wool," a testament to the British woolen cloth indus-

try that had existed right up through the 1980s. The owner was re-
counting how a customer had bought a cone of vintage thread earlier
that day and said her father had been the dyer at the mill where it was
made. "She was saying how miserable he was when acrylics came,
he just hated it. She bought the last cone and said she would not unwrap it."

Looking at baskets full of balls of vintage yarn, I thought of Mary,
a woman who worked at the School of Energy Resources in Wyoming. She once told me that while she was in labor she imagined balls
of beautiful yarn to calm herself and deal with the pain.

lick it, and then draft out. You've got to keep it spinning, because
if you don't, it starts to spin the other way." It was early evening,
and women were gathering around me for the "Giant Knit and Spin,"
an event where everyone brought out their own personal projects,
and the organizers put out trays of flapjacks and shortbread, and hot
water for tea.

Debbie Zawinski produced some purple and pink roving. "My
grandson is autistic and he *really* likes using the drum carder," she
said. "He has produced this large amount of roving and I've given
myself the task of making it into something." Tricia Hutchinson said
her eight-year-old nephew was autistic too, and she had knit him a
sweater with eight stripes on the sleeve and eight on the chest, so that
he could remember how to count to eight.

Archeologist Elizabeth Wayland Barber points out that Iron Age
ruins show that, at times when people live at the brink of survival, elaborate ornamentation in clothing remains. This is because, she argues,
work devoted to producing symbolic advantages, like the embroider-
ing of protective motifs, prayers, talismans, into fabric, was as important as the work that would produce material advantages, like warmth.

The benefits of this type of handwork aren't only in the product,
but also in the process. American folklorist Mathilde Frances Lind
found, in a series of surveys carried out among hand spinners, that
people who spin overwhelmingly report that they like it because it is
calming. Some go so far as to say that it helps with depression and

other mental health issues, allowing them to cope with stress and anxiety. It serves as a form of alternative therapy for chronic health conditions that do not respond to conventional medical treatment. Others in the study pointed to the intellectual stimulation involved. The chemistry of dyeing, the mechanics of a spinning wheel, the botany of fiber structure and growth, the mathematics used to measure yarn characteristics, and knowledge of animal husbandry and biology all serve the spinner.

Another thing that spinning allowed in an atmosphere like this was the space in which to swap stories, share skills, and build networks. One relatively new coinage for the very old concept of making cloth close to home is the "fibershed." Just as *watershed* is an area of land that drains rainwater or snow into one stream, lake, or wetland, a *fibershed* is a geographically circumscribed region in which fiber producers and processors can join their products, skills, and expertise to produce cloth.

In the United States, an organization called Fibershed was begun in 2010 to link fiber producers, fabric makers, and dyers and enable them to build full regional supply chains. There is a Piedmont Fibershed, a Vancouver Island Fibershed, and a Rust Belt Fibershed. There is one for western Massachusetts, one for Bristol, U.K., and one for Erode, India. Woolfest and other festivals like it serve a similar function: they build connections between people whose skills and resources can regenerate local production networks. Local fabric-making systems create these networks, the kind that were destroyed, often by force, in the periods leading up to and following the Industrial Revolution.

After Woolfest ended, I headed back to London. From the top of the double-decker bus on the way back to Penrith, I saw sheep pick among thistle and rocks in little enclosures formed by hedges and stonewalls. The bus passed close to rock face grown over with moss and fern. Across the lake, a tiny stone church stood at the base of a mountain skirted with pines, and looked buried under the mountain's weight. My suitcase was full with misshapen mice and elephants knit by Sarah, the woman whose sheep each come when called by name. She had knit them from the wool she clipped off her sheep and washed in her bathtub. I knew my nieces and nephews would find them very curious.

14

Weavers

Our designs are our thinking.

——IRENE CLARK, CONTEMPORARY NAVAJO WEAVER

Many, perhaps most, Americans have been severed from ancestral knowledge by modernizing forces, or intentional assimilation. But in the case of the Navajo, these breakages were forced by explicit U.S. government policy.

As the Indian Wars were winding down in the late nineteenth and early twentieth centuries, U.S. policy turned its focus from annihilation to education. Carl Schurz, commissioner of Indian Affairs, estimated in 1881 that it cost nearly $1 million "to kill an Indian in warfare, where it only cost 1,200 to enroll an Indian child for eight years of school." Off-reservation American Indian boarding schools established at the time removed Native youth from their families and communities, and forced them to learn English, accept Christianity, and adopt an "American" lifestyle. In 1900, the Phoenix Indian School housed more than seven hundred students. Ten to twenty ran away from the school each month, on average, and a corps of men was assigned to apprehend the fleeing children.

The deliberate separation of children from families was central to the boarding school experience, and clothing was central to its technology of control. Upon arrival, students were stripped of their clothes and given military uniforms or Victorian dresses, lace-up shoes, American names, and haircuts. In costumed school pageants, students played the roles of the colonizers and the colonized. Cholera was rampant in the close quarters in which the children lived. It is difficult to imagine what kind of comfort could possibly have been provided to the parents who received this letter from Richard Pratt, founder of the Carlisle Indian School: "Your son died quietly, without suffering, like a man. We have dressed him in his good clothes and tomorrow we will bury him the way white people do."

It is not inherently easier for the Navajo to reestablish traditional weaving techniques and their attendant lifeways than it is for any other modern American to take the effort to master traditional competencies, particularly after these skills were nearly wiped out by a genocidal colonial state. Native Americans were handed, in exchange for their cultural practices, the competencies and culture of the twentieth-century United States: a menu that included, as the century wore on, such dubious treasures as canned goods, television, and employment in radioactive uranium mines.

Mending broken lines of transmission is difficult. It is especially difficult for those who have experienced residual and compounding poverty. And yet, as farmers like Simon Bland have been working to improve the health of the soil by returning to ancient lifeways, and Scottish women in Cumbria are relearning traditional art forms like tapestry weaving, some people among the Navajo are reestablishing connections with ancestral knowledge. On July 4, 2019, I flew to Phoenix to meet some young Navajo weavers.

I drove out to Velma's house in Mesa, a suburb of Phoenix, the morning of the fifth. Palm trees lined the Phoenix highway, and I stepped out of the car into Velma's driveway in a 106-degree morning, with wind gusting like a blow-dryer to the face. Velma had purple hair, eyeliner, matching purple cat eyeglasses, pink lipstick, and black nail polish. Velma and her kids had been at Ikea the day before, buying a bed.

I had come across Velma's work in a book at the New Museum in New York. Her husband, Dustin (technically, her ex-husband; "it's complicated," as she says), put up the dog gate behind us as we walked through the living room and into the hallway toward her bedroom. Velma's loom stood next to a large well-organized desk. The weaving she had started on it had cream yarn at the base threaded with strands of blue, and then the beginning of a row of crosses.

One of the things that had attracted me to Velma's work was how densely layered with meaning each of her weavings was. In *Static*, Velma wove a television set. On its screen, the television displayed the banded colors of a traditional Navajo chief's blanket: brown, white, gray, and blue. Gray, brown, and white were all colors of undyed sheep's wool. Blue was made using indigo traded from the Spanish, who brought the dyestuff with them to the New World. In a visual pun, the weaving marked the way that Navajo weaving, or Navajo culture, is figured as stationary, or *static*, by the larger American culture.

Another of Velma's weavings features large strands of DNA. "Our lineage in Navajo runs through the mom," she explained, "so when we identify ourselves, we name our mom's clan first and then we name our dad's clan." Velma said that she made this piece after she read about mDNA. Scientists thought "they were going to be able to trace our lineage down to the first female, the lineage really was running through our cells to the matriarch, the mom." This struck her. And besides, Velma added, "DNA is two strands twisted together like yarn. It's a fiber."

The anthropologist Jane Schneider had argued that clothmaking under capitalism is unique in that it is "incapable of generating or sustaining ideas of benevolent spiritual or ancestral involvement." The potent metaphor linking fabrication and reproduction has been jettisoned by the capitalist West. And yet western science, as Velma had observed, arrived at an image of genetic coding that looked identical to a strand of yarn.

Velma's formation as a weaver required her to encounter breakages in the lines of transmission that pass skill from one generation to the next. It was a gap that I would become familiar with in speaking to Navajo weavers. Velma was born in Tuba City, an unincorporated town within the Painted Desert, near the western edge of the Navajo Nation. Raised in nearby Tonalea, she lived with her maternal grandmother until first grade. Her grandmother had processed wool from a small flock of sheep, but Velma said she did not know her grand-mother was a weaver until she herself started weaving. "I guess they didn't think it was that important to tell me about it," she said, or maybe the impulse was similar to the one that made her parents and grandparents speak Navajo to one another but English to the kids. "I think they thought I would be more successful," she said, "if we spoke English."

When she was six, Velma's family moved closer to her father's mother, in Klagetoh, near Ganado, also on the reservation. This grandmother wove often, and Velma watched her. "She had a big giant loom set up next to the television in the living room, and she would be weaving and she would be cooking, so I would just sit there and watch her." She offered to teach Velma to weave, but the lessons never came about. Years passed. Velma moved away, had her own children.

Velma was running a multimedia company with Dustin, making documentaries on tribes in the Southwest, when a friend, a TV writer and the daughter of celebrated Navajo weaver in the Two Grey Hills style, Barbara Teller Ornelas, told her it wasn't too late to learn. So, in 2011, Velma attended a two-week course at Idyllwild Arts Academy taught by Barbara and her sister, Lynda Teller Pete. Some of the other students were white, and some, like Velma, were Navajos who hadn't learned in "an organic way."

Some of the other Navajo weavers in her class began weaving in styles similar to those of the regions where their grandmothers were from. Velma didn't want to do that. "I don't want to weave anything if I don't really understand its meaning," she said. So, for her first weaving, Velma wove a tree. In the spaces between the branches, where she used a lot of white, she said, "I was trying to talk about how there are a lot of things existing that we don't know about." To Velma, weavings were like molecular combinations. The warp and the weft could be used to make any number of images, just as matter is composed of "the same molecules just bonded or woven together in a different combination." On the molecular level, Velma noted, things were not always as they appeared. "Things *seem* to be woven together so tightly but yet there are these spaces in between things that are immense."

Velma made weavings using cassette tape as a weft. She wove a large square QR code into the corner of an American flag, where the stars are normally placed. However, the idea of calling what Velma does less "traditional" than what some of her former classmates were doing begs the question of what "traditional" Navajo weaving really is. Indeed, what is now understood as "traditional" Navajo weaving was shaped by a long legacy of colonial interaction.

The fiber used in the earliest Navajo weavings was cotton, which reached the tribe from Mexico via the Pueblos, who began weaving with it as early as AD 800. Navajo textiles were highly sought after in the intertribal trade that preceded the arrival of the Spanish. Extensive networks of trade connected the Southwest with the east, south, west, and north, and when the Spanish entered New Mexico there were major trade centers at Zuni and Pecos Pueblo. The Navajos traded with the Pueblos, Utes, Comanches, Mescalero, Chiricahua, San Carlos, Jicarilla, and White Mountain Apaches, among others.

In the late sixteenth century, the Spanish brought sheep to the region, and by the eighteenth century, the Navajo were using wool in their clothing and blankets. By 1706, when the first written reference to Navajo weaving is made, the Navajo were weaving wool from flocks acquired in raids on Spanish ranches along the Rio Grande. From the Spanish, they also took on the practice of making weavings that were taller than they were wide. Previously, the Navajo had woven tapestries that were wider than they were high.

In 1821, the Mexican nation won its independence from Spain, and in 1846, the U.S. government took over New Mexico and adjacent territories from Mexico. As the lands changed hands, the Navajo continued to raid the settlements and ranches of Anglo Americans as they had raided the Spanish and Mexican settlements before them. This was unacceptable to the United States, which could not afford to send military protection to settlers in the midst of the Civil War.

In the summer of 1863, volunteers under Lieutenant Colonel Christopher "Kit" Carson, ordered to neutralize the perceived Navajo threat, began a brutal campaign. Carson forced the Navajo on an eighteen-day march across three hundred miles, a march on which at least two hundred people died of starvation and cold, and during which the Navajos' herds of sheep were decimated. The Navajo were then held in captivity at Bosque Redondo, a 1,600-square-mile reservation adjacent to Fort Sumner, until 1868. At Bosque Redondo, Navajo weavers were first introduced to bright chemically dyed yarns.

Among the annual shipment of goods that the United States government provided to the Navajos during and after their internment in the 1860s were woolen yarns manufactured in Germantown, Philadelphia. Philadelphia had emerged as a major textile-manufacturing center in the mid-nineteenth century, and by 1850 it held as many textile workers as did Lowell in Massachusetts—about twelve thousand. In the 1860s, the city became a center of wartime production, home to two federal arsenals and privy to major government contracts. Germantown manufacturers produced stockings worn by the Union troops and supplied yarn to manufacturers in other Philadelphia districts. In order to meet wartime demand, many manufacturers switched from cotton—no longer available from the South—to wool. By the end of the nineteenth century, Philadelphia was the nation's largest manufacturer of woolen and knit goods.

When these early products of modern chemistry were received by the weavers in the Southwest, captured at Basque Redondo, a creative explosion occurred. Bright orange, purple, red, and yellow threads appeared in weaving palettes. At the same time, these weavers were coming into increased contact with serapes and ponchos produced by the Saltillo weavers of northern Mexico, as interpreted by the Spanish colonial weavers of the Rio Grande. They began to incorporate many of the geometrical motifs and serrated edges found in these weavings into their work. The weavings from that period were of extraordinary complexity and originality.

But the explosive range of colors in Navajo weaving was to be short-lived. Traders, the first of whom arrived on Navajo territory soon after the Navajo-U.S. treaty and the Navajo return from Bosque

Redondo in 1868, encouraged a return to "traditional" dyeing and spinning techniques.

Lorenzo Hubbell, who owned a trading post in Ganado from 1878 to 1930, disapproved of the use of Germantown yarns, now a metonym for any aniline-dyed, industrially produced yarn, and sought out works that featured a "natural" color palette. He made an exception for "Ganado red." Hubbell understood that eastern customers wanted, or needed, an idealized idea of the Navajo as a reserve against the industrial, every bit as much as the Lake District poets needed the shepherd as a reserve against Manchester. The brief period of efflorescence of these bright rugs, the period after aniline dye was introduced to the Navajo, and before it was made anathema by traders, became known as the "Transitional Period" in their weaving history.

Velma had recently co-curated a show of Transitional Period weavings at the Heard Museum in Phoenix. The curatorial team called it "Color Riot: How Color Changed Navajo Textiles." The weavings on view were made between 1870 and 1900, a period when highly complex geometric patterns were developed and elaborated by weavers with a multitudinous palette. The wall tags beneath each work read, "Unidentified artist."

Velma and I met at the Heard Museum at night. Before looking at her exhibition, we took in the opening of Diné composer and artist Raven Chacon's sound installation, *Still Life Number 3*. The sound of elders narrating the Navajo creation story traveled across an arc of speakers while the lights in the gallery changed from white, to yellow, to blue, to red, signaling the passage of the Diné up through multiple worlds. Color was central in Navajo cosmology, which affiliated each of these worlds, and each cardinal direction, with a color.

Inside "Color Riot," which filled the main exhibition space, Velma and I stopped before a rug made up of a simple repeating pattern of squares inside of squares. Purple, black, yellow, orange, and red squares alternated across the weaving. No row was perfectly even, no square perfectly straight. Some bowed in and others out. Some of the dyes had a mottled effect because the wool had taken the dye unevenly, or showed variance in the color underneath. The black was sometimes on the outside, sometimes in the middle. Although it was a weaving from the late nineteenth century, the effect was strikingly reminiscent of American modern art. This was not surprising, because this type of work had been a central influence on the creation of modern art.

"This is one of the pieces we pulled for the Albers show," Velma said. Before it had evolved to fill the main exhibition space, "Color Riot" had been originally conceived as a small show to supplement a display of works by Josef Albers, a German-born artist who emigrated to the United States when the Nazis closed the Bauhaus, where he had been a professor. Albers, whose paintings and "color theory" had a deep impact on American modern art and arts education, had spent time in the Southwest, and his paintings, like *Homage to the Square*, bear the clear imprint of the influence of Navajo tapestries.

Albers's wife, the textile artist Anni Albers, headed a weaving workshop at the Bauhaus, one of the few women to hold a senior role at the school. Anni Albers described weaving this way: "Like any craft it may end in producing useful objects, or it may rise to the level of art." She implies that "useful objects" fell below "art" on a hierarchy of importance. For the Navajo, however, weavings were to become "art" when the violent intervention of the U.S. government robbed the Navajo of subsistence, and they were forced to cater to western taste by producing weavings that had no other purpose than to hang on a wall.

When the Navajo returned to their lands following their internment at Bosque Redondo, they had no food. Their sheep had been killed, their agriculture interrupted. They were forced to rely upon commodities purchased from trading post owners who moved onto the reservation alongside the returning Navajo. Flour and lard had been totally unknown to the Navajo prior to Basque Redondo. Now they became reliant on these products of industrial America, along with tinware dishes, tools, canned goods, coffee, and fabric.

As the Navajo rebuilt their flocks, trading posts eagerly bought their wool, and eventually evolved into marketers for Navajo goods, selling Navajo rugs and silver to an increasingly interested public. By the turn of the century, weavings had become the staple trade item.

As traders took more woven goods in trade, Navajo artisans devoted more time to their weaving. As it became more economically important, the Navajo stopped wearing their own woven blankets. These formed a ready way to earn cash to buy much needed commodities, and so it became less practicable to devote time to weaving cloth for wear.

Incursions on traditional clothing also came from the manufacture of Pendleton woolen blankets for the Indian market, the new availability of western clothes at trading posts, and the pressure to wear Anglo American clothing in school and at work. As their weavings shrank to fit on the walls of their western customers, the Navajo themselves began to wear machine-made cloth. Did Navajo weaving then, in Anni Albers's terms, "rise to the level of art"? Or was art, rather, a term imposed on it by a culture that had cleaved in two the creative and the productive acts?

In the first decades of the twentieth century, the increased exposure, through tourism, to the Southwest contributed to a growing demand for Navajo and Pueblo crafts. This demand spawned copycat goods, made in factories sometimes using Native American labor. In an effort to combat these copycat goods, the Indian Arts and Crafts Board, created in 1935, devised a stamp for silver and a tag for weavings to authenticate quality. The board was the U.S. government's main effort to boost the Indian economy through the work of artisans.

In 1936, René d'Harnoncourt was hired as the assistant manager of the board. In this capacity, d'Harnoncourt staged huge, influential exhibits. In 1939, he set up the "Indian Exhibit" at the Golden Gate Exposition in San Francisco, to which 1.5 million visitors came. In 1941, he created the exhibit "Indian Art of the United States" at the Museum of Modern Art in New York. The exhibit took up the entire museum, and framed the work of Indian crafts in the context of both Native American culture and American art—modern art in particular. Although the 1941 show at MoMA was correct to assert that Navajo images were every bit as full of creative genius as other types of modern art, it imposed a western conception of art—a conception that had been, since the Industrial Revolution, willing to strip creativity from the making of everyday objects like clothes and furniture and corral that creativity all within one small ghetto: the making of useless objects known as "art."

The next morning around eleven, I visited Velma at the weaving class she taught, in Tempe, just east of Mesa. The class was held in a former elementary school that had been turned into a continuing education center. Six Navajo women in shorts and tank tops or jersey dresses sat at long tables in front of their looms, which Velma's ex-husband, Dustin, had constructed. On the wall, posters listing rules about using the classroom computers—"Always wash your hands before using the Chromebook. Carry the Chromebook with two hands at all times . . ."—pointed to the room's use at other times. Now, the brushing and thudding sound of the beater bar, the murmur of women's voices, transformed it.

"Can I have another candy?" asked one of the weaving students' daughters, having finished her Twizzler.

Velma took me around, showing me each student's loom. Tia "had tension issues," so she was going back and reworking some of the lines of the weaving. On another loom, a student was working on twill, a textile weave that creates parallel ribs on the diagonal.

Some of her students, Velma had told me the day before, had the same apprehensions about learning to weave in a classroom that she herself had felt. They thought that they should have learned to weave "organically," from their parents or grandparents. She said part of what she wanted to do was to let her students know: "it's yours, you have it now."

Sometimes students brought their mothers or their grandmothers to class, Velma said, and some of these elders were weavers themselves. "They're living with my students out here in the city, but for some reason they don't feel confident. They didn't pass it on. So, they're sitting with their children in the classroom, validating that the process is right."

Sometimes the influence could move the other way too. One of Velma's more advanced students, Sheena, told me about her grandmother, Happy Cly, who lived in Monument Valley. Happy Cly had been featured in the movie *Navajo Boy*, which chronicled the devastating effects of radiation from uranium mines built on reservation lands. "My grandma didn't weave for a really long time," Sheena told me. "She was very closed off and wouldn't talk to me about it. I would ask her questions like, 'What's this? What's that?' And she would pretend she didn't know." When Sheena began weaving on her own, something changed. She gave her grandmother her second weaving as a gift, along with a loom she had warped for her, and Happy Cly started to weave again.

That afternoon I headed north out of Phoenix, up toward the reservation. I passed through an eerie desert suburb filled with outlet shopping: a Nike outlet, a Banana Republic outlet, a Van Heusen outlet. The heat finally loosened its grip as I got into the mountains, then the pine forest in the national parklands, and then the High Plains. As I got close to Winslow and passed signs for "Meteor Crater," the Painted Desert with its mesas appeared sandy pink, full of light, like an apparition.

I checked into the Rodeway Inn, which was run by a couple from India and their two teenaged children, on the old Route 66. Winslow is small, located on the edge of the reservation. It is what the Navajo and Hopi refer to as a "border town."

In the morning, I went to meet Marlowe Katoney at the Falcon, a 1970s-looking diner in the downtown area. Marlowe was known for his almost photorealistic, Gerhard Richter–like weavings of breakdancers and skateboarders. The first piece I saw of his featured a traditional tree of life motif, but the birds in the tree were Angry Birds, from the popular cell phone game.

Marlowe was fine-featured, with a flat cap, and he had brought both his brother Yancey and his mother, Pearl, to the interview. He wasn't feeling well, and left before the food arrived, leaving me with Pearl and Yancey. Pearl ended up doing most of the talking. She spoke fast, like one afraid of being interrupted before an important transmission had been made. Born in 1945, Pearl grew up near Sunflower

Butte, on the reservation, as the oldest of ten. Pearl's mother had been a celebrated weaver who favored the Ganado Ridge style. Ganado rugs usually feature one or two diamonds at the center with concentric diamonds around them, and a geometric border. They are red, gray, cream, and sometimes brown. I asked Pearl what her mother thought of Marlowe's weaving. "I don't know what kind of weaving he's doing," Pearl remembered her mother saying about Marlowe's weaving style. To her, "it was not right."

Pearl's mother wouldn't let her near the loom, she said, although she did rely on her to card the wool. "That was the grunt work." She was also often tasked with watching the sheep. She had no time to be a child, she said, because she had to change her siblings' diapers, care for the babies, help make the beans, do the dishes. Her father was very particular about the dishes, because he was afraid of tuberculosis, which ran rampant on the reservation, and so she had to boil the water to wash them every day.

The years of Pearl's youth had been lean times on the reservation. After their internment, the Navajo had enjoyed a period of prosperity, largely thanks to high wool prices during World War I. The Depression, however, hit them hard. Then, in the 1930s, federal officials worried that overgrazing by the sheep on the Navajo Reservation in Dust Bowl conditions would cause silting in the machinery of the Hoover Dam project. The government implemented a livestock reduction program that resulted in the slaughter of more than 250,000 sheep and goats, and more than 10,000 horses. The effects were lasting. This cull disproportionately hurt Diné women and girls, who owned virtually all of the goats, and the majority of the sheep (men owned more horse and cattle). John W. Kennedy, who was working for the Atarque Sheep Company, south of the Zuni Reservation, in the spring of 1931 recalled that "over behind one ridge, there was a mountain of old sheep carcasses and bones. . . . They were so dependent on their sheep that when you took away sixty or so percent of their income, it was a real blow."

Pearl suggested that, since it didn't look like I would be interviewing Marlowe that day, I might as well go with Yancey to Flagstaff, to the Hopi show. On the drive, Yancey told me about going to see ska shows in Flagstaff in high school, held in the woods with generators and speakers. The venues wouldn't host them because the pit was too rowdy. Later, in prison, some Navajo guys had taken issue with his knuckle tattoos spelling out S-K-A P-U-N-K, because they weren't traditional, and so he had them tattooed over.

As we got close to Flagstaff, the San Francisco Peaks rose up before us. Velma had told me that the four corners of the loom were symbolically connected to the four corners of Navajo country, which were once marked by the San Francisco Peaks in the west, Mount Hesperus in the north, Mount Blanca in the east, and Mount Taylor in the south. By these markers it is also possible to see how much diminished the Navajo lands were when they returned to them from Bosque Redondo.

The Hopi Reservation is an island within the Navajo Reservation. Hopi kids used to come to the ska shows too, Yancey said. At the Hopi show—an arts and culture festival—Yancey made the rounds to catch up with his friends—jewelers, a painter—and I stopped to chat with a weaver named Ivan, who was working on a cotton shawl, in the traditional black and white plaid.

Yancey and I ate Navajo tacos—fry bread with beans, cheese, lettuce, tomato—and then watched a Hopi ceremonial dance. He said that he and Marlowe had both spent a lot of time with his uncle, a jeweler, at events like this when they were young, but it was Marlowe who paid attention. Marlowe was interested in art from a young age. "I wasn't. I was playing in the dirt, playing with trucks and Transformers," said Yancey. He had worked for a while on the reservation doing sandblasting. "In an astronaut suit all day with oxygen circulating through it, no fun. They wouldn't even let me set the pressure," he said. "I am just a cog."

Marlowe on the other hand had gone on to art school, and used the techniques of painting in his weavings. His "ply splitting" technique, where he peeled apart yarns to get even smoother gradients in places where blocks of colors merged, owed more to his training in oils than it did to weaving as he had learned it from his maternal grandmother.

In the car on the way back, Yancey told me about the day his friend Jesús died. They had worked together, and Yancey had just texted Jesús to remind him to bring the Bluetooth speaker. Jesús was nowhere to be found. His parents wanted to file a missing person report, but not enough time had passed. The next day Jesús was found dead in front of a store, of a fentanyl overdose.

I thought about that story the next day when I met Marlowe again, and he told me he was weaving a Pietà—an image of the Virgin Mary holding her son's dead body—as a way to cope with the number of friends he had lost that year to accident and illness. Unlike Yancey, Marlowe had found a livelihood through which he could speak about his experiences. That was the problem, I thought, with dividing people into artists and, as Yancey had put it, "cogs."

Marlowe's opinion of his weavings was different from his grandmother's: he did not see them as a rupture from tradition. There is, he pointed out, a tradition of image making in Navajo weaving known as "pictorial weaving." Early pictorial weavings depicted, for instance, scenes from the life of a trading post. "If you look at, historically, what pictorial weavers were doing, they were depicting what was going on around them," Marlowe said. Their subjects were simply "what people are doing, what they're up to."

Marlowe said his work ought to be viewed as an extension rather than a rupture. The real rupture, according to him, was when Navajo weavings first began to be treated like wall pieces, when they began to be—sometimes literally, sometimes conceptually—framed as art. "Those first rugs that came out were utilitarian. They were wearing blankets." Then, later on, "the rugs got smaller and rather than being utilitarian, the owners of trading posts started to encourage them to make them as wall hangings." Eventually, rugs began to have borders which functioned "like a picture frame around the design. That idea has really transformed what Navajo weaving is. And now it's looked at more as an art form. And I think what I'm doing now is just taking it one step further."

nside R. B. Burnham & Co., a trading post in Sanders, Arizona, skeins of wool milled in Pennsylvania and dyed using vegetable dyes by a local woman named Mary Beguay stood out next to the Kool-Aid,

Honeybuns, Moon Pies, and Hamburger Helper displayed next to them on shelves. Mary Beguay used local plants to make her dyes, so her colors change over the course of the year, explained one of the employees.

R. B. Burnham & Co. is one of the last Navajo trading posts left, serving the dual purpose of selling Navajo rugs and jewelry to outsiders, while selling supplies, like yarns, to Navajo weavers, as well as basic groceries, lamb dips, formula, and farming implements.

Sherry was the store's fifth-generation proprietor, but the first woman in that line. She noted the differences between the way the men in her family had run the post and the way she was running it now. For example, she told me that her forefathers dictated what the Navajo weavers would make for sale. Today, the Navajo weavers did what they wanted, she said, and she just marketed it. Marlowe, who was here to buy yarn and also sold his rugs at the post, was a good example. She said if she didn't have the money to buy a rug from a weaver to sell in her store, she just didn't buy it. But she didn't sit there and critique the rug, a classic tactic that her predecessors used to drive prices down. Sherry's mother was Navajo, her father was an Anglo. His people were Mormons originally, like many early trading post owners.

Sherry opened a door in the back, and led me into a room filled with antique silver and turquoise jewelry and Navajo rugs. Sometimes Japanese people came through and bought up a bunch of stuff, she said. She told the story of a British couple who asked for the best rug she had, and bought it, even though it meant they had to be absentee bidders at the auction where she had already placed the rug on the bill. It was made by perhaps the most famous Navajo weaver, Daisy Taugelchee. She said Taugelchee could buy a car with one of her weavings. Pearl, who had been sitting silently on a bench while we talked, confirmed this. She had worked for many years at a Chevy dealership, and she had seen many of the more celebrated weavers trade weavings for trucks.

That evening, when Pearl and Marlowe and I arrived back at Pearl's, Yancey was coming across the street with a bunch of romaine lettuce that a neighbor had given him. We all went inside together and Marlowe took out a sack of brown churro wool he had picked up at his studio. Pearl got out some carders she borrowed from a relative on the reservation so that she could show me the part of the job that she had done for her mother, as a child.

She began to card the wool. She hadn't done this since she was a little girl, she said. Unsteady at first, her movements soon found a rhythm. Carding wool is a bit like brushing hair, only there are two brushes and the wool is between them. Next, Pearl got out the spindle that Marlowe had brought over and she approached it with familiarity even after a trance of fifty years. She wrapped the roving around the bottom and eventually made a knot. She began pulling out small sections of roving and giving them a little twist. Stretching a little more, twisting, winding the yarn on the spindle.

In the story of the Minotaur, Theseus is handed a ball of yarn by Ariadne along with a knife with which to slay the beast. He trails the thread behind him so that he can find his way out of the labyrinth. Thread is just as powerful a tool and weapon as the blade. Hand over hand, in the dark, through the maze, he can find the way back to safety by following the thread. Safety, it felt to me then, had something to do with thread *itself*, or the ability to make thread. Spinning is the act of taking many fragments and transforming them into a long continuous whole. Trauma can liquidate that ability for a time, fracturing experience into disconnected parts. If the spinner could adhere these fragments, little by little, wasn't that a way toward healing?

The boys were making fun of Pearl because her yarn was so lumpy. Marlowe said, "Well, maybe I could weave a saddle blanket out of that."

"He's trying to take down my work," she said. "Well, I won't let him." As she practiced, Marlow took out the skeins of yarn that he bought at the trading post and began to make one of the skeins into a ball, untangling it patiently as he went. Even Yancey took a try at the spindle after watching first his mother, then Marlow, give it a go. Mostly, though, Yancey watched BMX videos on his phone, or played with a cat on the rug, or showed us funny videos of Yoda saying things about Navajo tacos. He had said he was going to go out to see *Spider-Man*, but he wordlessly changed his plan, and sat with us in the twilight, while his mother carded and spun. It was as though the spindle created a small center of gravity.

Nikyle was in the hogan—a round or octagonal one-room structure traditionally used by the Navajo as dwellings or ceremonial sites—where there were churro fleeces laid out on the table. Nikyle wore a tie-dyed shirt with a jean shirt over it, and had a big frame, a soft voice, and feminine eyebrows. I realized Nikyle was transgender when they recounted to me a traditional Navajo story in which transgendered deities, for whom there exist multiple terms in Navajo, were playing a critical part in saving humanity, inventing tools for agriculture.

"My grandmother's brother died last night," Nikyle explained when I first arrived. "So, I can't weave. We're matrilineal, so when anybody dies on your maternal grandmother's side, you have to mourn." No traveling at night, no digging holes, no washing hair, and no weaving.

Nikyle had learned to weave as a child from their *shi'nali*, or paternal grandmother, and from her also how to care for a flock of sheep. "The first thing she really taught me how to do was saddle up the horse," Nikyle recounted. "There was a gentle older horse and she would say as the sun was going up, 'Just watch me,' and I watched her and the next morning I did it on my own."

Nikyle's grandmother kept Rambelais sheep, but spoke of another kind of sheep, called *Deé' dįį'*, or "four horns." These were the kind of sheep that had been on the reservation at the time when the government demanded stock reductions. Some people, Nikyle said, had preserved their sheep from the culls by leading them up into the buttes until the officials had gone. Similarly, some children escaped removal to boarding school by hiding out on the buttes, among the sheep. Nikyle didn't come across the Deé' dįį' until they were thirteen, when they joined the FFA (Future Farmers of America) and 4-H, organizations that were then raising Navajo churro sheep. "These were *my* sheep that I needed to have," Nikyle thought the moment they laid eyes on the sheep. "I am their person that will raise them and help them." While still in high school, Nikyle started a flock with a ram named Chester and a ewe named Misty.

Misty had come from a flock called the Navajo Sheep Project, which was founded in the 1970s by Lyle McNeal, a professor at Utah State University in Logan. The number of Navajo churro sheep had by that time dropped below five hundred. McNeal traveled to the reservation and bought and traded with the Navajo to start his own nucleus flock. From these, Nikyle said, McNeal had returned thousands of sheep to the rez, and helped restore the breed.

Even before becoming a teenaged shepherd, Nikyle had nurtured a secret weaving habit. As a child, their job was to stuff down the wool in large burlap sacks at shearing time, and this provided a chance to siphon off little scraps of wool to spin surreptitiously on a tiny handmade spindle. When Nikyle's grandmother found a loom they had made, instead of getting angry as Nikyle expected she would, she was supportive. She taught Nikyle how to make a traditional lap spindle out of an old axe handle.

Nikyle's grandmother told them, "If you want to do this, this is all it takes. Just, everything has to be in harmony. You can't have any negative thoughts towards your sheep, towards the wool, towards your loom. Even while you're weaving, you have to think very positive and you can't treat this like, 'Oh my gosh I have to do this and make money.'" It was also important to show a proper attitude to the sheep, she said. "In every aspect, they're life. So, you don't mistreat it. You don't talk down on them. You have to cherish them. When you no longer have your grandparents, when you no longer have your actual parents, the sheep will be your parents. They'll feed you, they'll clothe you. They'll provide you with a livelihood."

Nikyle spent two years at a local community college, and two more years at a university farther from home, always coming back home for lambing and shearing, to care for the flock that had begun with Misty and Chester. After graduating, they took a job inspecting circuit boards. When the company they worked for moved overseas, Nikyle came home and committed to making a livelihood from the sheep themselves.

This traditional life is now the exception in Navajo country, as it is everywhere else.

According to Nikyle, however, keeping traditional arts like weaving alive is a central component of the Navajo trans identity. In Navajo clan stories, "you know, whether it was gay or transgendered or even hermaphrodites—these were sacred people who would be like the backbone of the family. They would keep the family together. They would continue the sheep, continue weaving, even becoming medicine people, and keeping rituals and songs and prayers."

The English term Two-Spirit has been used in recent years in an attempt to incorporate and honor a concept that exists in hundreds of North American indigenous languages for a person whose persona projects both masculine and feminine spirits. As an identity, Two-Spirit denotes more than someone who eludes western gender binaries, but also someone who has a particular capacity as a ceremonial leader, caregiver, shaman, and in some tribes, those who were particularly skilled in crafts like weaving. Within the Navajo tradition, which includes at least five genders, they are an integral part of creation stories.

"People who are keeping traditions alive are people who are just like me. Who are gay, who are trans," Nikyle said. They said I would see this for myself if I went to a ceremony: "Here we call them the dolls. You'll see a group of them, running the show. Taking over, so no one has to worry."

Nikyle told me a story about a famous trans woman from Navajo lore who remained in her own hogan while the others surrendered and marched to Fort Sumner. Desperate, the interned Navajo sent two scouts back to beg her to come and help them. "*You* wanted to surrender, so you should go enjoy it," said the woman. "You know she was being catty, she was throwing shade." According to the legend, when the scouts entered her hogan they saw with amazement that she had a wall of dried rabbit meat, and a big blanket on the loom. Her goats were fat and plump although it was the dead of winter, and her storage cellars full of corn and squash. She refused, however, to be budged. She slaughtered a few goats for the others to take back to sustain the prisoners that winter.

Nikyle was a skilled weaver, and traded their weavings for live-stock, selling wool, and yarn, and breeding stock.

"Would you consider yourself an artist?" I asked Nikyle.

"Well, there's no word in Navajo for art," Nikyle said. "I weave for horses. My grandma always said, 'Your horses want to look pretty too! So, weave them something beautiful, so they can feel proud.'"

Just as the Gnostics saw the stars as tiny pinpricks revealing a radiant outer sphere, *holes* in the Navajo visual lexicon have a positive valence. The people who became the *Diné*, or Navajo, traveled upward through three different worlds, each time through a hole in the sky of one world, which was a hole in the ground of another. It was thought that one could find Spider Woman—the Navajo weaver goddess and a great helper, teacher, and protector of humans, through a hole in the ground. Small holes were sometimes left in weavings as a reference to her.

In a perforated world, there is possibility for transcendent solutions. According to economist E. F. Schumacher, it is typical of a society that has been cosmologically flattened to remain locked in stubborn dualisms like male and female, mind and matter, east and west, capitalist and communist, craft and art. Ironically too, the civilization that does not believe in any plane but this one is the first to have actually, literally perforated our world, creating holes in our sky and at the bottom of our seas.

Weaving is a transformative process with many functions. It involves clearing thought, and organizing personal energy and emotion. A handwoven work resists becoming mere product, or mere art.

Anthropologist Jane Schneider noted that even though cloth, in today's world, has lost many of its former meanings and connections to rituals of life and death, it is still used in important ways "to mobilize human emotions in support of large-scale institutions." Think of the flag, or the military uniform, or the pussy hat, or a red cap with white lettering that reads, "Make America Great Again." Our clothes are never neutral, and cannot be.

The severe and prolonged violence that has annihilated the world's weaving traditions cannot be separated from the destruction of agricultural systems, sovereignties, communal values, and identities. Neither should the resurrection of weaving traditions be seen in isolation: cloth cannot be viewed separately from the entire material and social basis from which it springs. Unerringly, cloth tells the story of the rise and fall of our societies and our cultures. And, perhaps, it does so more accurately than any words can.

Conclusion

It has been well said that mythology is the penultimate truth—penultimate because the ultimate cannot be put into words.

—JOSEPH CAMPBELL, *THE POWER OF MYTH*

We must believe in the existence of the spider, the experience behind the myth, though it is indeed true that we can never see this sort of spider at work; we can only find the webs, the myths that human authors weave.

—WENDY DONIGER, *THE IMPLIED SPIDER:*
POLITICS AND THEOLOGY IN MYTH

No other animal gets dressed. Food, clothing, and shelter—that triptych of human needs is only two thirds shared with the animals. No other animal tells stories, either. These two capacities are, it seems, deeply connected. Spinning and weaving goddesses are the great storytellers. Some concern themselves with individual fates, the story of each life. The Norns, of the old Norse tradition, spin the destinies of men, and for the greatest heroes spin a golden thread. The three Greek Fates determine the course of a life as follows: Clotho spins the thread for every person, and Atropos (the *unturnable*) cuts it at the moment of death, which is determined by Lachesis, *the allotter*. The Romans called these women the Parcae: Nona, Decuma, and Morta.

Not just storytellers, these goddesses were also arbiters of civilization, justice, law, and art. They were upholders of a collective life bound by values other than that of individual survival, or the combat of wills through violence. The weaver goddesses rule over fibers and fabrics, but also over passions, and they bring the various forces within society into harmony.

These goddesses are often associated with the spider. The spider connects people in a web, weaving the social order just as it weaves cloth, and holding chaotic forces at bay. The Navajo weaver goddess Spider Woman encounters the wiles of the trickster Coyote in a popular tale. The Japanese weaver goddess Amaterasu confronts her brother, the storm god, who destroys her loom and kills her weaving attendants when he hurls a flayed pony into her weaving room. Because Amaterasu is also the sun, the world is plunged into darkness when she retreats into a cave to mourn this senseless destruction. Athena, the Greek weaver goddess and the goddess of civilization and the city, art, wisdom, and the law, comes up against the more anarchic powers of Poseidon. She takes Odysseus's side on his journey home, protecting him each time Poseidon raises stormy seas against his fleet. The Norns guard the world tree, Yggdrasil, from the creatures that try to gnaw at it or scrape it with sharp claws. Where there is a cut or a tear, the weaver goddess mends, just as cobwebs were once used to stanch wounds. Ixchel, the Mayan weaver goddess, is associated with medicine.

In this correspondence between the weaver, the storyteller, and the values of common life, it seems almost as though humans, knowing some of their uniquely destructive capacities, tried to brandish some of their unique competencies to counteract them: the weaving spider tangles deftly with destructive forces.

Dressing is an individual act, but it is also a deeply social one. Clothing is not merely a demonstration of our relations to one another, it is a crystallization of these relationships. It is not surprising, then, that myths and stories about cloth and clothing are a place where people grapple with what ought to be their correct relationship with one another: with ethics. Myths and stories about cloth and clothing contain warnings: about locking women up and forcing them to spin ("Rumpelstiltskin") or weave ("The Crane Wife"), about the idiocies of the powerful ("The Emperor's New Clothes"). They explore the limits of human cruelty ("Snow White"), as well as the limits of human changeability and the relationship between the interior and the exterior self ("Cinderella," "Cap-o'-Rushes").

Cultural debates about clothes become proxy wars for other issues. In any historical period or region, to study a culture's conflicts and debates about clothes is to watch them approach the basic questions of civic life. How much inequality should exist between people, and should they be able to rise in the world? How does a society treat its women and men? Children and adults? Mortals and gods? What is the appropriate relationship between the individual person and the collective? How much more powerful should the powerful be than the weak?

In the contemporary United States, the culture is glutted with language about clothes, but the vast majority of this language belongs to the advertisers, or the para-advertisers in the form of magazines whose revenue stream is driven by apparel marketing. Clothing is offered to modern consumers both as an opportunity for creative expression, and a solution to every possible ill. Clothes exist for exercise: to achieve health. For yoga: to achieve peace of mind. For beauty: to attract a mate. For career advancement: to secure an income. For self-renovation: to heal a broken heart. Clothes *do* have power. The power of the branding apparatus, though, rests in making people believe that various ways of processing oil and cotton somehow yield distinctive objects. In this, the fashion industry parallels the U.S. food industry, which, as Michael Pollan has shown, reconstitutes a very few agricultural commodities: corn, soy, rice, and wheat, into an ever-shifting panoply of miracle products. With clothing, as with food, there is a vast secondary industry in guiding consumers in their purchases: magazines, stylists, subscription shopping services, and other "experts."

Fortunately, in an age of false myths, there also persist reliable sources of information. These are, of course, the clothes themselves. The biologist M. L. Ryder, tracing the evolution of sheep breeds in Britain, noted, "a parchment may have written records and painted miniatures of sheep on its surface, but the true history of sheep lies within the parchment itself." Parchment is made from sheepskin. The garment does not lie, though the writing on it may. A shirt may say "Wisconsin" while its tag reads "Made in India," but the real political story lies in its polycotton blend. To read objects carefully and accurately is to read the world itself: its systems and its systems-level failures.

Sometimes the clothes we wear tell truer stories than we do. For instance, those about the limits of human cruelty. In the U.S., I was raised to believe in the myth of progress: the idea that people and institutions that once were cruel and rapacious are no longer. The record shows that our cultural capacity for cruelty and exploitation, rather than improving along a straight line, waxes and wanes like the moon. In 1850, it was a commonplace for women seamstresses to live near starvation levels while working fourteen-hour days making shirts. In 1950 this kind of life was unthinkable for a seamstress defended by a union. Today it is a commonplace again.

Text and *textile* come from the same Latin root, *texere,* which means "to weave." Sometimes cloth, when used as a text, can say things that are impossible to say in any other way. Philomela, a princess of Greek mythology whose tongue was cut from her head so that she could not tell the story of her rape, wove that story instead.

Some fabrics have systems encoded within them that make them just as capable of transmitting complex historical events and concepts as a language is. One example is kente, a strip-woven cloth made by the Asante* peoples of Ghana and the Ewe peoples of Ghana and Togo. Warp strip patterns in kente are given names for important chiefs or queen mothers,† plants, animals, and natural phenomena. Warp patterns also often commemorate particular events. For

---

* The Asante, who still occupy a significant portion of south-central Ghana, are the most populous of the Akan (Twi-speaking) peoples in the country.

† Descent, inheritance, and succession among the Akan are all matrilineal, a system that provides considerable power and prestige to the queen mother.

instance, one pattern, Oyokoman, Ogya da mu, documents a civil crisis that occurred within the Oyoko family after the death of Osei Tutu, king and founder of the Asante Kingdom. The literal meaning of the pattern's name, art historian Paul Ofori-Ansah writes, is: "There is fire (crisis) in the Oyoko nation." Green and yellow represent the two branches of the Oyoko family and the red between them symbolizes "fire"—civil crisis.

Kente weft patterns also have names: often those of objects, although these objects also have resonance with proverbs. For instance, one weft design, Makowa, means "little peppers," which is identified with the proverb, "All peppers do not ripen at the same time." Thus, simply by selecting a warp pattern and a weft pattern, the weaver is able to make reference to specific historic events or personages, and given access to the range of more pliable philosophical concepts embedded in the parables. But that is not all.

Kente is not just made up of one rectangle of fabric. Rather, it is comprised of hundreds of strips of fabric sewn together to produce one field. Relationships between different strips within the field also have meanings, and the strips themselves can take different meanings depending on how they are combined. There is a warp pattern, for instance, called Afoakwa Mpua, or "Afoakwa's nine tufts of hair." This name conjures a hairstyle once worn by court officials, likely sword bearers. When strips of cloth containing this design are joined to produce a patterned field, it takes on another signification: Akyempem, or "A thousand shields." Considering that the total corpus of designs in Asante strip-woven cloth contains over five hundred warp patterns, and a similar amount of weft patterns, it is easy to see what a vast semiotic system this fabric represents.

We have to become good readers of cloth. Even, and especially, of the monochrome, mass-produced fabric bolt. And we might learn to approach our clothes with certain questions. Where did they come from? From what histories? From whose hands? From what fields? Where will they go when they break down? I hope this book can begin to provide some of those answers, but perhaps more important, to provoke the frequent asking of these questions.

After we have learned to read clothing, where do we go from

there? Can technology save us? This seems unlikely. Raw acquisitive urge is often joined to the most advanced technology. In this respect, Athena and Arachne's contest becomes a warning. Arachne was a woman who bragged that she could weave more skillfully than anyone, and in a contest with Athena, she proved this claim true. Nonetheless, Athena punished her for her lack of humility. Technology might be a place to demonstrate human virtuosity, but alone it cannot save us from jealous gods.

Nor is the answer as simple as a return to the handmade. In Oaxaca, where tourists from Europe and America have created a large market for embroidered dresses, local entrepreneurs have reconstituted the kind of putting-out system that impoverished home sewers in the nineteenth century. Human rights activist Rigoberta Menchú noted with grief in the 1980s that touristic attention to the Guatemalan Maya extended to the colorful clothing, but not to the people themselves. Good fabric requires us to rebuild entire systems of water use and conservation, distribution of wealth and resources, trade regimes, and agriculture.

Efforts to save handcraft are important, but we must be careful that those efforts treat the disease, and not merely the symptom. The making of good fabric cannot happen in isolation: it cannot happen without good communities and good agriculture. It cannot happen in the context of brutal, extractive trade regimes.

Human beings have long relied on the metaphors of spinning and weaving. In the sciences: *string* theory. In the humanities: the *fabric* of society, reality's *warp* and *woof*. In the press: communities are *rent* apart, alliances *stitched* together. If, as this omnipresent metaphor suggests, we are part of a social fabric, this should be one good indication that cloth can't be either destroyed, or restored, without completely altering our orientation toward one another, and to the land.

I do not believe there is any unitary answer to the question of how to fix our clothes system. The answer to the problem of clothes demands the attention of farmers, engineers, ranchers, dyers, weavers, spinners, artists, lawmakers, economists, writers, educators, environmental activists, community organizers, seamstresses, tailors, and dressers of all types. Which is to say, all of us. There are thousands of ways to go about this project, and many have made a start already.

I can tell a story about one idea I had, and where it led me.

At some point in my twenties, I imagined that a way to solve the problem of clothing would be to return to tailoring. To every hundred people or so, a tailor. It would be interesting, skilled work, a way to make a living and provide a valuable good. Perhaps a training program could be provided as an extension of high school or community college. The tailor could be provided with fabric by local co-ops, with an emphasis on regional materials, or fairly traded imported goods. I set out to learn tailoring myself. In the fall of 2010, I enrolled in a tailoring class at the Fashion Institute of Technology.

My classroom was large and lit with fluorescent lights, and on the tables stood JUKI sewing machines. These are Japanese-made industrial machines, and they are an altogether different animal than a Singer or a Bernina. You can feel the force in them as if you had taken hold of a leash attached to a dog much stronger than you.

My teacher had grown up and learned tailoring in the Dominican Republic and worked in what he called "the industry" for decades before coming to teach at FIT. He had an inexplicable but powerful passion for Charlie Sheen, who admittedly is often quite well tailored in some of his movies. Outside the building in which the class was held, there were always groups of students in ostentatious outfits smoking Parliament Lights, which is, to be fair, what I had smoked as an undergraduate too. Their misery, their posturing, their manic energy, made me both sympathetic to them and filled me with aversion.

The precise objects of the classroom were what moved me most. The triangular tailor's chalk with its rounded edges as it slid across a piece of charcoal gray wool, the muscular steel scissors. The pattern pieces were cut from a thick manila paper far more stable than the wafery paper used by at-home-sewing patterns, which often don't last for more than one project. There was even a special tool designed to punch a keyhole-shaped slot in the pattern pieces, through which was strung another special implement: a metal hook that could hang on a nail or on a rack. I fastidiously kept all of my sewing supplies—the tailor's chalk, the pins, the extra sewing machine needles, even the pressure foot—in a plastic fishing tackle box.

I was also moved by the intense focus we placed on each part of a garment: on the hip pocket, for example, of a skirt. I felt a kind of childlike satisfaction when the dozen or so of us gathered at the end of a long table to watch our teacher demonstrate the four different ways that one could hem a pocket opening.

To do my homework, I set up my sewing machine, a Bernina bought for me as a birthday present when I was twelve or thirteen, on the long table that one of my roommates at the time had made from old oak floorboards rescued from a demolished factory.

The first couple of times you incorrectly stitch in a pocket lining, it makes you feel honest and hardworking and ready to try again. The third time you wonder if you really have what it takes to be a tailor. The fourth time renders you philosophical. Since everything is difficult, I thought, since everything worth doing is agonizing and painstakingly difficult, I might want to choose this thing very carefully. And for me, that one thing turned out to be not tailoring, but writing.

I consoled myself by considering how many things there are that link the tailor and the writer. Hadn't Henry Miller's father been a tailor? And hadn't Thomas Mann said that the artist does not spring into his being and vocation out of a void, but rather forms himself as an artist in the pattern of his father's vocation?

Besides, how many of the writers that I loved, loved clothes. It could perhaps be said that the writer wants to undress the world more than she wants to dress it. Nonetheless, Sappho's poetry, or rather the fragments of it that remain, regularly center on some article of clothing. Oscar Wilde was a notorious clotheshorse. Virginia Woolf maintained a kind of negative fixation. Edith Wharton, when asked as a child what she wanted to be when she grew up, replied: "the best dressed woman in New York." Some writers have drawn me to them by the pure, melodious ravishment with which they treat the descriptions of the clothing of their characters. Colette's "pair of strong soled brown boots and a tweed coat and skirt, smelling of alpine meadows and pine forests." Thomas Mann's "Florentine cinquecento frock of claret coloured velvet."

When I first began to publish my writing, it was for the calendar section of a local newspaper, usually profiles of people in the community. One of these first profiles I wrote was of a woman who was helping people organize around alternatives to the industrial food system. She had worked to get fresh produce gleaned from local farms into the school cafeterias. She had started a nonprofit initiative to support farmers starting CSAs (community-supported agriculture). She was launching a magazine to tell stories about local food producers.

During our interview, we talked for a long time about the industrial food system. This is a system that has much in common with the contemporary garment industry. It carries goods across long distances. It relies on a labor pool of agricultural workers who, like garment workers, often toil in dangerous conditions without hope of union protections. The products travel along pathways carved by centuries of colonial control. The system devastates the land, it is wasteful, and as we learned when the COVID-19 crisis erupted—it is insecure. It is designed to realize returns on capital rather than to nurture bodies. It is cheap for the consumer because it externalizes cost. Avoiding the system entirely can have connotations of privilege and elitism. As we spoke, I felt more and more hopelessness over the situation. I asked her how she held on to optimism, or hope, or how she found the endurance to keep on working.

She told me, "Well, every meal is another opportunity."

Since then, I have come to see the wisdom in this way of thinking. A search for the delicious marks a bright part of the day, which lifted her spirits. She might eat fresh eggs from her neighbor's chickens, or good corn from a local farm, or find that her own basil was doing well. The vastness of the problem was met by the repetitive, quotidian nature of the small part she played in the solution.

I think that dressing may be the same. We can try to find something nearby and good to wear. Maybe somebody you know makes clothes. Maybe somebody else tracks the progress of a company making a good pair of pants. Somebody works on a certification scheme that would allow clothes made under fair conditions to be clearly marked for the consumer, as a way to help support the rights of workers. You yourself may make clothes. Even if it becomes just one emblem of the possibility of better clothes, this one emblem can make dressing heartening.

The fifty years before the French Revolution was a period prolific in fictional utopias. Fantasylands were filled with fantastical clothes: protective sun lotion in *Relation du monde de Mercure,* salamander skin in *Le voyageur philosophe,* cloth made from butterfly wings, asbestos, crystal, or hummingbird down in *L'Eldorado.* On the fictional island of Galligènes in *Histoire des Galligènes,* European refugees land on an island with no usable plants or animals for making fabric. Almont, the city's founder, discovers "aerial flax," a seaborn plant that "rose in the air and floated on the wind," "composed of imperceptible filaments, with no strength on their stem, no stiffness in their parts, are supported by the water and sway in the waves." This sea plant produced a fabric that was not only beautiful and of a brilliant color, but that exuded a sweet scent "exactly as needed."

The aerial flax of Galligènes is a fantasy. But it bears a strong resemblance to a type of fabric that is quite real: byssus, or "sea silk." Byssus is the filament extruded by a mollusk that, when properly processed, can then be spun and woven into a sea silk the color of gold. There is only one woman left in the world who knows how to produce byssus. She lives on a tiny Sardinian island and her name is Chiara Vigo. The knowledge of how to make byssus is passed down within a particular clan, to which Vigo belongs, and the Italian authorities forbid harvesting of byssus by anyone else.

Prized in antiquity, byssus is today one of the world's rarest substances. Passed down with the knowledge of how to make byssus, however, is the instruction that it must never be sold. One Japanese businessman approached Chiara Vigo in 2017 with an offer to purchase her most famous piece, *The Lion of Women,* for €2.5 million. Vigo had stitched the 45 x 45 cm piece with her fingernails over the course of four years, and she dedicated it to women everywhere. Although she lives in a small apartment on her husband's pension, Vigo refused the offer flat out.

Capital may seem to have penetrated every corner of the earth, but into that golden territory the size of a small tea towel, it cannot trespass. I do not think that money and clothes must be kept scrupulously separate for clothing to be meaningful and good. But I am glad for Chiara and others who know the real value of their work.

Not far from where the British built their first fortified settlement in India at Fort St. George, I met a man named Kannan who said he liked to argue with Gandhi in his head. Kannan Lakshminarayan was the founder and chief technology officer of Microspin, which produces a group of small machines that can allow farmers to spin their own cotton into thread. The machines are about the height of a man, and could fit in an American garage. They work with a wide variety of native seed types, which allows farmers to plant different species of cotton better suited to their soil than American varieties and avoid chemical inputs. It also allows farmers to earn more, selling processed thread, than they would if they sold raw cotton.

Kannan said that Gandhi had held a contest to create a better charkha, or spinning wheel, design, and offered a huge sum of money to the winner, but put impossible strictures on the contest. "Gandhi wanted to move from here, to here," said Kannan, tapping the side of his hand on one end of the desk, lifting it up, and placing it down a yard away. "But things progress," he said, making a motion as if he was sliding a pile of poker chips across the table: slowly and deliberately. What struck me most about Kannan was how he treated the world he worked to create as though it were already here. "Mass production," he said with a laugh. "That *anachronism*."

When you watch a spider spin a web it appears for a time to be walking over air. How does it get from point to point, how does it travel the distance between two firm holds when there is nothing connecting them? It makes a bridge as it goes, with the thread it produces. The thread itself is what provides safe passage between two impossible points, over an untraversable distance.

Some argue that the reason spinner goddesses were made responsible for making life is that it looks like a spinner is making something from nothing when you watch her work, just like a baby seemed to appear out of thin air to the ancients. An everyday, ordinary miracle.

Acknowledgments

This book was too heavy to hold on my own and I am grateful that I did not have to.

To the many guides who welcomed me into your countries, businesses, homes, and lives, you made this book what it is. There are too many to name, but I will name a few. In India, Ramesh Sivanpillai, Bamini Narayanan, Parimala Rao, and Sarojini Murthy. In Honduras, Javier Andino, Allan Duron, and Gustavo P. In China, David Crook, Carl Crook, Matt Lowenstein, Mrs. L., Mr. S, and Mr. Bo. In Vietnam, James Poleski, Carol Malony, and Tom Robinson. In the U.S., Edwin Lewis; Evan Morrison; Ralph Tharpe; Velma Kee Craig; Marlowe Katoney, Pearl Katoney, and Yancy Katoney; Nikyle Begay; Rabbit Goody; Luke Davis; Jay Ardai; and Shannon O'Hara.

This work rests on the work of scholars who have taken textiles and women's labor history seriously. In particular Ellen Rosen, Xinru Liu, Elizabeth Wayland Barber, Laurel Thatcher Ulrich, Jane Schneider, Alice Kessler-Harris, Silvia Federici, Eric Hobsbawm, Sven Beckert, Daniel Roche, Dana Frank, Stuart Ewen, and Paul David Blanc.

I would like to thank the dream team: my editor, Maria Goldverg, whose questions, precision, rigor, and enthusiasm have transformed this work several times over, and my agent, Laura Usselman, who helped this book take shape in almost every sense of that term, and who has been an incomparable ally in matters large and small. Thanks to Josephine Greywoode, who made several brilliant interventions, and Daisy

Parente, who believed in the relevance of this book for England. Laura Bullard did the fact checking, and was a very good traveling companion through the sprawling city that is this book's endnotes. Thank you to Stuart Krichevsky at SKA agency for your words of advice and encouragement, and to the late Dan Frank at Pantheon, whose enthusiasm for this project at an early stage was incredibly meaningful to me.

I don't know of anybody who becomes an artist without a few people who believe in their work before it even exists. Beth Loffreda, a person who works extremely hard to make artists' lives more possible in America, has been one of those people for me. So have Geraldine Brooks and Tony Horwitz, who showed me what it looks like to live as a writer, and encouraged me to be bold, and Ali Berlow, who gave me my first serious writing assignments.

To the artists and scholars I encountered at the University of Wyoming's MFA Program, both faculty and students, I thank you for incubating this project during years of research and experimentation. Isa Helfgot and Rattawut Lapcharoensap read an early draft, and Andy Fitch read many. Harvey Hicks and Alyson Hagy read sections, and Danielle Pafunda championed the project. Christopher Sweeney provided the translations from Old English in the Linen section. Joy Williams gave me words of encouragement on an early draft that are still framed and hanging on my wall.

Without learning how to sew, I wouldn't have understood what this book was about, nor would I have written it. I thank Hannah Calley, who taught me, and Molly Gray, who learned alongside me. Lila Fischer and Rachel Curtin, with whom I made Lunarwear, and Kate Hubbell, with whom I learned quilting, you taught me reverence for making things collectively. Christa Fischer provided space in her home for us to sew, and introduced me to the work of Elizabeth Wayland Barber.

I'd like to thank my family: my mother, April, with whom I have consulted on the prevalence of spinners and weavers in fairy tales and myths and who has been my informant on the clothes of the 1950s and '60s, as well as a reader, and a partner in touring old mills. My passion for dressing and the thrill of the thrift store took shape alongside and certainly in emulation of my sister, Chaya. My brother, Micah, hosted me, along with his wife, Emily Thanhauser, while I wrote the last section of this book. My late father, Sardar Thanhauser, gave me a great curiosity for supply chains, and the material basis of the social and political world.

I am indebted to friends who wouldn't let me forget about this book during the many times that I gave up on it. These include Adrian Shirk, Kelly Hatton, and Mikko Harvey, who also read drafts. Hannah Vahl, who kept saying she was excited to read it. Sarah and Charlie Calley, who sent relevant books and clippings. Sam Bungey, who believed in it. Sean Fitzpatrick, on whose tech support, enthusiasm, and optimism I have leaned heavily. I'd also like to thank some of the many people who have supported me as a human being over the course of making this book: Kelly Merklin, Catie Ballard, Esau Lozano, Korie Johnson, Jane Resnick, Jane Warrick, Annie Baker, Alison MacLean, Grace Kredell, and Sally Howe.

Much of this book was written at residencies at the MacDowell Colony, Ucross Foundation, Jentel Residency Program, Millay Colony, Virginia Center for the Creative Arts (VCCA), and Brush Creek Foundation. Thank you for providing me with the time and space in which to do this work. It was critical.

Notes

INTRODUCTION

xii In 2019, global retail sales: Shahbandeh, "U.S. Apparel Market—Statistics & Facts."

xii more than double that year's global sales: Statista, "Consumer Electronics Report 2020"; Fleurant, "The SIPRI Top 100 Arms-Producing and Military Services Companies, 2018."

xii Nike's market capitalization: "NIKE, Inc. (NKE)," "Ford Motor Company (F)," *Yahoo! Finance.*

xii Over the course: United Nations Economic Commission for Europe, "UN Alliance Aims to Put Fashion on Path to Sustainability."

xii By 2017: "A New Textiles Economy," Ellen MacArthur Foundation.

xii Textile and garment work: Solidarity Center, "Global Garment and Textile Industries."

xii Textile making has: United Nations Economic Commission for Europe, "UN Alliance Aims to Put Fashion on Path to Sustainability."

xv Women represent: International Labour Organization, "Wages and Working Hours in the Textiles, Clothing, Leather and Footwear Industries."

xv Cotton is an incredibly: Vartan, "Fashion Forward."

xv Between 2000 and 2008: Food and Agriculture Organization of the United Nations and International Cotton Advisory Committee, "World Apparel Fiber Consumption Survey."

1. THE LAST LINEN SHIRT IN NEW HAMPSHIRE

3   "Flax should be sowed": Wily, *A Treatise on the Propagation of Sheep*, 36.

5   The advent of string: Barber, *Women's Work*, 147.

5   Researchers using the: "UF Study of Lice DNA Shows Humans First Wore Clothes 170,000 Years Ago," *University of Florida News.*

6   A small number: Balter, "Clothes Make the (Hu) Man."

7   "picked up a compact lump": Glory, "Débris de corde paléolithique à la grotte Lascaux," 51–52.

7   The first intact cloth: Wilford, "Site in Turkey Yields Oldest Cloth Ever Found," C1.

8   Growing flax: Keller, "From the Rhineland to the Virginia Frontier," 488.

8   "Better skinner than": Quataert, "The Shaping of Women's Work in Manufacturing," 1129.

8   "carried the ladders": Quataert, "The Shaping of Women's Work in Manufacturing," 1129.

10 They lost ground: Federici, *Caliban and the Witch*, 92.

10 "Comedies and satires": Howell, *Women, Production, and Patriarchy in Late Medieval Cities*, 182.

11 Meanwhile, over the course: Kessler-Harris, *Women Have Always Worked*, 4.

11 "In pre-industrial societies": Kessler-Harris, *Women Have Always Worked*, 1.

12 "where any man": Ulrich, *The Age of Homespun*, 95.

12 "Break flax for Jam Henry": Diary of John Campbell, 17.

12 "which is exported": Belknap, "Manufactures," 22.

12 "Eastern parts": Minutes of "A Meeting with the Delegates of the Eastern Indians," 95.

13 "Nits become lice": Lapham, *History of the Town of Bethel, Maine, 1891*, 269.

13 At Amoskeag Falls: Eaton, *The Amoskeag Manufacturing Company*, 17.

13 "more Salmon": Macphaedris, Papers, 97.

14 "deceit practiced": Browne, *Early Records of Londonderry, Windham, and Derry, New Hampshire, 1719–1762*, 15.

14 "the Credate of": Browne, *Early Records of Londonderry, Windham, and Derry, New Hampshire, 1719–1762*, 15.

14 "a Certain Bundle": Massachusetts Supreme Judiciary Court, Case Papers, 202.

15 "Sarah Bartlet that Lived": Diary of Elizabeth (Porter) Phelps, 202.

15 "For she will neither": *Weekly Wanderer*, 367.

16 "I have been knitting": Diary of Elisabeth Foot, 211.

16 "stay'd at home": Diary of Elisabeth Foot, 214–15.

16 "I went to Robert": Diary of Matthew Patten of Bedford, N.H., 195.

16 "The Property of": Hannah Matthews Book, 199.

17 "the defect": Hamilton, *The Papers of Alexander Hamilton*, 253, 327.

18 "fine specimen": Eaton, *The Amoskeag Manufacturing Company*, 23.

19 "a domestic manufactured": *New England Farmer*, "Flax."

19 "the flax dresser": Judd, *History of Hadley, Massachusetts*, 27–28.

20 "I have tended": American Textile History Museum, "October 8, 1845."

21 "The great mass": Brownson, "The Labouring Classes," 13.

2. UNDERTHINGS

22 "Ed Sheeran": Sheeran, *Shape of You*.

22 "Wash everything": Grimm, "17 Ways to Take Care of Yourself After a Breakup."

22 "Schene vnder schete": *The Proverbs of Ælfred*.

22 "No down of fetheres": Chaucer, *The Former Age*.

23 "In France, the word": Roche, *The Culture of Clothing*, 152.

23 Women in Europe: Phillips and Phillips, *History from Below*, 133.

24 "Alle þei fled": Mannyng, *Mannyng's Chronicle*.

24 "He and the Duchesse": Middleton, *The Revenger's Tragedy*.

24 "Harlots and their": *Holinshed's Chronicles*.

25 "for if your clothes": Rimbault, "Le corps à travers les manuels," 373.

25 In the early 1780s: Chrisman-Campbell, *Fashion Victims*, 192.

25 "a fineness": Vaublanc, *Mémoires*, 192.

26 "a parcel": Winthrop, *The Journal of John Winthrop*, 352.

26 Women prepared: Schneider, "The Anthropology of Cloth," 411.

26 The matrilineal side: Matthews, "Distaff, Worldwide, Deep Antiquity."

27 "The possession of real": Ulrich, *The Age of Homespun*, 130.

27 Upon Marriage: *Ancrene Riwle*.

27 The word "coverture": *Ancrene Riwle*.

27 Under coverture, women: Allgor, "Coverture."

27 "two pair of sheets": Hampshire County Probate Records, 139.

28 "When I am dead": Ulrich, *The Age of Homespun*, 116–17.

28 Caring for children: Barrett, *Women's Oppression Today*, 179–80.

28 "the company will": Brandon, *Singer and the Sewing Machine*, 41.

29 "unsexes the man": Engels, *The Condition of the Working Class in England*, 155–56.

30 "We know of no class": Brandon, *Singer and the Sewing Machine*, 68–99.

31 "With fingers weary": Brandon, *Singer and the Sewing Machine*, 68.

31 "No inveterate habits": Brandon, *Singer and the Sewing Machine*, 32.

32 "one of the best Richards": Brandon, *Singer and the Sewing Machine*, 19.

32 "crude and bombastical": Brandon, *Singer and the Sewing Machine*, 19.

33 "What a devilish machine": Brandon, *Singer and the Sewing Machine*, 44.

34 "A little further on": Brandon, *Singer and the Sewing Machine*, 58.

36 "so exactly alike": *New York Daily Tribune*, 108.

36 "In the United States": *Mechanic's Journal*, 109.

36 "Mr. Plumley": *Frank Leslie's Illustrated Weekly*, 120–21.

37 "A most Wonderful": *Harper's Weekly*, 121.

37 "The great importance": Singer Sewing Machine Company booklet, 126–27.

38 In 1888: U.S. Commission of Labor, *Working Women in Large Cities*, 78.

39 "He recalled the history": Chekhov, *The Portable Chekhov*, 242–43.

39 "underpants on women": Ewen and Ewen, *Channels of Desire*, 110.

39 "cater to this particular": Hollander, *Seeing Through Clothes*, 133.

3. TEXAS FIELDS

43 "Modern humanity's governing": Berry, *The Unsettling of America*.

44 Cotton exists in: Foley, *The White Scourge*, 3.

45 At the time: Karda, "Lubbock Region Cotton Industry Impacts Economy."

45 The land in Lubbock: U.S. Department of Agriculture, "2017 Census of Agriculture County Profile: Lubbock County."

45 In 1790: Beckert, *Empire of Cotton*, 104.

46 "I fought through": Mooney, *Historical Sketch of the Cherokee*, 124.

46 "the great question": *Macon Telegraph*, 281.

46 "cannot be seriously": Agee and Evans, *Let Us Now Praise Famous Men*, xxi.

47 "rising tide": Stoddard, *The Rising Tide of Color*, 5–6.

47 "Poor whites in Texas": Foley, *The White Scourge*, 6.

47 "racial hygiene": Davis, *The White Scourge* and "Cotton Crisis," 6–7.

48 A huge mass: Little, "The Ogallala Aquifer."

48 "almost wholly unfit": Meinig, *The Shaping of America*, 76.

48 A 2017 study: Frankel, "Crisis on the High Plains."

48 This excessive growth: Mitsch et al., "Reducing Nitrogen Loading to the Gulf of Mexico from the Mississippi River Basin."

48 The size of: National Oceanic and Atmospheric Administration, "Large 'Dead Zone' Measured in Gulf of Mexico."

50 In 2015, seven: Hakim, "A Weed Killer Made in Britain, for Export Only."

51 The use of paraquat: Monge et al., "Parental Occupational Exposure to Pesticides and the Risk of Childhood Leukemia in Costa Rica," 293.

51 It has been banned: Prada, "Paraquat."

51 They maintained: Brueck, "The EPA Says a Chemical in Monsanto's Weed-Killer Doesn't Cause Cancer."

51 By then the world's: Schlanger, "Monsanto Is About to Disappear."

51 Bayer ought to: Andrews, "I.G. Farben."

52 In August 2018: Gillam, "I Won a Historic Lawsuit."

52 This was the first: Brodwin and Bendix, "A Jury Says That a Common Weed-Killer Chemical at the Heart of a $2 Billion Lawsuit Contributed to a Husband and Wife's Cancer."

52 Bayer made perfectly: Bellon, "Bayer Asks U.S. Appeals Court to Reverse $25 Million Roundup Verdict."

52 "It is unlawful": Ponnezhath, Klayman, and Adler, "U.S. Government Says Verdict in Bayer's Roundup Case Should Be Reversed."

52 Epidemiological studies: Pouchieu et al., "Pesticide Use in Agriculture and Parkinson's Disease," 299.

53 Estimates vary: Jordan, "Farmworkers, Mostly Undocumented, Become 'Essential' During Pandemic."

53 The average life: Holthaus, *From the Farm to the Table*, 140.

54 In one Navajo: Monroe and Williamson, *They Dance in the Sky*, 31–34.

54 In 2017, total: Gro Intelligence, "US Cotton Subsidies Insulate Producers from Economic Loss."

54 Critics have: Kinnock, "America's $24bn Subsidy Damages Developing World Cotton Farmers."

55 "Ekistman, GA": Gillette and Tillenger, *Inside the Ku Klux Klan*, 36.

55 "Photographers say": Gillette and Tillenger, *Inside the Ku Klux Klan*, 65.

55 "Murders of Negroes": Gillette and Tillenger, *Inside the Ku Klux Klan*, 26.

56 Robed Klan members: Wuthnow, *Rough Country*, 174–76.

56 The first members: Rice, *White Robes, Silver Screens*, 17.

56 "assigns an inherent power": Rice, *White Robes*, 17.

4. THE FABRIC REVOLUTION

58 "I claim that in losing": Gandhi, *Young India*.

58 The vast majority: Beckert, *Empire of Cotton*, 15.

59 "garments are made": Textile Narratives and Conversations.

59 "so much cash": Beckert, *Empire of Cotton*, 18.

60 "at least not": Beckert, *Empire of Cotton*, 36.

61 "The Company's Gumashta": Beckert, *Empire of Cotton*, 45.

61 "unprecedented mortality": British East India Company, 45.

61 "crept into": Defoe and McVeigh, *A Review of the State of the British Nation*, 33.

61 The flying shuttle: Mirsky and Nevins, *The World of Eli Whitney*, 83.

62 "bag-cheeked": Mirsky and Nevins, *The World of Eli Whitney*, 84–85.

62 He hired a clockmaker: Hills, "Sir Richard Arkwright and His Patent Granted in 1769," 257–60.

62 The immense power: Hobsbawm and Wrigley, *Industry and Empire*, 24, 87.

63 "Material prosperity": *Bremer Handelsblatt*, 133.

63 "While acknowledging": Mann, *The Cotton Trade of Great Britain*, 56.

63 "we are strongly impressed": *Times of India*, February 12, 1863, in Beckert, *Empire of Cotton*.

64 "Nothing could be": Beckert, *Empire of Cotton*, 123.

64 "The Native weavers": Charles Wood to Sir Charles Trevelyan, 297.

65 "India was systematically": Hobsbawm, *The Age of Revolution*, 35.

65 "The more the area's": Department of Agriculture, Memo to the Home Department, 336.

65 As mass nationalism: Trivedi, "Visually Mapping the 'Nation,'" 11.

66 The Indian National: Singhal, "The Mahatma's Message."

66 "[The exhibition]": "The Exhibition," 11.

66 "Nationalist debates": Chari, *Fraternal Capital*, 164–65.

70 Production costs rose: Branford, "Indian Farmers Shun GM for Organic Solutions."

70 Bt cotton entered: Seetharaman, "These Two Issues Could Put the Brakes on the Bt Cotton Story."

70 Thousands of cattle: Venkateshwarlu, "Genetically Modified Cotton Figures in a New Controversy in Andhra Pradesh."

70 "The entire biotechnology": Bhardwaj and Jadhav, "After Monsanto Patent Ruling, Indian Farmers Hope for Next-Gen GM Seeds."

71 The global ban: Stafford, "Endosulfan Banned as Agreement Is Reached with India."

72 "In early reports": Attar et al. "Paraquat poisoning."

76 While this scheme: Solidaridad—South & South East Asia, "Understanding the Characteristics of the Sumangali Scheme."

78 Indigenous goats: Hema et al., "Genotoxic Effect of Dye Effluents," 269.

78 River fish: Kumar and Achyuthan, "Heavy Metal Accumulation in Certain Marine Animals," 637.

78 In January 2011: "HC Orders Closure of Tiruppur Dyeing Units."

79 "The whole town": Chari, *Fraternal Capital*, 1.

79 "the most temporary": Chari, *Fraternal Capital*, 62.

80 A 2005 UNESCO: Hoekstra, "The Water Footprint of Cotton Consumption," 23.

81 Cotton is a thirsty: Soth, Grasser, and Salerno, "Background Paper: The Impact of Cotton," 1.

81 During this same: Hinrichsen and Tacio, "The Coming Freshwater Crisis Is Already Here."

5. DROUGHT

82 "They filled that place": Holdstock, *China's Forgotten People*, 99.

83 It was a political: Holdstock, *China's Forgotten People*, 40.

83 Its strategic importance: Bequelin, "Xinjiang in the Nineties," 65.

83 The Han ethnic: Bequelin, "Staged Development in Xinjiang," 359.

83 "the complex interplay": Holdstock, *China's Forgotten People*, 12.

84 Before its push: Richards, "Frontier Settlement in Russia," 255, 258.

85 "prevent all those": Shipov, "Khlopchatobumazhnaia promyshlennost," 345.

85 "would be our": Beckert, *Empire of Cotton*, 345.

85 Between 1865: Rashid, "The New Struggle in Central Asia," 36.

85 "the aim": Beckert, *Empire of Cotton*, 346.

85 Toward this end: Rashid, "The New Struggle in Central Asia," 36.

85 As early as 1918: Tal, "Desertification," 153.

87 Freshwater supplies are: Gray, "A Scarcity Adds to Water's Appeal."

87 Water consumption increased: Perrin, "Water for Agriculture," 20.

87 Cotton is the most: "Ecological and Social Costs of Cotton Farming in Egypt."

88 "Xinjiang has since": State Council, "Xinjiang de Fazhan yu Jinbu," 20.

88 "no Chinese would": Millward, *Eurasian Crossroads*, 20.

88 The modern-day heir: Kiely, *The Compelling Ideal*, 126–27.

88 "corporation whose purpose": Seymour, "Xinjiang's Production and Construction Corps and the Sinification of Eastern Turkestan," 188.

89 When snow melts: Jiang et al., "Water Resources, Land Exploration and Population Dynamics in Arid Areas," 473–75.

90 "almost all plants and animals": Jiang et al., "Water Resources, Land Exploration and Population Dynamics in Arid Areas," 482–83.

90 "Our investigation during the fieldtrips": Jiang et al., "Water Resources, Land Exploration and Population Dynamics in Arid Areas," 491–92.

90 "[Members of the XPCC] believe": Joniak-Lüthi, "Han Migration to Xinjiang Uyghur Autonomous Region," 163.

90 "experienced enormous changes": Jiang et al., "Water Resources, Land Exploration and Population Dynamics in Arid Areas," 485–86.

90 So many cultures: Liu, *The Silk Road in World History*, 47.

91 In a matter of: Jiang et al., "Water Resources, Land Exploration and Population Dynamics in Arid Areas," 473–74.

91 "the comprehensive engineering": Bequelin: "Xinjiang in the Nineties," 75.

91 "the chief vehicle": Bequelin, "Staged Development in Xinjiang," 360.

91 By 2019, Xinjiang became: Holdstock, *China's Forgotten People*, 107.

92 A 2019 Human: Caster, "It's Time to Boycott Any Company Doing Business in Xinjiang"; Human Rights Watch, "China's Algorithms of Repression."

92 One hundred sixty thousand cameras: Cockerell, "Inside China's Massive Surveillance Operation."

92 After 2016, textile: Byler, "How Companies Profit from Forced Labor in Xinjiang."

93 *The Wall Street Journal:* Dou and Deng, "Western Companies Get Tangled in China's Muslim Clampdown."

93 "What?! They're actually": Handley and Xiao, "Japanese Brands Muji and Uniqlo Flaunt 'Xinjiang Cotton.'"

93 "Many Uyghurs love": Handley and Xiao, "Japanese Brands Muji and Uniqlo Flaunt 'Xinjiang Cotton.'"

93 In December 2020: Zenz, "Coercive Labor in Xinjiang: Labor Transfer and the Mobilization of Ethnic Minorities to Pick Cotton."

94 "It's important that we manage": U.S. Department of State, "Secretary Antony J. Blinken, National Security Advisor Jake Sullivan, Director Yang and State Councilor Wang at the Top of Their Meeting."

95 In 2017, the United States: "China Textiles and Clothing Exports by Country in US$ Thousand 2018," World Bank.

95 As China's policy: Rosen, *Making Sweatshops*, 209.

6. YANGTZE SILK

99 "When you see the silkworms": Song Ruozhao, "Analects for Women," 827–31.

99 Anatomically modern: Boudot and Buckley, "Cultural and Historical Context," 8.

100 These agriculturalists: Chi and Hung, "The Neolithic of Southern China," 315–18.

100 At an archeological: Pearson and Underhill, "The Chinese Neolithic," 813.

100 A 2016 study: Gong, "Biomolecular Evidence of Silk from 8,500 Years Ago."

100 "I will inform": Pankenier, "Weaving Metaphors and Cosmo-Political Thought in Early China," 30.

100 "the guiding threads": Pankenier, "Weaving Metaphors and Cosmo-Political Thought in Early China," 14.

100 "Just as a skein": Pankenier, "Weaving Metaphors and Cosmo-Political Thought in Early China," 16.

101 "Heaven's grandchild": Pankenier, "Weaving Metaphors and Cosmo-Political Thought in Early China," 8.

102 "the area is rich": Wang, *Ke Yue zhilue*, 195.

102 According to the: Brook, *The Confusions of Pleasure*, 195.

103 Silk is extruded: Joy, "Spinning Apparatus of Silk Worm Larvae *Bombyx Mori* L the Spinneret," 872.

104 Overproduction caused: "China Silk Industry Hit by Overproduction."

106 Before the creation: Boudot and Buckley, "Cultural and Historical Context," 8.

106 In the 400s BC: Liu, *The Silk Road in World History*, 1.

107 "Now your majesty": Sima Qian, *Shi Ji*, 2.

108 The technology: Sheng, "Determining the Value of Textiles in the Tang Dynasty," 185–86.

109 On grand occasions: Ebrey, "Taking Out the Grand Carriage," 33.

109 "Each of the seven": *Dongjing menghua lu zhu*, 40.

110 "women spun": Zhang Tao, sixteenth-century chronicle, 17.

110 "only spin": *Jiujiang fuzhi*, 113–14.

110 "in every village": *Zhenze Xianzhi*, 114.

110 Francesca Bray has argued: Bray, "Le travail féminin dans la Chine impériale."

110 The canal connected: Moll-Murata, "Chinese Guilds from the Seventeenth to the Twentieth Centuries," 218.

111 Canal bridges: Brook, *The Confusions of Pleasure*, 197–98.

111 "If it isn't splendid": Zhang Han, "Baijong ji," 221.

113 "even the big merchants": Brook, *The Confusions of Pleasure*, 197.

114 After repeated efforts: Robins, *The Corporation That Changed the World*, 145.

114 In 1839, William: Dong, *Shanghai*, 8.

114 One eyewitness: Hanes and Sanello, *Opium Wars*, 6.

115 Between 1850 and 1930: Ma, "Between Cottage and Factory," 195–213.

115 In 1881 South Chinese: So, *The South China Silk District*, 116.

115 "all the old ideas": Dikötter, *The Cultural Revolution*, 81.

115 Silk, velvet: Dikötter, *The Cultural Revolution*, 83.

7. COSTUME DRAMA

117 In the 1130s: Bray, *Technology, Gender, and History in Imperial China*, 1–3.

117 The trend was: Riccardi-Cubitt, "Chinoiserie."

118 Sericulture began: Jacoby, "Silk Economics and Cross-Cultural Artistic Interaction," 199.

118 The Crusades acquainted: Dufrenoy, "Sericulture," 133–34.

118 The French artist: Lee-Whitman and Skelton, "Where Did All the Silver Go," 33.

119 "MONSIEUR JOURDAIN": Molière, *Middle-Class Gentleman*, 31–32.

119 "from the ladies": Roche, *The Culture of Clothing*, 479.

119 "the body's body": Erasmus, *De civilitate*, 6.

120 "the real and the imaginary": Roche, *The Culture of Clothing*, 7.

12 Louis XIV sought: De Colyar, "Jean-Baptiste Colbert and the Codifying Ordinances of Louis XIV," 60–65.

121 Louis XIV took the throne: Chrisman-Campbell, "Fit for a King."

121 "it was designed": Chrisman-Campbell, *Fashion Victims*, 93.

122 "was inseparable from": Roche, *The Culture of Clothing*, 281.

122 During Louis's reign: Chrisman-Campbell, "The King of Couture."

122 Over the course: DeJean, *The Essence of Style*, 6.

122 "Fashions were to France": Chrisman-Campbell, *Fashion Victims*, 317.

122 Enriched by state: Miller, "Mysterious Manufacturers," 87.

122 "The first thing": Adams, *Diary and Autobiography*, 75.

123 The first valet: Elias, "Etiquette and Ceremony," 53–54.

124 "Prohibiting absolutely": Roche, *The Culture of Clothing*, 49.

124 "The way in which": Roche, *The Culture of Clothing*, 49.

124 "You see the same": Rousseau, *Oeuvres Complètes*, 412.

125 "The sergeant's wife": Boursault, *Oeuvres Complètes*, 410.

125 "every social category": Roche, *The Culture of Clothing*, 147.

126 These decades witnessed: Flügel, "The Great Masculine Renunciation and Its Causes," 107–8.

126 "A man's clothes": de Beauvoir, "Social Life," 128.

127 They drafted regulations: Crowston, *Fabricating Women*, 4–5.

128 "the French have never": Sontag, *A Susan Sontag Reader*, 438.

129 "This profane age": Voltaire, "Le Mondain," 62.

129 "Tell me, celebrated Arouet": Rousseau, "Discourse on the Arts and Sciences," 44–45.

130 "woman dressed as a court": *Magasin des modes*, 20e, 177.

130 "The superb manufacture": Proudhomme, *Les Crimes des reines de France*, 31.

131 "a debate between": Rodgers, *The Dandy: Peacock or Enigma?*

131 "How many curious": Chrisman-Campbell, *Fashion Victims*, 3.

131 "I saw a suit embroidered": Chrisman-Campbell, *Fashion Victims*, 3.

131 "those without breeches": Roche, *The Culture of Clothing*, 139.

131 "we ought to make": Roche, *The Culture of Clothing*, 464.

132 "My mother makes": Roche, *The Culture of Clothing*, 315.

132 "It has been alleged": Abrantès, *Memoirs of Napoleon, His Court and Family*, 285.

8. THE RISE OF MASS FASHION

133 "As they have no understanding": Poiret, *King of Fashion*, 266.

135 A government report: Ewen and Ewen, *Channels of Desire*, 115–16.

136 "find it greatly": Ewen and Ewen, *Channels of Desire*, 121.

136 "SEWING BY MACHINERY": *Boston Daily Times*, 50.

136 "new, improved sewing": Ewen and Ewen, *Channels of Desire*, 121.

137 "Never see the factory": Woodward, *Through Many Windows*, 80.

138 "beyond their station": Richardson, *The Woman Who Spends*, 116–17.

138 "I'd like them better": Hoyt, *The Consumption of Wealth*, 95.

138 "shop apprentices": Richardson, *The Woman Who Spends*, 157.

139 "Did you ever go down": Richardson, *The Woman Who Spends*, 157.

139 "Mass fashion provided": Ewen and Ewen, *Channels of Desire*, 158.

139 "Where working people": Ewen and Ewen, *Channels of Desire*, 172–73.

139 "Mass production": Filene, *Successful Living in the Machine Age*, 92.

140 "disappointment with achievements": Nystrom, *Economics of Fashion*, 85.

140 "To those who cannot change": Woodward, *Through Many Windows*, 86.

140 "The *Toaster* that FREED": *Saturday Evening Post*, 161.

140 "A man expects to find": *Ladies' Home Journal*, 178–79.

141 "How many of them": Poiret, *King of Fashion*, 273.

141 "To sell common merchandise": Poiret, *King of Fashion*, 266.

141 "that in America": Poiret, *King of Fashion*, 272.

141 "on the pretext that": Poiret, *King of Fashion*, 276.

141 "propensity of all their manufacturers": Poiret, *King of Fashion*, 273.

142 "The head monkey": Thoreau, *The Portable Thoreau*, 280.

142 "for the average Soviet": Schiaparelli, *Shocking Life*, 101.

142 "Newspapers carried the sensational": Schiaparelli, *Shocking Life*, 108–9.

143 "One of the most important": Nystrom, *Fashion Merchandising*, 170.

143 "The robes were specially": Schiaparelli, *Shocking Life*, 102–3.

144 "Our modern clothing": Hegel, "On Drapery," 149.

145 "Starting last spring": "The Chinese Look," *Time*.

146 "have taken on the power": Dryansky, "What's in a Name?," 300.

146 "The June cover": Cronberg, "Will I Get a Ticket?"

148 "American traders": Poiret, *King of Fashion*, 266.

148 "wore a superb costume": Brandon, *Singer and the Sewing Machine*, 215.

9. RAYON

153 "It's no crime in the South": Huber, "Mill Mother's Lament," 102.

153 "Russia with its heartland": Mendeleev, *Uchenie o promyshlennosti*, 27.

154 "there is too much reason": "Our Overseas Trade," *Advertiser*, 63.

154 "So let alkaline": Blanc, *Fake Silk*, 130–31.

155 "The chemist is fast": Parkinson, "The Latest Member of Our Textile Family," 112.

155 "given to women to-day": Courtaulds Ltd., *National Rayon Week*, 63.

155 "He was thinking of Lenina": Huxley, *Brave New World*, 164.

156 "short weekend cruises": "Mystery," *Fortune*, 69.

158 "Read and Foster's": "Death to Squirrels and Gophers!" *Los Angeles Times*, 21.

158 "I have delayed": Peterson, "Three Cases of Acute Mania from Inhaling Carbon Bisulphide," 18.

159 "you have to do to repair": Dupin, "Rattier et Guibal—Caoutchouc," 438.

159 "Cinderella's rubber slippers": "Courrier de la mode," 436.

159 "In Cherbourg, all": Charpy, "Craze and Shame," 434.

160 "a curious pattern": Blanc, *Fake Silk*, xii.

161 "We have very good sanitary": Heaton, *Scraps of Work and Play*, 89.

161 American Bemberg Corporation: Tedesco, "Claiming Public Space, Asserting Class Identity, and Displaying Patriotism," 56.

162 "We believe the employment": "Labor Survey of Washington and Carter Counties and Adjacent Territories," 56–57.

162 In 1912, the massive: Watson, *Bread and Roses*, 12.

163 "Working in these two plants": Lindsay, "Rayon Mills and Old Line Americans," 89.

163 The July issue of: "The National Guard and Elizabethton," 90.

164 "Textile mill strikes flared": "Southern Stirrings," *Time*, 86.

164 More than three thousand strikes: Zieger, Minchin, and Gall, *American Workers, American Unions*, 37.

164 By assigning more looms: Huber, "Mill Mother's Lament," 87.

165 Two days after: Draper, "Gastonia Revisited," 11.

165 "seeks the overthrow of capital": Huber, "Mill Mother's Lament," 87–88.

166 "From experience": Beal, *Proletarian Journey*, 90.

166 "The bosses will starve you": Greenway, *American Folksongs of Protest*, 136.

166 "No evening passed": Beal, *Proletarian Journey*, 101.

167 "Her rather gaunt face": Hubert, "Mill Mother's Lament," 101.

167 "I never made no": Larkin, "The Story of Ella May," 97.

167 "One woman carried a baby": *Gastonia Daily Gazette*, 90.

168 "We leave our home": *Labor Defender*, 100.

168 The introduction of machine: Eller, *Miners, Millhands, and Mountaineers*, 110–11.

168 "neat and accurate": Larkin, "The Story of Ella May," 94.

169 "The bosses hated": Huber, "Mill Mother's Lament," 102.

169 "It's no crime in the South": Beal, *Proletarian Journey*, 102.

169 "Mill Mother's Lament" was: Baeza, "Book Review: The Last Ballad."

169 Ella May Wiggins: Campbell, "Portraits of Gastonia," 11.

170 "the workers will serve": Hamilton, "Nineteen Years in the Poisonous Trades," 80–81.

170 "it is certainly possible": Hamilton, *Industrial Poisons Used in the Rubber Industry*, 79.

170 "he told a rambling tale": Hamilton, *Industrial Poisons Used in the Rubber Industry*, 79.

171 "He did not wish": Hamilton, *Industrial Poisons in the United States*, 45.

171 "an investigation of": Susan Kingsbury to Dean Helen Taft Manning, 94–95.

171 "that for some unknown reason": "Bryn Mawr Study of Occupational Disease in Pennsylvania," 95.

172 "convincing proof": Erskine, "Report to Ralph M. Bashore," 102.

173 "behind every other volume": Orleck, *Common Sense and a Little Fire*, 18.

174 "What the woman who labors wants": Brooks, Minerva K., "Rose Schneidermann in Ohio," 288.

174 Samuel Gompers had: Stein, *The Triangle Fire*, 163–65.

176 The ILGWU gained: Appelbaum and Lichtenstein, "An Accident in History," 62–63.

176 Its educational department: Coit and Starr, "Workers' Education in the United States," 194, 197.

176 "Verdi arias and Rooseveltian": "Laboring Voice," *Time*, 62.

176 In 1937–40 union: "Longest-Running Shows on Broadway," *Playbill*.

177 "You can't stand still": Rome, "Status Quo."

177 "Roosevelt, Our Greatest": Simon, "General Textile Strike."

177 Dan Beacham, the mill: "SC Site of Bloody Labor Strike Crumbles," Associated Press.

177 Seven strikers were: Riddle, "Walls of Silence."

177 Roosevelt announced: Murray, "Textile Strike of 1934."

178 The backlash: Davis, "Walking Out."

180 "she remembers the communal": Applebome, *Dixie Rising*.

180 "Irrationality, unconscious spells": Blanc, *Fake Silk*, 85.

181 Their physicians: Tasca et al., "Women and Hysteria," 111.

181 "RAYON FACTORY": Petricha E. Manchester telegram to Dr. Alice Hamilton, 78.

10. NYLONS

183 "I'll be happy": Waller, "When the Nylons Bloom Again."

183 DuPont chemist: Knight, "The Tragic Story of Wallace Hume Carothers."

183 Nylon, which has: "Polyamide Fibers (Nylon)."

183 When the U.S.: Spivak, "Stocking Series, Part I."

184 "They are the women": Kessler-Harris, *Women Have Always Worked*, 155.

184 On August 6: Hersey, *Hiroshima*, 2–6.

185 Over the course of the war: Rosen, *Making Sweatshops*, 29.

186 "Isn't this the first time": U.S. Senate, Trade Agreements Extension Act of 1951, 70.

186 "our allies need": U.S. Senate, Problems of the US Textile Industry, statement of W. J. Erwin, 49.

186 "Must there be closed": Fowler, "Imports Shroud Cotton Outlook," 82.

188 Worldwide, the total: Schneider, "In and Out of Polyester," 7.

189 Nylon quickly became: Blaszczyk, "Styling Synthetics," 486–87.

191 "We were so charmed": Melinkoff, *What We Wore*, 57–58.

191 Previously, laundry had: Melinkoff, *What We Wore*, 39.

191 In 1856, an eighteen-year-old: Fagin, "Dye Me a River."

191 Like coal tar itself: World Bank, "How Much Do Our Wardrobes Cost to the Environment?"

191 Textile dyeing relies on chromium: Kant, "Textile Dyeing Industry as an Environmental Hazard," 22.

192 Dumped into waterways: Derisi, "Reviewed Work: The Dirty Side of the Garment Industry," 87–89.

192 "crude, livid—and cheap": Vallance, *The Art of William Morris*, 73.

192 "Now that purple": Isager, *Pliny on Art and Society*, 125.

192 Color used to carry: Barber, *Women's Work*, 113, 115–16.

192 "Once only the Rich": Quant, *Quant by Quant*, 10.

194 "In most business": Euse, "The Revolutionary History of the Pantsuit."

195 "We may be approaching": Chafe, *The Unfinished Journey*, 425.

197 They were soon joined: Green, "The Asian Connection," 11.

11. EXPORT PROCESSING ZONES

202 "I see America": Miller, "Third or Fourth Day of Spring," 23.

204 The Caribbean Basin: Green, "The Asian Connection," 13–14.

204 His two-pronged: Rosen, *Making Sweatshops*, 133.

205 "The Caribbean": Milman, "It's Working," 148.

205 A 1992 report: Briggs, Cook, McCay, and Kernaghan, "Paying to Lose Our Jobs," 150.

207 "the most successful": Green, "The Asian Connection," 35.

208 "You can say I'm ugly": Rosenblum, "Farewell to Kathie Lee, Sweatshop Queen."

208 "As long as there is greed": "Announcement by President Bill Clinton on Fair Labor Practices."

208 For instance, Grupo Kattan: Kattan Group, Investment Summary.

209 Grupo Kattan also owns: Castano Freeman, "Grupo Kattan Mulls $70m Wovens Facility"; "Apparel," Kattan Group.

210 Many of the elite: Paley, "The Honduran Business Elite One Year After the Coup."

210 Former Honduran president: Frank, *The Long Honduran Night*, 11.

212 "My clients represent the CEAL": Lovato, "Our Man in Honduras."

212 The Canahuatis own: "ZIP Choloma–ZIP Buena Vista."

212 "There is no doubt": Cable, Hugo Llorens to Department of State, 18.

214 "Urban violence and out-migration": Chayes, "When Corruption Is the Operating System," 8.

214 "churn out New Balance": Brodzinsky, "Inside San Pedro Sula."

214 The tower houses call: Rico, "Who Are the Richest Men in Central America and Why"; Tucker, "In Honduras Grupo Karim's Is Not Waiting Around."

215 There, his holdings: "Apparel Manufacturing Division," Grupo Karim's.

217 "Micro" was "the fashion": Schneider, "In and Out of Polyester," 5.

217 "the diets of marine animals": Resnick, "More than Ever, Our Clothes Are Made of Plastic."

217 "The average person": Resnick, "More than Ever, Our Clothes Are Made of Plastic."

218 Every year, half a million: World Bank, "How Much Do Our Wardrobes Cost the Environment?"

218 "If you only deliver": Wallach, *A World Made for Money*, 9–10.

219 As recently as 1997: Desai, Nassar, and Chertow, "American Seams," 53.

219 In 1984, 6.2 percent: Ross, "The Twilight of CSR," 76.

219 According to the Bureau: U.S. Bureau of Labor Statistics, Occupational Outlook Handbook.

219 In 2007 Ann Taylor: O'Connell, "Retailers Reprogram Workers in Efficiency Push."

220 "because it gave a personality": Wallach, *A World Made for Money*, 25.

220 These codes proliferated: Appelbaum and Lichtenstein, "An Accident in History," 60.

220 "exits were blocked": Ross, "The Twilight of CSR," 88.

220 "specific references to": Ross, "The Twilight of CSR," 88.

12. ARMY OF THE SMALL

226 The university's Wool: Kruger, "University of Wyoming Wool Laboratory and Library," 2.

226 The ones they developed: "Wool Products Labeling Act of 1939," Federal Trade Commission.

226 Access to plentiful grass: Western, "The Wyoming Sheep Business."

226 "away from the settlements": Western, "The Wyoming Sheep Business."

227 A career in wool: Burns, "Guide to Wyoming and the West Collection."

228 "enough to light": Braasch, "Powder River Basin Coal on the Move."

228 Black Thunder Mine: Bleizeffer, "Wyoming's First Coal Bust."

229 Zawi Chemi Shanidar: Dohner, "Sheep," 69.

229 A comparative analysis: Perkins, "Prehistoric Fauna from Shanidar, Iraq."

229 In what is now Syria: Barber, *Women's Work*, 73.

231 Wyoming was, in fact: Amos, "Mission Jurassic."

231 This is because: Raymo, Ruddiman, and Froelich, "Influence of Late Cenozoic Mountain Building on Ocean Geochemical Cycles," 649.

231 Textile production is one: United Nations Economic Commission for Europe, "UN Alliance Aims to Put Fashion on Path to Sustainability."

231 More than three thousand: Paerregaard, *Peruvians Dispersed*, 117.

231 Peruvian shepherds legally: Lee and Endres, "Overworked and Underpaid."

232 Sheep and wool are: Lind, "Handspinning Tradition in the United States," 161.

233 "idealized historical narratives": Lind, "Handspinning Tradition in the United States," 153.

234 Socially and politically: Bratich and Brush, "Fabricating Activism," 245.

234 "based on material": Bratich and Brush, "Fabricating Activism," 234–35, 240.

234 "set out to explore": Bratich and Brush, "Fabricating Activism," 244.

237 "high quanta of energy": Illich, *Toward a History of Needs*.

237 "Preindustrial ethics": Gardels, "Interview with I. Illich."

239 By the end of the 1980s: Howe, "The Secret to Vintage Jeans."

239 To achieve the effect: *"Indigofera tinctoria,"* Missouri Botanical Garden.

239 Natural indigo did: Reed, "British Chemical Industry and the Indigo Trade," 114.

239 Japanese dyers achieved: Howe, "The Secret to Vintage Jeans."

248 In America, the first revival: Ulrich, *The Age of Homespun*, 17.

248 The next big revival: Alvic, "Other Mountain Weaving Centers," 113.

13. WOOLFEST

250 "Sympathy nowadays": Woolf, "On Being Ill," 35.

250 Changes in agriculture: Rebanks, *The Shepherd's Life*, 40, 115.

250 By the 1970s, the Bampton: Dohner, "Sheep," 78.

250 Atmospheric carbon makes: Hodgson and Collie, "Biodegradability of Wool."

251 When disposed of, wool: McNeil, Sunderland, and Zaitseva, "Closed-Loop Wool Carpet Recycling," 220–24.

251 In 2001, an outbreak: Bates, "When Foot-and-Mouth Disease Stopped the UK in Its Tracks."

252 Sheep were not domesticated: Ryder, "The History of Sheep Breeds in Britain," 2.

253 "half the value": Bell, Brooks, and Dryburgh, *The English Wool Market*, 8.

254 Ironically, the excellent: Bowden, *Wool Trade in Tudor and Stuart England*, 26–27.

254 "fifteen women including": Federici, *Caliban and the Witch*, 73.

255 The Highland Clearances: Richards, *Debating the Highland Clearances*, 6, 8.

255 "in rustic hospitality": Smith, *An Inquiry into the Nature and Causes of the Wealth of Nations*, 897.

255 "thefts, outrages": Marx, *Capital, Volume One*.

257 The Bayeux Tapestry: Hoops, "What Is the Bayeux Tapestry? Why Is It in France?"

258 "she was weaving": Lattimore, *The Iliad of Homer*, 103.

258 In the 1980s and 1990s: Hmong Cultural Center and the Hmong Archives in Saint Paul, Minnesota.

260 "'prefigurative politics'": Bratich and Brush, "Fabricating Activism," 249.

261 The wall, which: "The Sheep," Orkney Sheep Foundation.

263 "A man doth *sand*": Johnson, *An Improving Prospect?*, 40.

265 Scientists call this: Berger, "Group Size, Foraging, and Antipredator Ploys," 91.

14. WEAVERS

269 "Our designs are": McLerran, ed., *Weaving Is Life*, 10.

269 "to kill an Indian in warfare": "Remembering Our Indian School Days," Heard Museum.

270 "Your son died quietly": Hoerig, "Remembering Our Indian School Days," 643.

271 "incapable of generating": Schneider, *Cloth and Human Experience*, 11.

273 The fiber used: Williams, *A Burst of Brilliance*, 6–7.

273 Extensive networks: Powers, *Navajo Trading*, 23.

274 Philadelphia had emerged: Scranton, "An Immigrant Family and Industrial Enterprise," 365–66.

276 "Like any craft": Albers, *Anni Albers: On Designing*.

280 The government implemented: "Dust Bowl Slaughter of the Navajo Sheep," Southwest Indian Relief Council.

280 This cull disproportionately hurt: Farmer, "Erosion of Trust."

280 "over behind one ridge": John W. Kennedy interview, Cline Library, 40.

287 "The English term Two-Spirit": Peters, "Navajo Transgender Women's Journey of Acceptance in Society."

288 "to mobilize human emotions": Schneider, *Cloth and Human Experience*, 11.

CONCLUSION

290 "It has been well said": Campbell, *The Power of Myth*, 206.

290 "We must believe": Doniger, *The Implied Spider*, 68.

292 "a parchment may": Ryder, "The History of Sheep Breeds in Britain," 1.

293 One example is kente: Ross and Adedze, *Wrapped in Pride*, 20.

294 "There is fire": Ross and Adedze, *Wrapped in Pride*, 113.

294 "All peppers do not": Ross and Adedze, *Wrapped in Pride*, 117.

297 "the best dressed woman": Wharton, *A Backward Glance*, 20.

297 "pair of strong soled brown": Colette, *Cheri*, 122.

298 "Florentine cinquecento frock": Mann, "The Blood of the Walsungs," 89.

299 "rose in the air": Tiphaigne de La Roche, *Histoire des Galligènes*, 426.

299 She lives on a tiny: Stein, "The Last Surviving Sea Silk Seamstress."

Bibliography

Abrantès, Laura, duchesse d'. *Memoirs of Napoleon, His Court and Family,* 1836. In Chrisman-Campbell. *Fashion Victims: Dress at the Court of Louis XVI and Marie-Antoinette* (New Haven: Yale University Press, 2015), 285.

Adams, John. *Diary and Autobiography,* October 26, 1782. In Chrisman-Campbell, *Fashion Victims: Dress at the Court of Louis XVI and Marie-Antoinette* (New Haven: Yale University Press, 2015), 75.

Agee, James, and Walker Evans. *Let Us Now Praise Famous Men.* Boston: First Mariner Books, 2001.

Albers, Anni. *Anni Albers: On Designing.* Middletown: Wesleyan University Press, 1971.

Allgor, Catherine. "Coverture—The Word You Probably Don't Know but Should." National Women's History Museum, September 4, 2014. http://www.womenshistory.org.

Alvic, Phillis. "Other Mountain Weaving Centers." In *Weavers of the Southern Highlands,* 113–34. Lexington: University Press of Kentucky, 2003.

American Textile History Museum. "October 8, 1845." Transcribed: University of Massachusetts, Lowell, Center for Lowell History, Lowell Mill Girl Letters, UMass Lowell Library Guides. https://libguides.uml.edu.

Amos, Jonathan. "Mission Jurassic: Searching for Dinosaur Bones." BBC, August 15, 2019. https://www.bbc.co.uk.

Ancrene Riwle, 1225. In "Coverture," *Encyclopaedia Britannica,* October 8, 2007. http://www.brittanica.com.

Andrews, Edmund L. "I.G. Farben: A Lingering Relic of the Nazi Years." *New York Times,* May 2, 1999.

"Announcement by President Bill Clinton on Fair Labor Practices," Rose Garden, The White House, Washington, D.C., 11:36 a.m., August 2, 1996. C-SPAN clip, 22:15. https://www.c-span.org.

"Apparel." Kattan Group. https://www.kattangroup.com.

"Apparel Manufacturing Division." Grupo Karim's. http://www.grupo karims.com.

Appelbaum, Rich, and Nelson Lichtenstein. "An Accident in History." *New Labor Forum* 23, no. 3 (Fall 2014): 58–65.

Applebome, Peter. *Dixie Rising: How the South Is Shaping American Values, Politics, and Culture.* New York: Crown, 2012.

Attar, N. R., S. Arsekar, M. N. Pawar, and V. Chavan. "Paraquat Poisoning—A Deadly Poison: A Case Report." *Medico-Legal Update* 9, no. 2 (July 2009): 43–47.

Baeza, Gonzalo. "Book Review: The Last Ballad, by Wiley Cash." *The WV Independent Observer,* September 10, 2017. https://wearetheobserver.com.

Balter, Michael. "Clothes Make the (Hu) Man." *Science* 325, no. 5946 (September 2009): 1329.

Barber, Elizabeth Wayland. *Women's Work: The First 20,000 Years.* New York: W. W. Norton, 1994.

Barnard, Joseph. Account Book, June 30 and December 8, 1762. In Laurel Thatcher Ulrich, *The Age of Homespun: Objects and Stories in the Creation of an American Myth* (New York: Alfred A. Knopf, 2001), 202–3.

Barrett, Michèle. *Women's Oppression Today: Problems in Marxist Feminist Analysis.* London: Verso, 1980.

Bate, Roger, and Aparna Mathur. "Corruption and Substandard Medicine in Latin America." *RealClear Health,* October 26, 2016. https://www.realclearhealth.com.

Bates, Claire. "When Foot-and-Mouth Disease Stopped the UK in Its Tracks." *BBC News Magazine,* February 17, 2016. https://www.bbc.com.

Beal, Fred E. *Proletarian Journey: New England, Gastonia, Moscow,* 1937. In Patrick Huber, "Mill Mother's Lament: Ella May Wiggins and the Gastonia Textile Strike of 1929." *Southern Cultures* 15, no. 3 (2009): 90, 101.

Beckert, Sven. *Empire of Cotton: A Global History.* New York: Vintage, 2015.

Belknap, Jeremy. "Manufactures," report #325, in *American State Papers* 6, *Finances,* 1832, 435. In Katherine Koob and Martha Coons, *All Sorts of Good Sufficient Cloth: Linen-Making in New England, 1640–1860* (North Andover: Merrimack Valley Textile Museum, 1980), 22.

Bell, Adrian R., Chris Brooks, and Paul R. Dryburgh. *The English Wool Market, c. 1230–1327.* Cambridge: Cambridge University Press, 2007.

Bellon, Tina. "Bayer Asks U.S. Appeals Court to Reverse $25 Million Roundup Verdict." Reuters, December 16, 2019. http://reuters.com.

Bequelin, Nicholas. "Staged Development in Xinjiang." In "China's Campaign to 'Open Up the West': National, Provincial and Local Perspectives." *The China Quarterly,* no. 178 (June 2004): 358–78.

———. "Xinjiang in the Nineties." *The China Journal* 44 (July 2000): 65–90.

Berger, Joel. "Group Size, Foraging, and Antipredator Ploys: An Analysis of Bighorn Sheep Decisions." *Behavioral Ecology and Sociobiology* 4, no. 1 (1978): 91–99.

Berry, Wendell. *The Unsettling of America: Culture & Agriculture.* Berkeley: Counterpoint Press, 2015.

Bhardwaj, Mayank, and Rajendra Jadhav. "After Monsanto Patent Ruling, Indian Farmers Hope for Next-Gen GM Seeds." Reuters, January 10, 2019. https://www.reuters.com.

"Black Thunder Thermal Coal Mine, Wyoming." *Mining Technology.* https://www.mining-technology.com.

Blanc, Paul David. *Fake Silk: The Lethal History of Viscose Rayon.* New Haven: Yale University Press, 2016.

Blaszczyk, Regina Lee. "Styling Synthetics: DuPont's Marketing of Fabrics and Fashions in Postwar America." *The Business History Review* 80, no. 3 (Autumn 2006): 485–528.

Bleizeffer, Dustin. "Wyoming's First Coal Bust." *The Online Encyclopedia of Wyoming History.* Wyoming State Historical Society, June 1, 2020. WyoHistory.org.

Boston Daily Times, November 8, 1850. In Ruth Brandon, *Singer and the Sewing Machine: A Capitalist Romance* (New York: Kodansha International, 1996), 50.

Boudot, Eric, and Chris Buckley. "Cultural and Historical Context." In *The Roots of Asian Weaving,* 8–19. Oxford: Oxbow Books, 2015.

Boursault. *Oeuvres Complètes,* 1721. In Daniel Roche, *The Culture of Clothing: Dress and Fashion in the Ancien Régime* (Cambridge: Cambridge University Press, 1996), 410.

Bowden, Peter J. *Wool Trade in Tudor and Stuart England.* Abingdon: Routledge, 2013.

Braasch, Gary. "Powder River Basin Coal on the Move." *Scientific American,* December 9, 2013. https://www.scientificamerican.com.

Brandon, Ruth. *Singer and the Sewing Machine: A Capitalist Romance*. New York: Kodansha International, 1996.

Branford, Sue. "Indian Farmers Shun GM for Organic Solutions." *The Guardian*, July 29, 2008. https://www.theguardian.com.

Bratich, Jack Z., and Heidi M. Brush. "Fabricating Activism: Craft-Work, Popular Culture, Gender." *Utopian Studies* 22, no. 2 (2011): 233–60.

Bray, Francesca. "Le travail féminin dans la Chine impériale." *Annales: Histoires, Sciences Sociales*, no. 4 (1994). In Timothy Brook, *The Confusions of Pleasure: Commerce and Culture in Ming China* (Berkeley: University of California Press, 1999), 202.

———. *Technology, Gender and History in Imperial China: Great Transformations Reconsidered*. London: Routledge, 2013.

Bremer Handelsblatt, 1853. In Sven Beckert, *Empire of Cotton: A Global History* (New York: Vintage, 2015), 133.

Briggs, Barbara, David Cook, Jack McCay, and Charles Kernaghan. *Paying to Lose Our Jobs*, National Labor Committee, 1992. In Ellen Israel Rosen, *Making Sweatshops: The Globalization of the U.S. Apparel Industry* (Berkeley: University of California Press, 2002), 150.

British East India Company. Letter from Board of Directors, London, April 20, 1796, to Our President in Council at Bombay. In Sven Beckert, *Empire of Cotton: A Global History* (New York: Vintage, 2015), 45.

Brodwin, Erin, and Aria Bendix. "A Jury Says That a Common Weed-Killer Chemical at the Heart of a $2 Billion Lawsuit Contributed to a Husband and Wife's Cancer." *Business Insider*, May 14, 2019. https://www.businessinsider.com.

Brodzinsky, Sibylla. "Inside San Pedro Sula—The Most Violent City in the World." *The Guardian*, May 15, 2013. https://www.theguardian.com.

Brook, Timothy. *The Confusions of Pleasure: Commerce and Culture in Ming China*. Berkeley: University of California Press, 1999.

Brooks, Minerva K. "Rose Schneidermann in Ohio." *Life and Labor, Volume 2*, September, 1912. Chicago: National Women's Trade Union League.

Browne, George Waldo. *Early Records of Londonderry, Windham, and Derry, New Hampshire, 1719–1762*. In Katherine Koob and Martha Coons, *All Sorts of Good Sufficient Cloth: Linen-Making in New England, 1640–1860* (North Andover: Merrimack Valley Textile Museum, 1980), 15.

Brownson, Orestes Augustus. *The Labouring Classes, an Article from the Boston Quarterly Review*. Fifth Edition. Boston: Benjamin H. Greene, 1842.

Brueck, Hilary. "The EPA Says a Chemical in Monsanto's Weed-Killer Doesn't Cause Cancer—But There's Compelling Evidence the Agency

Is Wrong." *Business Insider*, June 17, 2019. https://www.businessinsider.com.

"Bryn Mawr Study of Occupational Disease in Pennsylvania," 1937. In Paul David Blanc, *Fake Silk: The Lethal History of Viscose Rayon* (New Haven: Yale University Press, 2016), 95.

Burns, Robert Homer. "Papers, 1910–1973: #400002." In "Guide to Wyoming and the West Collections." American Heritage Center, University of Wyoming. http://www.uwyo.edu/ahc/files/collectionguides/wy-west2014-ed2019june.pdf.

Byler, Darren. "How Companies Profit from Forced Labor in Xinjiang." SupChina, September 4, 2019. https://supchina.com.

Cable, Hugo Llorens to Department of State. "Open and Shut: The Case of the Honduran Coup," July 24, 2009. In Dana Frank, *The Long Honduran Night: Resistance, Terror, and the United States in the Aftermath of the Coup* (Chicago: Haymarket Books, 2018).

Campbell, Joseph. *The Power of Myth with Bill Moyers*. Edited by Betty Sue Flowers. New York: Doubleday, 1988.

Campbell, Patricia R. "Portraits of Gastonia: 1930s Maternal Activism and the Protest Novel." A dissertation presented to the Graduate School of the University of Florida, 2006, 11.

Carroll, Chris. "Wyoming's Coal Resources: Wyoming State Geological Survey Summary Report." Wyoming State Geological Survey, February 2015. https://www.wsgs.wyo.gov.

Castano Freeman, Ivan. "Grupo Kattan Mulls $70m Wovens Facility in Honduras." *Just-style*, February 25, 2020. https://www.just-style.com.

Caster, Michael. "It's Time to Boycott Any Company Doing Business in Xinjiang." *The Guardian*, October 26, 2019.

Chafe, William. *The Unfinished Journey: America Since World War II*. Oxford: Oxford University Press, 2003.

Chari, Sharad. *Fraternal Capital: Peasant Workers, Self-Made Men, and Globalization in Provincial India*. Stanford: Stanford University Press, 2004.

Charles Wood to Sir Charles Trevelyan, April 9, 1863. In Sven Beckert, *Empire of Cotton: A Global History* (New York: Vintage, 2015), 297.

Charpy, Manuel. "Craze and Shame: Rubber Clothing During the Nineteenth Century in Paris, London, and New York City." *Fashion Theory: The Journal of Dress, Body & Culture* 16, no. 4 (2012): 433–60.

Chaucer, Geoffrey. *The Former Age*, 1347. In OED Online, "sheet, n.1," March 2021. Oxford University Press. https://www.oed.com.

———. *The Wife of Bath*. Boston: Bedford/St. Martin's, 1996.

Chayes, Sarah. "When Corruption Is the Operating System: The Case of Honduras." Carnegie Endowment for International Peace, May 30, 2017. https://carnegieendowment.org.

Chekhov, Anton Pavlovich. *The Portable Chekhov.* London: Penguin, 1968.

Chi, Zhang, and Hsiao-Chun Hung. "The Neolithic of Southern China—Origin, Development, and Dispersal." *Asian Perspectives* 47, no. 2 (2008): 299–329.

"China Silk Industry Hit by Overproduction." United Press International, May 8, 1995. https://www.upi.com.

"China Textiles and Clothing Exports by Country in US$ Thousand 2018." World Integrated Trade Solution, World Bank. https://wits.worldbank.org/.

"The Chinese Look: Mao à la Mode." *Time,* July 21, 1975.

Chrisman-Campbell, Kimberly. *Fashion Victims: Dress at the Court of Louis XVI and Marie-Antoinette.* New Haven: Yale University Press, 2015.

———. "Fit for a King: Louis XIV and the Art of Fashion." Lecture at Harold M. Williams Auditorium, Getty Center, August 23, 2015.

———. "The King of Couture: How Louis XIV Invented Fashion as We Know It." *The Atlantic,* September 1, 2015. https://www.theatlantic.com.

Cockerell, Isobel. "Inside China's Massive Surveillance Operation." *Wired,* May 9, 2019. https://www.wired.com.

Coit, Eleanor G., and Mark Starr. "Workers' Education in the United States." *Monthly Labor Review* 49, no. 1 (1939): 1–21.

Colette. *Cheri* and *The Last of Cheri.* New York: Farrar, Straus & Young, 1951.

"Consumer Electronics Report 2020." Statista Consumer Market Outlook, August 2020. https://www.statista.com.

"Courrier de la mode." *L'Artiste* 5 (1858). In Manuel Charpy, "Craze and Shame: Rubber Clothing During the Nineteenth Century in Paris, London, and New York City." *Fashion Theory: The Journal of Dress, Body & Culture* 16, no. 4 (2012): 436–60.

Courtaulds Ltd. *National Rayon Week* promotional pamphlet, 1936. In Paul David Blanc, *Fake Silk: The Lethal History of Viscose Rayon* (New Haven: Yale University Press, 2016), 63.

Cronberg, Anja Aronowsky. "Will I Get a Ticket? A Conversation About Life After *Vogue* with Lucinda Chambers," July 3, 2017. Vestoj. http://vestoj.com.

Crowston, Clare Haru. *Fabricating Women: The Seamstresses of Old Regime France, 1675–1791.* Durham and London: Duke University Press, 2001.

Davis, B. J. "Walking Out: The Great Textile Strike of 1934." NCPEDIA. https://www.ncpedia.org.

Davis, Edward Everett. *The White Scourge*, 1940, and *The Cotton Crisis: Proceedings of Second Conference Institute of Public Affairs*, 1935. In Neil Foley, *The White Scourge* (Berkeley: University of California Press, 1999), 5–7.

Davis-Young, Katherine. "For Many Native Americans, Embracing LGBT Members Is a Return to the Past." *Washington Post*, March 29, 2019. https://www.washingtonpost.com.

de Beauvoir, Simone. "Social Life." In Daniel Leonhard Purdy, ed., *The Rise of Fashion* (Minneapolis: University of Minnesota Press, 2004), 126–36.

De Colyar, H. A. "Jean-Baptiste Colbert and the Codifying Ordinances of Louis XIV." *Journal of the Society of Comparative Legislation* 13, no. 1 (1912): 56–86.

Defoe, Daniel, and John McVeigh. *A Review of the State of the British Nation, Volume 4, 1707–08*. In Sven Beckert, *Empire of Cotton: A Global History* (New York: Vintage, 2015), 33.

DeJean, Joan E. *The Essence of Style: How the French Invented High Fashion, Fine Food, Chic Cafés, Style, Sophistication, and Glamour*. New York: Free Press, 2005.

Department of Agriculture, Revenue and Commerce, Fibres and Silk Branch. Memo to the Home Department, Calcutta, June 24, 1874. In Sven Beckert, *Empire of Cotton: A Global History* (New York: Vintage, 2015), 336.

Derisi, Stephanie. "Reviewed Work: The Dirty Side of the Garment Industry: Fast Fashion and Its Negative Impact on Environment and Society by Nikolay Anguelov." *Modern Language Studies* 46, no. 1 (2016): 87–89.

Desai, Anuj, Nedal Nassar, and Marian Chertow. "American Seams: An Exploration of Hybrid Fast Fashion and Domestic Manufacturing Models in Relocalised Apparel Production." *Journal of Corporate Citizenship* 45 (2012): 53–78.

Diary kept by Elizabeth Fuller, Daughter of Rev. Timothy Fuller of Princeton. In Laurel Thatcher Ulrich, *The Age of Homespun: Objects and Stories in the Creation of an American Myth* (New York: Alfred A. Knopf, 2001), 285.

Diary of Elisabeth Foot. In Laurel Thatcher Ulrich, *The Age of Homespun: Objects and Stories in the Creation of an American Myth* (New York: Alfred A. Knopf, 2001), 211, 214–15.

Diary of Elizabeth (Porter) Phelps. In Laurel Thatcher Ulrich, *The Age of Homespun: Objects and Stories in the Creation of an American Myth* (New York: Alfred A. Knopf, 2001), 202.

Diary of John Campbell. In Katherine Koob and Martha Coons, *Linen-Making in New England, 1640–1860: All Sorts of Good Sufficient Cloth* (North Andover: Merrimack Valley Textile Museum, 1980), 17.

Diary of Matthew Patten of Bedford, New Hampshire. In Laurel Thatcher Ulrich, *The Age of Homespun: Objects and Stories in the Creation of an American Myth* (New York: Alfred A. Knopf, 2001), 195.

Diary of Ruth Henshaw, 1792. In Laurel Thatcher Ulrich, *The Age of Homespun: Objects and Stories in the Creation of an American Myth* (New York: Alfred A. Knopf, 2001), 287.

Dikötter, Frank. *The Cultural Revolution: A People's History, 1962–1976.* New York: Bloomsbury, 2017.

Disher, M. L. *American Factory Production of Women's Clothing.* London: Deveraux Publications, 1947.

Display advertisement, "Death to Squirrels and Gophers!" *Los Angeles Times,* May 26, 1883. In Paul David Blanc, *Fake Silk: The Lethal History of Viscose Rayon* (New Haven: Yale University Press, 2016), 21.

Dohner, Janet Vorwald. "Sheep." In *The Encyclopedia of Historic and Endangered Livestock and Poultry Breeds* (New Haven: Yale University Press, 2001), 159–64.

Dong, Stella. *Shanghai: The Rise and Fall of a Decadent City.* New York: Harper Perennial, 2001.

Dongjing menghua lu zhu. In Patricia Ebrey, "Taking Out the Grand Carriage: Imperial Spectacle and the Visual Culture of Northern Song Kaifeng." *Asia Major* 12, no. 1 (1999): 40.

Doniger, Wendy. *The Implied Spider: Politics and Theology in Myth.* New York: Columbia University Press, 2011.

Dou, Eva, and Chao Deng. "Western Companies Get Tangled in China's Muslim Clampdown." *Wall Street Journal,* May 16, 2019. https://www.wsj.com.

Draper, Theodore. "Gastonia Revisited." *Social Research* 38, no. 1 (1971): 3–29.

Drew, Michael. "The Death of the $2 Trillion Auto Industry Will Come Sooner than Expected." July 6, 2020. https://www.oilprice.com.

Dryansky, G. Y. "What's in a Name? Behind the Label—An Insider's Guide to European Style." *Vogue,* October 1986.

Dufrenoy, Marie-Louise. "Sericulture." *Scientific Monthly* 71, no. 2 (1950): 133–34.

Dupin, Charles. "Rattier et Guibal—Caoutchouc." In *Exposition universelle de 1851: Travaux de la Commission française* (Paris: Imprimerie impériale, 1862). In Manuel Charpy, "Craze and Shame: Rubber Clothing During the Nineteenth Century in Paris, London, and New York City." *Fashion Theory: The Journal of Dress, Body & Culture* 16, no. 4 (2012): 438.

"Dust Bowl Slaughter of the Navajo Sheep." Southwest Indian Relief Council. http://www.nativepartnership.org.

Eaton, Aurore. *The Amoskeag Manufacturing Company: A History of Enterprise on the Merrimack River.* Charleston: The History Press, 2015.

Ebrey, Patricia. "Taking Out the Grand Carriage: Imperial Spectacle and the Visual Culture of Northern Song Kaifeng." *Asia Major* 12, no. 1 (1999): 33–65.

"Ecological and Social Costs of Cotton Farming in Egypt." University of British Columbia Open Case Studies. https://cases.open.ubc.ca.

Elias, Norbert. "Etiquette and Ceremony: Conduct and Sentiment of Human Beings as Functions of the Power Structure of Their Society." In Daniel Leonhard Purdy, ed., *The Rise of Fashion* (Minneapolis: University of Minnesota Press, 2004), 49–63.

Eller, Ronald D. *Miners, Millhands, and Mountaineers: Industrialization of the Appalachian South, 1880–1930.* Knoxville: University of Tennessee Press, 1995.

Engels, Friedrich. *The Condition of the Working Class in England.* David McLellan, ed. Oxford: Oxford University Press, 1993.

Erasmus. *De civilitate morum puerilium.* In Daniel Roche, *The Culture of Clothing: Dress and Fashion in the Ancien Régime* (Cambridge: Cambridge University Press, 1996), 6.

Ernst, Jeff, and Elisabeth Malkin. "Honduran President's Brother, Arrested in Miami, Is Charged with Drug Trafficking." *New York Times,* November 26, 2018. www.nytimes.com.

Erskine, Lillian. "Report to Ralph M. Bashore," March 21, 1938. In Paul David Blanc, *Fake Silk: The Lethal History of Viscose Rayon* (New Haven: Yale University Press, 2016), 102.

Euse, Erica. "The Revolutionary History of the Pantsuit." *Vice,* March 21, 2016. http://www.vice.com.

Ewen, Stuart. *Captains of Consciousness: Advertising and the Social Roots of the Consumer Culture.* New York: McGraw-Hill, 1976.

Ewen, Stuart, and Elizabeth Ewen. *Channels of Desire: Mass Images and the Shaping of American Consciousness.* Minneapolis: University of Minnesota Press, 1992.

"The Exhibition." *Young India,* July 14, 1927. In Lisa Trivedi, "Visually Mapping the 'Nation': Swadeshi Politics in Nationalist India, 1920–1930." *Journal of Asian Studies* 62, no. 1 (2003): 11.

Fagin, Dan. "Dye Me a River: How a Revolutionary Textile Coloring Compound Tainted a Waterway: When Aniline Dye Was Synthesized from Coal Tar, Few Studied What the Manufacturing Process Left Behind." *Scientific American,* March 22, 2013. https://www.scientificamerican.com.

Farmer, Jared. "Erosion of Trust." *American Scientist* 98, no. 4 (July/August 2010): 348. https://www.americanscientist.org.

Federici, Silvia. *Caliban and the Witch.* Brooklyn: Autonomedia, 2014.

Filene, Edward A. *Successful Living in the Machine Age,* 1931. In Stuart Ewen, *Captains of Consciousness: Advertising and the Social Roots of the Consumer Culture* (New York: McGraw-Hill, 1976), 92.

Fleurant, Aude, Alexandra Kuimova, Diego Lopes da Silva, Nan Tian, Pieter D. Wezeman, and Siemon T. Wezeman. "The SIPRI Top 100 Arms-Producing and Military Services Companies, 2018." SIPRI, December 2019. https://www.sipri.org.

Flügel, J. C. "The Great Masculine Renunciation and Its Causes." In Daniel Leonhard Purdy, ed., *The Rise of Fashion* (Minneapolis: University of Minnesota Press, 2004), 102–8.

———. *The Psychology of Clothes.* In Kimberly Chrisman-Campbell, *Fashion Victims: Dress at the Court of Louis XVI and Marie-Antoinette* (New Haven: Yale University Press, 2015), 8.

Foley, Neil. *The White Scourge: Mexicans, Blacks, and Poor Whites in Texas Cotton Culture.* Berkeley: University of California Press, 1999.

Food and Agriculture Organization of the United Nations and International Cotton Advisory Committee. "World Apparel Fiber Consumption Survey." July 2013. https://www.icac.org.

Fowler, Glenn. "Imports Shroud Cotton Outlook: Japanese Textiles Are Said to Pose a Life or Death Question for Industry." *New York Times,* April 6, 1956. In Ellen Israel Rosen, *Making Sweatshops: The Globalization of the U.S. Apparel Industry* (Berkeley: University of California Press, 2002), 82.

Frank, Dana. *The Long Honduran Night: Resistance, Terror, and the United States in the Aftermath of the Coup.* Chicago: Haymarket Books, 2018.

Frankel, Jeremy. "Crisis on the High Plains: The Loss of America's Largest Aquifer—the Ogallala." *University of Denver Water Law Review,* May 17, 2018. http://duwaterlawreview.com.

Frank Leslie's Illustrated Weekly, July 30, 1859. In Ruth Brandon, *Singer and the Sewing Machine: A Capitalist Romance* (New York: Kodansha International, 1996), 120–21.

Gandhi, Mohandas. *Young India,* October 13, 1921. *Bombay Sarvodaya Mandal.* https://mkgandi.org.

Gardels, Nathan. "Interview with I. Illich." Special issue: "Dialogues on Civilization." *NPQ: New Perspectives Quarterly* 26, no. 4 (Fall 2009): 80–89.

Gastonia Daily Gazette, April 25, 1929. In Patrick Huber, "Mill Mother's Lament: Ella May Wiggins and the Gastonia Textile Strike of 1929." *Southern Cultures* 15, no. 3 (2009): 90.

Gillam, Carey. "I Won a Historic Lawsuit, But May Not Live to Get the Money." *Time*, November 21, 2018. https://time.com.

———. "Revealed: Bayer AG Discussed Plans to Give Not-for-Profit Funding for Influence." *The Guardian*, November 21, 2019. https://www.theguardian.com.

———. "Thailand Wants to Ban These Three Pesticides. The US Government Says No." *The Guardian*, November 10, 2019. https://www.theguardian.com.

Gillette, Paul J., and Eugene Tillenger. *Inside the Ku Klux Klan*. New York: Pyramid, 1965.

Glass, Brent D., and Michael Hill. "Gastonia Strike." *Encyclopedia of North Carolina*. University of North Carolina Press, 2006. https://www.ncpedia.org.

Glory, A. "Débris de corde paléolithique à la grotte Lascaux." *Mémoires de la Société préhistorique française* 5 (1959): 137–38. In Elizabeth Wayland Barber, *Women's Work: The First 20,000 Years* (New York: W. W. Norton, 1994), 51–52.

Gong Y., L. Li, D. Gong, H. Yin, and J. Zhang. "Biomolecular Evidence of Silk from 8,500 Years Ago." *PLOS One* (2016).

Gray, Tim. "A Scarcity Adds to Water's Appeal." *New York Times*, July 11, 2019.

Green, Cecilia. "The Asian Connection: The U.S.-Caribbean Apparel Circuit and a New Model of Industrial Relations." *Latin American Research Review* 33, no. 3 (1998): 7–47.

Greenway, John. *American Folksongs of Protest*. Philadelphia: University of Pennsylvania Press, 1953.

Grimm, Beca. "17 Ways to Take Care of Yourself After a Breakup so You Can Move On in the Healthiest Way Possible." July 2, 2015. http://www.bustle.com.

Gro Intelligence. "US Cotton Subsidies Insulate Producers from Economic Loss." June 6, 2018. https://gro-intelligence.com.

Grose, Timothy. "Beautifying Uyghur Bodies: Fashion, 'Modernity,' and State Power in the Tarim Basin." University of Westminster, October 11, 2019. http://blog.westminster.ac.uk/.

Hakim, Danny. "A Weed Killer Made in Britain, for Export Only." *New York Times,* December 20, 2016, A1.

Hall, Jacquelyn Dowd. "Disorderly Women: Gender and Labor Militancy in the Appalachian South." *Journal of American History* 73, no. 2 (1986): 354–82.

Hamilton, Alexander. *The Papers of Alexander Hamilton, Volume 10, December 1791–January 1792.* Harold C. Syrett, ed. New York: Columbia University Press, 1966.

Hamilton, Alice. *Industrial Poisons in the United States,* 1925. In Paul David Blanc, *Fake Silk: The Lethal History of Viscose Rayon* (New Haven: Yale University Press, 2016), 45.

——. *Industrial Poisons Used in the Rubber Industry.* Bureau of Labor Statistics Bulletin 179, 1915. In Paul David Blanc, *Fake Silk: The Lethal History of Viscose Rayon* (New Haven: Yale University Press, 2016), 79.

——. "Nineteen Years in the Poisonous Trades." *Harper's Magazine,* October 1, 1929. In Paul David Blanc, *Fake Silk: The Lethal History of Viscose Rayon* (New Haven: Yale University Press, 2016), 80–81.

Hampshire County Probate Records. In Laurel Thatcher Ulrich, *The Age of Homespun: Objects and Stories in the Creation of an American Myth* (New York: Alfred A. Knopf, 2001), 139.

Handley, Erin, and Bang Xiao. "Japanese Brands Muji and Uniqlo Flaunt 'Xinjiang Cotton' Despite Uyghur Human Rights Concerns." ABC News, November 3, 2019. https://www.abc.net.au/news.

Hanes, William Travis, and Frank Sanello. *Opium Wars: The Addiction of One Empire and the Corruption of Another.* Naperville, IL: Sourcebooks, 2002.

Hannah Matthews Book, 1790–1813. In Laurel Thatcher Ulrich, *The Age of Homespun: Objects and Stories in the Creation of an American Myth* (New York: Alfred A. Knopf, 2001), 199.

Hargis, Peggy Griffith, and Larry J. Griffin. *The New Encyclopedia of Southern Culture, Volume 20: Social Class.* Chapel Hill: University of North Carolina Press, 2012.

Harper's Weekly, March 10, 1866. In Ruth Brandon, *Singer and the Sewing Machine: A Capitalist Romance* (New York: Kodansha International, 1996), 121.

"HC Orders Closure of Tiruppur Dyeing Units." *Economic Times of India,* January 29, 2011. https://economictimes.indiatimes.com.

Heaton, Ida. *Scraps of Work and Play.* In Paul David Blanc, *Fake Silk: The Lethal History of Viscose Rayon* (New Haven: Yale University Press, 2016), 89.

Hegel, Georg W. "On Drapery." In Daniel Leonhard Purdy, ed., *The Rise of Fashion* (Minneapolis: University of Minnesota Press, 2004), 145–52.

Hema, L., N. Murali, P. Devendran, and S. Panneerselvam. "Genotoxic Effect of Dye Effluents in Chromosomes of Indigenous Goats (*Capra hircus*)." *Cytologia* 76, no. 269 (September 2011).

Hersey, John. *Hiroshima*. New York: Vintage, 1989.

Hills, Richard L. "Sir Richard Arkwright and His Patent Granted in 1769." *Notes and Records of the Royal Society of London* 24, no. 2 (1970): 254–60.

Hinrichsen, Don, and Henrylito Tacio. "The Coming Freshwater Crisis Is Already Here." In "Finding the Source: The Linkages Between Population and Water." Wilson Center. https://www.wilsoncenter.org.

Hmong Cultural Center and the Hmong Archives in Saint Paul, Minnesota. www.HmongEmbroidery.org.

Hobsbawm, Eric. *The Age of Revolution, 1789–1848*. New York: Vintage, 1962.

Hobsbawm, Eric J., and Chris Wrigley. *Industry and Empire: From 1750 to the Present Day*. New York: New Press, 1999.

Hodgson, A., and S. Collie. "Biodegradability of Wool: Soil Burial Biodegradation." Presented at 43rd Textile Research Symposium in Christchurch, New Zealand, December 2014.

Hoekstra, Arjen. "The Water Footprint of Cotton Consumption." Value of Water Research Report Series No. 18, September 2005. UNESCO Water Footprint Report, September 2005. UNESCO-IHE Institute for Water Education.

Hoerig, Karl A. "Remembering Our Indian School Days: The Boarding School Experience." *American Anthropologist* 104, no. 2 (2002): 642–46.

Holdstock, Nick. *China's Forgotten People: Xinjiang, Terror and the Chinese State*. London: I. B. Taurus, 2015.

Holinshed's Chronicles, 1587. In OED Online, "sheet, n.1," July 2018. Oxford University Press. http://www.oed.com.

Hollander, Anne. *Seeing Through Clothes*. New York: Avon Books, 1978.

Holthaus, Gary. *From the Farm to the Table: What All Americans Need to Know About Agriculture*. Lexington: University Press of Kentucky, 2014.

Homer. *The Iliad of Homer*. Translated by Richard Lattimore. Chicago and London: University of Chicago Press, 1961.

Hoops, Kat. "What Is the Bayeux Tapestry? Why Is It in France?" *Express*, January 17, 2018. https://www.express.co.uk.

Howe, Brian. "The Secret to Vintage Jeans." *Craftsmanship Quarterly* (Fall 2017). https://craftsmanship.net.

Howell, Martha C. *Women, Production, and Patriarchy in Late Medieval Cities*. Chicago: University of Chicago Press, 1986.

"How Much Do Our Wardrobes Cost to the Environment?" World Bank. September 23, 2019. https://www.worldbank.org.

Hoyt, Elizabeth Ellis. *The Consumption of Wealth*, 1928. In Stuart Ewen, *Captains of Consciousness: Advertising and the Social Roots of the Consumer Culture* (New York: McGraw-Hill, 1976), 95.

Huber, Patrick. "Mill Mother's Lament: Ella May Wiggins and the Gastonia Textile Strike of 1929." *Southern Cultures* 15, no. 3 (2009): 81–110.

Human Rights Watch. "China's Algorithms of Repression: Reverse Engineering a Xinjiang Police Mass Surveillance App." May 1, 2019. https://www.hrw.org.

———. "Honduras: Accusations by Military Endanger Activist." December 19, 2013. https://www.hrw.org.

Huxley, Aldous. *Brave New World*. London: Chatto & Windus, 1932.

Illich, Ivan. *Toward a History of Needs*. New York: Pantheon, 1978.

Indian Health Service. "Two Spirit." https://www.ihs.gov.

"Indigofera tinctoria." Missouri Botanical Garden. https://www.missouribotanicalgarden.org.

International Labour Organization. "Wages and Working Hours in the Textiles, Clothing, Leather and Footwear Industries." September 2014. https://www.ilo.org.

Isager, Jacob. *Pliny on Art and Society: The Elder Pliny's Chapters on the History of Art*. Abingdon: Routledge, 1991.

Jacoby, David. "Silk Economics and Cross-Cultural Artistic Interaction: Byzantium, the Muslim World, and the Christian West." *Dumbarton Oaks Papers* 58 (2004): 197–240, at 199.

Jiang, Leiwen, Tong Yufen, Zhao Zhijie, Li Tianhong, and Liao Jianhua. "Water Resources, Land Exploration and Population Dynamics in Arid Areas: The Case of the Tarim River Basin in Xinjiang of China." *Population and Environment* 26, no. 6 (July 2005): 471–503.

Jiujiang fuzhi, 1527. In Timothy Brook, *The Confusions of Pleasure: Commerce and Culture in Ming China* (Berkeley: University of California Press, 1999), 113–14.

Johnson, David. *An Improving Prospect?: A History of Agricultural Change in Cumbria*. Gloucestershire: Amberley, 2016.

Joniak-Lüthi, Agnieszka. "Han Migration to Xinjiang Uyghur Autonomous Region: Between State Schemes and Migrants' Strategies." Special Issue: "Mobility and Identity in Central Asia," *Zeitschrift für Ethnologie* 138, no. 2 (2013): 155–74.

Jordan, Miriam. "Farmworkers, Mostly Undocumented, Become 'Essential'

During Pandemic." *New York Times,* April 10, 2020. http://www.nytimes .com.

Joy, Omana. "Spinning Apparatus of Silk Worm Larvae *Bombyx mori* L the Spinneret." *Current Science* 55, no. 17 (1986): 872.

Judd, Sylvester. *History of Hadley, Massachusetts,* 1905. In Katherine Koob and Martha Coons, *All Sorts of Good Sufficient Cloth: Linen-Making in New England, 1640–1860* (North Andover: Merrimack Valley Textile Museum, 1980), 27–28.

Kant, Rita. "Textile Dyeing Industry an Environmental Hazard." *Natural Science* 1 (2012): 22–26.

Karda, Sarah. "Lubbock Region Cotton Industry Impacts Economy." *Daily Toreador,* September 15, 2016. http://www.dailytoreador.com.

Kattan Group. Investment Summary, IDB Invest, Inter-American Development Bank. https://www.idbinvest.org.

Keller, Kenneth W. "From the Rhineland to the Virginia Frontier: Flax Production as a Commercial Enterprise." *Virginia Magazine of History and Biography* 98, no. 3 (July 1990): 487–511.

Kennedy, John W. Cline Library interview, December 1998. In Willow Roberts Powers, *Navajo Trading: The End of an Era* (Albuquerque: University of New Mexico Press, 2001), 40.

Kessler-Harris, Alice. *Women Have Always Worked: A Concise History.* Urbana: University of Illinois Press, 2018.

Kiely, Jan. *The Compelling Ideal: Thought Reform and the Prison in China, 1901–1956.* New Haven: Yale University Press, 2014.

Killing, Alison. "China's Camps Have Forced Labor and Growing US Market." *Buzzfeed,* December 28, 2020. https://www.buzzfeednews .com.

Kingsbury, Susan M., to Dean Helen Taft Manning. Bryn Mawr College, February 26, 1935. In Paul David Blanc, *Fake Silk: The Lethal History of Viscose Rayon* (New Haven: Yale University Press, 2016), 94–95.

Kinnock, Glenys. "America's $24bn Subsidy Damages Developing World Cotton Farmers." *The Guardian,* May 24, 2011. https://www .theguardian.com.

Knight, Sam. "The Tragic Story of Wallace Hume Carothers." *Financial Times,* November 28, 2008. https://www.ft.com.

Koob, Katherine, and Martha Coons. *All Sorts of Good Sufficient Cloth: Linen-Making in New England, 1640–1860.* North Andover: Merrimack Valley Textile Museum, 1980.

Kruger, David. "University of Wyoming Wool Laboratory and Library:

1907–2012." Paper presented at "Transforming Food and Fiber," Agricultural History Society Annual Meeting, Provo, Utah, June 2014.

Kumar, K. A., and H. Achyuthan. "Heavy Metal Accumulation in Certain Marine Animals Along the East Coast of Chennai, Tamil Nadu, India." *Journal of Environmental Biology* 28, no. 637 (July 2007).

Labor Defender, October 1929. In Patrick Huber, "Mill Mother's Lament: Ella May Wiggins and the Gastonia Textile Strike of 1929." *Southern Cultures* 15, no. 3 (2009): 100.

"Laboring Voice." *Time,* June 27, 1949, 62.

"Labor Survey of Washington and Carter Counties and Adjacent Territories." North American Rayon and American Bemberg Records. In Marie Tedesco, "Claiming Public Space, Asserting Class Identity, and Displaying Patriotism: The 1929 Rayon Workers' Strike Parades in Elizabethton, Tennessee." *Journal of Appalachian Studies* 12, no. 2 (2006): 57.

Ladies' Home Journal, January 1922. In Stuart Ewen, *Captains of Consciousness: Advertising and the Social Roots of the Consumer Culture* (New York: McGraw-Hill, 1976), 178–79.

Lakhani, Nina. "How Hitmen and High Living Lifted Lid on Looting of Honduran Healthcare System." *The Guardian,* June 10, 2015. https://www.theguardian.com.

Lapham, William B. *History of the Town of Bethel, Maine, 1891.* In Laurel Thatcher Ulrich, *The Age of Homespun: Objects and Stories in the Creation of an American Myth* (New York: Alfred A. Knopf, 2001), 269.

"The Largest Indigenous Pride in the United States to Be on the Navajo Nation." Diné Pride. https://www.navajonationpride.com/.

Larkin, Margaret. "The Story of Ella May." *New Masses* 5 (November 1929). In Patrick Huber, "Mill Mother's Lament: Ella May Wiggins and the Gastonia Textile Strike of 1929." *Southern Cultures* 15, no. 3 (2009): 97.

Lee, Jennifer J., and Kyle Endres. "Overworked and Underpaid: H-2A Herders in Colorado." A Report by the Migrant Farm Worker Division of Colorado Legal Services. January 12, 2010.

Lee-Whitman, Leanna, and Maruta Skelton. "Where Did All the Silver Go: Identifying Eighteenth-Century Chinese Painted and Printed Silks." *Textile Museum Journal* 22 (January 1983): 33–52.

Li, Lillian M. "Silks by Sea: Trade, Technology, and Enterprise in China and Japan." *Business History Review* 56, no. 2 (1982): 192–217.

Lind, Mathilde Frances. "Handspinning Tradition in the United States:

Traditionalization and Revival." *Journal of American Folklore* 133, no. 528 (2020): 142–64.

Lindsay, Matilda. "Rayon Mills and Old Line Americans." *Life and Labor Bulletin,* 1929. In Paul David Blanc, *Fake Silk: The Lethal History of Viscose Rayon* (New Haven: Yale University Press, 2016), 89.

Little, Jane Braxton. "The Ogallala Aquifer: Saving a Vital U.S. Water Source." *Scientific American,* March 1, 2009. https://www.scientific american.com.

Liu, Xinru. *The Silk Road in World History.* Oxford: Oxford University Press, 2010.

"Longest-Running Shows on Broadway." *Playbill,* March 9, 2020. https://www.playbill.com/.

Lovato, Roberto. "Our Man in Honduras: The Backers of the Honduran Coup Have an Inside Man in Washington." *The American Prospect,* July 22, 2009. https://prospect.org.

Ma, Debin. "Between Cottage and Factory: The Evolution of Chinese and Japanese Silk-Reeling Industries in the Latter Half of the Nineteenth Century." *Journal of the Asia Pacific Economy* 10, no. 2 (2005): 195–213.

Macon Telegraph, May 31, 1865. In Sven Beckert, *Empire of Cotton: A Global History* (New York: Vintage, 2015), 281.

Macphaedris, Alexander. Papers, Portsmouth, New Hampshire. In Laurel Thatcher Ulrich, *The Age of Homespun: Objects and Stories in the Creation of an American Myth* (New York: Alfred A. Knopf, 2001), 269, 272.

Madani, Dorsati. "A Review of the Role and Impact of Export Processing Zones. Policy Research Working Paper 2238." World Bank Publications, 2003.

Magasin des modes, 20e Cahier des Costumes Français. In Kimberly Chrisman-Campbell, *Fashion Victims: Dress at the Court of Louis XVI and Marie-Antoinette* (New Haven: Yale University Press, 2015), 177.

Malkin, Elisabeth. "Who Ordered Killing of Honduran Activist? Evidence of Broad Plot Is Found." *New York Times,* October 28, 2017. https://www.nytimes.com.

Manchester, Petricha E., to Dr. Alice Hamilton, telegram, March 11, 1933. In Paul David Blanc, *Fake Silk: The Lethal History of Viscose Rayon* (New Haven: Yale University Press, 2016), 78.

Mann, James A. *The Cotton Trade of Great Britain: Its Rise, Progress, and Present Extent.* London: Frank Cass, 1968.

Mann, Thomas. "The Blood of the Walsungs." *Death in Venice, and Seven Other Stories.* New York: Vintage, 1989.

Mannyng, Robert. *Mannyng's Chronicle*. In OED Online, "sheet, n.1," July 2018. Oxford University Press. http://www.oed.com.

Marx, Karl. *Capital: Volume One: A Critique of Political Economy*. Mineola: Dover Publications, 2019.

Massachusetts Supreme Judiciary Court, Case Papers. In Laurel Thatcher Ulrich, *The Age of Homespun: Objects and Stories in the Creation of an American Myth* (New York: Alfred A. Knopf, 2001), 202.

Matthews, Mera. "Distaff, Worldwide, Deep Antiquity." Smith College Museum of Ancient Inventions: Distaff. https://www.smith.edu.

McCubbin, Tracy. "How to Cleanse Your Home After a Breakup: A Pro Declutterer Explains." January 29, 2018. http://mindbodygreen.com.

McKinsey & Company. "The State of Fashion 2019." www.mckinsey.com.

McLerran, Jennifer, ed. *Weaving Is Life: Navajo Weavings from the Edwin L. & Ruth E. Kennedy Southwest Native American Collection*. Athens, OH: Kennedy Museum of Art, Ohio University, 2006.

McNeil, Steve, Matthew Sunderland, and Larissa Zaitseva. "Closed-Loop Wool Carpet Recycling." *Resources, Conservation and Recycling* 51 (July 2007): 220–24.

Mechanic's Journal, April 1, 1858. In Ruth Brandon, *Singer and the Sewing Machine: A Capitalist Romance* (New York: Kodansha International, 1996), 109.

"A Meeting with the Delegates of the Eastern Indians," Minutes. In Laurel Thatcher Ulrich, *The Age of Homespun: Objects and Stories in the Creation of an American Myth* (New York: Alfred A. Knopf, 2001), 95.

Meinig, D. W. *The Shaping of America: A Geographical Perspective on 500 Years of History, Volume 2: Continental America, 1800–1867*. New Haven: Yale University Press, 1993.

Melinkoff, Ellen. *What We Wore: An Offbeat Social History of Women's Clothing, 1950–1980*. New York: Quill, 1984.

Mendeleev, Dimitri Ivanovich. *Uchenie o promyshlennosti* [Studies on Industry], 1900. In Paul David Blanc, *Fake Silk: The Lethal History of Viscose Rayon* (New Haven: Yale University Press, 2016), 27.

Middleton, Thomas. *The Revenger's Tragedy*. In OED Online, "sheet, n.1," July 2018. Oxford University Press. http://www.oed.com.

Miller, Henry. "Third or Fourth Day of Spring." *Black Spring*. New York: Grove Atlantic, 2007.

Miller, Lesley Ellis. "Mysterious Manufacturers: Situating L. Galy, Gallien et Compe. in the Eighteenth-Century Lyons Silk Industry." *Studies in the Decorative Arts* 9, no. 2 (2002): 87–131.

Millward, James. *Eurasian Crossroads*, 2007. In Nick Holdstock, *China's*

Forgotten People: Xinjiang, Terror and the Chinese State (London: I. B. Taurus, 2015), 20.

Millward, James A. "Historical Perspectives on Contemporary Xinjiang." *Inner Asia* 2 (2000): 121–35.

Milman, Joel. "It's Working." *Forbes,* February 19, 1990. In Ellen Israel Rosen, *Making Sweatshops: The Globalization of the U.S. Apparel Industry* (Berkeley: University of California Press, 2002), 148.

Mirsky, Jeannette, and Allan Nevins. *The World of Eli Whitney.* New York: Macmillan, 1952.

Mitsch, William J., et al. "Reducing Nitrogen Loading to the Gulf of Mexico from the Mississippi River Basin." *BioScience* 51 no. 5 (2001): 373–88.

Molière. *The Middle-Class Gentleman,* 1670. Translated by Phillip Dwight Jones. Middletown: CreateSpace Independent Publishing Platform, 2019.

Moll-Murata, Christine. "Chinese Guilds from the Seventeenth to the Twentieth Centuries: An Overview." *International Review of Social History* 53 (2008): 213–47.

Monge, Patricia, et al. "Parental Occupational Exposure to Pesticides and the Risk of Childhood Leukemia in Costa Rica." *Scandinavian Journal of Work, Environment and Health* 33, no. 4 (August 2007): 293–303.

Monroe, Jean Guard, and Ray A. Williamson. *They Dance in the Sky: Native American Star Myths.* Boston: Houghton Mifflin, 1987.

Mooney, James M. *Historical Sketch of the Cherokee.* Chicago: Aldine Publishing Company, 1975.

Munro, John H. "Medieval Woollens: Textiles, Textile Technology and Industrial Organisation, c. 800–1500." In D. T. Jenkins, ed., *The Cambridge History of Western Textiles, Volume 1* (Cambridge: Cambridge University Press, 2003), 181–227.

Murray, Jonathan. "Textile Strike of 1934." NorthCarolinahistory.org: An Online Encyclopedia, North Carolina History Project. https://northcarolinahistory.org/encyclopedia/textile-strike-of-1934/.

"Mystery: The American Viscose Corps." *Fortune,* July 1937. In Paul David Blanc, *Fake Silk: The Lethal History of Viscose Rayon* (New Haven: Yale University Press, 2016), 69.

"The National Guard and Elizabethton." *Life and Labor Bulletin,* 1929. In Paul David Blanc, *Fake Silk: The Lethal History of Viscose Rayon* (New Haven: Yale University Press, 2016), 90.

National Oceanic and Atmospheric Administration. "Large 'Dead Zone' Measured in Gulf of Mexico." August 1, 2019. https://www.noaa.gov.

New England Farmer. "Flax," February 9, 1831. In Katherine Koob and Martha Coons, *All Sorts of Good Sufficient Cloth: Linen-Making in New England, 1640–1860* (North Andover: Merrimack Valley Textile Museum, 1980), 27.

"A New Textiles Economy: Redesigning Fashion's Future." Ellen MacArthur Foundation, 2017. www.ellenmacarthurfoundation.org.

New York Daily Tribune, May 23, 1862. In Ruth Brandon, *Singer and the Sewing Machine: A Capitalist Romance* (New York: Kodansha International, 1996), 108.

Nystrom, Paul. *Economics of Fashion*, 1928. In Stuart Ewen, *Captains of Consciousness: Advertising and the Social Roots of the Consumer Culture* (New York: McGraw-Hill, 1976), 85.

———. *Fashion Merchandising*, 1932. In Stuart Ewen, *Captains of Consciousness: Advertising and the Social Roots of the Consumer Culture* (New York: McGraw-Hill, 1976), 170.

O'Brien, Sharon. "20 Ways to Survive (and Feel Better) After a Breakup." July 24, 2014. http://msn.com.

O'Connell, Vanessa. "Retailers Reprogram Workers in Efficiency Push." *Wall Street Journal*, September 10, 2008. https://www.wsj.com.

Orleck, Annelise. *Common Sense and a Little Fire: Women and Working-Class Politics in the United States, 1900–1965*. Second Edition. Chapel Hill: University of North Carolina Press, 2017.

"Our Overseas Trade." *Advertiser*, April 22, 1936. In Paul David Blanc, *Fake Silk: The Lethal History of Viscose Rayon* (New Haven: Yale University Press, 2016), 63.

Paerregaard, Karsten. *Peruvians Dispersed: A Global Ethnography of Migration*. Lanham, MD: Lexington Books, 2008.

Paley, Dawn. "The Honduran Business Elite One Year After the Coup." *NACLA*, June 23, 2010. https://nacla.org.

Pankenier, David W. "Weaving Metaphors and Cosmo-Political Thought in Early China." *T'oung Pao* 101, no. 1/3 (2015): 1–34.

Parkinson, N. A. "The Latest Member of Our Textile Family." *Scientific American* 135, no. 2 (1926): 112–14.

Pearson, Richard, and Anne Underhill. "The Chinese Neolithic: Recent Trends in Research." *American Anthropologist*, New Series, 89, no. 4 (1987): 807–22.

Perkins, Dexter. "Prehistoric Fauna from Shanidar, Iraq." *Science* 144, no. 3626 (1964): 1565–66.

Perrin, Anne. "Water for Agriculture: New Resource Management Strategies." *Spore* 181 (2016): 20–24.

Peters, Pamela J. "Navajo Transgender Women's Journey of Acceptance in Society." *Medium,* October 7, 2018. https://medium.com.

Peterson, Frederick. "Three Cases of Acute Mania from Inhaling Carbon Bisulphide." *Boston Medical and Surgical Journal,* 1892. In Paul David Blanc, *Fake Silk: The Lethal History of Viscose Rayon* (New Haven: Yale University Press, 2016), 18.

Phillips, Janet, and Peter Phillips. "History from Below: Women's Underwear and the Rise of Women's Sport." *Journal of Popular Culture* 27 (Fall 1993): 129–48.

Poiret, Paul, and Stephen Haden Guest. *King of Fashion: The Autobiography of Paul Poiret.* Philadelphia: J. B. Lippincott, 1931.

"Polyamide Fibers (Nylon)." Polymer Properties Database, 2015–2020. https://polymerdatabase.com.

Ponnezhath, Maria, Ben Klayman, and Leslie Adler. "U.S. Government Says Verdict in Bayer's Roundup Case Should Be Reversed." Reuters, December 21, 2019. http://reuters.com.

Postan, M. M. *Medieval Trade and Finance* (London, 1973), 342. In A. R. Bell, P. Dryburgh, and C. Brooks, *The English Wool Market, c. 1230–1327* (Cambridge: Cambridge University Press), 8.

Pouchieu, Camille, et al. "Pesticide Use in Agriculture and Parkinson's Disease in the AGRICAN Cohort Study." *International Journal of Epidemiology* 47, no. 1 (February 2018): 299–310.

Powers, Willow Roberts. *Navajo Trading: The End of an Era.* Albuquerque: University of New Mexico Press, 2001.

Prada, Paulo. "Paraquat: A Controversial Chemical's Second Act." Reuters, April 2, 2015. https://www.reuters.com.

Proudhomme, L. *Les Crimes des reines de France* (Paris: Bureau des Révolutions de Paris, 1791). In Chrisman-Campbell, *Fashion Victims: Dress at the Court of Louis XVI and Marie-Antoinette* (New Haven: Yale University Press, 2015), 31.

The Proverbs of Ælfred in *An Old English Miscellany, 1200–1425.* In OED Online, "sheet, n.1.," March 2021. Oxford University Press. https://www.oed.com.

Quant, Mary. *Quant by Quant.* In Jane Schneider, "In and Out of Polyester: Desire, Disdain and Global Fibre Competitions." *Anthropology Today* 10, no. 4 (August 1994): 10.

Quataert, Jean H. "The Shaping of Women's Work in Manufacturing: Guilds, Households, and the State in Central Europe, 1648–1870." *American Historical Review* 90, no. 5 (1985): 1122–48.

Rashid, Ahmed. "The New Struggle in Central Asia: A Primer for the Baffled." *World Policy Journal* 17, no. 4 (Winter 2000–2001): 33–45.

Raymo, Maureen E., William F. Ruddiman, and Philip N. Froelich. "Influence of Late Cenozoic Mountain Building on Ocean Geochemical Cycles." *Geology* 16, no. 7 (1988): 649.

Rebanks, James. *The Shepherd's Life: A Tale of the Lake District.* London: Penguin, 2016.

Reed, Peter. "The British Chemical Industry and the Indigo Trade." *British Journal for the History of Science* 25, no. 1 (1992): 113–25.

Reichart, Elizabeth, and Deborah Drew. "By the Numbers: The Economic, Social and Environmental Impacts of 'Fast Fashion.'" World Resources Institute, January 10, 2019, https://www.wri.org/.

"Remembering Our Indian School Days: The Boarding School Experience." Curated by Margaret Archuleta. Heard Museum, Phoenix, Arizona, 2000; ongoing exhibition.

Resnick, Brian. "More than Ever, Our Clothes Are Made of Plastic. Just Washing Them Can Pollute the Oceans." *Vox*, January 11, 2019. https://www.vox.com.

Riccardi-Cubitt, Monique. "Chinoiserie." Oxford Art Online, 2003. https://www.oxfordartonline.com.

Rice, Tom. *White Robes, Silver Screens: Movies and the Making of the Ku Klux Klan.* Bloomington: Indiana University Press, 2016.

Richards, Eric. *Debating the Highland Clearances.* Edinburgh: Edinburgh University Press, 2007.

Richards, John F. "Frontier Settlement in Russia." In *The Unending Frontier: An Environmental History of the Early Modern World* (Berkeley: University of California Press, 2003), 242–73.

Richardson, Bertha June. *The Woman Who Spends: A Study of Her Economic Function*, 1913. In Stuart and Elizabeth Ewen, *Channels of Desire: Mass Images and the Shaping of American Consciousness* (Minneapolis: University of Minnesota Press, 1992), 116–17, 157.

Rico. "Who Are the Richest Men in Central America and Why." *The Q Media*, October 24, 2017. https://qcostarica.com.

Riddle, Lynn. "Walls of Silence: 86 Years Later, Anniversary of Violent Mill Strike Passes Largely Unnoticed." *Greenville News*, September 6, 2014. http://greenvilleonline.com.

Rimbault. "Le corps à travers les manuels." In Daniel Roche, *The Culture of Clothing: Dress and Fashion in the Ancien Régime* (Cambridge: Cambridge University Press, 1996), 373.

Robins, Nick. *The Corporation That Changed the World: How the East India Company Shaped the Modern Multinational*. London: Pluto Press, 2012.

Roche, Daniel. *The Culture of Clothing: Dress and Fashion in the Ancien Régime*. Cambridge: Cambridge University Press, 1996.

Rodgers, Nigel. *The Dandy: Peacock or Enigma?* London: Bene Factum Publishing, 2012.

Rome, Harold. "Status Quo." *Pins and Needles*. Columbia Records, 1962.

Rosen, Ellen Israel. *Making Sweatshops: The Globalization of the U.S. Apparel Industry*. Berkeley: University of California Press, 2002.

Rosenblum, Jonathan D. "A Farewell to Kathie Lee, Sweatshop Queen." *Chicago Tribune*, July 30, 2000. https://www.chicagotribune.com.

Ross, Doran H., and Agbenyega Adedze. *Wrapped in Pride: Ghanaian Kente and African American Identity*. UCLA Fowler Museum of Cultural History, Textile Series, No. 2, 1998.

Ross, Robert J. S. "The Twilight of CSR: Life and Death Illuminated by Fire." In Richard P. Appelbaum and Nelson Lichtenstein, eds., *Achieving Workers' Rights in the Global Economy* (Ithaca: Cornell University Press, 2016), 70–92.

Rousseau, Jean-Jacques. "Discourse on the Arts and Sciences." In Daniel Leonhard Purdy, ed., *The Rise of Fashion* (Minneapolis: University of Minnesota Press, 2004), 37–48.

———. *Oeuvres Complètes*. In Daniel Roche, *The Culture of Clothing: Dress and Fashion in the Ancien Régime* (Cambridge: Cambridge University Press, 1996), 412.

Ruwitch, John. "Pompeo Accused China of Genocide. Experts Say That Term Is Complicated." NPR, January 21, 2021. https://www.npr.org.

Rybczynski, Witold. *Home: A Short History of an Idea*. New York: Penguin, 1987.

Ryder, M. L. "The History of Sheep Breeds in Britain." *Agricultural History Review* 12, no. 1 (1964): 1–12.

Sarah Weeks Sheldon Papers, February 1805. In Laurel Thatcher Ulrich, *The Age of Homespun: Objects and Stories in the Creation of an American Myth* (New York: Alfred A. Knopf, 2001), 287.

Saturday Evening Post, December 7, 1929. In Stuart Ewen, *Captains of Consciousness: Advertising and the Social Roots of the Consumer Culture* (New York: McGraw-Hill, 1976), 161.

"SC Site of Bloody Labor Strike Violence Crumbles." Associated Press, October 5, 2009.

Schiaparelli, Elsa. *Shocking Life*. New York: E. P. Dutton, 1954.

Schlanger, Zoë. "Monsanto Is About to Disappear. Everything Will Stay Exactly the Same." *Quartz*, June 5, 2018. https://qz.com/.

Schneider, Jane. "The Anthropology of Cloth." *Annual Review of Anthropology* 16 (1987): 409–48.

———. *Cloth and Human Experience*. Washington, D.C.: Smithsonian Books, 1991.

———. "In and Out of Polyester: Desire, Disdain and Global Fibre Competitions." *Anthropology Today* 10, no. 4 (August 1994): 2–10.

Scranton, Philip. "An Immigrant Family and Industrial Enterprise: Sevill Schofield and the Philadelphia Textile Manufacture, 1845–1900." *Pennsylvania Magazine of History and Biography* 106, no. 3 (1982): 365–66.

Seetharaman, G. "These Two Issues Could Put the Brakes on the Bt Cotton Story." *Economic Times* (India), January 21, 2018. https://economictimes.indiatimes.com/.

Seymour, James D. "Xinjiang's Production and Construction Corps, and the Sinification of Eastern Turkestan." *Inner Asia* 2, no. 2, Special Issue: "Xinjiang" (2000): 171–93.

Shahbandeh, M. "U.S. Apparel Market—Statistics & Facts." Statista, April 26, 2021, https://www.statista.com.

"The Sheep." Orkney Sheep Foundation. https://www.theorkneysheep foundation.org.

Sheeran, Ed. "Shape of You," ÷ (album). Asylum Records, 2017.

Sheng, Angela. "Determining the Value of Textiles in the Tang Dynasty: In Memory of Professor Denis Twitchett (1925–2006)." *Journal of the Royal Asiatic Society* 23, no. 2 (2013): 175–95.

Shipov, Aleksandr. "Khlopchatobumazhnaia promyshlennost 'I vazhnost' eco znacheniia v Rossi, otd I," 1857. In Sven Beckert, *Empire of Cotton: A Global History* (New York: Vintage, 2015), 345.

Sima Qian. *Shi Ji*. In Xinru Liu, *The Silk Road in World History* (Oxford: Oxford University Press, 2010), 2.

Simon, Bryant. "General Textile Strike." *South Carolina Encyclopedia*. University of South Carolina, Institute for Southern Studies, August 9, 2016. https://www.scencyclopedia.org.

Singer Sewing Machine Company booklet. In Ruth Brandon, *Singer and the Sewing Machine: A Capitalist Romance* (New York: Kodansha International, 1996), 126–27.

Singh, Khushboo, Punita Raj Laxmi, and Shakti Singh. "Reviving Khadi: From Freedom Fabric to Fashion Fabric." *Man-Made Textiles in India* 42, no. 11 (November 2014): 409–13.

Singhal, Arvind. "The Mahatma's Message: Gandhi's Contributions to the

Art and Science of Communication." *China Media Research* 6, no. 3 (July 2010): 103–6.

Smith, Adam. *An Inquiry into the Nature and Causes of the Wealth of Nations*, 1776. Project Gutenberg, 2010.

Snipes, Shedra A., et al. "'The Only Thing I Wish I Could Change Is That They Treat Us Like People and Not Like Animals': Injury and Discrimination Among Latino Farmworkers." *Journal of Agromedicine* 22, no. 1 (2017): 36–46.

So, Alvin Y. *The South China Silk District: Local Historical Transformation and World-System Theory*. Albany: State University of New York Press, 1986.

Solidaridad—South & South East Asia. "Understanding the Characteristics of the Sumangali Scheme in Tamil Nadu Textile and Garment Industry and Supply Chain Linkage." Fair Labor Association, 2012. https://www.fairlabor.org/.

Solidarity Center. "Global Garment and Textile Industries: Workers, Rights and Working Conditions." August 2019. https://www.solidaritycenter.org.

Song Ruozhao. "Analects for Women." In William Theodore de Bary, *Sources of Chinese Tradition*, Second Edition, Volume 1 (New York: Columbia University Press, 1999), 827–31.

Sontag, Susan. *A Susan Sontag Reader*. New York: Farrar, Straus & Giroux, 2014.

Soth, Jens, Christian Grasser, and Romina Salerno. "Background Paper: The Impact of Cotton on Fresh Water Resources and Ecosystems, a Preliminary Synthesis." Report prepared for World Wildlife Foundation, May 1999.

Southern Indian Mills, Association. *SIMA: A Journey Through 75 Years* (2008): 153.

"Southern Stirrings." *Time*, April 15, 1929. In Patrick Huber, "Mill Mother's Lament: Ella May Wiggins and the Gastonia Textile Strike of 1929." *Southern Cultures* 15, no. 3 (2009): 86.

Spivak, Emily. "Stocking Series, Part 1: Wartime Rationing and Nylon Riots." *Smithsonian Magazine*, September 4, 2012. www.smithsonianmag.com.

Stafford, Ned. "Endosulfan Banned as Agreement Is Reached with India." *Chemistry World*, May 6, 2011. https://www.chemistryworld.com.

Stagg, Natasha. *Sleeveless: Fashion, Image, Media, New York, 2011–2019*. South Pasadena: Semiotext(e), 2019.

State Council, "Xinjiang de Fazhan yu Jinbu" [The Progress and Development of Xinjiang], 2009. In Nick Holdstock, *China's Forgotten People: Xinjiang, Terror and the Chinese State* (London: I. B. Taurus, 2015), 20.

Stein, Eliot. "The Last Surviving Sea Silk Seamstress." BBC, September 6, 2017. http://www.bbc.com.

Stein, Leon. *The Triangle Fire*. Centennial Edition. Ithaca and London: Cornell University Press, 2011.

Stoddard, Lothrop. *The Rising Tide of Color Against White World-Supremacy*. New York: Charles Scribner's Sons, 1916. In Neil Foley, *The White Scourge: Mexicans, Blacks, and Poor Whites in Texas Cotton Culture*. (Berkeley: University of California Press, 1999), 5–6.

Tal, Alon. "Desertification." In Frank Uekoetter, ed., *The Turning Points of Environmental History* (Pittsburgh: University of Pittsburgh Press, 2010), 146–61.

Tasca, Cecilia, et al. "Women and Hysteria in the History of Mental Health." *Clinical Practice and Epidemiology in Mental Health* 8 (2012): 110–19.

Tedesco, Marie. "Claiming Public Space, Asserting Class Identity, and Displaying Patriotism: The 1929 Rayon Workers' Strike Parades in Elizabethton, Tennessee." *Journal of Appalachian Studies* 12, no. 2 (2006): 55–87.

Textile Narratives and Conversations: Proceedings of the 10th Biennial Symposium of the Textile Society of America. "Cotton to Cloth: An Indian Epic." October 11–14, 2006, Toronto, Ontario.

Tiphaigne de La Roche. *Histoire des Galligènes ou, mémoires de Duncan*, 1765. In Daniel Roche, *The Culture of Clothing: Dress and Fashion in the Ancien Régime* (Cambridge: Cambridge University Press, 1996), 426.

Thoreau, Henry David. *The Portable Thoreau*. Carl Bode, ed. New York: Penguin, 1982.

———. *Walden*. Boston: Houghton, Mifflin, 1884.

Trivedi, Lisa N. "Visually Mapping the 'Nation': Swadeshi Politics in Nationalist India, 1920–1930." *Journal of Asian Studies* 62, no. 1 (2003): 11–41.

Tucker, Duncan. "In Honduras, Grupo Karim's Is Not Waiting Around for Someone Else to Act on Talent Demands." *Nearshore Americas*, January 7, 2014. https://nearshoreamericas.com.

"UF Study of Lice DNA Shows Humans First Wore Clothes 170,000 Years Ago." *University of Florida News*, January 6, 2011. https://news.ufl.edu.

Ulrich, Laurel Thatcher. *The Age of Homespun: Objects and Stories in the Creation of an American Myth*. New York: Alfred A. Knopf, 2001.

United Nations Economic Commission for Europe. "UN Alliance Aims to Put Fashion on Path to Sustainability." July 13, 2018. https://www.unece.org.

U.S. Bureau of Labor Statistics. Occupational Outlook Handbook, Retail Sales Workers. BLS.gov.

U.S. Commission of Labor. *Working Women in Large Cities, Fourth Annual Report, 1888*. In Alice Kessler-Harris, *Women Have Always Worked: A Concise History* (Urbana: University of Illinois Press, 2018), 78.

U.S. Department of Agriculture, National Agricultural Statistics Service. "2017 Census of Agriculture County Profile: Lubbock County." https://www.nass.usda.gov.

U.S. Department of State, Office of the Spokesperson. "Secretary Antony J. Blinken, National Security Advisor Jake Sullivan, Director Yang and State Councilor Wang at the Top of Their Meeting." March 18, 2021. http://www.state.gov.

U.S. Senate. Problems of the US Textile Industry, 77. Statement of W. J. Erwin, president of Dan River Mills, Danville, chairman, Foreign Trade Committee, American Cotton Manufacturers' Institute. In Ellen Israel Rosen, *Making Sweatshops: The Globalization of the U.S. Apparel Industry* (Berkeley: University of California Press, 2002), 49.

U.S. Senate, Committee on Finance. Trade Agreements Extension Act of 1951, June 1951. In Ellen Israel Rosen, *Making Sweatshops: The Globalization of the U.S. Apparel Industry* (Berkeley: University of California Press, 2002), 70.

Vallance, Aymer. *The Art of William Morris*. Mineola: Dover, 1988.

Vartan, Starre. "Fashion Forward: How Three Revolutionary Fabrics Are Greening the Industry." *JSTOR Daily*, December 19, 2017. https://daily.jstor.org.

Vaublanc, comte de. *Mémoires de M. le comte de Vaublanc* 1857. In Chrisman-Campbell, *Fashion Victims: Dress at the Court of Louis XVI and Marie-Antoinette* (New Haven: Yale University Press, 2015), 192.

Venkateshwarlu, K. "Genetically Modified Cotton Figures in a New Controversy in Andhra Pradesh as Livestock Die After Grazing on Bt Cotton Fields." *Frontline* 24, no. 8 (April 21–May 4, 2007). https://frontline.thehindu.com/.

Voltaire. "Le Mondain," 1736. In Alicia Montoya, *Medievalist Enlightenment: From Charles Perrault to Jean-Jacques Rousseau* (Suffolk, U.K.: Boydell & Brewer, 2013), 62.

Wallach, Bret. *A World Made for Money: Economy, Geography, and the Way We Live Today*. Lincoln: University of Nebraska Press, 2015.

Waller, Fats. "When the Nylons Bloom Again." *Ain't Misbehavin'*. WB Music Corp and Chappell & Co., INC, 1943.

Wang Zhideng. *Ke Yue zhilue* [Brief Account of My Journey Through Zhejiang]. In Timothy Brook, *The Confusions of Pleasure: Commerce and Culture in Ming China* (Berkeley: University of California Press, 1999), 195.

Watson, Bruce. *Bread and Roses: Mills, Migrants, and the Struggle for the American Dream*. New York: Penguin, 2005.

Weekly Wanderer, July 23, 1804. In Laurel Thatcher Ulrich, *The Age of Homespun: Objects and Stories in the Creation of an American Myth* (New York: Alfred A. Knopf, 2001), 367.

Western, Samuel. "The Wyoming Sheep Business." November 8, 2014. wyohistory.org.

Wharton, Edith. *A Backward Glance*. New York: Scribner, 1964.

Wilford, John Noble. "Site in Turkey Yields Oldest Cloth Ever Found." *New York Times*, July 13, 1993.

Williams, Lucy Fowler. *A Burst of Brilliance: Germantown, Pennsylvania and Navajo Weaving: Catalog of an Exhibition, November 12, 1994 to February 12, 1995*. Arthur Ross Gallery, University of Pennsylvania, 1994.

Wily, John. *A Treatise on the Propagation of Sheep, the Manufacture of Wool, and the Cultivation and Manufacture of Flax* (Williamsburg: F. Royle, 1765), 31–32. In Katherine Koob and Martha Coons, *All Sorts of Good Sufficient Cloth: Linen-Making in New England, 1640–1860* (North Andover: Merrimack Valley Textile Museum, 1980), 36.

Winthrop, John. *The Journal of John Winthrop*. Richard S. Dunn and Laetitia Yeandle, eds. Cambridge: Belknap Press of Harvard University Press, 1996.

Wolfe, Patrick. "Settler Colonialism and the Elimination of the Native." *Journal of Genocide Research* 8, no. 4, (2006): 387–409.

———. "Structure and Event: Settler Colonialism, Time, and the Question of Genocide." In Moses A. Dirk, ed., *Empire, Colony, Genocide: Conquest, Occupation, and Subaltern Resistance in World History* (New York: Berghahn Books, 2010), 102–32.

Woodward, Helen. *Through Many Windows*, 1926. In Stuart Ewen, *Captains of Consciousness: Advertising and the Social Roots of the Consumer Culture* (New York: McGraw-Hill, 1976), 80, 86.

"The Wool Products Labeling Act of 1939." Federal Trade Commission. 15 U.S.C. § 68. https://www.ftc.gov.

Woolf, Virginia. "On Being Ill." *The New Criterion* 4, no. 1 (January 1926). London: Faber & Gwyer, Limited, 32–45.

"World of Change: Shrinking Aral Sea." NASA Earth Observatory. https://earthobservatory.nasa.gov.

World Water Council. "World Water Vision: Making Water Everybody's Business." https://www.worldwatercouncil.org.

Wuthnow, Robert. *Rough Country: How Texas Became America's Most Powerful Bible-Belt State*. Princeton: Princeton University Press, 2014.

Xiao, Eva. "China Pushes Inter-Ethnic Marriage in Xinjiang Assimilation Drive." AFP, May 17, 2019.

Zenz, Adrian. "Coercive Labor in Xinjiang: Labor Transfer and the Mobilization of Ethnic Minorities to Pick Cotton." December 14, 2020. *Newslines Institute*. https://newlinesinstitute.org.

Zhang Han. "Baijong ji." In Timothy Brook, *The Confusions of Pleasure: Commerce and Culture in Ming China* (Berkeley: University of California Press, 1999), 221.

Zhang Tao, sixteenth-century chronicle. In Timothy Brook, *The Confusions of Pleasure: Commerce and Culture in Ming China* (Berkeley: University of California Press, 1999), 17.

Zhenze Xianzhi, 1746. In Timothy Brook, *The Confusions of Pleasure: Commerce and Culture in Ming China* (Berkeley: University of California Press, 1999), 114.

Zieger, Robert H., Timothy J. Minchin, and Gilbert J. Gall. *American Workers, American Unions*. Baltimore: Johns Hopkins University Press, 1994.

"ZIP Choloma–ZIP Buena Vista." In "Export Mall Central America," Central American Business Consultants (CABC S.A.). http://www.ca-bc.com.

Index

Greensboro, N.C., 239, 242–43
Greenville, S.C., 178–80
Greenville News, The, 179–80
Griffith, D. W., 56
Grupo Karim, 215
Grupo Kattan, 203, 208–9, 212
Grupo Lovable, 209, 212
Guangxi, China, 83, 105
Guardian, The, 214
Guatemala, 205, 207, 211, 295
guilds, 9–10, 127–28
Gulf of Mexico "dead zone," 48–49

Haiti (Saint-Domingue), 25
Hamilton, Alexander, 17–18
Hamilton, Alice, 170–73, 181
Han Chinese, 83, 89, 91
handcrafts, *see* crafts, fiber
hand spinning, 76, 233–34, 260–61,
  267–68, 284–85
handweaving, 66–67, 248
Han Dynasty, 100, 107–8, 116
Hangzhou, China, 111, 113
Hardeman, Edwin, 52
Harper's Weekly, 37, 170
Hartford Denim Company, 240, 241
health benefits of crafting, 267–68,
  284
Heard Museum (Phoenix), 275
Hebridean Sheep Society, 257
Hegel, Georg W., 144
herbicides, 50–54
Highland Clearances, Scottish, 255
Hill, Sue Cannon, 180
hill farming, Cumbrian, 263–64
Hiroshima, bombing of, 184–85
Hobsbawm, Eric, 65
Holdstock, Nick, 83–84
Hollander, Anne, 38
homemade cloth, 9–10, 14, 58, 65–66,
  85, 268, 295

homemade clothing, x, xiii, 135, 136,
  295
Honduran Manufacturers Association,
  214, 215
Honduras
  activists and protests in, 211, 216
  coup and corruption in, 212–14
  EPZs in, 202, 203–6, 207–16
  Kathie Lee Gifford apparel and, 208
  living conditions in, 202–3, 209–10,
    213–14
  port in, 215–16
  power of oligarchy in, 210–13
  U.S. garment production in, 203–6,
    207–8, 214–17
  U.S. imperialism in, 204, 211–14
Honea Path, S.C., 177–80
Hong Kong, 187, 193, 195, 197, 204,
  205–6
Hood, Thomas, 31
Hopi arts and culture festival, 281
horizontal looms, 7
Howe, Elias, 33, 34–35
Howell, Martha C., 10
human rights abuses, 92–93, 94, 95
  see also exploitation, labor
human trafficking, 232
Hunt, Walter, 34
Hutchins, Grace, 155

Illich, Ivan, 237
immigrants in U.S., 138–39, 162,
  173–75, 196, 213–14
imports to U.S.
  from Asia, 95, 185–88, 193, 195, 204,
    219
  garments, 95, 187–88, 193, 195–96,
    204–6, 219
  from Honduras with CBI, 204–6
  quotas on, 188, 194, 195, 204, 218–19
  textiles, 185–87, 188, 219

A Note About the Author

Sofi Thanhauser was born in Hanover, New Hampshire, in 1984. She has received fellowships from the Fulbright Program, MacDowell Colony, and Ucross Foundation. Her writing has appeared in *Vox*, *Essay Daily*, *The Establishment*, among other publications. She teaches in the writing department at Pratt Institute. She studied U.S. history at Columbia University, and creative writing and environment and natural resources at the University of Wyoming.

A Note on the Type

Pierre Simon Fournier le jeune (1712–1768), who designed the type used in this book, was both an originator and a collector of types. His services to the art of printing were his design of letters, his creation of ornaments and initials, and his standardization of type sizes. His types are old style in character and sharply cut. In 1764 and 1766 he published his *Manuel typographique*, a treatise on the history of French types and printing, on typefounding in all its details, and on what many consider his most important contribution to typography—the measurement of type by the point system.

Typeset by Scribe, Philadelphia, Pennsylvania

Printed and bound by Friesens, Altona, Manitoba

Designed by Betty Lew